Family Realities

Family Realities

A Global View

BETTY YORBURG

The City College and the Graduate Center
The City University of New York

Upper Saddle River, New Jersey 07458

Library of Congress Cataloging-in-Publication Data

Yorburg, Betty
    Family realities : a global view / Betty Yorburg
      p.   cm.
    Includes bibliographical references and index.
    ISBN 0-13-578105-1
    1. Family. 2 Family—Cross-cultural studies. 3. Multiculturalism. I. Title.

HQ728 .Y656 2001
306.85—dc21

                    2001034369

VP, Editoral director: Laura Pearson
AVP, Publisher: Nancy Roberts
Managing editor (editorial): Sharon Chambliss
Executive managing editor (production): Ann Marie McCarthy
Production liaison: Fran Russello
Project manager: P.M. Gordon Associates, Inc.
Compositor: DM Cradle Associates, Inc.
Prepress and manufacturing buyer: Mary Ann Gloriande
Art director: Jayne Conte
Cover designer: Bruce Kenselaar
Marketing manager: Chris Barker

This book was set in 10/12 Sabon by DM Cradle Associates
and was printed and bound by Hamilton Printing Co., Inc.
The cover was printed by Pheonix Color Corp.

© 2002 by Pearson Education Inc.
Upper Saddle River, New Jersey 07458

Printed in the United States of America
10 9 8 7 6 5 4 3 2

ISBN 0-13-578105-1

PEARSON EDUCATION LTD., *London*
PEARSON EDUCATION AUSTRALIA PTY, LIMITED, *Sydney*
PEARSON EDUCATION SINGAPORE, PTE. LTD
PEARSON EDUCATION NORTH ASIA LTD, *Hong Kong*
PEARSON EDUCATION CANADA, LTD., *Toronto*
PEARSON EDUCACIÓN DE MEXICO, S.A. DE C.V.
PEARSON EDUCATION–JAPAN, *Tokyo*
PEARSON EDUCATION MALAYSIA, PTE. LTD
PEARSON EDUCATION, *Upper Saddle River, New Jersey*

To my granddaughters,
Jessica and Maggie Uschakow,
with special love

Contents

Part II   Changing Family Realities   47

Chapter 3   Families in Time and Place   49

Chapter 4   U.S. Families in Time and Place   69

Part III   Transitions and Future Developments   91

Chapter 5   Love and Attachment   93

Chapter 6   Finding a Partner   111

List of Tables

Preface

I have written this book for a number of reasons. To begin with, after more than 100 years of social scientific research and observation of family life, we now know more about family realities than we have ever known. This information can be helpful in making decisions and diminishing unnecessary stress in our closest relationships. At the beginning of the 21st century, we can make much more informed choices than we could in the past; we can prevent mistakes and cope more effectively with problems in our family relationships than ever before. At this point in time, unrealistic expectations, ineffective defenses, and unnecessary provocations are preventable or even curable conditions.

The interdisciplinary social science research information on families that we now have can improve our ability to communicate, confide, reduce conflict, manage stress, and avoid crises in our family relationships. We can use these insights and this information to build, maintain, and strengthen relationships we value; or we can use this knowledge to terminate unsalvageable, unrewarding, and destructive relationships.

Even more important, perhaps, is the accumulated social scientific research information we now have about how family relationships have changed in major kinds of societies since the beginnings of human history. I have used what sociologists call the *comparative cross-cultural method* to classify societies on the basis of the scientific and technological discoveries and inventions that distinguish them and to describe typical family relationships in these societies. I have done this for three reasons.

First, by comparing families in different societies, or in the same society at different times, we can gain a much needed perspective on contemporary family life—a more positive perspective than many people now have. We can better appreciate certain advantages that most families, at least in advanced industrial societies, take for granted. In the past, hunger, disease, unrelieved pain, disability, infertility, untimely death, and other agonizing frustrations were commonplace. With developments in science and technology, we can now do far more to relieve human suffering; we can prevent, control, or postpone devastating and unnecessary losses and separations in family life. Given current concerns about where family life is headed, in the United States and elsewhere, it can be helpful to keep this larger picture in mind.

Second, we can also find some much needed guidelines about what to do and what to expect in family life by looking at the past. We live in a time when we have lost the comfort and security of knowing exactly what to do in the most important areas of our lives—in our family, work, love, and friendship relationships. Cultural guidelines more often now are absent, ambiguous, competing, or irrelevant. These guidelines are constantly being challenged or outdated by a flood of new scientific inventions and discoveries in both the psychological and material realms of life. Eternal truths, especially in family life, evade us. Folk wisdom survives but is in disrepute; and experience is no longer viewed as the best teacher—quite the contrary. Knowing what worked and did not work in the past—and why—can provide helpful guidelines that are based on fact rather than fiction and collective illusions.

Finally, an understanding of historical changes and trends in family life can provide some valuable clues about what to expect in the future. If we understand how and why the roles, values, power, and conflicts of family members have changed historically, in all parts of the world, we can make more accurate predictions about the likely future of families everywhere. If we know where we are going and why, governments can plan for this future more rationally and effectively, given the standard of the greatest good for the greatest number of people—ideally. Planning on an international scale becomes especially appropriate now that nationalism and national borders are becoming obsolete and the idea of *one world* is more a reality than an ideal.

At a more personal level, my other reasons for writing this book have to do with my philosophy of teaching.

My primary goal in teaching has been to open up new horizons for students: to teach them how the social sciences in general, and sociology in particular, can *liberate* the mind and promote critical thinking. This is the goal, after all, of the liberal arts. I have also tried to train my students to think *sociologically*, that is, to apply an insight, a concept, or a theory we are discussing in class (or have discussed in the past) to the news events that break daily in the media. If the course has to do with families, I bring in a news item about a family; if it has to do with ethnic minorities or women, I bring in articles on these topics. My aim is to help students relate current news events to the culture, the stage of scientific and technological development, and the government and economy of the country in which these events are happening. The next step is to apply these insights to their own lives and to the current situation in the United States.

Finally, I have tried to promote greater identification, empathy, and understanding in my students with people who are different, culturally or physically, who have lived in other times and places in the past, or who live in other countries or in different geographic or cultural spaces in the United States today. My goal here has been to promote more tolerance and acceptance of people whose traditions, beliefs, and behavior may be different, but whose differences are quite legitimate, as long as they are not being destructive to themselves or to other people.

My academic career reflects these goals. I started out majoring in cultural anthropology and shifted to sociology when it became clear that I would not be able to pursue this interest because I had married someone who was not an anthropologist. Given my values, and those of most college-educated women of my generation, I would not be able to go off alone to study exotic cultures in faraway places, intriguing as this might be, because of family responsibilities. This was the post-

World War II 1940s, and urban anthropology had not yet been invented. As an anthropologist, it was not possible at that time to study convenient communities in our own industrial society, since this was then the separate domain and the major distinction (now gone) between cultural anthropology and sociology.

As an undergraduate student in the two-year core curriculum program at the University of Chicago, I was exposed to literature, philosophy, and most of the physical and social sciences. I loved anthropology, was fascinated by history, did my best work in psychology, but found my calling, finally, in sociology. I have drawn from all of these disciplines in my portrait of family realities—here and around the world, today and long ago.

I want to thank the many people who have helped with this project—those I know and those I have never met in person but whose input was essential to the successful completion of my venture. But most of all, I am grateful to my students. They were the first to hear the accepted explanations of many of the facts about family life described here. Their questions and comments taught me to go back, reread, rethink, and make things clearer and more reasonable to them—and to myself.

Betty Yorburg
The City College and the Graduate Center
The City University of New York

Family Realities

PART 1
SOCIOLOGICAL APPROACHES

Introduction

Sociology as a separate and distinct scientific discipline arose in the middle of the 19th century. It was a time of great human suffering from the fallout of rapid industrialization in Europe, a time of chaos and catastrophe, of revolutionary political movements and revolts by serfs, slaves, workers, and -women. It was a time of widespread violent crime, family breakdown, prostitution, and destitution among factory workers and self-employed craftsmen and -women, who were displaced by machines, were hungry and unemployed, and were subject to the vast and never-ending insecurities of unregulated capitalism and recurring economic recessions.

The European founders of sociology were deeply concerned by the human suffering they observed. They hoped to relieve this suffering by providing accurate scientific information that could be used as a basis for rational, effective government policy. In the United States, initially at least, sociologists tended to be the academic counterparts of the muckrakers at the turn of the 20th century. Many of the founders of sociology in the United States (and leaders of various reform movements at the turn of the century) were former ministers, or the sons of ministers, who had decided to redirect their attention and energies to this-worldly concerns.

Since the end of the Second World War, sociologists in the United States have been more likely to pursue their special research interests, regardless of any direct or immediate implications of their work for government policy or personal decision making. They are most interested in collecting valid information about various social realities. Other sociologists, myself included, continue to build on the earlier traditions of the founders of our discipline by emphasizing the usefulness of our research in promoting a more satisfying life for people everywhere. Also, given my specific academic history and interests, I have used research information from anthropology, history, and psychology, as well as from sociology, to tell the story of family realities in other times and places and in the United States today.

Since many of you are coming to this course from different academic backgrounds, I have started with a chapter explaining what is unique about the sociological approach to family life. To do this, I have explained how we use ordinary language—terms such as *culture, subculture, values, role, power*, and *conflict*—in a quite special and precise way. I have also made clear how our approach to families differs from that of the other social sciences, and why all social scientists contribute to filling in the large outlines and small details of the overall picture.

The information on family life in the remainder of the book falls into three parts, on a time frame going from the past, to the present, and—with some caution but with optimism—to the future. I have used what anthropologists and sociologists call the *sociocultural evolution perspective* to explain basic historical trends in family life in major types of societies, including our own. This is a model that classifies societies, historically and today, according to certain distinguishing features: their level of scientific knowledge about the world; the efficiency and effectiveness of their technology in controlling the environment and in meeting basic human needs for food, shelter, clothing, and protection; and their cultural complexity.

Historically, the material aspects of human reality have tended to evolve in the direction of increased efficiency and effectiveness. But all aspects of human reality have tended to change in interrelated ways over time—though not always in the same way, or in a direct line in specific countries. Values play a crucial role in affecting the speed and direction of scientific and technological change in specific countries.

As for the present, my focus is mainly on families in the United States and on national trends in family life here and now, especially as these reflect the latest developments in science and technology. I have brought in comparisons with other contemporary societies, in all stages of development, as these comparisons help explain what is happening now or could happen in the United States in the future.

In this part of the book, I have also pointed out important differences in the life histories and experiences of families in the various subcultures of class, ethnic origin, race, religion, gender, and generation in the United States today. My focus, here also, has been on what is common in family relationships everywhere, regardless of social location, as well as what is unique in various locating subcultures. This is especially important in describing a society as diverse as the United States; too often we forget the essential humanity of all humans, regardless of differences in their ethnic origins, nationality, and life situations.

At the group level of actual, ongoing family relationships, I have used what sociologists and psychologists call the *family development, family life cycle,* or *family life course perspective*. I have looked at the changing roles, conflicts, stresses, and rewards family members experience, typically, during the various stages of their history after a new family is founded—as family members age and as new members enter, leave, and sometimes return to the family group.

Here, my approach also has included changing scientific, technological, economic, and political conditions in the wider society, and changes in human conditions (in prejudice or acceptance, discrimination or equal opportunity) in the United States today, as these impinge on various family realities and destinies. How have new discoveries and inventions in contraceptive and reproductive technologies affected fertility rates in the United States, for example? How have the latest anthropological and biogenetic discoveries about ethnic origins and genetic mixing affected thinking about races and race differences?

I have also reviewed other scientific discoveries in the realm of human relationships, drawn mainly from sociology and psychology. What do we know now about finding an appropriate partner, on testing and correcting illusions and unrealistic expectations, on improving communication, reducing role conflict, stress, and violence, and on dealing more effectively with the problems of partners, parents, and children in all social locations during the various stages of family life? This is where my goal of promoting more educated, informed choices and decisions in family relationships applies. I also discuss the importance of government policies in promoting or subverting real choices and alternatives in family life—especially in the areas of day care and other supports for dependent children.

My take on the future of families is optimistic. Much that has happened and is now happening to men, women, and children in families around the world is sad, appalling, even outrageous; but it is nowhere near as destructive and devastating as what most people, in and out of families, experienced and accepted in the good old days that never were.

In industrial societies, most people have more possibilities for changing their life circumstances and their destinies than humans have ever had. And we have more effective tools for making these changes than ever before: factual information about our society and our own personal situations that we can seek out and apply. We can do this informally, on our own, or more formally, in educational or therapeutic settings especially designed for that purpose. In the United States, we can do this for as long as our lives continue; continuing education for people of all ages is flourishing in all parts of the country.

Private solutions do not solve social problems directly and immediately. But if enough people make conscious, deliberate, and informed changes in their roles and relationships, cultures change, governments and laws change, schools, religious institutions, and economic institutions change. These changes accelerate in human societies as literacy and education become universal—for the young and the old, for women and men, and for all social classes and all ethnic populations everywhere in the world. Sociologists have been in the forefront of research indicating that educated people tend to be less susceptible to propaganda and less prone to fatalism. Educated women and men are more likely to know what they want, and to fight for what they want.

I have laid out an ambitious plan in this short preview of what is to come. But we now have more good information about family life than we have ever had, information that is documented by thousands of social scientific research studies that go back to the late 19th century. These studies and the insights they provide build on one another; they become more sophisticated, accurate, and reliable as research methods improve and scientific knowledge accumulates. Ultimately, they point to the possibility of making more informed choices and decisions in the conduct of our lives—as individuals, as members of a family, and as citizens of a society.

Chapter I
Sociological Reality

How do sociologists look at families? What do we try to understand and explain about family life? What questions do we ask and how do we answer these questions? Also, what is unique about our approach, and how does it differ from that of the other social sciences—especially from psychology?

Sociological Awareness

Sociologists ask questions such as: What was it like to be a mother, father, son, or daughter when humans lived in caves and suffered agonizingly painful diseases for which there were no lasting relief and no possible cures? What was it like when more than half of the children mothers bore died during infancy and parents were fortunate if they themselves survived to the age of 30? What was it like when women in some societies were (and still are) killed for losing their virginity, even when they were raped, and children could be killed for being disobedient, even when they were right? And, on the other hand, what is it like to live in advanced industrial societies where change, stress, ambiguity, and ambivalence are commonplace.

One way to get the answers to these and other questions about family relationships is to identify with the people we are studying and empathize with them: We imagine ourselves in their place and try to think what they are thinking and feel what they are feeling. We do this to increase our understanding of why people behave as they do—what makes people ambitious or fatalistic, optimistic or pessimistic, tolerant or prejudiced, for example.[1] Not all sociologists use this technique, nor would they agree with the need to identify and empathize with the people we are trying to understand; but many of us have found this approach quite helpful in our pursuit of answers to the riddles of time and of history.

Research Methods

It is not easy to get into the minds and hearts of those we are studying, and it is extraordinarily difficult when the people we are identifying with are long gone and left no written evidence of their stay on earth. We use many methods in doing sociological research: survey questionnaires; lengthy and detailed face-to-face "depth" interviews; detached observation, or observation as a participating member of the group or the community we are studying; library research (analyzing information collected by other researchers); experiments in laboratories or *natural* experiments carried out in the field (Table 1.1).

Research out in the field is done in natural settings that we do not create—a neighborhood, a school, a hospital or psychiatric facility, a factory. As in the classic laboratory experiment, we *compare* two groups (matched in age, gender, ethnic origin, and social class), one of which experiences a change, such as Head Start training, sex education, drug intervention, or a crime-prevention program, while the other group does not. We compare the two groups over time and measure the short- and long-term results of these programs so that we can judge whether or not the programs have been effective or how they need to be improved.[2]

TABLE 1.1   Research Methods in Sociology

SURVEYS

1. Large amounts of information can be gathered quickly, easily.
2. Necessary for defining national and regional trends; economic, educational needs of various segments of the population; government planning for the future; evaluation of social programs.

Limitations

Respondents may lie (give socially acceptable responses), refuse to answer, give defensive replies, misunderstand the questions.

DEPTH INTERVIEWS, CASE STUDIES

1. Can penetrate defenses, reveal deeper motives, feelings.
2. May yield unexpected, new, valuable insights that can then be tested on larger populations.

Limitations

• Greater danger of emotional involvement of researcher; less objectivity in observations, interpretations, reporting results.
• Results may not be representative of other examples of the single case that is intensively studied (other families, suburbs, schools, hospitals, street gangs).

EXPERIMENTS—LABORATORY, OR NATURAL (IN THE FIELD)

1. Can determine the relative importance of different variables.

Limitations

Difficulty re-creating very complex social realities, selecting the most important variables to observe, measure.
2. Subjects may change their behavior when being observed.

SECONDARY ANALYSIS, LIBRARY RESEARCH

1. Integrates, builds on available research information.

Limitations

Incomplete records, inaccuracies, omissions.

Note: All methods can be used in cross-cultural research.

Comparative Cross-Cultural Research

Another way of doing natural experiments is to compare societies at different stages of development or to compare the same society at different times in its own history—before and after industrialization, for example.[3] Again, the differences among these societies are natural, that is, they are *given*; we do not introduce these changes—we can't, certainly, in societies that no longer exist, let alone in societies that do exist. If our focus is on the past, we call this *cross-cultural research*; if we are comparing contemporary societies, we usually call what we are doing *cross-national research*.

The Uses of the Comparative Method

This method is especially useful if we are trying to answer certain questions about contemporary family life, such as the importance of genetic factors as opposed to cultural and economic factors in determining the sexual behavior, personalities, and power of women and men in families. Take the question "Is there a hormonally determined maternal instinct?" If biology is destiny—that is, more important than learning and social circumstance in determining behavior—then women at all times, in all societies, and during all periods of their lives should be nurturing toward infants. But if we do cross-cultural comparisons and find even one society in which women dread pregnancy, practice infanticide whenever possible, and nurse newborns grudgingly and unwillingly, we can conclude that learning and experience can override hormonally and genetically grounded predispositions—whatever these may be.[4]

Family violence is another important question that cross-cultural research can shed light on. Is male aggression inevitable in human societies, for genetic reasons and regardless of social conditions? If we compare societies at different stages of economic development, we find that male aggressive behavior, such as domestic violence and the abuse of children, is widespread in agricultural societies but becomes much less frequent as these societies industrialize.[5] Moreover, rates of male aggression are lower in societies where women and children produce valuable economic resources—but only if they can maintain ownership or control over what they produce.

In the old heredity versus environment controversy, most (but not all) sociologists tend to give more weight to the environment. This would seem reasonable given the fact that humans have a larger, more developed cortex (the seat of learning and memory in the brain) than any other animal and are more dependent on and more strongly affected by learning experiences. But newer technological breakthroughs that have improved the measurement of biological factors in human behavior have revived research and renewed controversies on this issue.[6]

The Universal and the Unique

Another reason for comparing families in different times and places is to see what is universal and, presumably, essential in family life. If we know this, we are in a better position to argue about whether or not other kinds of groups (such as friendship, government-sponsored, and professionally led groups) can satisfy basic human needs and to what extent they can replace family groups.

Moreover, when we compare families in different societies, we can better understand in what ways families appear to be better or worse off now (physically or emotionally) than they were in the past. This can give us a more realistic perception of current changes and trends in family life—such as the growth of family groups that are not based on marriage and the increase in nonmarital childbearing in the United States. Is this new? It is not. Is this more widespread now than it was in the past? Again, it is not. Compared to the 19th century, more people in the United States are getting married, more married people are having children, and more married couples are staying married longer than ever before.[7] Comparative historical information can help us place what we may currently define as a social problem in a more realistic perspective.

Predicting the Future

Finally, if we compare societies and understand *why* recent trends in family life are happening, we can be more confident about predicting family relationships in the future. An example is the economic role of women as this affects their prestige and power in societies. Historically, in most societies, women who produced economic resources and maintained independent control over these resources have had higher status, more authority in family decision making, and have experienced less family violence and abuse.[8] This pattern holds true to this day and is supported by social scientific research from all Western countries that have been surveyed.

Given the increased tendency for women in industrial societies to earn independent income in the nonfamily economy, we can predict that women in these societies will continue to have more prestige and authority in their family relationships. This trend has been slower and has even been reversed, temporarily, in certain staunchly patriarchal Eastern and Middle Eastern societies. But even in these countries, the prestige and authority of women are now rising as literacy and higher levels of education, essential for economic development, become more widespread—for women as well as for men.[9]

Why is it so important to predict the probable future of family relationships? All scientists predict on the basis of their research. Given the fact of individual variability, social scientists cannot predict with the same level of certainty as can natural scientists; we have no laws of human behavior comparable to the laws of physics and chemistry. Psychiatrists try to predict the behavior of patients released from prisons or mental hospitals, but they are often wrong. We do make predictions, however, backed up by the best research available; we do this so that democratic governments can anticipate and plan more rationally for the future needs of their citizens.[10]

The research techniques we use help us confirm or deny the insights and hunches we get when we try to create other people's realities in our imaginations. But whatever focus and methods sociologists use to understand various human realities, we need the input of all of the social sciences to understand and explain reality; there is too much to know, and no single social science has all the answers.

Sociology and the Social Sciences

How does each of the social sciences contribute to an understanding of family realities, and how do these contributions differ from a sociological view of families (Table 1.2)? Briefly, historians are more likely than sociologists to focus in great and very specific detail on people who have lived during a certain period of time in a particular society. More recently, they have tried to portray the daily lives of ordinary people (in addition to kings, queens, and other privileged and powerful people), an approach historians call *social history*. This brings them closer to the sociological approach because we have always tried to bring the lives of all people in a society into the picture—if we can.

Psychologists focus mainly on individuals rather than on total societies or parts of societies. They do research on motivation, perception, emotions, thinking, learning, and personality development. They also study abnormal behavior and how mental illness develops as people relate to their families and to other important people throughout their lives. Sociologists are also concerned with mental illness, but we are more interested in how and why *rates* of and *reactions* to mental illness vary among people in different social locations—among different ethnic populations, classes, men and women, and so on.

Cultural anthropologists come closest to the comparative cross-cultural focus of sociologists who use this approach, especially now that anthropologists are studying all kinds of societies, including urban industrial societies. Anthropologists use the same language: They focus on cultures, roles, values, conflicts, and power in families and societies; and, in fact, they invented many of the

TABLE 1.2 Sociology and the Social Sciences

SOCIOLOGY: Focus on groups and large categories of people. Social location in time and place: historical eras, centuries, generations; in types of societies; in cultures and subcultures.

PSYCHOLOGY: Focus on individuals; biological and psychological maturation and personality development over time. Relationships with important people as this affects development.

ANTHROPOLOGY: Focus on communities and cultures, subcultures. Cross-cultural comparisons.

HISTORY: Focus on accurate reconstruction of the human past, starting with agricultural societies and the invention of writing. Understanding and explaining social change over time.

ECONOMICS: Focus on economic inequality; on the amount, flow, and distribution of goods and services in societies.

POLITICAL SCIENCE: Focus on power and politics in societies, on government structure and functioning, on policy-making procedures.

concepts we use, such as *culture*.[11] How, then, would I describe our particular window on reality?

Sociological Reality

Sociologists look at the life experiences and the typical ways of thinking, feeling, and behaving of people who live or have lived in a particular time and place. We locate the people we are studying in time: in a particular century or historical era and according to their age or generation; and we locate them in place: on a continent, in a country, and in a region, community, or neighborhood in that country. We focus on both the material (economic, geological, climatic) and the human conditions (the actions and reactions of other people) that impinge on the people we are studying; and we try to explain how and why these surrounding circumstances affect their typical experiences, outlook, and behavior.

The knowledge we contribute is scientific because we do our best to collect information that is valid and reliable. *Valid* means accurate or true; *reliable* means that our conclusions can be confirmed by other researchers using the same or similar methods. The standards of validity and reliability guide all research efforts that are scientific, more obviously in the natural sciences, but in the social sciences as well.[12]

Social Conditions

Why do we locate people in time and in geographic and social space? *Social space*, incidentally, refers to class, ethnic origin, age, gender, and other social statuses that define how people regard themselves, typically, and how they are regarded by others. Location in time and place—determined, initially, by when, where, and to whom we are born—also determines the typical *social conditions* we experience. And these conditions strongly shape the way we live, love, and relate. More specifically, then, what are these social conditions?

Science and Technology

The level of scientific and technological development in a society is a major social condition. Sociologists ask: How much scientific knowledge about the world do people in a society have, and how efficient and effective are its tools and weapons in adapting to and controlling the environment? This affects the typical economic activities in the society (basically, cooperative or competitive) and the distinctive political conditions in the society (mainly autocratic or democratic in terms of who has power, why they have it, and what they do with it). The level of scientific, technological, political, and economic development in a society profoundly affects all aspects of life, including family relationships.[13]

These social conditions tend to reinforce each other over the centuries. As scientific knowledge about the world accumulates and technology (tools, weapons, human skills, and sources of energy) becomes more efficient, societies become more complex (modernized, developed). By *increased technological efficiency* I mean that people achieve their goals of producing or obtaining food and other economic resources and fulfilling human material needs in shorter periods of time using higher levels of skills. This has been a major trend in human history.

Climate and Natural Resources

Other surrounding conditions also affect our family and individual realities. Depending on when we are born and where we live, our physical environment (climate and natural resources) differs. In the United States, pioneer women and men, who pushed westward in the 17th, 18th, and 19th centuries, experienced brutal physical conditions in their encounters with wild animals, parasitic insects, and inhospitable climates, not to mention the resistance of American Indians, who were there first.

The Human Environment

Social conditions also include the human environment we live in. Immigrants to the United States over the centuries experienced great differences in the human environments they encountered when they arrived: in the attitudes and behavior of the people who were already here.[14] Our human environment (acceptance or rejection by other people in the society) strongly affects how we live and what we can hope for. During colonial times, Protestant immigrants to the United States from northern and western Europe (who were not slaves, indentured servants, or convicts shipped here from prisons) were welcomed and well treated by the English and other Protestant western and northern European Americans who had arrived earlier.

Two centuries later, by the end of the 19th century, Catholic and Jewish immigrants from southern and eastern Europe experienced a high degree of prejudice and discrimination when they arrived, even as their labor in factories was needed and welcomed in a rapidly industrializing United States.[15]

Chinese laborers, who were needed to work on the railroads and in the mines, experienced an even more ambivalent reception when they arrived. By the 1880s, prejudice against these workers was so strong that despite a great need for their labor, Chinese immigration to the United States was cut off by the Chinese Exclusion Act of 1882, the first law of this kind. Up to that time, the United States had an open-door policy: Anyone who wanted to come to the United States from any other country could come, without visas or other legal requirements or constraints.

For over 400 years on this continent, African slaves were routinely beaten and killed, especially when they rebelled or attempted to escape. In the 1990s, in an atmosphere of declining prejudice and the discovery of new historical sources of information, writers produced dozens of new books documenting the abusive historical experiences of African slaves in the United States, Latin America, and the Caribbean.

The human environment that immigrants and their descendants experienced when they arrived had a profound effect on their destinies. And it still does, but in different ways. Upper-class African immigrants (diplomats, usually) can buy homes in exclusive suburbs and can join the most exclusive fraternities at Ivy League colleges more easily than talented, highly motivated native-born African Americans from the inner cities of the United States. We don't choose the human and material conditions we are born into; they come with the time and place where we are born.

Location in Time

The year we are born locates us in time: in a major historical era—in prehistorical times before the invention of writing or in ancient, medieval, or modern times. It also locates us in a specific century and in a particular generation. In industrial societies, a generation is a period of about 25 years, or the average age of mothers who give birth to a new generation of children in that society.

Generations

In rapidly changing industrial societies, location as a member of a specific generation strongly affects how we think, feel, and behave and makes for distinct differences in the skills and opportunities of the generations that follow one another.[16] Think of some of the major inventions in communication in advanced industrial societies over the past 50 years and how they have affected the typical life experiences of succeeding generations in the United States. Typically, grandparents grew up with radios; parents grew up with television; and grandchildren grow up with computers.

This makes for quite a difference in the knowledge and skills of succeeding generations. Compare this with the experience of three generations growing up 200 years ago in the United States. How much difference was there, at that time, between parents and children (and grandparents if they survived and were still around)? Not much, because the United States was still an agricultural society. Most children grew up to do pretty much what their parents did, and they didn't differ much in other ways either: in education, religion, values, morality, sexual behavior, and tastes in food, dress, and recreation.

Stages and Transitions

At the level of the group or the individual, we also locate people according to their stage in life; and this too is based on time, ultimately. Psychologists study individuals as they grow, mature, and age during the developmental stages of infancy, childhood, adolescence, adulthood, and old age. Sociologists use the term *family development* to trace changes in family histories over time. For most people, in families that remain intact, there are typical changes among family groups that start when a young couple marries or moves in together or when an unmarried woman has a child.[17]

Other major changes occur as the years go by when couples (or unmarried parents) bear children (if they do), raise children, get older, see their children depart (and sometimes return), retire, and die. Many transitions or changes that occur in families as time passes are marked by the entrance or exit of family members: separation, divorce, and death remove members; newborns, adoptions, marriages and new in-laws add members.

STAGES AND CHANGING REALITIES   The various stages in family histories that locate families are usually associated with certain typical rewards and satisfactions, as well as conflicts and stresses. Practically anything we are interested in understanding and explaining will vary during specific stages of family life, and locating the family in this way can be quite helpful in explaining why families are experiencing certain stresses or satisfactions at any particular time. On national surveys, for example, reported marital satisfaction is highest in the earliest years before the birth of children; it is lowest when children are adolescents; and it increases once again when children are grown and gone—a stage sociologists have waggishly labeled the *empty nest* stage.[18] The presence of children in a marriage is a challenge, especially in industrial societies.

BECOMING A PARENT   How do things change when a first child is born? We can't fully anticipate this change until it actually happens. In fact, we can never know what *any* major change in status (taking our first adult full-time job, getting married, becoming a parent or a grandparent) will be like until it actually happens.

When we become a parent for the first time, financial pressures increase (especially if one or both parents cut back on their employment); and sleep, privacy, freedom to come and go, and time for recreation, sex, and companionship decrease. The roles of mother and father tend to become more traditional (the work of parents in the home becomes more separated and segregated), even if the mother continues to work outside of the home, as most mothers do in postindustrial societies.[19] For women in the United States, having it all (marriage, children, career) has meant doing it all, or almost all—though this is changing now.

OLDER FIRST-TIME PARENTS   The age when we become a parent is a locating factor that strongly affects our reactions. To begin with, parents are more likely to be economically secure when they are older and less likely to feel as financially pressed. Older first-time fathers tend to be more nurturing toward their infants and children, and older first-time mothers are more likely than younger mothers to be tolerant of their loss of freedom. They have lived longer, seen and done more, and are usually less stressed by the new restrictions and obligations that go with having the never-ending, 24-hour-a-day responsibility for a new human being.[20]

But since they are older, they usually have less energy and bringing up children is more exhausting, especially when their infants start moving: when they start crawling and, even more so, when they start walking. Toddlers move fast, recklessly, and endlessly; they require huge amounts of energy to watch and to chase after when they are in motion. The luxury of sitting and relaxing during the day is confined largely to the toddler's nap time or time in the play pen—both of which most toddlers abhor.

Other Locating Factors

In addition to how old we are, the experience of becoming a first-time parent also varies greatly depending on the society we live in, our social class, our ethnic and racial origins, our religion, and whether or not we are married, living together, or single. These locating statuses strongly affect our life satisfaction during any stage in our history. The reported feeling of personal well-being at any stage in a family's life history is higher for middle-class than for working-class people; and it is higher for whites than for blacks in all social classes, according to replies on national surveys.[21]

Why? For one thing, conflicts, frustrations, and stresses (especially financial stress) differ significantly in various social locations or places. Since blacks are more likely than whites to be in the working class and to experience more financial insecurity at all class levels, it is not surprising that more blacks report lower feelings of well-being.

A change or transition from one stage to another involves making new adaptations; even a positive change (overcoming a disability, winning the lottery, finding a better job, getting a promotion, becoming a grandparent) is usually stressful in some ways. In later chapters, when I focus largely on family life in the United States today, I use the family development model to organize the research information we now have; this approach helps explain some of the stresses families typically go through as family members live out their lives.

Transitions in Industrial Societies

In an advanced industrial society such as ours, the stages that families and individuals go through over time are different from transitions in agricultural societies. There are more stages (people live longer); the boundaries between stages and the timing of stages are more flexible (adults change careers, go back to school, or marry, divorce, remarry, and start new families); and cultural traditions about age-appropriate behavior are less binding. Individuals are less likely to "act their age," and people are increasingly likely to be "off time" rather than "on time"—in finishing school, taking a first adult full-time job, getting married, and so on.[22] But these tendencies toward greater flexibility and more choices are strongly related to socioeconomic status—to membership in a particular class.

CLASS AND TRANSITIONS Depending very strongly on our social class location (as defined by level of education, income and wealth, and occupational prestige), our ethnic origins, and our religion, we marry or move in together for the *first* time during adolescence, or after the age of 30, 40, or even 50. We have our first child at 14 or 40, and we may have one, two, or six children, again depending largely on our social class and other statuses. Over time, we stay married or we divorce; we remain single or we remarry and start all over again. This, too, is strongly related to class, ethnic origin, religion, and gender.

Divorced working-class men are less likely than middle- or upper-class men to remarry; professional women are less likely to remarry than working-class women.[23] And, again, depending largely on class and ethnic origin, we become grandparents for the first time anywhere from our 30s to our 60s or even older. Lower-income single mothers are more likely to have daughters who become single mothers, and this often happens when the maternal grandmother is still in her 30s. At the other end of the class and ethnic prestige hierarchy, middle- and upper-class daughters usually wait until they have completed college and established themselves in a career before they become mothers. And grandmothers in the higher social classes consider themselves fortunate to become grandmothers by the time they are 60—if they become grandmothers at all.

Location in Place

Not only do the time we are born and our stage in life affect how we think, feel, and act, but the geographic area and the type of society we live in also profoundly affect our typical outlook, experiences, and behavior. Anthropologists classify major types of societies primarily on the basis of the level of scientific knowledge and technological development in these societies, their major sources of energy (fire, muscle power, animal, wind, water, electric, or atomic power), and the typical economic and political activities of people in these societies (Table 1.3).[24]

Types of Societies

Anthropologists distinguish four major types of societies: hunting and gathering, horticultural, agricultural, and industrial societies.

TABLE 1.3 Types of Human Societies

Types of Society	Technology	Energy	Economics
Hunting and gathering	Stone, wood, bone; spears, bow and arrow	Fire, human muscle power	No economic surplus, specialization, inequality
Horticultural, herding	Planting, hoe	Animal (for transport)	Some surplus, trading, specialization, inequality, slavery, war
Agricultural	Plow, irrigating, writing	Animal (oxen), water, wind	Emergence of literacy, money, middle class, cities; extreme inequality
Industrial	Steam engine, rubber, autos, telephone, airplanes	Coal, gas, oil, electricity	Most workers in manufacturing industries, crafts
Postindustrial	Automation, TV, computers	Atomic, solar	Most workers in service industries. Middle class most numerous; widespread employment of women in nonfamily economy

NONLITERATE SOCIETIES   Hunting and gathering and horticultural societies had no written language. Briefly, for now, in hunting and gathering societies people hunt wild animals (men, mainly) and gather wild vegetation (women, mainly). In horticultural (or tribal) societies people know how to plant, but they do not have plows. Herding (or pastoral) societies are at about the same level as horticultural societies technologically, but since they usually live in desert or arctic areas, people do not plant food; they fish, hunt, or breed animals as a major source of food. They use domesticated animals (horses, camels, donkeys, and mules) for transportation, but not as a source of energy. In the past, since these societies did not have a written language, traditions, knowledge, and skills were passed down orally from generation to generation. And in horticultural societies, certain human conditions make their first appearance: economic inequality (rich and poor families), organized group warfare, and slavery—after more than 5 million years of human existence on this planet.

AGRICULTURAL SOCIETIES   In agricultural (or agrarian) societies, the first of which appeared about 10,000 or 12,000 years ago in Egypt, people also plant food. But they do this far more efficiently because they use plows, and they harness the energy of oxen to pull these plows. They can produce enough food to feed much larger populations, and cities make their first appearance. Colonizing and collecting taxes from conquered and occupied territories also make their first appearance, as do bureaucracies created to administer these occupied territories, and a written language to keep records of taxes paid and taxes owed. With these developments, the economic and political inequality of families and societies becomes even more extreme.

INDUSTRIAL SOCIETIES   People in industrial societies harness other, more efficient sources of energy to run machines that produce goods, and most people in the work force are factory or crafts workers rather than farmers. The middle classes grow in number, and economic inequality becomes somewhat less extreme. Sociologists now distinguish between industrial and advanced industrial or *postindustrial* societies.[25] In postindustrial societies, atomic power is a new source of energy and a majority of people in the work force do not extract raw materials from land or sea, nor do they make goods (food, cloth, or other crafts) at home or in factories to use or to trade.

In this type of society, most people sell their services: They work as janitors, waitresses, salespeople, record keepers, teachers, preachers, healers, and so on. And the educated middle class becomes the largest class in these societies. Only a handful of societies such as the United States, Canada, Japan, Singapore, Sweden, Switzerland, and Germany are postindustrial societies—so far.

Development and Reversals

Social conditions and family realities are different, typically, in each type of society. But some things about family life—the human need for attachment, nurturing, teaching, and acceptance—are universal, regardless of the size and complexity of societies. The level of scientific knowledge and technological development in a society makes these needs easier or harder to satisfy for fewer or greater numbers of people. But, historically, developments in science, technology, and other social conditions do not occur in a straight line—from the simple to the complex, from the less efficient to the more efficient, from the less effective to the more effective.

LOSSES AND MIXED DEVELOPMENT   There are reversals in scientific and technological development that usually occur after a defeat in war, when major scientific and technological discoveries and inventions are lost.[26] The defeat of Rome that ushered in the Dark Ages is an example. Also, there are societies that are mixed in their level of development: They have high levels of scientific knowledge and technology (advanced medical treatment procedures or atomic energy and weapons) that they have borrowed or stolen from other societies, but, at the same time, most employed workers in the society are farmers, crafts workers, and traders. China, Iraq, Pakistan, and India are current examples.[27]

The Genetic Factor

It is important to know that most sociologists and other social scientists who use this evolutionary perspective in classifying human societies do not believe that different rates of cultural, scientific, technological, and economic development in specific societies, historically, are due to differences in the genetic intelligence of the populations in these societies. They do not accept the assumption of white superiority in explaining the course of human history.

VARIETIES OF DEVELOPMENT   To give some examples, as far as we know at this stage in archeological research, agriculture was first invented in ancient Egypt. The Egyptians were of mixed African and Semitic (Middle Eastern and Asian) ancestry. Other major human inventions, such as paper, porcelain, printing, gunpowder, and the compass, first appeared in China. But Chinese leaders valued the learning of Chinese literature and Confucian ethics—an emphasis on learning that persists to this day among Chinese families, in China and wherever else ethnic Chinese immigrants and their descendants live. In the tenth century, the Chinese established yearly civil service examinations that enabled men with ability, drive, and hard work (merit) who passed these examinations to obtain the most prestigious government positions. The Chinese valued learning far more than they valued industrialization. In the 15th century, Chinese emperors banned clocks, water-powered machines, and ocean liners in China; and China did not begin to industrialize until the early 20th century.[28]

Values and Development

It is now generally accepted that *values*—what people believe is important, right, and desirable (what they value)—can have a powerful effect in slowing or speeding up scientific, technological, economic, and political change in human societies.

Other factors such as climate and geography, war and conquest, and levels of communication between societies also affect the direction and rate of scientific and technological development in human societies.

MORE QUESTIONABLE DEVELOPMENT   But we can't claim that there has been a progressive trend toward greater morality, happiness, justice, and freedom in human societies, although we can make a better case for this trend than we could in the past. The means of killing and maiming have changed—from cannibalism, scalping, and human sacrifice to far more efficient techniques such as atomic and germ warfare. But cruelty and hatred persist. We no longer hang people for stealing a loaf of bread, but justice continues to favor the rich and the powerful. In the United States, upper-class people have been convicted of murder, but relatively few have been executed for murder. As for happiness, the reasons for unhappiness have changed, but dissatisfaction, frustration, and hopelessness persist—for less obvious reasons.

In advanced industrial societies, poverty declines for most people, but newspapers, books, magazines, movies, and television increase materialistic desires far beyond what people who lived in the isolated rural societies of the past could imagine. As for freedom, people in economically and technologically advanced societies have far more opportunities and choices in determining their ultimate station in life, especially if they start out in the middle class. But the poor have fewer choices; and involuntary servitude persists in prisons and in other less obvious places—in dull, routine, dead-end jobs, for example.

CURRENT DECLINES   Scientific and technological advances have greatly improved the material quality of life for most people in industrial societies, but material well-being is declining dramatically in developing countries.[29] Also, and at the same time, we have far more efficient and effective ways to destroy the world we have made, not only by weapons of war, but also by exhausting or poisoning our supplies of air, water, food, forests, and fields.

Other Locating Factors

Geography not only locates us in a major type of society, in technologically more advanced agricultural and industrial societies, it locates us in a particular region of that society: rural, urban, north, south, east, west. And this too determines the social conditions that affect us. What else locates us in place?

Ethnic Origin, Race, and Class

Once societies go beyond the nonliterate stages of hunting and gathering and horticulture, means of transportation improve. This happens very gradually at first, and then with increasing speed and ease: We advance from horses, camels, and canoes, to ocean liners, trains, and automobiles, and, finally, to jet and supersonic airplanes. Techniques of communication also improve: from drums and smoke signals, to letters, telegrams, telephones, movies, and television, and, finally, to instant global contact by satellite, internet, and e-mail.

EXPANDING HORIZONS   People get more information about other societies, or other parts of their own society, faster and their psychological frontiers expand: They can more easily identify with people *outside* of their community, their country, and their continent. With developments in transportation, they can move to other places faster and less expensively, if they need to, want to—or are permitted to. Migration, the movement of people from one geographic area to another, and immigration, the migration of people across national borders, speeds up; and this, too, creates more subcultures and greater diversity in nations.

INCREASED DIVERSITY   As more people move into new countries, these countries become more differentiated in terms of ethnic origin—the country or continent where most of the ancestors of inhabitants came from originally. Tribal societies may be quite diverse, but they do not differ, usually, in terms of the continent where the ancestors of the various tribes come from. In the late 1600s, there were over 200 politically autonomous tribes in the United States, but these tribes were all descendants of immigrants from the Asian continent.[30] Immigrants from other countries or continents also bring new religious beliefs and practices with them, and other values and customs that may be quite different from those in the new country.

As tools and weapons become more efficient in horticultural and herding societies, societies produce more economic goods than they can consume, and we begin to get rich and poor families. We don't know why certain families became richer than others, historically. Probably the richer families produced more children, initially. In horticultural and agricultural societies, children (and women) are regarded as property: They are willing workers and breeders, who increase family wealth. In advanced industrial societies, women earn independent incomes and children become a luxury. Like women, children also go out to work in the nonfamily economy, and they become increasingly expensive to raise and to educate.

At this point, I have introduced the models I have used to organize the research information described in the rest of the book. Models are frameworks for looking at data; and the building blocks of these frameworks are a set of interrelated concepts. Concepts are the language of science. Scientific concepts vary, depending on the science, the scientist, and the state of scientific knowledge at a particular time in history. What are some of the concepts that are currently useful to sociologists in their research on families?

The Language of Sociology

Much of the language sociologists use is the same as that used by most people in a society, but we try to define our terms or concepts more precisely. We do this so that others will know exactly what we mean when we refer to a family, a class, a role, or a culture.

Concepts

Concepts are abstract terms or phrases that sensitize us to certain aspects of reality; they determine what we look for and, to a large extent, what we see. If we didn't have the concept of *class*, for example, we might miss an important factor in explaining differences in family realities. Certain concepts help explain why people who live or have lived at various times and places think, feel, and behave in expected and more or less predictable ways. These terms are *culture, subculture, status, role,* and *socialization.*[31]

Culture and Socialization

Culture is a social condition that deeply affects people in a society. As new discoveries and inventions in human societies increase and accumulate, cultures and all other social conditions change faster and faster.

Characteristics of Culture

A *culture* consists of the language, norms, values, beliefs, knowledge, and skills that most people in a society learn by a process we call *socialization*. The contents of cultures are learned; they are not in the genes. Socialization involves identifying with parents, teachers, friends, and other models whom we admire and respect and internalizing their values and norms. Books, the mass media, and cyberspace are also important socializing influences in modern times.

Cultures are attached to specific societies, and the basic aspects of cultures are passed on to *most* people in the society from generation to generation. A fad or a fashion does not usually become part of the culture, since it doesn't last and doesn't affect most people in the society. Also, simpler societies do not have fads and fashions; contact with other societies is minimal. They have fewer new inventions and discoveries, and social conditions change slowly, if at all. Moreover, the prestige, resources, and identity of members in these societies are fixed; they don't need fashions to confirm who they are, how much they have, or what they have achieved.

Socialization from Birth to Death

Our culture affects us from the moment we are conceived until the end of our lives. It affects what our mothers eat and drink during pregnancy, whether they smoke or take drugs, whether they have good prenatal care (or no prenatal care), how much stress they experience, and their attitudes and beliefs about bearing and bringing up children. An example is the contrast between immigrant and native-born Mexican American mothers. First-generation immigrant Mexican mothers are more likely to produce healthy, normal birth weight infants than second-generation Mexican American women, who were born in the United States and are much more likely to smoke and to drink.[32]

The first thing newborn infants must learn is to control their hunger and sleep through the night and, later, to eat three meals a day. Depending on their culture, they learn to eat with their fingers, chopsticks, or forks and knives. They learn what foods to prefer and, later, also depending on their culture, when and where to get rid of bodily wastes. In agricultural societies there is no specific emphasis on toilet training; toddlers use the fields and, later, outhouses. In industrialized societies they learn to use flush toilets, usually after a long, tedious, and stressful toilet-training process.

At the end of life, our culture affects how we react to pain, how we face death, and how much help and support we get from our family and community. It defines the proper way to mourn, bury our dead, and carry on the functions of those we have lost. In some tribal societies, those who are about to die go off alone to a distant hill to await death; in agricultural and industrial societies, with much greater material resources, death is celebrated with elaborate, impressive, and enormously costly rituals, especially among the rich and famous. As for dying voluntarily, in 2001 it became legal for physicians in the Netherlands to assist terminally ill people to commit suicide. Before that time, the practice was illegal in both the Netherlands and most of the United States. But because of a difference in cultural values, some physicians in the United States who assist in the suicide of terminally ill patients have been prosecuted and imprisoned; in the Netherlands, the practice was widespread and ignored, even before it became legal.[33]

Personality and Culture

As I pointed out earlier, psychologists focus mainly on individuals and on individual development as this results from particular relationships with important authority figures, friends, and other models during infancy, childhood, adulthood, and old age. But sociologists are more likely to look at how these relationships vary, typically, according to location in time and place—during different historical periods and in different cultures, social classes, and ethnic populations. We are usually more interested in the setting than the scene; though the scene changes as the setting changes, and we need to look at both.

Gender Differences

Take gender differences in personality as an example of how changes in the setting—in this case the economy, mainly—affect the family scene. How has the socialization of males and females changed over the past 40 or 50 years in the United States and why? Most sociologists, incidentally, distinguish between sex and gender when referring to males and females. *Sex* refers to the biological differences between girls and boys and men and women: differences in hormones, chromosomes, and anatomy, especially. *Gender* refers to the socialized aspects of the male and female personality: what people define and label *masculine* or *feminine* in a particular culture at a particular time and place.

Since women in industrial countries are expected to work in the nonfamily economy, many parents are now encouraging daughters as well as sons to be assertive and achieving. They are trying to break down age-old stereotypes in childrearing that discouraged girls from being "tomboys" and, even more strenuously, discouraged boys from being "sissies." But differences in the typical socialization experiences of boys and girls persist, in spite of major changes in cultural values and gender roles in recent decades.[34]

In their research on sex differences, psychologists are more likely to focus on specific genetic differences between males and females—on differences between the functions of the left and right sides of the brain in males and females, for example. Or they study specific childrearing practices that extinguish or reinforce gender differences in personality development. Sociologists are more likely to focus on *why* childrearing practices change during different historical periods; and we usually relate these changes to economic and political conditions and to changes in cultural or subcultural values.

Most parents in any society try to bring up children who will be able to function successfully as adults in the society in which they live. Adult employment in the nonfamily economy is now a given for women of almost all classes and ethnic origins in the United States. In marital relationships, shared interests and values, companionship, and emotional support are now more important to women than economic support from their husbands, though economic support is not unimportant.[35] Girls will need to be more ambitious and assertive if they are to succeed at higher levels in the work force when they grow up; boys will need to be more emotionally available if they are to succeed in their relationships with their wives and children.

Status and Roles

We are born with a variety of widely recognized, socially locating *statuses*, or positions, in a group (daughter, son, sister, brother) or in a total society (female, male, rich, poor, white, black, Catholic, Protestant, Muslim, Jew, or Buddhist). As occupants of particular statuses, we learn culturally defined *roles*: scripts we are supposed to follow in acting out the dramas of our daily lives. Roles are attached to statuses. We occupy a status; we play a role.

The culture defines the rights and obligations of the roles attached to statuses. Through the process of socialization, we learn what our rights and responsibilities are supposed to be as occupants of a particular status: what we can expect from others and what they can expect from us, at least ideally. This is how human social life goes on in more or less orderly fashion; if we were not taught to conform to roles, unpredictability and uncertainty, even chaos and catastrophe, could be the result.

Cultural Ideals and Reality

Take the roles of parents and children. Ideally, at least, in the United States at the beginning of the 21st century, mothers and fathers should be loving, nurturing, supportive, and encouraging toward their children. Children should be loving, cooperative, and reasonable in relating to their parents. In relationships between parents and children today, to be loved is a right; to give love is a responsibility—again, ideally. But this, too, varies according to time, place, and person. When reality is overwhelmingly oppressive—psychologically, physically, financially—love becomes a luxury.[36]

Personality and Role

No two people will play out a role in exactly the same way, since no two people are identical psychologically (not even identical twins raised together or apart). No two people have exactly the same life experiences, no matter where they are located in time and place, and no two brothers or sisters grow up in the same family. Each has a different relationship with parents or parent substitutes: favorite, family scapegoat or bully, substitute mother or father, first born, youngest, and so on.[37] These statuses fall through the cracks of culturally defined role prescriptions. But socialization, starting at birth and continuing to the end of our lives, if it is successful, enables us to function in our society and relate to others in fairly predictable ways.

Subcultures

In more complex, technologically advanced societies, statuses multiply. Locations such as gender, class, ethnic origin, religion, and generation place us in subcultures.

Different but Not Inferior

Members of a subculture conform to most of the basic cultural norms of a society, but their customs differ in some ways. The prefix *sub* in *subculture* does not mean lower or inferior; it simply means *different* in some ways. Most people in the United States speak English; people in subcultures usually have a different language or use special terms that are not understood by outsiders.

Members of some subcultures can be recognized by their distinctive language and dress. This is especially true of age and ethnic subcultures.[38] Young adults in the United States do not wear grass skirts or loin cloths, for example, but young women wear cutoff jeans, miniskirts, string bikinis, and low-cut gowns held in place with spaghetti straps or two-sided tape. These fashions are not common among women over 65.

Territories

People who share a similar subculture, especially age, class, and ethnic subcultures, usually share a common territory—Wall Street; exclusive suburbs; Koreatowns, Chinatowns, or barrios; high school and college campuses; gay and lesbian neighborhoods; or retirement communities. One of the latest subcultures in the United States is based on a computer-connected *virtual community*.[39] Here, the shared territory is cyberspace. Community members are joined together by the Internet and the need for instant and constant non–face-to-face communication. As in other subcultures, members have a special language, shared interests, values, and a feeling of belonging.

Whatever the differences in the focus and language of sociologists, psychologists, and other social scientists, we all need a working definition of family groups that is not culture bound. That is, we need a definition that transcends a specific time, place, and culture and is universal.

Defining Families

All known human societies have family groups, ultimately for biological reasons. Two major biological distinctions of humans when they first appeared on this planet were a completely upright posture and a larger cortex—that part of the brain that is responsible for memory and learning. The upright posture meant a narrowing of the pelvis to hold in the stomach and the intestines. And this, in turn, meant that larger-skulled human infants had to be delivered when they were smaller in size and less mature than other animals. Humans are born more dependent and in need of physical care, teaching, and emotional support for a longer period of time than any other animal. Families have fulfilled these functions, in various ways, everywhere and at all times. How, then, do we define this very important group?[40]

Family Groups

The United States Bureau of the Census defines families as groups related by blood, marriage, or adoption who share the same household. A major problem with this definition is that it doesn't include unmarried couples, with or without children. Unmarried couples (heterosexual or same-sex) who share a common household are not related by blood, marriage, or adoption. This definition also doesn't include families whose members do not spend most of their time in the same household.

In what sociologists call *commuter marriages*, husbands and wives work in different cities and are together only on weekends, if then. Some husbands and wives work on different continents and spend even less time together in the same household. People in certain occupations, such as sailors, truck drivers, manufacturers' representatives (formerly known as traveling salesmen), corporate troubleshooters, and entertainers and sports figures are most likely to find themselves in commuter marriages. Also, divorced fathers who do not have custody of their children (and about eight out of ten do not) live in different households from their closest biological relatives—their children.[41]

Varieties of Family Groups

Given these conditions, I define *families* as groups related by marriage, birth, adoption, or *mutual definition*. If people define themselves as a family, they *are* a family. Mutual definition is an essential feature because if people feel they belong to a family group, if they have a deep, personal, emotional involvement (negative or positive) with this group, and if their identity is defined by the group, then we must accept them as a family. They are families even if their relationships are not recognized by tradition, law, or custom.[42]

We can't omit or ignore these groups in our research; there are too many of them in the United States today and, in fact, all over the world. This is not to say that marriage as the basis for forming a new family has no advantages; we now have accumulating evidence that it does. I'll return to this question later, when I review research studies that point to physical, emotional, and economic differences between married and unmarried people.

We turn now to some additional concepts that need to be clearly defined; these concepts are essential for explaining how families have changed historically, and how they are changing now, all over the world.

Chapter 2
The Language of Family Change

Families in industrial societies, and especially in postindustrial societies, are experiencing dramatic changes in forms, functions, expectations, and values. In Chapter 3 I trace the cross-cultural origins of these changes in greater detail. For now, I need to make clear the concepts I use to describe these worldwide trends in family life.

Changing Family Forms

Traditionally, marriage between a man and a woman has been regarded as the basis and foundation of family life. This is reflected in the early definitions of the family by anthropologists and sociologists that I have described. *Marriage* is a more or less exclusive sexual relationship, celebrated by ritual, that is expected to last. It is found in all known human societies and has been a way to control sexual behavior, reduce competition for sexual partners, and guarantee the care of very young and highly dependent children—at least ideally.

Nuclear and Extended Families

Social scientists have classified families as *nuclear*, *extended*, or somewhere in between. In deciding whether a family is nuclear or extended, we look at the amount of contact, influence or control, economic help, and emotional support families receive from, or give to, relatives. We make these distinctions in family forms because they point to certain important changes in family functioning, historically.[1]

Nuclear families are parents (including single parents) and their children: the *immediate* family. Extended families are relatives (sisters, brothers, aunts, uncles, cousins, and in-laws) who live nearby and are in daily, or almost daily, contact. The amount of face-to-face *contact* is the most important factor in deciding whether a family is nuclear or extended. This definition is different from the one used by many anthropologists and historians in the past; it does not require that three generations of a family live in the *same* household (Table 2.1).[2]

The masses of people in agricultural societies had large families and did not have the living space to accommodate three or more generations in the same modest household. If we insist on this rigid definition, we define away the extended fam-

TABLE 2.1   Family Forms: Contact, Authority, Economic Dependence, Emotional Support

Truly Extended	Semiextended	Seminuclear	Isolated Nuclear
1. Daily *contact*	Daily contact	Regular visiting, weekly usually, but no daily contact	Infrequent visits on ceremonial occasions
2. Oldest members exert strict *authority* over younger generations	Nuclear family authority, but influence of relatives on nuclear family decisions is strong	Influence of relatives on nuclear family decisions is weak	Relatives exert no influence on nuclear family decisions
3. Complete *economic* interdependence of related nuclear families	Economic independence of nuclear family, but daily exchange of goods and services with relatives	Largely self-sufficient nuclear family; help from relatives in emergencies	Nuclear family is completely self-sufficient economically; no help from relatives
4. Complete *emotional* interdependence	Relatives most important in providing emotional support, protection, socialization; some reliance on outsiders	Nuclear family reliance on relatives for emotional support is weak but not absent	Nuclear family and a variety of outsiders provide socialization, emotional support, and protection

Source: Adapted from Betty Yorburg, "The Nuclear and the Extended Family: An Area of Conceptual Confusion." 1975. *Journal of Comparative Family Studies*, 6:1–14.

ily in many societies where relatives lived *near* but not *in* the same household as nuclear families. They exercised authority or had strong influence over their relatives, providing protection (blood revenge), economic goods (food, clothing), emotional support, child care, and advice on a daily basis. But they did not live in the same household.

In urban, industrial societies, members of the extended family may live upstairs or downstairs (in two-family houses), down the street, or around the block. In these societies, nuclear families earn independent income in a nonfamily setting— except for a small and disappearing number of families where two or more generations work on the family farm or in a family business that is owned by the oldest generation. But the more important criteria for defining the extended family in industrial societies are daily contact, strong influence (advice), emotional support, and help with money, cooking, cleaning, and child care.

Today in the United States, immigrants, ethnic minorities, and lower-income families are most likely to live in extended family situations because they are most likely to need help from one another. But many such families are increasingly unable to provide help to their relatives. "The lack of available childcare has led to a crisis among poor women, particularly minority women. Policy makers can no longer assume that poor women can endure infinite hardship . . . and will simply rely on extended kinfolk for their survival."[3] Welfare reform acts in various states and cities have overwhelmed the capacity of homeless shelters to provide refuge and protection for low-income minority women and children who do not have relatives who are able or willing to provide food, shelter, and other kinds of essential support.

At this point in time in the United States, higher-income middle- and upper-class parents, grandparents, and in-laws, who do not live next door or down the street, are providing more help, when needed, by sending money—which they can better afford to do. Their adult children, grandchildren, and other relatives use this money to buy the goods and services that relatives, who no longer live nearby, can't provide in person. Relatives continue to be a major support network in the United States today, in whatever way they can, wherever they are.[4]

Family Forms

At the other extreme, if there are no relatives within easy visiting distance (defined by most researchers as less than 1 hour away in traveling time), we speak of an *isolated nuclear family*. This family form usually results from a geographic move to another part of the country in response to a job offer, a racial or religious inter-marriage that parents disapprove of, or a need to escape psychological conflicts with parents, brothers and sisters, or other relatives. The isolated nuclear family is completely independent, economically and emotionally, of the extended family. Family members borrow from banks rather than relatives. If they are in trouble, they seek advice from outsiders (friends, therapists, or other experts). Relatives exert no influence on nuclear family decisions. Visiting with relatives is infrequent, limited mainly to holidays and ceremonial occasions such as weddings and funerals. This type of family is found mainly among white Protestants; it is not typical in the United States and is uncommon among minority and working-class families, whatever their ethnic origins.[5]

In-Between Forms

Most nuclear families in the United States today are in between in form; they are not truly extended or isolated. But they are closer to one pole or the other. *Semiextended nuclear families* earn independent income, but they have *daily* contact and exchange goods and services with relatives, who have a strong influence on their personalities and decisions. This form is especially common among ethnic minority families who are recent immigrants from Asia—from China, Korea, Vietnam, and India.[6] Seminuclear families visit regularly (weekly usually) but are pretty self-sufficient and self-reliant, except in emergencies. A mother may come in to babysit when her daughter goes into the hospital to deliver another child, for example. In the United States, a majority of native-born families of European descent are seminuclear in form.[7]

Three-generation, extended-family *households* are increasing in the United States today, mainly for economic reasons. In fact, as a temporary arrangement, they are probably more frequent now than they were in the 19th century. Many adult children are remaining at home longer or are returning home, temporarily, because of economic or personal reversals. Between 1969 and 1984 in the United States, about one-third of a national sample of middle-aged married women in this country experienced the return of an adult child to their households for varying lengths of time. The comparable figure for African American women was close to two-thirds. These figures are even higher now because of delays in leaving home by young adult children and the return home of other relatives because of the decline in federal government aid to single mothers, children, older people, immigrants, and the disabled.[8]

Polygamous Forms

Historically, another family form has also been widespread among wealthier families in Africa, Asia, and the Middle East. *Polygamy* is a family form in which one man or woman is married to several husbands or wives. *Polygyny* refers to a family in which a husband has several wives. This family form was the ideal in a majority of tribal societies, but only wealthier men could afford more than one wife, and these wives usually had economically productive roles. *Polyandry* is a situation (quite rare) in which one woman has several husbands—usually brothers. Polyandry is usually found in societies with few natural resources (in desert or arctic areas), where women do not plant or care for livestock, and where it takes more than one husband to support one wife and her children.[9]

In advanced industrial societies, high divorce rates result in an increase in *binuclear families* or stepfamilies.[10] This refers to a splitting up of a nuclear family into two forms after a divorce and remarriage—one containing the original father and one containing the original mother of a single nuclear family. Both new households contain children. These family forms have become relatively common in contemporary industrial societies; divorce and remarriage rates are high, and stepparents are common (the United States and Sweden are examples).

Alternative Family Forms

In the United States today, large numbers of unmarried people live together in heterosexual or homosexual relationships, with or without children. We also have a large variety of other nontraditional, sexually active groups, with single or multiple partners, married or unmarried, in communes and elsewhere. They, too, define themselves as families. The growth and increasing acceptance (but not necessarily approval) of these groups are reflected in our language. They are now called *alternative* family forms, rather than pathological or deviant, as they were in the past.

We also have a large number of divorced or never-married single parents of many different ages and all economic circumstances. And we have vast numbers of remarried families and stepfamilies, whose problems are unique because the biological parent as well as the stepparent are both still alive. In the past, death broke up most marriages; today divorce does.

In the capital of the United States, more than half of the newborns are born to mothers who are not married—although this figure is declining sharply now, especially among teenagers. In the country as a whole, about one-third of all children are living with single parents; about 90 percent of single parents are women; and most single parents are divorced rather than never married.[11]

Decline or Change?

Many people believe that the large increase in nontraditional single-parent and unmarried-partner family groups is a serious social problem in the United States today. This particular change has triggered a major controversy among family sociologists, as well as among other researchers and writers on family life. The controversy centers on whether the family as a necessary social group in human societies is in decline or whether the family is changing but will not disappear as an essential social group.[12]

A Focus on Change

Researchers with a historical perspective argue that families, in all their infinite variety, are not about to disappear and, in many ways, are better off than most families in the past. As I pointed out earlier, which bears repeating: In the 19th century, compared to today, a higher percentage of children in the United States lived in poverty; nonmarital pregnancy rates were even higher among the working classes; and a much higher percentage of children lost their parents through death, desertion, and disease and grew up in orphanages, foster homes, or the homes of relatives.[13]

A Focus on Decline

Researchers with a more conservative view are troubled by the decline in what they perceive as traditional family values: marriage, duty, commitment, and responsibility. They see an increase in selfishness and self-indulgence, especially among the baby boom generation, which they believe underlies the high divorce rate and the increase in unmarried parents in the United States today. They believe the relentless pursuit of careers, money, success, and other personal goals is incompatible with the demands of responsible parenting. Other researchers believe that at least part of the increase in divorce, living together, and single parenting has less to do with changing values than with inadequate government support for families in the United States, especially compared to other advanced industrial countries.

Some Newer Trends

Actually, certain trends in family life in the United States today do not support the idea of a decline in the traditional values of commitment and responsibility among most parents in family households. According to nationwide statistics, fathers are now more likely than grandparents or other relatives to be the primary caregivers to their preschool children if mothers are employed full time during the day or have highly demanding careers.[14] In the working class, they do this by working split shifts with their wives. Also, three-job families are increasing faster now than two-job families, and fathers are the ones who are taking on the additional jobs.

Commitment and Responsibility

There are other indications that the values of commitment and responsibility in family life are not declining among most people in the United States today. In the middle classes, more fathers and mothers work at home doing self-employed work, so they are not away from their children as much as those working outside the home. Growing numbers of parents employed by large corporations are connected to their offices by modems, faxes, and video telecommunications while they work at home. Women list personal and family responsibilities first as their reason for working at home; men list a desire to have control over their work situation first, but family responsibilities are next in rank.[15] Parents are spending as much time as possible with their young children, taking them along on visits with friends or staying home rather than leaving them with sitters or relatives. Divorce and separation rates are declining, and marital counseling is booming.

The evidence does not support a decline in the values of commitment and responsibility in the family relationships of most people in the United States today; if anything, these values are as strong as or stronger than ever before. The present generation of parents with young children reports more stress than their parents experienced when they were at the same stage in family life. They are more pressed financially, they have more severe work-family conflicts (more mothers with children of all ages, including infants, are employed full-time), and they argue more about who should do what around the house (roles are more negotiable). But they also report a stronger commitment to maintaining the marital relationship for life, whatever the problems in their marriages.

Changing Functions

How is what family members do for one another changing? Are there universal functions that families have always performed, everywhere and in all societies? Families have functioned in most societies to provide new members, so that societies do not die out. But we have had societies where unmarried women who did not live in families were used as breeders of new, supposedly superior, members (Germany during the Nazi era). We have societies in which parents do not directly support their children economically (commune settlements in the People's Republic of China and in Israel). We have societies where most children are cared for, most of the day, by paid professionals rather than by family members (the Scandinavian countries). In the past, going back to the first stone age cultures of over 5 million years ago, families were responsible for fulfilling *all* of the needs of their members. Family groups provided food, clothing, housing, healing, protection, education, worship, recreation, childrearing, and emotional support, albeit with much help from other members of their small communities.

The Rise of Experts

Very gradually, but more rapidly as societies industrialized, full-time specialists—traders, farmers, artisans, factory owners, storekeepers, builders, and record keepers—took over the production and distribution of food, clothing, housing, household objects, tools, and weapons. Doctors, nurses, drug companies, and hospitals replaced most folk medicines, many home remedies, and much home care.

Teachers and schools became essential for educating and reeducating young and old. Clergy and houses of worship took over most religious functions. Police, lawyers, and governments became the dispensers of justice and the providers of protection. Social workers, psychologists, marriage counselors, and psychiatrists became the confidants and experts on family relationships. And commercial entertainers replaced many home recreational activities. All have cut into the family's near monopoly over the fulfillment of human needs.

More Sharing of Functions

Since the 1920s, many researchers have referred to this change as a *loss* of functions.[16] What has happened, actually, is not a loss but an increased *sharing* of functions with outsiders who have expert knowledge, training, and skills in fulfilling particular needs. Family members work outside of the home to purchase these goods or services. The family still produces goods and services within the home that have economic value, however, and it is still very much involved in these and other functions. Cooking, cleaning, laundering, marketing, child care, nursing, tutoring, chauffeuring, and repairing are expensive services to buy in the nonfamily marketplace.

Changing Expectations

With the rise of experts, and with more leisure time and less brutal daily living conditions for most people in advanced industrialized societies, there has been a gradual shift in the priorities of family life.

The Emotional Factor

People now place more importance on love, friendship, and companionship in family relationships than they do on economic support—although the satisfaction of basic physical needs remains an important aspect of family life.[17] Parents in industrial societies do not sell their children into slavery or prostitution out of economic necessity or gain. Also, there was far more brutality toward children (and women) of all social circumstances in agricultural societies, although less so in the United States. This trend goes back to colonial times, when women were in short supply and more highly valued; patriarchal traditions were imported from Europe, but these traditions were not as strong in the United States.[18]

Women and children in industrialized societies are more likely to be valued as sources of love, emotional gratification, and enjoyment. As the daily physical struggle to stay alive decreased for the masses of ordinary people and as they became more educated, they became freer to pursue the luxury of the examined and more satisfying life. Nowhere has this tendency and preoccupation been stronger than in the United States. The United States is in the forefront of research and publications on how to increase satisfaction in close relationships and how to resolve individual and family problems. And until recently, personal happiness and marital happiness have been more closely linked together in people's hopes and expectations in the United States than in other societies. This situation seems to be changing, now, however.[19]

Unrealistic Expectations

Some researchers believe that the inability to separate personal from relational problems is a major reason for unrealistic expectations in marriages and the high rate of divorce in the United States today.[20] It may also be one of the reasons why the divorce rate in second marriages is slightly higher than that in first marriages. In the United States, unhappy people tend to blame their marriages for their unhappiness. But when emotional problems are severe, deep-seated, and psychological in origin (depression, low self-esteem, high levels of anxiety or rage, psychosis, or addictions), neither marriage nor divorce will solve these problems, any more than a new job or a major move will. To disentangle the personal from the relationship and situational sources of dissatisfaction is a major challenge in family life today.

A More Fragile Tie

Emotional interdependence is a far more fragile bond than economic interdependence in family relationships. The pressures are different, the challenges are more subtle, the possibilities for exhilaration, disillusionment, and conflict are greater. The temptation to give up, flee, or retreat is stronger. This is certainly more possible in advanced industrial societies. But so, too, is the possibility of changing and strengthening our relationships and ourselves in ways that were unknown and unimaginable to our ancestors. They did not have the opportunities that we now have for getting good information and trained help to change family relationships and reduce conflict and stress.

Optimistic writers on family life have welcomed the increased emphasis on emotional support, friendship, and companionship in family relationships. Others have been more concerned about the new problems in family life, especially for women, as expectations change and the possibilities for psychological frustration and conflict increase.[21] And still others have achieved fame and notoriety, at least for a while, by tuning in to the family's failures in the areas of the emotions and mental health.

Families survive, nevertheless. Few people would now question their continued existence as human groups, however they are defined. The United States is returning to basics: the three Rs, natural foods, herbal medicines, and the family—in all its various manifestations. Threats to the environment are different now and more dangerous than ever. At the same time, awareness of the universal human need for strong, enduring, close relationships is also increasing. In the field of psychology, this is the basic assumption of attachment theory, a highly influential school of psychological theory and practice that traces its origins, ultimately, to Sigmund Freud and his followers in England.[22] Some people thrive on solitude, and a highly conflicted relationship can be more depressing than living alone. But most humans need close, stable, secure attachments—from whatever source, from birth to death.

Changing Values

Certain widespread changes in values have also had a profound effect on family realities in industrial societies. Values are crucial in determining the goals we seek and the decisions we make in all areas of life. Values are difficult (but not impossible) to change, and they determine our choices and priorities as well as our goals.

Role Models

We learn our values from *role models*. These are people with whom we identify and want to be like. We identify with them because we feel close to them or because they have resources we admire and want. Our models may have any of a number of resources: intelligence, education, money, friends, beauty, youth, physical and emotional strength, warmth, kindness, generosity, selfishness, ruthlessness, a sense of humor. Whatever they have or are, we admire and respect them; and we would like to be like them.

Models may be family members, friends, neighbors, teachers, religious or political leaders, co-workers, or celebrities in the mass media. We do not have to know the people we identify with. But our basic values, such as individualism or familism, conservatism or liberalism, as well as our general outlook on life, usually come from our families; they are there first. Adolescent peer groups exert strong influence on dress, speech, and sexual behavior. But parents continue to transmit their values to their children. This is especially true of major life decisions children make: education, career, marital choice, and religious and political beliefs and behavior.

This may not become obvious until the children are well into adulthood (not until they have their own children, in fact). Sociologists Peter and Alice Rossi have referred to the often delayed reappearance of parental values in adult children as a *sleeper effect*.[23] It is strongest in families that are emotionally close.

Values tend to be shared by people in similar statuses or social locations: people who are of the same gender, nationality, historical era, social class, ethnic origin, religion, age, and generation. Our strongest values are reinforced by religion and by friends and other support groups that we know or seek out. As societies industrialize, there has been a broad tendency for cultural values to shift: away from traditional rural values such as familism, fatalism, and authoritarianism toward modern urban values such as increased individualism, activism, and egalitarianism (Table 2.2).[24]

TABLE 2.2   From Traditional Rural to Modern Urban Values

Values are beliefs about what is good, right, desirable, or important. Values affect behavior, choices, goals, emotions.

PATRIARCHY—The belief that males are biologically superior to females (intellectually, emotionally, and morally) and should have complete and absolute power in families and in societies.

EGALITARIANISM—The belief that humans should have power, prestige, and economic rewards on the basis of merit (education, intelligence, talent, and drive) rather than gender, ethnicity, physical strength, inherited wealth, or other inherited statuses.

FAMILISM—The belief that the needs of the family as a group are more important than the personal needs or desires of individual members of the family (sacrifice vs. self-fulfillment).

INDIVIDUALISM—The belief that the needs and desires of individuals should take precedence over the needs of the group or the society (extreme individualism—narcissism, materialism—greed is good; more is never enough; the public be damned).

FATALISM—The belief that one should accept and not fight to change one's life circumstances.

ACTIVISM (Achievement, Ambition)—The belief that one has the right to improve one's social circumstances. One should fight to increase wealth, power, prestige, happiness, good health (the American Dream: anyone can be president; be all that you can be).

From Familism Toward Individualism

As educational and occupational opportunities expand for more people in industrial societies, families lose absolute control over the economic destinies of their children. *Familism*—the belief that the needs of the family group are more important than the needs and desires of any individual member—declines. People who value *individualism* are more inclined to pursue their own interests and develop their own talents and abilities, regardless of family needs or demands. They are more independent, self-reliant, and ambitious. But they are usually not without conflict and guilt about pursuing their personal goals if these goals are strongly disapproved of by their families. Self-reliance and resourcefulness are important traits in rapidly changing industrial societies where more economic, political, and personal choices and opportunities are available, especially in the middle class. Most middle-class parents try to encourage these personality traits in their children.[25]

Family members who are strongly individualistic will marry whom they please, even against family wishes. They will pursue higher educational opportunities and job openings, even if this means leaving their families. Husbands will leave economically dependent wives whom they married when they were very young; wives will leave husbands, and sometimes children, to pursue personal goals. Older siblings may not support younger brothers or sisters, or even elderly parents, if this means sacrificing personal goals and desires for education, marriage, career advancement, or material comfort. These are extreme examples and are not typical of most families, though they are more common among families that are not close emotionally.[26]

Ethnic Differences

I should point out that regardless of the general trend toward increased individualism in industrial societies, familism is still quite strong among most ethnic minorities in the United States, and not only among the more recent immigrants from Asia and their descendants. In bringing up children, African American parents and parents of Asian and Mexican descent are more likely than native-born European American parents to emphasize cooperation, sharing, obligation, and interdependence. Asian parents are most likely to emphasize obedience to family authority, respect for elders, and the sacrifice of personal goals for the good of the family.[27]

Ambivalence

It is also important to understand that individualism and familism tend to exist side by side, at the same time, in most people; and the pull between these opposing values is constant and relentless for some. Rarely are people totally individualistic or totally familistic in their family relationships. The result is *ambivalence*—mixed emotions (love and hate, for example) and internal conflict—opposing internal impulses or a contradiction between the way we feel and the way we must behave.

Ambivalence is another trait that is more prevalent among humans than among other animals, especially in modern times. Many humans do things that they think are right but resent doing; other animals act as they feel. They do not worry about conflicts between their values, their feelings, and their behavior. But humans often have inconsistent or unrealistic beliefs and feel totally opposite emotions toward the same person at different times: love and hate, anger and gratitude, trust and fear, respect and disgust, pride and envy toward a husband, wife, partner, child, parent, brother, or sister.

Denial in Times Past

Ambivalence is normal, natural, and widespread in industrial societies; but this was less true in earlier times. Cultural definitions of the proper way to think, feel, and act were more binding; family, religious, and community control was more effective; and people were more likely to deny or suppress unacceptable feelings.

The evidence for denial in previous times can be found in histories, literature, letters, diaries, and other documents of the past. Idealization of human motives and relationships was rampant, at least among those who knew how to write and had the time and inclination to think about these things. Not until the beginning of the 20th century did more realistic notions about human motivation and family relationships develop, and this was only the beginning.[28] Developments in social science, especially in psychology, have lifted the veil on idealization, ambivalence, and illusions: "What is characteristic of illusions is that they are derived from human wishes. In this respect they come close to delusions."[29] But recognizing illusions and delusions (false beliefs), admitting ambivalence, and talking about negative feelings in family relationships is more difficult, by far, than making small talk about distant people, faraway places, or remote news events.

Historically, becoming aware of unconscious feelings and impulses has been an important focus of psychoanalytic psychotherapy, the "talking cure." The basic assumption of psychoanalytic therapy is that awareness leads to control: that by helping patients become more aware and more accepting of ambivalent and negative feelings and impulses, in themselves and in others, guilt, self-blame, anxiety, and defensive behavior will be diminished.[30]

Guilt and Self-Blame

Another important consequence of increased individualism, especially in advanced industrial societies, is an increase in self-blame. If we are more likely to value independence, self-reliance, and self-control in industrial societies, we are also more likely to blame ourselves for our failures and misfortunes. This has been particularly true in the United States, where individualism seems to be stronger perhaps than in other industrialized societies.[31]

There are many possible reasons for the pronounced individualism in the United States, but at least one important reason often cited by historians is the fact that the United States is a nation of immigrants and descendants of immigrants. Even American Indians were originally immigrants to this country. They came from Siberia, about 12,000 years ago, during the last ice age. They crossed over the then frozen Bering Straits into Alaska, over into Canada, down through what is now the United States, and on down to the southernmost tip of Latin America.[32]

Except for those who were forced to come here as prisoners or slaves, there probably was a selective factor operating in the personalities of the people who came. It takes a great deal of courage, self-reliance, and independence to uproot oneself and leave family, friends, familiar places, a familiar language, and customary ways of doing things. These traits seem to have passed into and became an important part of the culture in the United States. Humans are not simply blank tablets upon which the culture writes its messages. They act back, and they change cultural values and role definitions, at an ever-accelerating rate in advanced industrial societies.

The continuing importance of individualism in the United States is revealed in repeated nationwide surveys that ask, "Why are there poor people in this country?" Most people rank individual personality factors—lack of thrift, low ability, laziness—rather than external factors such as poor schools, lack of jobs, or even bad luck as "most important." For example, in yearly surveys conducted by the National Opinion Research Center from 1977 to 1989, lack of motivation (not lack of ability) was the predominant reason given by the general public in explaining the greater poverty of African Americans in the United States.[33] Also, many social scientists attribute the failure of political reform movements, such as socialism, in the United States to the strong value placed on individualism.

Personal responsibility is the cornerstone of the American Dream and the burden of people who are failures. According to the American Dream, success is possible for everyone, and failure is the fault of the individual and not of economic and political conditions or government policies that maintain or increase inequality.

Large numbers of business managers and skilled workers who have been fired as a result of takeovers, mergers, cutbacks, or plant closings (over which they had no control) blame themselves for their "failure." As anthropologist Katherine Newman, who studied these individuals, has observed: "One can play by the rules, pay ones dues, and still be evicted from the American Dream."[34] In a more recent study, she reaches similar conclusions about fast-food workers in Harlem.

What bearing does all this have on family life? Self-blame is the basis of much unnecessary stress and torment in contemporary family relationships. Strengthening families requires increased understanding of self and society, clarifying values, reducing conflict, improving communication, and devising rational techniques for managing stress and preventing crisis. But it also requires adequate support for families from governments—especially in the areas of subsidized child care, preschool education, housing, health care, and higher education. In this respect, the United States lags behind other advanced industrial societies. At the moment, the United States has the highest percentage of poor families of any advanced industrial country.[35]

The strong value placed on individualism is not the only reason for the increase in guilt and self-blame in modern times, especially among women. Research developments in psychology that have emphasized the importance of early childhood experiences and good mothering in healthy emotional development of children have also played a role. Mothers, especially working mothers of preschool children, have been mightily affected by this point of view. They are more likely to take the blame for their children's problems, insecurities, and failures now than in the past.

> My family's been very supportive but I don't think they realize what they have and how much easier it is for them. My days are very long, you know. I have to do all the stuff it takes two of them to do. You know—cooking, cleaning, laundry, keeping the house up. And, I mean it gets really rough. Emotionally, I'm on a roller coaster. I feel guilty when I'm at work. I feel guilty when I'm at home. I feel guilty that he doesn't have a father.[36]

Compared to the past, it is harder now to blame evil spirits, God's will, inborn instincts, or faulty heredity for our disturbed or troubled children, though genetic explanations are making a comeback in social scientific thinking today. Valid or not, blaming it on the genes helps take beleaguered parents off the hook: Their children were "born that way."

Some Consequences

Women are twice as likely as men to be treated for severe depression in the United States. But men commit suicide at more than four times the rate women do, and the actual extent of depression among men is probably much greater than official statistics indicate.[37] One reason why depression is less likely to be diagnosed in men is that men are less likely than women to seek professional help. Also, doctors and clinicians have found that depressive symptoms (sadness, fatigue, sleep and appetite disorders, inability to function adequately) are more likely to be covered up by irritability and hostile behavior in men. Hence their higher rates of violence: Three out of four victims of murder in the United States are women who are killed by their current or former husbands or lovers.[38]

As for female suicides, guilt, self-blame, and anger turned in on the self in a dominance-submission situation are major reasons for depression, and the socialization of women continues to reinforce these traits, although less so than in the past. But women make many more unsuccessful suicide attempts. Psychologists interpret these attempts as cries for help, but here, too, we are seeing changes. Younger women are now more likely to use guns in their suicide attempts. This is the male method of choice, and it is more likely to succeed than swallowing a bottle of pills half an hour before someone in the family is due home.[39]

Social scientists cannot directly solve the problem of the increase in guilt and self-blame in industrial societies. But we can provide more insight into societal sources of human suffering and, at the level of family relationships, more effective guidelines and suggestions for reducing objective and subjective stresses and conflicts.

From Fatalism Toward Activism

Another major change in values that profoundly affects family life in advanced industrial societies is the decline in fatalism. *Fatalism* is the belief that we can't change our destiny (fate) or our life circumstances and we shouldn't try. Fatalistic people value passive acceptance; they don't fight to change their situations. They turn the other cheek; they pursue their daily rounds waiting for the next blow to fall. For them, hope does not spring eternal: "I was born poor and I will die poor;" "That's life;" "What will be, will be;" "That's the way the ball bounces, the banana peels, the cookie crumbles;" "There's nothing to be done about it;" "There'll be pie in the sky when you die."

Passive acceptance of one's circumstances is a realistic reaction among peasants in agricultural societies and among the urban poor in authoritarian industrializing societies. In the past, peasants did not have the power to change their fate. Today, in the polluted, corrupt urban slums of rightist, militaristic developing societies, the poor can't move to less polluted, drug-free, or crime-free places; and they tend to be fatalistic about protesting against their circumstances: The politicians wouldn't listen.

Fatalism declines in industrial societies for pretty much the same reasons as the decline in familism. Developments in science, technology, and economics provide new opportunities and more alternatives for more people. Education provides the possibility of more accurate understanding, active mastery, and rationalism in controlling our lives. *Active mastery* means an orientation toward changing our perceptions, behavior, and social conditions in dealing with problems.[40]

Rationalism implies a means-end orientation toward problems and the selection of the logically most effective means for solving these problems.[41] Increases in scientific knowledge in human societies provide us with more effective means for solving our problems, at least ideally. If an infant develops a devastating, life-threatening illness, a mother may seek help from God by praying, doing penance, and making a contribution to her church. Or she may use a scientifically established, logically effective, and efficient means: She takes the child to a clinic or to a pediatrician (if she has health insurance). Most mothers in the United States today do both.

From Patriarchy Toward Egalitarianism

Patriarchy refers to the complete and absolute domination of men over women in families and societies. Patriarchy is most extreme in agricultural societies. *Matriarchy*—rule by women as a class—has never existed in any known human society and is uncommon in individual families.[42] The ultimate basis of power is physical force; and, on average, men are bigger and stronger than women. But in industrial societies, size and strength become less important in determining power; as weapons and tools become more efficient and effective, anyone (even a child) can push a button, pull a trigger, throw a bomb, and drive a tank or a tractor. Historically, however, control over economic resources has reinforced the power of men over women.

In agricultural societies, the power of the deceased patriarch passes to the oldest son usually, rather than to the surviving wife. Higher levels of education for women and paid work in the nonfamily economy are the major reasons cited by most researchers for the change in the values and increasing power of women in industrial societies. Also, in industrial societies, even if a husband or father has died, deserted, or become incapacitated, wealthy women are unlikely to have matriarchal power over younger generations who live in their own independent nuclear families.

Education and Modern Values

Large-scale studies of value changes in a number of industrializing societies have found that the spread of formal education to the masses of people is the single most important factor affecting changes in the values, power, and outlook of women and men. When we compare societies, education and literacy are even *more* important than urbanization and industrialization per se in diminishing the strength of patriarchal values—but patriarchy is most resistant to change.[43]

The Importance of Clarifying Values

If we value commitment, loyalty, and duty more than we value freedom, rights, and rewards, we will make very different decisions in family relationships: decisions about whether to give up or fight, stay or leave, help or ignore. These decisions may seem irrational to those who do not share our values, and, in fact, they may be if we use objective standards such as needs, costs, and rewards in evaluating our relationships. Values affect what we want and what we feel we have a right to expect. They are usually conscious, although we may not be fully aware of them until they are put to a test. In these situations, we often have conflicting values and must decide which value is more important. And usually this is not easy.

It is better to know what we want and need, and what our values are, *before* we make the wrong choices, pursue the wrong goals, and establish unrewarding relationships. And here, unlike the past, family members can now get much better information and insight into their own and other people's motives; or they can turn to highly skilled therapists and counselors to provide effective help if they need to do so.

Changes in Cultural Values

Clarifying values doesn't necessarily mean that people don't know what their values are before they make choices. But values were more clearly defined and more binding in the past. Many older middle-class men and women in the United States were quite clear about why they made the choices they made in the 1940s and 1950s. Changes in cultural values and economic circumstances since then have tended to make the traditional roles of women as full-time homemakers and men as sole breadwinners obsolete.[44] Nevertheless, compared to many developing countries, most industrial countries are second-chance societies. For example, divorced middle-aged women, who were full-time homemakers with few or outdated job skills, find work or return to school after they recover from their divorce; burned-out middle-aged fathers may start new less-demanding careers. Continuing education is booming for women and men in the later years.

Relative Deprivation and Rising Expectations

In industrializing and industrial societies, as communication between societies improves, humans experience *rising expectations* and a feeling of *relative deprivation*. Ironically, in these societies, at the same time that actual physical deprivation (hunger, disease, disability, and premature death) decreases, the subjective feeling of deprivation tends to increase. The more we have, the more some of us want. Expectations rise; deprivation becomes relative. Whatever our objective circumstances, we tend to feel rich or poor, depending on our *reference groups*—the people with whom we identify and compare ourselves.[45] Social climbers (for example, *The Great Gatsby*) admire and respect the upper class and try to live as they do; revolutionaries do not—at least not until they and their families become the new upper class.

Identifications and Comparisons

Students who do not do well in school feel less deprived if they identify with other unsuccessful students than if they identify with honors students. Poor people feel less deprived if they identify with other poor people, who experience the same deprivations. It is comforting to know that we are not alone. But it can also be inspiring to identify with people who are more favored or fortunate. This did not happen in the isolated agricultural villages of the past; people in these societies could not identify with anyone outside of the groups to which they belonged. For example, years ago, in a major interview study in the Middle East, peasants were asked: "If you were king . . ." The interviewers were interrupted, before they could finish the sentence, with the protest: "But I could not be king." When asked to "pretend" they were king, they could only repeat: "But I could not be king."[46]

In industrial societies, people can imagine being anyone, anywhere. Fantasy easily outpaces reality as modern visual messages—especially from television and movies—bring other people's social worlds (often idealized) closer. Our reference groups expand; ambition and desire become boundless; and envy, greed, frustration, and anger intensify. But an informed view of societal, family, and individual realities, now and in the past, can help moderate these trends. It can point to solutions based on fairness, tolerance, and hope; it can make us more aware of the likely long-range consequences of the choices we make; and it can help prevent unnecessary losses, costly mistakes, and discouraging disappointments—at all levels of reality.

After filling in some additional details about families in other times and places, I have concentrated mainly on families in the United States for the remainder of the book. My focus is on the major changes that families in different statuses and subcultures experience as they go through the early, middle, and later years of their lives. This done, we can be in a better position to understand the probable future of families, in the United States and throughout the world, as developments in science, technology, and culture march on—at an ever-intensifying pace.

PART II
CHANGING FAMILY REALITIES

Chapter 3
Families in Time and Place

What was it like to be a man, woman, or child in a family when humans first appeared on earth, sometime between five and six million years ago? (The date keeps getting pushed back as new fossil remains are discovered.) And how and why has this changed over the course of human history? We have no written records until the invention of agriculture, some six thousand years ago, but for many decades, anthropologists have tried to reconstruct family realities in nonliterate societies. They have done this on the basis of cave paintings, artifacts recovered by archaeologists, and direct observation of completely isolated hunters and gatherers and horticulturalists who survived into the late 19th and early 20th centuries. The assumption has been that these isolated societies have changed little, if at all, from the societies of their earliest ancestors.[1]

Families and Societies

If we take the broadest view of human history, from the beginnings of the human presence on earth to the present, an interesting pattern in family life emerges. Although vastly different in culture and conditions, family relationships in the simplest (hunting and gathering) and in the most complex (postindustrial) societies are startlingly similar.[2] We call this a *circular* or *curvilinear* pattern. This similarity occurs in all major aspects of family life: in family forms or structure (nuclear, extended), gender roles, premarital sexual behavior, marital choice, and husband-wife and parent-child relationships. This kind of comparison is a natural experiment: If we compare these two vastly different types of societies and look for anything at all that they have in common, we can come that much closer to explaining why the relationships of partners, parents, and children in these societies are similar (Table 3.1).

The only exception to this circular pattern is in the area of family functions: what family members do for one another. Generally, in most societies and with more or less help from other members of the community, families provide physical care and protection for dependent members, teach the young how to adapt and survive in their environment, and support members of all ages—economically, physically, and emotionally.

But here the pattern is not circular: As societies become more complex, these family functions are increasingly shared by paid experts and other outsiders, as well

TABLE 3.1 Families in Major Types of Societies

	Hunting and Gathering	Horticultural	Agricultural	Industrial and Postindustrial
FAMILY FUNCTIONS	All-inclusive: physical care, intellectual development, emotional support	All-inclusive	Some sharing with experts, specialists	Sharing with experts, specialists in all spheres, including emotional support; emotional support becomes most important
FAMILY STRUCTURES (FORMS)	Nuclear	Extended	Extended and semiextended	Nuclear and seminuclear
PREMARITAL SEXUAL ACTIVITY	Unrestricted	Mixed, depending on social status; higher-status females restricted	Restricted; double standard for all females	Unrestricted, except for the deeply religious
MARITAL CHOICE	Personal preference, free choice, personal qualities	Arranged by family; social background most important	Arranged by family on basis of social status	Romantic love, personal preference, personal qualities, shared interests and values most important
HUSBAND–WIFE RELATIONSHIP				
Power	Egalitarian	Varies, depending on social status	Authoritarian	Egalitarian; senior partner/junior partner roles
Gender Roles	Work and leisure activities shared	Separate work and leisure activities	Physically and emotionally separate	Shared leisure activities, two-earner households, shared child care, less sharing of household chores
Communication	High, talking, confiding, joking	Mixed, depending on social status	Low	High, closeness, sharing, companionship, friendship most highly valued
PARENT–CHILD RELATIONSHIPS	Permissive	Mixed, depending on social status	Authoritarian	Permissive/authoritative (democratic)

as friends and neighbors. This includes protection, teaching, and support of all kinds provided by paid therapists, doctors, teachers, police officers, and other specialists. It is more rational to ask scientifically trained, highly skilled, impartial people to teach, heal, protect, or advise us than to rely on magic, superstition, or other unproven or unprovable means. True? Well, maybe.

For example: The problem with delegating emotional support to paid experts is that, by definition, relationships with professionals are temporary, impersonal, and limited. Teachers are not supposed to have pets, and therapists do not usually form lasting friendships and are not supposed to have sexual contact with their clients or patients. Physicians don't treat members of their immediate family for serious or life-threatening illnesses; their emotions would get in the way. Friends may have their own problems and may be unable or unwilling to help or advise us. The point here is one I made earlier. The family has not lost its functions. In the realm of emotional support, in fact, it can't be replaced, however imperfectly it fulfills this need at times and however much help family members may seek from outsiders.

What, then, are the similarities in family life in the simplest and most complex societies? Why do these similarities exist? And how do they help us understand and explain what's happening in families today—in the United States and everywhere else?[3]

Family Structure

The nuclear family is the predominant family form in hunting and gathering and in postindustrial societies.

Life Expectancy, Mobility, and the Economy

In hunting and gathering societies, with average life expectancies of less than 30 years, three generations rarely survived to form an extended family. Also, since hunting and gathering societies ranged in size from about 20 to 50 people, young people often needed to look outside of the small band for eligible partners. Moreover, these societies had what we call *subsistence economies*: There was no surplus food or other resources to trade or fight over, and there was usually not enough food to feed large extended families. Most hunters and gatherers were constantly on the move, as local supplies of animals and wild vegetation were exhausted. And relatives tended to break off from the band to form new bands that forged for food in other, more promising places.

Increased Mobility

The nuclear family becomes the typical form in advanced industrial societies also, largely because certain kinds of mobility become commonplace. When family members move away, extended family ties are broken and nuclear families become more detached from relatives geographically and emotionally; reaching out by telephone or e-mail is faster and more efficient than the letters of days gone by, but it is not the same as face-to-face contact.

GEOGRAPHIC MOBILITY   Geographic mobility, or migration, increases as people pursue better economic opportunities in other areas of their country or in other countries. Wars, famines, plagues, and floods also inspire immigration and create refugees. But historically, the search for economic resources has been a more constant reason for the geographic uprooting of families and individuals. The lure of a better life in faraway places is irresistible for the hungry and the hopeful.

In the United States, the two world wars created factory jobs that impelled huge numbers of African Americans to move from the South to the North, Midwest, and Far West (California) in pursuit of these jobs. Now, as economic opportunities in the South are increasing, there has been a reversal in this pattern of migration. African Americans are returning to the South in record numbers. Many are skilled college graduates, but most are avoiding the areas where their ancestors were most heavily concentrated in the past and where they suffered the most: the rural Deep South.[4]

Geographic mobility loosens family, community, and religious control over family members, and nonconformity to traditional norms increases. Migrants to new areas are more likely to marry out of their class, ethnic group, race, and religion.[5] In the long run, migration loosens emotional ties as well, as family members have less face-to-face contact over the years.

SOCIAL MOBILITY   Movement up or down in class standing also increases in postindustrial societies, and this, too, tends to disrupt extended family relationships. If for no other reason, this happens because a major change in socioeconomic status usually results in a move to better (or worse) living accommodations away from relatives. Also, even if basic values don't change when people move up or down in class standing, prestige, tastes, interests, and buying power do change. Conflicts between relatives are more likely to increase, and less attractive emotions such as envy and guilt may also surface. Instant wealth or fame (when a star is born, or when a family member wins the lottery or cashes in on a new public stock offering, for example) tends to weaken extended family ties, although immediate family ties usually remain strong in families that have been close.

PSYCHOLOGICAL MOBILITY   Finally, in postindustrial societies, as the masses of people become more educated and less isolated, psychological mobility—identification with models outside of the family or local community and comparison with reference groups to which we do *not* belong—also increases. This, too, may promote conflict between the generations and becomes a major factor in the weakening of extended family bonds. Conflict of this kind is especially likely when family members are trying to move up and out of the class they are born into or when the sons and daughters of immigrants adopt the language, customs, and disapproved values of the new culture.

Horticultural and Agricultural Societies

In contrast to both hunting and gathering and postindustrial societies, tribal (horticultural or herding) societies and agricultural societies tend to be less mobile. Most people are bound to the land that produces their food. Because planting and herding provide a larger and more dependable source of food than wild vegetation and animals, these societies increase in size. Some horticultural societies had as many as 2,000 people in their settlements (the Aztecs and the Incas are examples). In nonindustrial societies, population tends to increase in direct proportion to the availability of food—wars, plagues, famines, floods, and other natural and unnatural disasters permitting.

In these societies, extended families became the norm—less so in Europe than on other continents, but there too, especially in southern Europe (Portugal, Italy, Greece). In Asia, Africa, and the Middle East, the extended family structure was reinforced by the practice of polygamy.[6] But while this was the cultural ideal, it was practiced mainly by the wealthiest families; whatever the cultural norm, monogamy has been the reality for most families historically and today.

In matrilineal societies, descent was traced through the female line and polygyny (multiple wives) added to family wealth by providing more workers, since women did the planting in these societies. In arranged marriages, the groom's family paid a bride price to the bride's family to compensate them for the loss of a valuable worker. In patrilineal and patriarchal (male-dominant) herding and horticultural societies, where descent was traced through the male line, polygyny was used by ruling families to increase their wealth and power by uniting them with other ruling families through marriage. In societies where women were not the major economic producers, the bride's family paid a dowry to the groom's family. In India today, the practice of dowry payment has spread to all castes, but the fathers of employed professional women usually pay less: The daughter's potential earning power is a valuable asset.

In European agricultural societies, monogamy became the law as well as the norm, but the ruling families, and those who would be aristocrats, continued to arrange their daughters' marriages with an eye to increasing family wealth, power, and prestige. The practice is still common in Muslim and Arab agricultural societies today. Monogamy became nearly universal in Christian agricultural societies. In these societies, women were more likely to be food processors than food producers (although most did both), and it became difficult for one man to support more than one wife. But the wealthiest men in these societies were less restricted to monogamous sexual relationships than poorer men. Prostitutes, concubines, slaves, and female members of poorer families provided additional sexual outlets for upper-class men.[7]

Gender Roles

In the simplest and most complex societies, economic activities, housekeeping, child care, and leisure activities are more likely to be shared: Women and men do similar things, separately or together. In herding, horticultural, and agricultural societies, these activities are more likely to be segregated, or separated, on the basis of gender: What women do, men don't do. When males and females do the same kinds of things, especially when they are both economic providers, they tend to be more equal in their relationships and to be closer emotionally. Women and men in postindustrial societies do more sharing of work and leisure activities, but major differences persist in the life experiences and outlook of men and women.[8] For now, I'll describe just a few of these differences in the United States, since I have returned to this topic throughout the book.

Persisting Differences

First, despite major changes in values and culturally defined roles, most women continue to assume major responsibility for household chores and child care, no matter how many hours a week they work and regardless of the prestige and demands of their jobs.[9] Women also tend to experience greater guilt and distress over family problems; men are more likely to deny these problems. In the United States, if a boy is in trouble for bullying other children or vandalizing school property, a father will say: "Boys will be boys" or "He'll grow out of it." Mothers are more likely to seek help from therapists and are more willing than men to talk about problems in therapy sessions.[10]

At the highest income and educational levels (graduate degrees), women are more likely to divorce; wealthier, better-educated men are more likely to stay married or to remarry after a divorce. Women tend to experience greater economic difficulties after a divorce; men report more loneliness. In remarriages, stepmothers have far greater difficulties than stepfathers.[11] Among other things, they are usually more involved in conflicts over the disciplining and loyalty of stepchildren, especially when the divorced biological mother is around. Also, stepmothers must contend with the "wicked stepmother" stereotypes that are part of the folklore of most cultures.

The Major Trend

Despite continuing and important differences in the family experiences of women and men, the major trend in postindustrial societies has been in the direction of increased sharing of activities and obligations and greater equality between men and women. Generally, the arbitrary, sometimes harsh, and frequently destructive distinctions between men and women in patriarchal societies are declining. And, in this respect also, we are approaching the patterns of our earliest ancestors in the simplest societies.

Premarital Sexual Activity

The sexual behavior of young, unmarried boys and girls is another area where norms in the simplest and most technologically developed societies are similar. In both types of society, premarital sexual contact has been relatively free from control by families and communities.

Hunting and Gathering Societies

In hunting and gathering societies, young, unmarried girls were as likely to be sexually active and to pursue sexual partners as boys.[12] Extended families were not common, all families were poor or pretty much equal in economic status, and families had no pressing need to control the sexual activities of their daughters. Also, puberty occurred much later in these societies: Girls were usually married before they became fertile, and families were not concerned about premarital pregnancies.

Advanced Industrial Societies

In postindustrial societies, scientific and medical advances, such as more effective birth control techniques and medical advances in the treatment and cure of sexually transmitted diseases (until the advent of AIDS), are usually cited as major reasons for the decline in virginity before marriage, especially among middle-class women (and men), where this change has been most striking.[13] Also, the marital choices of daughters and sons become much freer when the economic and political fate of families is less dependent on their choices. In advanced industrial societies, governments share in the care of older, dependent parents, and parents are more likely to have pensions to support them in their old age.

THE UNITED STATES TODAY   In the 1970s, more than half of the 19-year-old women in the United States were sexually active and virginity at marriage was not typical, except among deeply religious women. Then, in 1981, the first case of AIDS was diagnosed. And now, with the spread of sex education courses, the increased use of condoms, and the invention of long-term contraceptive devices, nonmarital pregnancies are declining, along with premarital (and extramarital) sexual activity.[14]

The Double Standard

In horticultural, herding, and agricultural societies, especially, and in the United States today, the double standard is used to judge sexual behavior. The standard allows sexual freedom to males but not to females. The premarital sexual activities of daughters of wealthier families in nonindustrial societies (daughters of tribal chieftains, sheiks, kings, and other landed aristocrats) have usually been more restricted than the activities of the daughters of poorer families. In the most patriarchal societies, where marriages are arranged for the purpose of maintaining or increasing family power and wealth, female virginity is a closely guarded, valuable family asset.

It is important to understand that female virginity and fidelity in these societies may not be consciously defined as economic or political assets. For centuries in the Arab world, female chastity has been tied to "family honor" rather than to family prosperity. In rural areas, where the traditional culture remains quite strong, a woman who has a premarital or extramarital affair must be killed by a member of her family to restore the reputation and esteem of her disgraced family.

> It took six years for the al-Goul family to hunt down their daughter Basma. She had run away with a man, afraid for her life after her husband suspected her of infidelity. Her husband divorced her and, in hiding, she married the other man.
>
> In the Arab village where the family lived, "We were the most prominent family with the best reputation. . . . Then we were disgraced. Even my brother and his family stopped talking to us. No one would even visit us. They would say only, 'You have to

kill.' " Basma's eight sisters were deemed unmarriageable by neighbors and her five brothers were taunted for being "unmanly." In the end, it was Basma's brother, just 10 when she ran away, who pulled the trigger.[15]

Punishment for honor killings is light; honor killings are considered self-defense (family defense). Honor killings occur almost entirely in the tribal, rural areas in Jordan, Yemen, Lebanon, Syria, and the Palestinian territories; they are rare among educated adults living in the urban centers of these countries.

In strongly patriarchal societies, childhood engagements or marriages and the seclusion of women and children have also promoted the norm of female premarital virginity. Some societies in Africa and the Middle East took even more drastic measures. Female circumcision (the surgical removal of the clitoris and, sometimes, other parts of the genitalia) was practiced to reduce the capacity for sexual pleasure in young women, diminish their desire for disapproved sexual activities, and protect their virginity and "marriageability." The practice continues in many of these countries today, though opposition to it is becoming more organized and vocal. And while it is outlawed in this country, it continues among some immigrants to the United States from societies where the practice exists. Historically, female circumcision was not unknown in the United States, incidentally. In the 19th century, the operation was performed as a treatment for female "hysteria" and "eroticism."[16]

The sexual activities of low-income women in nontribal agricultural countries and in industrializing societies have been freer, as indicated by high illegitimacy rates in these countries. Also, in Europe, starting in the 16th century, and even earlier in some countries, half or more of adult women never married. This was due largely to the loss of eligible men who emigrated to colonized countries or to other, more affluent regions of their own country or who were killed in wars; marriage was a privilege in agricultural societies.[17]

Marital Choice

The same circular pattern applies to the choice of marriage partners in the simplest and most complex societies, and mainly for the same reasons: Personal preference and free choice is the norm in choosing partners. Societies that are in between have been characterized by marriages arranged by parents. Actually, even though parents in highly industrialized societies no longer arrange marriages, about nine out of ten people continue to find partners who are from the same major social class: upper, middle, or working. And this is even more true of mixed-race marriages; in the United States, less than 3 percent of the total number of marriages are between white and black partners.[18]

The fact is that most people continue to make choices, on their own, that parents approve: Sociologically, like marries like. And most people find partners who are similar in age, intelligence, physical attractiveness, height, and previous marital status as well. Widows tend to marry widowers and divorced people tend to marry divorced people: They live with similar disappointments and losses, and empathy comes more easily.

When friendship, communication, and emotional support become most important in finding someone to marry (and in staying married), this is understandable. People from similar backgrounds grew up with similar life experiences, advantages, or disadvantages. They are more likely to meet in the first place, and they are more likely to enjoy and value the same things. They can identify and empathize with one another more easily; talking to one another is easier when they first meet, and the relationship is more likely to develop.

Marital Power

Power in a relationship is the ability to make decisions, get your way in arguments or disagreements, and control the beliefs, feelings, and behavior of other people. Husbands and wives are most equal in the simplest and most complex societies.

Egalitarianism

This doesn't mean that married women and men have equal power to make decisions. This would result in standoffs (if not homicide), and nothing would get settled or done. It means that conflicts are negotiable and that decisions are made on the basis of the different needs, interests, and skills of partners. If the husband is more interested in and knowledgeable about decorating the apartment or house, he makes these choices and decisions; if the wife is more interested and skilled in financial matters, she makes investment decisions. In middle-class two-career families, if the husband gets a job offer in a distant city too far away and too expensive for him to commute home on weekends, and the wife can't find a job in the new area, the couple usually doesn't move. Husbands made these decisions in the past; they still do in less egalitarian relationships.

In households where power is shared (or irrelevant), conflicts are resolved by discussion, negotiation, and finding a compromise that is acceptable to both partners.[19] Cooperation and mutual support is the norm, and there are no winners or losers in these relationships, at least not as a rule. This makes sense, since we now know that power and love are incompatible motives. People who are strongly invested in power have difficulty loving other people.[20] The take-no-prisoners drive for power is another reason why governments have been more likely to be conservative than liberal and why love was considered irrelevant in arranged marriages.

Power in Patriarchal Societies

In herding societies and in those agricultural societies where women have been more dependent or have had less control over economic resources, authoritarian and patriarchal relationships have been typical. Males in these societies have absolute control; there is no discussion or compromise. Girls are subordinate to their fathers before marriage, women are subordinate to their husbands after marriage, and mothers are subordinate to their first-born sons if they become widowed.

In strongly patriarchal societies, there is little talking, confiding, and joking between husbands and wives. One jokes with friends and other status equals but not with authoritarian husbands (or fathers or teachers or bosses). The old adage "silence is golden" was a symptom and a symbol of authoritarian societies. Historically, in the most patriarchal societies, women were meek, spoke softly, kept their eyes downcast, spoke only when spoken to, sat on lower, less comfortable chairs, and ate leftovers or less choice portions of food. Where the marital tie was not emphasized, husbands and wives slept separately, walked separately, ate separately, and sat separately at public functions. Public display of affection—by look, gesture, speech, or touch—was taboo. And these patterns continue today in the most patriarchal cultures or subcultures.

Marital Power in the United States

In colonial times, immigrant women who arrived with little or no formal education from rural areas of strongly patriarchal societies were meek and submissive. But by the second generation (and sometimes sooner) and certainly by the third generation, this kind of behavior declined (and still does).[21] The shortage of women, at least initially, the lure of the frontier, and the absence of a medieval past seem to have blunted the more extreme forms of patriarchy in the United States. It is no accident that the women's movements of the 19th and 20th centuries were stronger in the United States than in most other countries.[22]

Reform (as distinct from revolutionary) movements occur when people believe in the possibility of improving their lives legally, and they are more likely to feel this way in tolerant environments. Greater tolerance of women's rights in the United States continues, compared to most other countries. Surveys going back to the 1970s report little difference between men and women in support for equal rights for women in the United States. The results of similar surveys in Great Britain, Germany, and Austria, where patriarchal traditions have been stronger, point to less male enthusiasm for equality between the sexes in these countries.[23] This is true in eastern European countries, as well, despite the Marxist heritage of the past.

Parents and Children

Relationships between parents and children also tend to be similar in the simplest and most complex societies. Most parents in hunting and gathering and in postindustrial societies have emphasized independence, resourcefulness, and self-control in their childrearing. Parents in authoritarian herding and agricultural societies have usually insisted on strict obedience to fixed rules. Independence and resourcefulness are essential for survival in the potentially dangerous environments of the simplest societies and the unpredictable or rapidly changing environments of the most complex societies. In advanced industrial societies, these personality traits are important, since class status is not guaranteed for life and it is quite possible to move up or down in prestige, power, and privilege. Resourcefulness—thinking fast, finding ways to resolve unexpected problems that are always coming up—is also important. Teaching children to blindly obey rules is not helpful if there are no rules, if rules are constantly changing, or if rules are ambiguous or unclear.

Childrearing Styles

Psychologist Diana Baumrind has classified childrearing techniques and relation-ships as authoritarian, permissive, or authoritative (democratic).[24] These *parenting styles* differ in the expression of emotion (warmth or reserve), rules (rigid or flexi-ble), discipline (physical or psychological punishment), values (obedience or inde-pendence and self-control), and type of parent-child attachment (secure, inconsistent, rejecting). Sociologists and anthropologists have located these kinds of parent-child relationships in different cultures and within the various subcultures of class, ethnicity, race, and generation in the same society.

And, as usual, when dealing with humans and their relationships, this classifi-cation isn't perfect: Parent-child relationships may be inconsistent; they may change over time; or they may differ for fathers and for mothers. In the same family (and culture) fathers may be authoritarian and mothers permissive; parents may be per-missive with young children and strict and demanding with older children. Still, this way of classifying parent-child relationships points to essential differences in child-rearing that persist today—cross-culturally and among families in different social locations within the same country (Table 3.2).

AUTHORITARIAN CHILDREARING   Authoritarian childrearing is adult centered: The child exists for the convenience and gratification of the parent first and foremost. Parents are demanding and controlling; they expect absolute obedience. Rules are not negotiable; the child obeys because "I say so." Discipline is physical: spanking,

TABLE 3.2   Parenting (Childrearing) Styles

FOUR ASPECTS
1. Expression of emotion (warmth or emotional reserve)
2. Rules (rigid or flexible)
3. Discipline (physical or psychological)
4. Values (obedience or independence and self-control)

AUTHORITARIAN (ADULT-CENTERED)
1. Emotional reserve, coldness
2. Rigid rules, no negotiation
3. Physical punishment
4. Obedience, subordination (many demands)

PERMISSIVE (CHILD-CENTERED)
1. Warmth
2. Very flexible, negotiable rules or no rules
3. Psychological punishment
4. Creativity, dependence—few or no demands

DEMOCRATIC (MUTUAL RIGHTS)
1. Warmth
2. Strict rules (explained, consistent, but child is consulted)
3. Psychological punishment
4. Independence, resourcefulness, fairness, cooperation (demands are discussed, negotiable)

beating, and depriving the child of food, shelter, and other necessities. Parents are not warm, supportive, or encouraging. In the United States, this pattern has been more prevalent in rural areas and among the lowest levels of the working class, but it is found in all classes.

PERMISSIVE CHILDREARING   Permissive childrearing is warm, affectionate, child-centered, and spontaneous. Parents and children express love and anger freely. There are few demands and no consistent rules (or no rules), and all rules are negotiable. Infants are fed when they are hungry, not according to a rigid schedule. Explanation, reasoning, and rewards for good behavior are emphasized; physical punishment is rare. In the United States, this pattern was widespread among the educated upper middle class after the Second World War. Dr. Benjamin Spock's *Baby and Child Care*, first published in 1946, was the manual for these parents. At its peak, it outsold the Bible.

DEMOCRATIC CHILDREARING   Authoritative, or democratic, childrearing falls somewhere in between the permissive and authoritarian styles. It is warm and supportive, but the rights of *both* parents and children are central to the relationship. Rights and obligations are *mutual*, or reciprocal: Infants are fed during the night if they wake up hungry, but the parent's need for sleep is not sacrificed to the infant's wakefulness or desire to play. There are more demands on children, and there is more control and discipline than in permissive households; but the child is encouraged to be independent, self-controlled, and resourceful. Children are seen and heard.

Historical and Current Trends

In the United States today, democratic or authoritative childrearing is the cultural norm, especially among college-educated, middle-class, native-born parents; but it is spreading to all subcultures. Many permissively reared baby boomers felt a need for more parental control in their own lives when they were growing up, and they are making more demands and setting more limits for their own children.[25]

Historically, where parental power (the power of the father, actually) has been central to the relationship with children, the spontaneous display of anger (as well as affection) is curbed. The hostility that the child cannot express at home may be displaced onto subordinates, strangers, and minorities in later life. The bully, the bigot, the sadist, and the murderer are often the products of brutal, authoritarian homes.[26]

In matrilineal societies, where the mother's brothers had more authority over a child than the father, father-son relationships were usually warm and less restrained. And in some agricultural societies, where opportunities to change one's fate exist, many values in family life that are modern—such as individualism, egalitarianism, and ambition—may be present even before industrialization.[27] The United States is an example: It has been a relatively open society from the beginning. The frontier, with its vast quantities of land and other resources, provided unusual opportunities for economic success and achievement, for sons especially. The land belonged to American Indians, who had arrived from Asia thousands of years earlier, but explorers and pioneers had the advantage of superior weapons and a strong conviction of white superiority to justify acts of genocide.

In the mid-19th century, Horace Greeley, an influential editor of the *New York Tribune*, who urged young men to "go West" to make their fortunes, had this opinion of Native Americans: "Their arts, wars, treaties, alliances, habitations, crafts, properties, commerce, comforts, all belong to the very lowest and rudest ages of human existence. . . . These people must die out—there is no help for them. God has given the earth to those who will subdue and cultivate it, and it is vain to struggle against his righteous decree."[28]

Foreign travelers to the United States, from colonial times to the present, have commented on the greater egalitarianism in husband-wife relationships and the relative lack of discipline and control in parent-child relationships in the United States compared to European and other societies. Children have been variously described as spoiled, rude, and not properly respectful and obedient to elders. This doesn't mean that patriarchal and authoritarian values and behavior were absent in this country. Certainly the laws of the land reflected these values. But laws, including the Bill of Rights, tend to reflect ideals rather than realities. "The practice of partible inheritance, in which the paternal estate was divided into equal portions for all children, made it difficult for farm or artisan families to pass on farms or family shops over time . . . this reduced the dependence of grown sons upon their parents. . . ." By the 19th century, "Foreign travelers and native commentators shared the opinion that the paternal role was characterized by an informality and permissiveness unknown in contemporary Europe or in America itself earlier in time."[29]

We've seen how family lives in the past were affected by location in time and place. What about the picture in other countries today? How do these countries compare with the United States? And in the United States, how do family realities vary in the subcultures of social class, ethnic origin, race, and religion?

Families: A Global View

With the globalization of economies, cultures, communication, transportation, environmental hazards and depletions, and weapons of mass destruction, relatively few people can now live in isolation—either splendidly or wretchedly.

The World Today

Increasingly, we live in one world, but a world in which human life is becoming more polarized: rich or poor, healthy or sick, powerful or powerless, secure or vulnerable, optimistic or pessimistic, satisfied or dissatisfied. Generally, the positive end of this continuum—rich, healthy, powerful, secure, optimistic—coincides with the wealth of nations and the wealth of families within these nations. But in industrial societies, satisfaction or dissatisfaction tends to depend more on reference groups, expectations, and the feeling of relative deprivation. The United States, one of the wealthiest nations in the world, has the highest proportion of women and children living in poverty among the advanced industrial societies, and, with the exception of contemporary Russia, it now has the highest degree of household income inequality.[30]

Some researchers contend that the vastly increased rewards of those at the top are acceptable as long as the economy is booming and the poor aren't hurt. But they are. Rates of child poverty have doubled in recent years because the purchasing power of the adults they live with has declined. Average wages were stagnant for more than 25 years, although they are increasing now. In the last ten years of the 20th century, the income of the top owners of capital (stocks, bonds, savings) rose spectacularly. The middle classes lost out as they mortgaged their homes and their futures to keep up with the new Wall Street and dot.com Joneses. Spending and debt increased; envy and resentment flourished. And how does this compare with the situation in other countries? What are the sources of content and discontent in other societies, and how do we gather this kind of information accurately—without exaggeration or distortion?

Cross-National Research

Most social scientists who study other countries (and our own) use survey questionnaires. We gather statistical information: on average income, life expectancy, birth rates (to married and unmarried women), divorce rates, literacy rates of males and females, unemployment, female employment rates, size and type of household, extended family contacts, rates of premarital sexual activity, rates of unmarried couples living together, and numbers of female-headed or supported households.

This is important and essential information. Survey research methods enable researchers to gather huge amounts of information quickly and easily. This information reveals demographic trends and the attitudes and beliefs of people in a society. Governments concerned about the needs of their citizens (or ways to maintain their power) use survey information to guide political policy and plan for the future. Statistical research is also essential for evaluating government programs and policies that are in place, such as family planning, literacy, job training, and health care programs.

But deeper information about actual family realities—about the power, conflicts, satisfactions, and stresses in families—is harder to measure by survey methods. People have a tendency to give socially acceptable false answers or answers that depend on the way the question was asked. If people are asked "Should the government spend more money on welfare?" most people in the United States answer "No." If they are asked "Should the government spend more money to help poor people?" they answer "Yes." Also, statistical research in industrializing countries may be inaccurate or unreliable because these countries do not have the technology, the trained personnel, or perhaps the willingness to conduct accurate statistical research.

Some of our deepest insights into family realities come from methods that involve prolonged contact and more intense involvement with the families we are studying. In sociology, as I mentioned earlier, this is called the *case study* method: We become a part of the group or community we are studying as a *participant observer*, or we interview people at great length. This kind of research is more expensive and time-consuming, but it can give us information that probes deeper and goes beyond possibly defensive replies on surveys; we can get a more realistic picture of what actually happens in day-to-day family life.

An example of what case study research can reveal is the question of how women who live in polygynous families feel about their situation. In Nigeria, when asked about this on a survey questionnaire, most women replied that they welcome the help and companionship of other wives.[31] But a more recent case study of polygynous families, by an anthropologist who moved into a Nigerian village and spoke to women at great length, revealed deeper, less acceptable feelings: jealousy, competition, and conflict in polygynous families, especially as the number of wives per husband increases.[32]

This seems logical. If our earliest and most intense emotional experiences are in a one-to-one relationship with a mother or other caregiver, we tend to look for this primary type of attachment in adult partner relationships—that is, if the earliest attachment to the caregiver was loving and secure. This is true regardless of culture and other locating differences; it is based on ultimate biological and psychological need. Sibling rivalry, especially when one child (or wife) is favored over another, is not a Western invention.

I asked one of my graduate students, who grew up in a polygynous Muslim family in Nigeria, whether he believes women in his country who are in polygynous marriages feel competitive with their co-wives, especially with first or favored wives. He told me that there is usually an intense rivalry between wives, and also between the children of the favored wife and the children of other wives. He also told me that the practice of polygyny, while still legal, is declining and is rare among urban, college-educated women in Nigeria. In his own household, the son of a younger wife was favored by his father, and he still (at the age of 46) feels enormous anger toward his father for favoring his half-brother. Is this typical in polygynous families?

Anthropologists or sociologists who live in the communities they are studying can provide us with a more vivid understanding of what is actually going on in families. Other sources for this kind of information are accounts in newspapers and magazines, movies, and documentaries. Novels and memoirs by natives of various countries are other sources that can be more revealing than replies on survey questionnaires.

A problem with all of these sources of information is that what is described may or may not be typical of what is actually going on among most families in all parts of the country. Also, it is more difficult to be objective if we become deeply involved with the people we are studying. But we now have better tools, such as tape recorders and video cameras, for collecting accurate information about other places and other people. This makes it harder to distort what we see and what we report; it is difficult to argue with a tape recorder or a moving picture.

Major Global Trends

What has our research revealed about families in other countries today? Generally, around the world, the average age at which women marry for the first time is increasing, as is the age at which women give birth to their first child.[33] Divorce rates are increasing, and birth rates and the average size of family households are declining. Support from extended family members is also declining. At the same time, the burden on working-age parents of providing for dependent family members (children and the elderly) is increasing. With huge increases in the knowledge and skills necessary to function successfully in adult occupations, children need more years of formal education. Moreover, with steady increases in life expectancy in recent decades, older parents (and grandparents and great-grandparents) are living longer and requiring more care when they become infirm.

People over 85 are the fastest-growing age category in the United States today. Even if they are in relatively good health and can get out of bed, bathe, dress, and feed themselves without help, most people at this stage in life need some help with their daily activities: shopping, cooking, housekeeping chores, transportation (to doctors' offices, mainly), and so on. And in the lower middle and working classes, this help is still provided mainly by middle-aged daughters, who live nearby.

Nonmarital childbirths, female-headed or -supported households, and the percentage of children living in poverty are also increasing in many parts of the world. Finally, the number of households where fathers are present but mothers are the primary source of support for the family is also increasing. Many of these changes are related to the level of economic development and the status of women in specific societies.[34] Where women have higher status—higher levels of education and occupational prestige, and where they have independent income (inherited or earned in the nonfamily economy) that they are allowed to keep—birth rates are lower, household size is smaller, the average age at first marriage is higher, and the divorce rate increases. But government policy has a great deal to do with trends in specific countries—whatever their stage of economic development.

The Importance of Government Policy

The availability of government-sponsored birth control information and technology and the role of government in subsidizing day care, education, medical care, and the care of the elderly, infirm, and disabled are crucial factors in explaining some of these trends.

The Swedish government provides more comprehensive support programs for its population than other postindustrial societies and makes no legal distinction between married and unmarried couples in providing benefits to parents. In fact, Sweden now has a higher percentage of unmarried than married parents in family households. It also has a very high divorce rate and the highest percentage of full-time employed mothers with preschool children. But, given the high level of government support, Sweden has a higher birth rate than most other industrialized European countries. It also has the lowest infant mortality rate and the lowest proportion of children living in poverty.[35]

Among economically developing countries, Mexico has experienced a sudden and spectacular decline in the birth rate among the present adult generation of women.[36] In fact, the birth rate in Mexico (an average of 2.5 children per adult woman) is now lower than it is among first-generation Mexican American immigrant women living in the United States (3.3 children). This change will have important consequences for immigration to the United States in the future if the Mexican economy improves. But it will take three or four decades for this to happen. Right now, almost two-thirds of the Spanish-speaking immigrants living in this country are from Mexico.[37] And Mexican immigrants are changing the ethnic demographic profile of the United States in a major way.

Why has the birth rate in Mexico and beliefs about ideal family size changed so dramatically in one generation? Demographers in Mexico attribute much of the decline to a major change in government policy. In the mid-1970s, the government, concerned about the exploding population, the inability of the economy to provide enough jobs for this population, and the possibility of revolution, established a network of government-sponsored birth control clinics. These clinics provide free birth control information and contraceptives. Attitudes in Mexico had already begun to change. Ignoring Roman Catholic doctrine in a deeply religious country, more educated, urban women had long been buying contraceptives on the black market.

With the decline in the birth rate, there will be fewer adult children (and aunts, uncles, and cousins) to care for needy children and older, infirm parents, grandparents, and great-grandparents in the future. Right now, most retired Mexicans live with their adult children, as do many older first-generation Mexican immigrants to the United States. But the Mexican family is shrinking, increasing numbers of older Mexicans live alone, and in the future older people may not be able to count on their fewer numbers of adult children and brothers and sisters for help.

Government Policy in the United States

The decline in the extended family as a source of support for the young and the old is a worldwide trend and has been a major public issue in the United States since the 1980s.[38] At the turn of the 21st century in the United States, a higher percentage of children are living in poverty than are people over 65 (mostly women). What is the responsibility of government, what is the responsibility of families, and what is the responsibility of individuals for educational failures, homelessness, poverty, and inadequate health care, especially at the level of prevention, in the United States today?

Currently, federal, state, and local governments are cutting back on welfare support for families. The debate over a decline in family values—duty and responsibility, especially—has been interpreted by some critics as an attempt to blame families for their economic problems and to shift the responsibility for solving these problems from government to families. Significantly, the welfare reform act of 1996 was called "The Personal Responsibility and Work Opportunity Reconciliation Act." This act turns control of federally financed welfare programs over to the states and sets a lifetime limit of five years on benefits. It also requires welfare recipients to work after two years of receiving benefits, obtain on-the-job or vocational training, or do community service. Unmarried mothers under 18 must live with a parent or guardian and remain in school in order to obtain benefits. Schooling in community colleges does not qualify as job training for welfare mothers. The intention of this welfare reform law is to decrease unnecessary welfare dependency, discourage nonmarital pregnancies, and raise families out of poverty.

Since 1996, the number of people on welfare has declined dramatically nationwide.[39] Opponents of the law point out that the jobs available to welfare recipients do not provide enough income to lift most welfare families out of poverty, and the percentage of the population defined as poor has increased since 1996. Also, about one-third of welfare recipients, labeled "hard to serve" by welfare professionals, are not easily employable because of lack of skills, illiteracy, or low levels of education, drug, alcohol, or mental health problems, criminal records, transportation and child-care problems, or lack of motivation to work.

As for discouraging nonmarital pregnancies, industrial societies such as Sweden, Germany, the Netherlands, Denmark, and France provide more generous benefits to single mothers but have fewer single-parent households. In the United States, the nonmarital pregnancy rate among adolescents is declining, but this is not happening among low-income, older unmarried women, who are continuing to have more children, even without welfare benefits, and poverty rates are not declining.

The decline in government support for poorer families is reinforced by the well-intentioned voluntary efforts of wealthy citizens to help out. Where private charities with old, upper-class, and celebrity sponsors step in to support parks, libraries, and magnet schools (in their own neighborhoods), city governments tend to abandon support for all neighborhoods, and poorer communities lose out. Corporations spend millions of dollars on lobbying efforts to prevent or remove federal regulation of the price and quality of consumer products and to reduce corporate taxes. At the same time, they expect high praise for public services such as planting trees on Main Street. Critics claim that it would be more logical to collect enough taxes from those who can afford it to provide better public services to the poor—and to other citizens as well. Tax increases to pay for the building and repair of deteriorating bridges, roads, tunnels, and other public facilities and greater government control over environmental hazards would benefit the rich, as well as the poor.

Government Policy in Developing Countries

Countries that are currently developing economically usually have large populations, widespread poverty, and little support from conservative, often corrupt, governments. At the same time, contact with industrial societies and rapid social change have often led to unprecedented conflicts and stresses in family life. Expectations are rising faster than material gains in many developing countries, and unlimited greed can have severely destructive consequences. In India, for example:

> Many women in my country are dying by burning, hanging, or poisoning. Their deaths are listed as accidents or suicides. But they are being destroyed by traditional practices that have been perverted by contact with Western cultures and the materialism and greed this can bring.
>
> In the past, when daughters married, Hindu fathers provided them with a dowry because they could not inherit family property. [Also] . . . Hindu wives in the past threw themselves on the burning funeral pyres of their dead husbands, a practice known as *sati*.

Today, the dowry system and *sati* are outlawed. Both are thriving, however, but in different forms and for different reasons . . . practiced in all castes, in all provinces, and by Muslims and Christians.

Where marriages are arranged, and most marriages in my country are, women often become commodities—a ticket to cars, stereos, imported watches, refrigerators, motor bikes. Whatever families desire to have but cannot afford, they rely on their son's marriage to obtain. The son is expected to fulfill all of his family's unfulfilled and never-ending ambitions.

The deaths of increasing numbers of young brides in "dowry deaths" or "kitchen accidents" are occurring because husbands kill their wives for failing to deliver on promised possessions. Or the wives kill themselves because they can no longer bear the pressures exerted on their fathers to provide more and more goods to greedy husbands.[40]

The Global Trend in Mother-Supported Households

Another major global trend, the increase in mother-headed households and in mother-supported family households (even when fathers are present), is also occurring in all types of societies, regardless of the level of economic development. Divorce tends to be the major reason in postindustrial countries, but not always; Japan has a low divorce rate. What are some other reasons, not so obvious perhaps, for the worldwide increase in mother-supported households? To begin with, mothers in all societies that have been studied are less likely to separate from or abandon their children or the fathers of their children. They are also less likely to squander family income on drugs or alcohol.

A lot of West Indian men like to drink. Those that do work to support their families usually do not make enough to support their drinking habits and their families. So women have to go to work too. . . . Women are used to supporting themselves, so they do it when the men are here and when the men are gone as well. They tell their daughters not to depend on men, but on themselves. They should tell their sons to have responsibilities, but they don't. It is the women who become responsible.[41]

Married women are more likely to be widowed, since they have higher life expectancies in all societies that do not practice female infanticide or neglect, and they are usually younger than the men they marry. In the United States today, more than two-thirds of women over 75 are widowed and widows outnumber widowers three to one.[42]

Two-Parent Households

Even in two-parent households, where fathers and dependent children are present, mothers in many countries are increasingly likely to be the primary source of economic support for the household. In the United States today, men over 55 are leaving the work force in greater numbers, while women over 55 are more likely to be working outside the home than ever before. Women in all societies that have been studied work more hours at home and in outside employment; they have less leisure time. This has always been true, incidentally, regardless of the type of society and women's economic roles.

Also, mothers who work in the nonfamily economy use more of their earned income to support the household. Fathers are more likely to reserve part of their earnings for personal use: gambling, drinking, sports, and other leisure activities. Even in cases where the father earns much more than the mother, he may be unwilling to contribute more than a fraction of his earnings to meeting basic household needs. Moreover, fathers may be supporting other women and children from previous or current sexual relationships—a pattern that is quite common in Central and South America and the Caribbean. Or, as is the case in some West African matrilineal countries, a father's primary financial obligation may be to support a sister's children rather than his own children.

Gender Differences

In economically developing countries, mothers with the lowest level of skills can usually find domestic work in middle-class households or in factories that require skills such as sewing or food processing. Fathers may not be able to find steady or full-time unskilled work, especially during economic recessions. In countries other than those of Central and South America and the Caribbean, fathers are more likely than mothers to migrate to areas where jobs are available. But unlike mothers who migrate to find jobs, as time goes by, fathers are more likely to stop sending money home to the families they left behind. Short separations make the heart grow fonder; long separations destroy relationships. In the United States, immediately after the Second World War, the divorce rate surged when service men and women, who had married hastily or impulsively during the war, returned home.[43]

Around the world today, about three-quarters of the world's poor are women, as are two-thirds of the world's illiterate adults. Two-thirds of the children who are not in school are girls, and 75 to 80 percent of the world's refugees are women and children. The status of women, as measured by average life expectancy, years of school completed, and average income compared to that of men in the same occupations, is highest in European and North American postindustrial societies: Sweden, Norway, Finland, Canada, and the United States.[44]

The status of women is rising in most industrial countries but has declined sharply in Russia since the breakup of the Soviet Union in 1991. Women in Russia are as literate as men (99 percent), but they are three times more likely to be unemployed. Their earnings, relative to those of men in the same occupations, declined from 75 percent in 1991 to 40 percent in 1996, the largest gap in the industrial world. The comparable figure in the United States also went down slightly, but in 1998 it was 75 percent. With the huge increase in unemployment, prostitution is flourishing in former Communist countries.[45]

We can now place some of the major trends in family life in a broad comparative framework historically and cross-culturally. How does the past influence the present, and how do family realities in the United States today vary according to class, ethnic origin, race, rural or urban residence, and religion?

Chapter 4
U.S. Families in Time and Place

Almost every aspect of family relationships in the United States differs in important ways, depending on the family's location in various subcultures. I will be returning to these differences in the remaining chapters as I review what we know about family relationships during the early, middle, and later years of family life. But first, we need some additional background information to help set the scene.

Social Class Differences

Regardless of the type of society, humans have always ranked each other on a scale from high to low prestige, depending largely on cultural values, political and economic conditions, and personal qualities of people in the society. In the simplest societies, age, sex, and personal qualities such as strength, bravery, resourcefulness, and temperament determined the overall prestige of individuals. Power differences (except for the shaman or the headman) and differences in property and wealth did not exist and were irrelevant in determining the prestige of families and individuals.

In the most complex societies, these differences do exist, and overall prestige is based on income and wealth (ownership of land, stocks, and other forms of property), level of education, and occupational prestige.[1] Most sociologists use the term *social class* in referring to class location because overall prestige in the society is based on more than just economic differences among families and individuals.

Our location in a particular social class affects every aspect of our lives every day of our lives. Another thing to keep in mind is that the major locating factors that determine membership in a social class—income, education, and occupational prestige—don't always go together. Drug dealers rank low on occupational prestige and, usually, low on years of education completed but they may rank quite high on income and property, depending on their status in the drug subculture. Truck drivers have less education and rank lower in occupational prestige than school teachers, but they usually earn more money.

Social Classes in the United States

Sociologists in the United States usually locate people within one of three major social classes—upper, middle, and working. They then divide each class into two levels: the old or the new upper class, the upper middle or lower middle class, and

TABLE 4.1 Social Classes in the United States

Percent of Population (Approximate)	Wealth and Income	Family	Education	Religion	Politics	Recreation
Old upper—.5%	Hereditary wealth, highest income, multimillionaires	Extended, semiextended, high birth rate	Liberal arts at prestigious colleges	Churchgoers, Episcopalian	Conservative	Lavishly expensive, sexually integrated, frequent traveling and entertaining, sponsors of the arts
New upper—1.5%	Achieved wealth, highest income, multimillionaires	Isolated nuclear, seminuclear, moderate or low birth rate	Varied, depending on occupation	Frequent change of church preference	Conservative or independent	Patterned after the old upper class
Upper middle—10%	High income, property, savings	Isolated nuclear or seminuclear, low birth rate	College graduates, professional training	Frequent change of church affiliation	Liberal or independent	Independent travel, entertaining friends
Lower middle—43%	Moderate income, small savings, little or no property	Seminuclear, low birth rate	Some college, high school graduates	Most frequent churchgoers	Conservative	Group travel, television, visiting relatives
Working—30%	Moderate income, little savings, little or no property	Semiextended or seminuclear, moderate birth rate	High school, high school dropouts	Religious faith strong, churchgoing moderate	Economically liberal, conservative on civil rights issues	Television, visiting relatives, sex-segregated leisure activities
Poor—15%	No savings, income inadequate to purchase essential goods and services	Extended or semi-extended, high birth rate	Largest percentage of school dropouts, widespread functional illiteracy	Religious faith very strong, particularly among women; churchgoing infrequent	Alienated, apathetic, nonvoting	Television, visiting relatives

the upper or lower working class (the poor) (Table 4.1). As with all attempts to classify human beings, our categories are not absolute and it is sometimes difficult to place people, especially if they are on their way up—or down.

The big divide between the upper and middle class is money—millions or billions of dollars. The major difference between middle- and working-class people is that middle-class people use information and communication skills in their work; working-class people work mainly with their hands. Surgeons work with their hands, but their work is based on an enormous amount of information and training that they acquire during long years of education and hands-on training.

The Old Upper Class

The old upper class (about 0.5 percent of the population) consists of multimillionaires who have inherited the bulk of their fortune from an ancestor and have managed to pass on their wealth over a period of several generations, at least. The Rockefellers, DuPonts, Roosevelts, Vanderbilts, and Fords are well-known examples.[2]

MODELS AND VALUES   In the past, old upper-class people tended to be traditional, politically conservative, familistic, authoritarian, and *ethnocentric* (the belief that your own cultural or subcultural customs and values are superior to all others). The models of the old upper class were white Anglo-Saxon Protestant (WASP) ancestors who immigrated to New England during the 17th century. Over time, the English and other Protestant immigrants from western and northern Europe succeeded in taking over the entire territory that is now the United States. They also succeeded in establishing their values—thrift, hard work, self-control, emotional reserve, physical endurance, politeness, and good manners—as part of the historically dominant culture in the United States.

The culture has changed, but as usual, when cultures change, some traditions survive. Values such as hard work, independence, emotional reserve, politeness, and civility are still prominent in the dominant culture, especially at the top levels. Materialism has edged out thrift, but manual laborers work harder and longer hours in the United States than anywhere in Europe. Emotional reserve is also strong among the descendants of Protestant European immigrants. The United States was a low-touch, hands-off society when this was the dominant culture. As for the survival of values such as politeness and emotional reserve, according to contemporary foreign visitors, New Yorkers are now more polite and courteous (more likely to say "thank you," less likely to jump lines or to close doors or elevators in other people's faces) and less likely to kiss and hug in public places than Londoners.[3]

SURVIVALS   Among the other traditional values that survive in the contemporary old upper class, familism is probably the most prominent. This is indicated by naming practices such as passing on the first name of the member who founded the family fortune to succeeding generations (with the suffixes Jr., II, III, or IV) or using the mother's maiden name as the first or middle name of children. Extended family closeness is reinforced by spending leisure time together at frequent large gatherings on family vacation compounds or by traveling together in extended family groups.

Family rituals such as debutante balls, formal engagements, large weddings, christenings, and Thanksgiving and Christmas gatherings of the clan are extremely important in this class.

CHANGING VALUES   Younger generations of the old upper class are less ethnocentric and authoritarian but are still highly familistic: not because they need help from each other but because of great pride in the family line. Husband-wife relationships are more egalitarian and companionate, and parent-child relationships are more emotionally involved and democratic among younger generations. Children are not bound to family businesses or land; they have more opportunity to strike out on their own in the nonfamily economy. Contact with other social classes increases as prestigious schools and colleges expand their recruitment to talented scholarship students, usually from the middle classes. The information economy requires a much wider base of talent than the old upper class can provide, and talent overcomes prejudice—slowly, but more effectively than in the past.

Many of the current generation of Kennedys have married (or remarried) talented women and men of middle-class origins. And more members of the latest generation of Protestant old rich are marrying men and women of minority, new or old upper class origins. The marriage of former President George Bush's son Jeb to a new upper-class Mexican national and the marriage of Vice President Al Gore's daughter Karenna to an heir of an old-line German-Jewish family are examples.

Mixed-class marriages are also more acceptable. In England, after three divorces among her older children, the last of Queen Elizabeth's four children married the talented and highly successful daughter of a lower-middle-class tire salesman—with the Queen's blessing. And this marriage is widely touted in the British media as one that is expected to last. Prince Edward and his new princess (countess, actually) had an eight-year courtship and share similar interests in the communications and entertainment industries.

The New Upper Class

The new upper class (about 1.5 percent of the population and growing fast) is newly rich and sometimes famous; but it also consists of multimillionaires, whatever the source of their wealth. The family member who made the fortune is still alive or has only recently died. Most members of this class have made their considerable fortunes in investment banking, computer industries, entertainment, or athletics. Bill Gates and Warren Buffet in business, Steven Spielberg and Julia Roberts in the movie industry, and Wayne Gretsky and Sammy Sosa in sports are examples.

MINORITIES   The new upper class contains more people of minority ethnic, racial, and religious origins, most of whom have succeeded in entertainment or sports. Extraordinary talent, ability, and drive are not limited to any class, although reaching the top is far more difficult for those who start life on the lower rungs of the prestige ladder. But whenever and however they came by their fortunes, old and new upper-class people usually have the highest level of prestige in the United States and, if they are gainfully employed, they occupy the top positions in government, business, sports, the arts, and the professions.

VALUES   Members of the new elite of self-made men and women tend to be more materialistic than the old upper class. Their social status is newer and less secure, and they are more likely to be conspicuous consumers: to buy costly diamonds, furs, art, cars, mansions, and other material possessions to display and confirm their new-found status. This pattern goes way back in human history, but it has graver consequences now because the excesses of this class are more likely to be publicized in the media and imitated by less fortunate people who can't afford to keep up with them.

Familism is not a strong value in the new upper class because the members of this class have been highly mobile—socially, psychologically, and geographically. New upper-class families are most likely to be isolated nuclear in form because of the huge gap in lifestyle between them and the relatives they left behind. But if family relationships in childhood and adolescence were strong and emotionally close, or if members of the new upper class come from a subculture where familism is still quite strong (even in the second, third, or fourth generation after immigrating to the United States), they may set up parents or brothers and sisters in homes nearby. Asian Americans, Italian Americans, Jewish Americans, and Latinos are more likely to do this than new-upper-class descendants of Protestant immigrants.

FAMILY RELATIONSHIPS   Nuclear family relationships reflect the middle-class origins of most members of this social class. Marital relationships are more egalitarian and less reserved than those of the more traditional old upper class. Parent-child relationships are more spontaneous, democratic, and emotionally involved. Divorce rates are also higher, although not as high as in the middle and working classes. Long separations are more frequent, as husbands (and wives) travel to multinational business offices in other parts of the world, or (among the sports and entertainment elite) when family members go on location to film movies or to train for and compete in games. Married women in the new upper class are more likely to be employed than women in the old upper class, most of whom continue to play the role of full-time companion, household manager, and fund-raiser for favorite charities.[4]

The Upper Middle Class

The upper middle class (about 10 or 12 percent of the population and also growing) consists of highly successful businesspeople, government employees, and professionals who are near, but not at the top of, the prestige, power, and wealth hierarchies in the United States. Some may be worth one million or even two million dollars, but mainly on paper because their houses and savings have appreciated to this level over the years.

Most are college graduates and many have graduate training in the higher professions, such as medicine, law, and college teaching. They have careers, not jobs, and they are highly invested in the work ethic. Exceptional drive, talent, and hard work (and a little bit of luck) may lead to national recognition, wealth, and movement into the new upper class. They usually work long hours, but they don't punch time clocks. They set up their own schedules, and they have more power and control in their work situations than lower-level workers. The most educated members of the upper-middle-class tend to be highly creative; they are a major source of cultural change in industrial societies.

MOBILITY Upper-middle-class people tend to be geographically mobile: They pursue new and better jobs in faraway places or they are transferred to new locations by their corporations. The isolated nuclear family is more common in this class. Two-career families are also becoming more frequent. (A career as opposed to a job requires more education, a higher level of communication skills, a greater degree of commitment, and usually longer hours of work.) But, although about two-thirds of the wives of higher professional men are employed, only about 5 percent of these couples are both higher professionals: lawyers, doctors, high-level business executives, or college teachers.[5] Commuter marriages are also on the increase in this social class.

VALUES Egalitarianism in husband–wife relationships is an important value in the upper middle class, as is rationalism, especially among the more educated. Upper-middle-class people are highly likely to pursue the latest scientific (and sometimes not so scientific) formulas and techniques for self- and relationship improvement. Materialism is more frequent among businesspeople in this social class than among professionals, who have their degrees and titles to validate their status. But the materialism in this class in no way comes close to that of the new upper class; they do not have the money to underwrite lavish expenditures on entertaining, travel, food, housing, cars, and clothes.

The Lower Middle Class

Lower-middle-class people (about 43 or 45 percent of the population) work at the less prestigious and lower-paying jobs that require communication skills: clerical and sales workers, lower-level management (foremen, office managers), semiprofessionals (case workers, parole officers), self-employed craftspeople, small storekeepers, and small farm owners. In these jobs, knowledge and communication skills are more important than tools, equipment, and machines. Secretaries work with machines but continue to use communication skills that have not yet been taken over by computers; salespeople use information about their products and persuasive conversation to sell their products. Skilled workers (e.g., plumbers, electricians) who own their small businesses are also among the lower middle class.

VALUES People in this class have usually completed high school and may have earned trade school or community college degrees, but most are not graduates of four-year liberal arts colleges. They have lower incomes and less savings, and are less socially and geographically mobile than the upper middle class, with which they identify. They value achievement, but their ambitions are centered on their children since their own mobility is limited by their lack of a four-year college education.

Familism and ethnocentrism are stronger than in the upper middle class. Most families do not live in daily contact with relatives, but they usually live close enough to visit regularly—about once a week, usually. Hired domestic help is rare in this class, and since husbands usually have less time-consuming jobs than upper-middle-class men, they are more likely to share homemaking obligations. In disciplining their children, they usually set stricter limits than the more affluent and individualistic upper middle class. But they are more likely than working-class parents to use reasoning, verbal threats, and withdrawal of privileges ("you're grounded," or "go to your room," or "no television for one week") rather than physical punishment in disciplining their children.[6]

Unsympathetic profiles of this class by upper-middle-class observers have tended to emphasize their conformity, political conservatism, exaggerated respectability, thrift, and petty striving.[7] But members of this class perform important functions as active and dedicated rank-and-file members and workers in religious, service, military, and political organizations in the United States. Their purchasing power has declined significantly in recent years, despite the increase in two-earner households in this class.

The Upper Working Class

The upper working class (about 30 percent of the population and declining in number) consists of skilled or semiskilled people who work mainly with their hands. They earn hourly wages rather than salaries. Skilled workers (plumbers, electricians, some types of construction workers) require vocational training, long apprenticeships, or extensive on-the-job training. Semiskilled workers (most factory employees) usually need only a few days of on-the-job training. Both categories of manual workers are more likely to be unionized than lower-middle-class employees, but their limited education, lack of savings, and lack of home, life, and catastrophic health insurance make them highly vulnerable to situational stresses.[8] Unemployment, hurricanes and floods, prolonged incurable illnesses, untimely deaths in the family, and fatalistic attitudes are more likely to precipitate crisis and despair in this class.

Also, the higher profits that result from new technological advances that lower production costs are passed on to managers and chief executive officers rather than to workers in the United States. Currently, fewer than one in ten factory workers in the United States earn more than workers in Germany, France, Italy, or the Scandinavian countries, where labor unions are stronger.

The percentage of high school dropouts in the working class is dropping but remains high. Wives often have more education than their husbands, since they are less likely to drop out of school and are more likely to attend and graduate from college. Authority in the home seems to be patriarchal ("wait 'til your father gets home!") But women have real authority in most day-to-day decision making, if only by default.

Other traditional values remain strong. The extended family is usually more important than experts, friends, clubs, and organizations as a source of emotional support, advice, and leisure activities. Working-class people are not likely to join clubs or other associations, except for labor unions and veterans' organizations, and, when they do join, their participation is minimal and marginal compared to that of the lower middle class. Religious beliefs are strong, especially among women, but churchgoing is less frequent than in the middle class.

Ethnocentrism is also strong, reinforced by lower levels of education, less geographic mobility, and less contact with unfamiliar people, places, and things.

Exposure to the mass media could possibly dispel some false beliefs about out-groups. But exposure to television and print in this class is limited largely to enter-tainment and sports rather than informational programs and articles.

New purchases provide temporary relief from frustration at home and at work. Working-class men and women are very vulnerable to credit-card debt. They tend to buy name brands and top-of-the-line products on the assumption that you get what you pay for; they are unlikely to subscribe to consumer information magazines.

As in other social classes, younger members of the upper working class are less likely to have traditional values. They have a higher level of education and are more geographically mobile, often moving to the suburbs in pursuit of jobs that are now more available there than in central cities. They are more likely to be separated from their relatives, and the extended family loses its previous influence and importance. Younger members tend to be more egalitarian, less fatalistic, and more knowledge-able and informed in managing the routine demands of daily life.

The Lower Working Class (The Poor)

In any particular year, the federal government sets the poverty line according to the changing cost of food, housing, and services, as measured by the Consumer Price Index. In 1999, the poverty line was defined as a household income of less than $16,000 for a family of four. This figure is adjusted according to how many people live in a household. Also, household income figures do not include noncash gov-ernment benefits such as food stamps, subsidized public housing, and other public services such as Medicaid (for the poor or the uninsured).

In the United States, the poor have the lowest income, the lowest levels of edu-cation and occupational skills, and are unemployed or underemployed—working part-time or irregularly, when they would prefer steady, full-time employment. Also included are the *working poor*, who work full time but in jobs that don't pay enough to keep the family above the poverty line. Finally, men and women who, regardless of level of education and occupational skills, sink into poverty as a result of physical or mental illness, loss of a job, divorce, widowhood, or other situational changes are also included among the poor.

Worst off, perhaps, are the *ghetto poor*, who are doubly vulnerable because of their minority status as well as their low economic status. Most people on welfare live in inner cities, but most new jobs in our current economy are being created out-side of large central cities. The poor can't afford to travel to these jobs—by trains, planes, or automobiles.

At this point in time, compared to white families, blacks are almost three times as likely to be living in poverty. And an even higher percentage of Latino families are now classified as poor. In part, this is because Latinos now have a higher rate of nonmarital childbirths than blacks. They also have higher fertility rates and lower rates of high school and college graduation than blacks. Mainly for these reasons, Latino males now have higher unemployment rates than African American females. And if present trends in immigration and fertility rates continue, Latinos will out-number African Americans early in the 21st century and become the largest minor-ity in the United States.[9]

THE HOMELESS   I have already pointed out that women, children, and older people are now more likely to be living in poverty in the United States than in any other advanced industrialized country in the world, with the exception of Russia. We also have the highest rate of homelessness of any postindustrial society—an overall rate that has been increasing for more than two decades. A majority of those who are homeless are single men still, but the number of single women, mothers, children, and adolescent runaways who are homeless will soon outnumber the traditional pillars of homeless society. The rate of homelessness has increased for a number of reasons: government cutbacks in public housing; a decline in the supply of low-rent, privately owned housing; cuts in public welfare programs; government programs to move mentally ill people out of hospitals and into communities (where those who are inadequately supervised and provided for become homeless); and the inability or unwillingness of stressed-out, impoverished extended families to take in their homeless relatives.

Keeping in mind this brief sketch of what sociologists mean when they refer to the various social classes in the United States today, I can now point out more specifically how this all-important locating factor affects family realities, and how it affects almost all other kinds of realities that people face as they live out their lives.

The Significance of Social Class

On national surveys, except for upper-class people (who do not respond to surveys), as we go up the social class structure, people are more likely to experience and report higher self-esteem and greater psychological security (less stress and anxiety), as well as greater economic security. With each increase in socioeconomic status (increases in income, level of education, and occupational prestige), people have better physical and mental health, lower rates of acute and chronic illness, fewer disabilities, and longer life expectancy. Higher-status people have better medical care and healthier diets, are more likely to exercise, are less likely to smoke, and are less likely to be overweight. They are less likely to be hospitalized or institutionalized for physical or mental illness, for crimes against society, or for crimes against other family members (murder, abuse, lack of support). And they are less likely to be the victims of violent crimes outside of the home as well.

The divorce rate goes down at each higher social class level, as does the fertility rate, except for old upper-class families; those with daughters only are more likely to continue having children until a son is born. Also, major life transitions (taking a first job, getting married for the first time, becoming a parent or grandparent, retiring) take place at older ages at successively higher class levels. People with high socioeconomic status are also more likely to change careers and go back to school for more training. And higher-income men are far more likely to remarry and start new families at an older age than men who are working class or poor.

The higher social classes are also less conventional, and they tend to look, feel, and act younger than their chronological age. On surveys, they are less likely to report themselves as "old," regardless of their chronological age, as long as they don't have a seriously disabling illness. They are also more socially connected:

They travel more, read more, get more mail, have more friends, do more entertaining, are less likely to retire if they are healthy, and are more likely to do volunteer work if they do retire. Also, they are more adventurous in their sexual practices: more likely to engage in foreplay, oral sex, masturbation, and variations in sexual positions. The working class is more likely to have an unadorned, no-nonsense, silent approach to sex.

Mixed-Class Families

Since social class is so important in understanding family realities, how do we classify a *mixed-class family* in which the employed husband and the employed wife have different occupational prestige—a secretary married to a factory worker, for example? This becomes an interesting question now that more than three-quarters of married women in the United States are in the labor force and almost half are married to men who work in less prestigious jobs.

In the past, married women derived their social status from their husbands' occupations, but not now. Even the Bureau of the Census no longer asks about the "head of the household." What is happening now is that the class *identifications* of people—men and women, single or married—are increasingly independent of their partners' or their parents' social class standing.[10]

What does this mean for family relationships? Probably, for predicting the values of a particular family, it would be best to classify that family according to the status of the more prestigious partner, regardless of gender. But in mixed-class situations, which are much more frequent now, we can also predict more family conflict stemming from class-based differences in values, interests, tastes, and goals. These conflicts show up in all sorts of decisions: how to discipline children, how to spend money, which movie to go to, what kind of vacation to take, how much time to spend with friends or in-laws, and so on.

Our location in a particular social class strongly affects the likelihood of meeting potential partners, living together, marrying, and remarrying. It affects how we raise our children, our satisfactions, amount of communication, and kinds and intensity of stresses we experience in family relationships. It affects the conflicts we have and how we resolve these conflicts. It affects our values, judgments, outlook, and opportunities. In short, it affects how we feel, where we can go, what we can do, what we want, and what we can have. Given the importance of social class location, I'll be returning to class differences in practically every aspect of family life I describe in future chapters.

Ethnic and Racial Differences

Recent trends in family life and in the immigration that results in ethnic family differences are major issues of public concern in the United States today. Concern about families centers on the increase in alternative family forms: in unmarried, same-sex or opposite-sex couple and family households and the increase in single, divorced, or never-married mothers with children. Huge increases in immigration to the United States from poorer, non-European countries since 1965 (when the federal government liberalized its immigration policy) are major reasons for increased public concern about immigration in recent years.[11]

These are not new concerns historically. But more information and better understanding of both trends, based on research rather than unfounded fears and misguided prejudices, can help put these trends in perspective, relieve public anxiety, and, hopefully, point to more rational and effective government policies to deal with these concerns.

This said, let's look at some basic concepts sociologists use in their research on ethnic family realities, concepts that are crucial to understanding and explaining these realities.

Ethnic Origin

Ethnic origin (from the Greek *ethnikos*, meaning "nation" or "people") refers to the country or continent where most of a person's ancestors originated. Since race usually coincided with continent, race could be included in the concept of ethnic origin. But given the enormous amount of migration and genetic mixing of various populations over the centuries, it becomes increasingly difficult to classify people as members of a distinct ethnic or racial population. According to the most recent DNA evidence provided by geneticists, the ancestry of Europeans, for example, is one-third African and two-thirds Asian. The physical differences associated with race are surface changes that occurred as various migrating populations adapted to different climates.[12] In tropical climates, darker skin protects against skin cancer; in colder climates, lighter skin protects against rickets.

Racially, how do we classify golf celebrity Tiger Woods? His mother was born in Thailand but is of Chinese ancestry. His father is African American but has European American and American Indian ancestors. In the United States he is classified as black because of the "one drop of blood" ruling, upheld by the Supreme Court in 1986. This ruling states that any individual who has African American ancestors, no matter how few or how many, is black. For the first time, the 2000 census allowed people to check more than one race to indicate their ancestry; but if they checked "Black, African American, or Negro" they were classified as black, no matter how many other categories they checked.

Minorities

Today in the United States, people whose ancestry is not western or northern European are defined as minorities. Long ago, sociologist Louis Wirth defined a *minority* as a large number of people "who, because of their physical or cultural characteristics, are singled out from others in the society in which they live for differential and unequal treatment."[13] We define, or try to define, different races in terms of visible, distinguishing physical traits such as skin color, shape of the eyes, nose, and lips, hair texture, and body build. Cultural differences consist of language, values, beliefs (religious beliefs, especially), customs, and tastes that differ from those of the dominant English-speaking, white, Protestant culture in the United States.

The major ethnic populations in the United States are of European, African, Asian, or Latino ancestry. Latino Americans are a mixed population with varying amounts of European, African, and Asian ancestry. (The Indian populations of North, Central, and South America are now believed to have migrated to this continent from Asia during the last ice age.)

Stereotypes and Generalizations

In describing ethnic families, it is important to know the difference between stereotypes and generalizations. *Stereotypes* are beliefs about a particular category of people that are applied indiscriminately to *all* people in that category; *generalizations* are conclusions based on scientific evidence. *Prejudice* (from the Latin *praejudicare* meaning "to prejudge") are stereotypes, or fixed images in people's minds, about others who are physically or culturally different; *discrimination* is actual hostile behavior toward others who are different physically, culturally, or both.

Generalizations about ethnic family differences are usually based on more than one research study, and conclusions about ethnic families are prefaced by the words *most, usually, tend to, are more likely to,* or *more often are.* Social scientists rarely use the word *all.* This isn't possible when we are dealing with individuals and their infinite small differences. Also, not only are ethnic families different in some ways, they change over time and in succeeding generations. But we don't despair; yesterday's generalizations are today's good history. And we can't understand the present or predict the future of ethnic families unless we understand their past—and our past.

Assimilation and Acculturation

Researchers find remarkably persistent ethnic differences among specific ethnic populations in the United States today: in values and attitudes, educational and occupational achievements, gender roles, childrearing practices, fertility, marriage and divorce rates, extended family relationships, and family histories. And these differences persist long after the time when immigrant ancestors first came to the United States. We are all immigrants or descendants of immigrants. With immigrants from over 400 different countries, historically and today, the United States is the most ethnically varied country in the world.

In explaining the persistence of ethnic family differences in this country, it helps to be clear about the meaning of two other concepts: assimilation and acculturation. *Assimilation* is the process by which new immigrants lose their ethnic identity and identification and become "100 percent American." This is the old "melting pot" ideal and, except for immigrants from England, Wales, and Northern Ireland, this hasn't happened here—or anywhere else in the world for that matter.

Historically, racial minorities from Africa and Asia were not expected to assimilate, but even European immigrants to the United States and their descendants are still distinguished and identified as Anglo American, Irish American, Italian American, and so on—generations after their ancestors originally came here.

But most immigrants and their descendants do *acculturate*. They learn the basic aspects of the dominant culture in the United States: the language, norms, values, knowledge, and skills that a majority of people must learn in order to function successfully in the mainstream economy and society (Table 4.2). This happens, more or less quickly, depending on where immigrants came from, when they came here, where they settled, and what they brought with them. What they brought with them is their socioeconomic status (education, occupational skills, money, and other property), their rural or urban origin, and their physical or cultural differences from the dominant population.

Rates of Acculturation

In the United States today, *cultural pluralism* is the standard. Ideally, this involves a live-and-let-live attitude toward those who are different, an unprejudiced acceptance of these differences, and increased pride in and respect for one's own particular cultural heritage. The belief that it is necessary or desirable to assimilate in order to acculturate is another myth undone by social science research. While pride in one's ethnic ancestry is the norm now, the acceptance of certain dominant cultural values in the United States (individualism and achievement, especially) tends to cross ethnic boundaries over time, as immigrant groups acculturate and are socially, psychologically, and geographically mobile—if they are.

TABLE 4.2   Factors Affecting Rates of Acculturation

1. Degree of physical and cultural difference from the dominant population in a society (in the United States, European Americans at the present time)
2. Willingness of minorities to acculturate (voluntary vs. involuntary segregation)
3. Strength of traditional values—fatalism, familism, patriarchy (related to social class, religion, urban or rural origins)
4. Attitudes, beliefs, and behavior of the dominant population (stereotypes, prejudice, discrimination, acceptance)
5. Costs of discrimination compared to the advantages of exclusion and subordination (the costs of welfare vs. the gains from economic exploitation)
6. Educational and economic opportunities available in the society (state of the economy; business cycle: bust, boom)
7. Degree of contact with or isolation from the dominant population (segregation from or exposure to the dominant culture via work, leisure activities)
8. Nearness to the country or geographic area of origin (going home: reinforcement of traditional cultural values, norms)
9. Recency of arrival, gender, and age at immigration (for the individual, affects goals, expectations, and opportunities)

Whether and how fast this happens for particular ethnic immigrants depends mainly on how different they are physically and culturally from the dominant population, the strength of their traditional values (familism and fatalism especially), the educational and occupational opportunities in the area where they settle, and the prejudice and discrimination they encounter. Also important are the degree of contact with or isolation from the dominant population and culture and the nearness to their country of origin. For individual immigrants, gender and age when they arrive are also important in determining when or whether they acculturate.[14]

Some examples will make this clearer. English and Irish immigrants are physically similar to the dominant population and both speak English, but Irish Catholic immigrants have had a slower rate of acculturation because of their religious beliefs and lower social class origins.[15] Immigrants from southern and eastern Europe at the turn of the 20th century experienced more prejudice because of their non-Protestant religion and their generally darker complexions. In fact, they were referred to as "black" in the popular newspapers of that time.[16]

Most Latino immigrants are Catholic and speak Spanish, but Cuban immigrants have acculturated much faster than Mexican immigrants. Here, the amount of European ancestry and class origins are major factors. The first generation of Cuban immigrants, who arrived shortly after the revolution in 1959 (when it became evident that Castro would establish a Communist government in Cuba), were largely European (Spanish) in ethnic origin, and were urban and of upper- and middle-class origin. The resources they brought with them (high levels of education, strong occupational skills, and middle-class values, emphasizing education and achievement) speeded their acculturation.

Moreover, the first Cuban immigrants were granted refugee status, since, like Vietnamese and other Southeast Asian and Russian immigrants since the 1970s, they were fleeing Communist regimes. Unlike other immigrants, refugees receive public assistance from the United States government in the form of subsidized housing, English language instruction, job retraining, Supplemental Security Income payments, and food stamps.

The first generation of Cuban immigrants encountered little prejudice when they arrived. Moreover, though they lived close to their country of origin, they could not go home again, and this, too, speeded up their acculturation. Compared to other Latino immigrants and their descendants, Cuban Americans now have the highest percentage of college and professional school graduates, the lowest birth rate, the lowest rate of mother-headed households, and the lowest poverty rate.[17]

In contrast, Mexican American immigrants are not refugees; most have come from rural areas, with low levels of education and limited technical skills. Increasingly, they are settling in large central cities where educational standards are low and low-skilled jobs have been declining. Over three generations, many have experienced a marked increase in family problems: higher rates of separation, divorce, nonmarital pregnancies, mother-headed households, delinquency, alcohol and drug addiction, and mental illness.[18]

Persisting Ethnic Differences

What are some persisting differences in values and customs that we find among various ethnic families today?

Unmarried Young Adults

The conflict between individualism (establishing independence) and familism is strongest during adolescence and young adulthood. Italian, Jewish, Asian, and Latino American families tend to place more emphasis on familism and continued contact, attachment, and interdependence in their relationships with adult children; English, German, and Scandinavian Americans are more likely to value geographic separation, emotional distancing, and parent-child independence.[19]

Husband–Wife Relationships

Asian Americans are more likely to maintain traditional relationships. Power, decision making, and coping with the outside world are regarded as male prerogatives. This usually also applies to Greek and Italian American families. Anglo Americans and Jewish Americans are more likely to be democratic (egalitarian) in their relationships. But the open display of affection is usually more restrained in Anglo American family relationships.[20]

Extended Family Relationships

The boundary around the nuclear family is quite strong among Anglo and Irish Americans: Advice and attempts to influence married children by parents and other relatives are usually regarded as an intrusion. In African and Italian American families, advice and help with the conflicts and problems of nuclear families are more often expected and sought from other members of the family. Italian American parents tend to expect their married children to live nearby. They absorb new in-laws into the extended family, and they expect their adult children to socialize mainly with them and with other members of the family rather than with friends.[21]

Childrearing Practices

Ethnic groups tend to differ in the degree of permissiveness or strictness used in bringing up children. They also tend to differ in the degree to which family relationships are child-centered or parent-centered. Some ethnic groups, such as Puerto Rican and Greek Americans, tend to indulge infants but become much more strict with children and adolescents, especially girls. African Americans are more likely to use physical punishment in disciplining children, although this pattern declines somewhat in the middle class.

Jewish Americans tend to be intensely involved in the intellectual and emotional development, educational achievements, and occupational success of their children. They are also more likely to seek professional help for children with problems. Now, however, Asian Americans—Chinese, Japanese, and Korean Americans, especially—are even more intensely involved in the academic achievements of their children.[22] Currently, they are more likely than Jewish Americans to limit TV watching and to enroll their children in after-school academic enrichment programs.

This reflects the survival of Confucian cultural values among many Asian immigrants and their descendants. The Confucian system of ethics, as I described earlier, emphasized unquestioning obedience to and great respect for parents and other older adults, extreme patriarchy, and formal education as a crucial means of social mobility. The survival of these values is reflected in the current family demographics and educational and occupational achievements of Asian Americans.

Compared to other minorities, Asian Americans have the lowest divorce, fertility, and unmarried pregnancy rates and the highest rate of racial intermarriage, and they are most likely to be living in three-generation households. And, compared to whites, they have a higher percentage of BAs, a higher percentage of workers in managerial and professional occupations, and the highest median income in the country.[23] Mainly, this is because median income is calculated in terms of total household income. Asian Americans are more likely than whites to have adult employed children and extended family members living in the same household and contributing to total household income.

Class and Ethnic Origin

Over the generations, socioeconomic status, especially level of education, tends to become more important than ethnic origin in affecting family relationships, despite persisting ethnic differences. A good example of this is found in more recent studies of African American families. These studies have focused on the middle class as well as on the inner-city poor. More than one-third of African American families are now middle class and, in some ways, their class standing brings them closer to whites than to their fellow African Americans who are poor or working class.[24]

Studies of African American families in this class correct images of a deteriorating family life among *all* African Americans. Middle-class African Americans work hard and emphasize achievement, independence, and self-reliance in their family relationships. They are almost as likely as European Americans to have two-parent family households.

But most African Americans don't conform to certain aspects of the patriarchal tradition. Wives and mothers in this subculture have been employed for generations. Females have been more self-reliant and assertive, and males have been more emotionally expressive than is typical among whites. Husbands are more willing to talk to their wives about how they feel, even in wife-dominant families, and they are more likely than white and Latino males to share housekeeping chores.[25] Traditional personality stereotypes about female passivity and male emotional reserve do not apply to African Americans.

Generally, and on repeated national surveys, whites report themselves to be happier than blacks, regardless of social class standing.[26] This probably has to do with the human conditions of prejudice and humiliation that African Americans experience, regardless of social class. In the wider society and at every class level,

TABLE 4.3   African Americans as Forerunners of Family Change

In the United States, African American families exhibited the following family patterns *before* European American families, who are now catching up, especially in the middle social classes:

1. Very low birth rates in the highly educated middle classes—no children or one-child families
2. Increase in single-parent households
3. Increase in never-married mothers
4. Widespread employment of married women with dependent children at home in all classes, including the middle class
5. Increase in the number of unmarried living-together couples
6. Delay in age at marrying for the first time; increase in permanent, never-married singles
7. Increase in rate of premarital sexual activity; lowering of age when genital sexual activity begins
8. Higher divorce rates at *all* class levels
9. Highly educated women married to less well-educated men
10. Prevalence of extended family structure
11. Smaller gap between the earnings of husband and wife
12. More sharing by fathers of childcare and homemaking responsibilities

blacks tend to have less prestige, power, and wealth than whites. They have greater difficulty gaining acceptance from neighbors and co-workers in racially mixed neighborhoods and work situations, and are often viewed as dangerous or subordinate because of the color of their skin, regardless of how they are dressed and how well they speak. They are more likely than whites to be ignored in stores and by doormen and cab drivers, mistaken for the help in exclusive stores, and given less desirable tables and poorer service in high-end restaurants.[27]

But in some ways, African American families have been forerunners of family change in the United States (Table 4.3). Certain features that have been true of African American family life for decades are now becoming increasingly widespread among middle-class white families: the large increases in mother-headed or mother-supported households; in unmarried living-together couples; in the employment of married women with infants and very young, dependent children at home; and in the tendency for women with higher levels of education and income to marry down.

Geographic Location and Family Life

Compared to class, ethnic origin, and race, the geographic area where families live is less important in affecting family realities than it was in the past, but some differences persist. Generally, New York and California are major centers of social change in the United States, where new divorce and child custody policies originated, for example, as well as laws to provide health care and other benefits to unmarried partners in same-sex or opposite-sex relationships. This is probably because these states contain many more people who have migrated from other countries, or from other parts of this country, and are less constrained by the families they left behind in the choices they make and the way they conduct their lives. The South and the Midwest continue to have lower rates of alternative family forms, lower divorce rates, and lower ethnic and racial intermarriage rates—although the gap is closing.

Also, most researchers agree that major differences in the family lives of city dwellers and rural residents in the United States are declining. The spread of industrialization to rural areas, the reverse migration trend from city to country, and the connecting influences of computer technology and the mass media are believed to be the most important reasons for this decline.

Urban–Rural Differences

In describing urban–rural differences in family life, small as they are at this point, we should bear in mind that the rural–urban classification is arbitrary and often blurred, except at the extremes of the huge metropolis and the small family-owned farm. The United States Bureau of the Census defines communities of less than 2,500 people as rural, but only if they are not close to a central city of 50,000 people surrounded by densely settled suburbs. At this point in time, only about 20 percent of the U.S. population is classified as rural and less than 2 percent of rural families are classified as farm families.[28]

Still, rural residents are somewhat more likely to marry, somewhat less likely to divorce, less likely to have female-headed households with young children present, less likely to have two-earner families, and have lower unemployment rates. But, again, these differences are small and are declining.

Older People in Rural Areas

The biggest differences among rural and urban people show up in statistics about older rural residents.[29] About the same percentage of older people live in urban and rural areas. But older people in rural areas are more likely to be living in poverty, especially those who are over 75 years old. Medical care of any kind is not as likely to be readily available in rural areas, nor are other support services, formal (from public or private agencies) or informal (from adult children or other relatives). The adult children of nonfarm, rural older people are more likely than urban children to have moved some distance away from their parents. This is especially true in the more impoverished rural areas, where jobs are hard to find.

The dependency needs of many older rural residents (economic, physical, and emotional) are greater. They tend to have lower incomes, poorer health, and less convenient means of transportation than city dwellers. Providing care for disabled older parents is a serious problem for middle-aged children everywhere in the United States today, but especially for those whose parents live in rural areas, where household help and nursing care are less available or not affordable. Many older parents with serious chronic illnesses are now following their children to metropolitan areas, where health-care services (and their children) are more available. Others, who have lived in their community for decades, rely on old friends for help.[30]

Gender Differences

Another difference between city and country dwellers shows up in studies of older unmarried people—mainly widowed, but also divorced or never married. Social scientists have long known that older single men are much less likely than older single women to be involved in family, friendship, and community activities. Unlike most older women, older men usually have no close friends to confide in.

Gender differences in isolation or contact are reinforced by size of place. Single urban older women are more likely than rural women to be involved in outside activities: friends, family, clubs, religious, and volunteer work. Single rural older men are least likely to be involved with other people and outside activities, and white men over 65 have the highest suicide rate in the United States today.[31]

Religion

Religion is a powerful force in guiding the behavior of deeply religious people, especially where questions of ethics are involved.[32] Ethics define what is good, bad, and obligatory for believers. In deeply religious families, duty outweighs impulse and temptation, strengthens commitment, and helps resolve conflicts. Strong religious beliefs provide powerful ways to cope with major life stresses: a disabling or life-threatening disease, the death of a family member or close friend, and divorce.[33] A growing number of research studies have found that people who are religious (as measured by weekly attendance at religious services) are less likely to suffer from high blood pressure and depression and to live, on the average, ten years longer than those who are not religious.[34]

Religion and Family Solidarity

Religious ritual reinforces individual and family identity and solidarity. Same-faith friends are a major source of nonfamily support in times of crisis, especially among minorities in impoverished inner-city areas, where crisis is endemic.[35] Among the lowest-income African Americans, strong religious beliefs and the influence of other church members reinforce the desire to fulfill family responsibilities and avoid infidelity, promiscuity, substance abuse, and criminal and delinquent behavior.[36]

Religion and Morality

In the United States, the importance of strongly held religious beliefs in guiding moral behavior is usually recognized and respected, even when the behavior is not the norm. Virginity before marriage and faithfulness after marriage are stronger among deeply religious people. In the 1970s, when sexual activity was less restrained than it is now, sociologist Mirra Kamarovsky found that deeply religious students at Barnard College who were virgins were accepted and respected; students who were not religious and were virgins were perceived by other students as having psychological problems.[37]

Religion and Family Violence

On the National Survey of Families and Households, a random survey of over 13,000 households conducted in the late 1980s and repeated five years later, it was reported that domestic violence was lower among regular churchgoers. There were no significant differences in same-faith or mixed-faith households. But rates of domestic violence were higher for men who held the most conservative theological beliefs and had a strongly patriarchal view of male authority in the home.[38]

Declining Religious Distinctions

In the past, religious affiliation (Catholic, Protestant, or Jewish) strongly affected birth rates, divorce rates, the choice of a marital partner, sexual behavior, the roles of husbands and wives, childrearing practices, and a belief in life after death.[39] Now, beliefs and behavior are converging in the United States; differences among the various religions appear to be less important than whether or not family members are religious.[40]

At the beginning of the 21st century, on a national poll sponsored by the *New York Times*, almost one-half of the respondents who were under 30 agreed with the statement "The best religion would be one that borrowed from all religions." (In contrast, less than one-third of those over 70 years of age agreed with this statement.)[41]

Roles

At this point in time, families who are religious are more likely than families who aren't to value virginity before marriage, fidelity after marriage, staying married, educating children, and maintaining contact with parents—regardless of whether they are Catholic, Protestant, or Jewish. Studies of veiled Islamic, fundamentalist Protestant, and Orthodox Jewish women in the United States indicate a basic similarity in their perceptions of women's roles, regardless of differences in religion and ethnicity.[42]

Childrearing

In older studies of childrearing practices in the United States, Catholics were more likely than Protestants to insist on unconditional obedience in disciplining their children. Protestant parents were more likely to value independence and self-reliance. More recent studies indicate a significant decline in the value of obedience among younger Catholic parents. The descendants of 19th- and early-20th-century Irish and Italian immigrants are now mainly middle class, and their childrearing is more democratic.[43]

In recent national studies of Protestant parents, even those with the most conservative theological beliefs are no longer authoritarian in their relationships with their children. In fact, they report more warmth, support, and encouragement in their childrearing than less religious Protestants do.[44] In religious intermarriages, there are fewer conflicts if neither partner is religious. But if one partner is religious and the other is not, conflicts are likely, especially after a child is born and the question arises of what the child's religion will be.

Identity, Crisis, and Community

In the United States, new recruits to fundamentalist religious groups experience a return to religion. This is usually interpreted as a reaction to personal crisis (the born-again experience). It also represents a search for family, community, belonging, and connectedness by those who do not have these attachments and identities. Whatever the reasons, strong religious beliefs continue to have a significant effect on family realities and on coping with loss and stress. For the deeply religious, common ethical standards may sometimes override differences in ethnic origin and specific religious rituals.

The following quote is from a newspaper interview with a deeply religious 95-year-old black woman. For generations in Ghana, her family practiced Jewish rituals but were considered Christian. In the 17th century, her family was brought to the Caribbean as slaves; they continued to believe in their ancestral Jewish origins and practiced Jewish rituals. She immigrated to New York in the 1920s and eventually settled in Harlem:

> And when I went to the [Jewish] temple on 128th Street, I realized I was in the right place. I did not join the Hebrew faith—I returned. I simply was on the wrong road and found my way back. That's my experience. In the Bible Jeremiah says he is black. Solomon says he is black. And David was and Samuel was and Jacob was. That's where I come from. . . . Complexion doesn't mean one thing for me. It's your character and your decency that counts. . . . I use a wheel chair now and a walker and a cane, but I still pray. It's like food for me—it allows me to survive.[45]

PART III
TRANSITIONS AND FUTURE DEVELOPMENTS

Chapter 5
Love and Attachment

Before going into the topics of love and attachment, both of which are extremely popular areas of research these days, I need to describe the approach I use to organize the information we have about families in the United States in the remaining chapters. Earlier, I referred to this approach as the family development, life cycle, life history, or life course model; researchers have used one or the other of these terms, with slight variations in meaning. In this chapter, I have used the term *family development*, to include both internal family changes and the external societal changes (in the economy, in government policy, and in the culture, for example) that affect families. The concept of development is consistent with the concept of individual development used by psychologists; both perspectives rely ultimately on the stages or transitions that individuals and families go through as they age over time.

The Family Development Model

The life history of an individual begins at birth, ends at death, and, in between, proceeds through various biologically grounded, but culturally shaped, developmental stages. Generally, these stages are called *infancy, toddler, childhood, adolescence, adulthood, middle age*, and *old age*. The life history of a new family begins when an unmarried woman has a child or when partners marry or move in together and take on varying amounts of economic, physical, and emotional responsibilities for one another. Families develop and change over time as the founding members of a new nuclear family age, face new demands and responsibilities in the early and middle years of their lives, and withdraw from some of these responsibilities in their later years—if they can.

A specific generation of a family ends when the founding members die, regardless of how the family was formed or whether the family remains intact over the years. A focus on families as they go through various stages over time is a major perspective in the social sciences (Table 5.1). Sociologists call this approach the *family development perspective*; at the level of the individual, it is called *child and adult development* by psychologists. The basis of both approaches is time and aging.

TABLE 5.1   The Family Development Model

1. A model of family change over time as members age
2. Family members include generations, siblings, couples (married, unmarried, separated, divorced, remarried, heterosexual, and same-sex), parents (including single parents), and children (as children grow and mature)
3. Focus is on changing relationships: roles (rights and obligations), values, power, conflicts, stresses, satisfactions during various stages
4. Stages are defined by status changes in family and work situations during the early, middle, and later years of life, especially as children and other members come and go, and as work roles change, up to and after retirement
5. Explanations of changing roles, conflicts, satisfactions, and stresses are internal (psychological) and external (related to changing cultural, economic, political, and human conditions in the wider society over time)

Stage Theories

Locating families in terms of the various stages they go through over time has two advantages. First, it is a logical way to organize research information on families that helps us answer questions such as how and why roles, conflicts, power, economic resources, satisfaction, and stress vary as family members age. Second, this approach helps us understand and explain certain stresses that families experience over the years, because the focus is on the *changes* that family members experience as they age. Over time, they confront new challenges and take on new obligations as family members come and go and circumstances change. This way of looking at families has a long history in the social sciences, going back to the beginning of the 20th century.[1]

For most adults who form new families in various subcultures in the United States today, a major change in the early years is the birth of a child. Coping with the death of parents and with the physical and emotional changes in adolescent children are typical changes in the middle years. Changes that result from the marriage and/or divorce of adult children now straddle the middle and later years. The typical changes associated with old age require adapting to loss: the gradual loss of strength and good health, and the loss of old friends and brothers and sisters if they die before we do. Separating from children emotionally as they develop and mature is a change that begins when children enter day care or preschool; it continues until the time they leave home (whenever this happens—temporarily or forever).

These changes are stressful. They involve feelings of pressure or anxiety because they require adapting to new circumstances—good or bad, expected and unexpected, internal and external.[2] Unexpected changes are such things as the sudden death of a family member, floods, fires, desertion, divorce, the loss of a job, the return home of an adult child, and involuntary retirement. No one deliberately plans for these changes; they are more stressful than expected changes such as the growth and maturing of children. And if changes and stresses pile up and the stress is severe enough, it can lead to *crisis.*[3]

Families in crisis are unable to function. Dishes and laundry pile up. Cooking, cleaning, and shopping for food become overwhelming chores. Bills go unpaid. Children and other dependents are neglected. No one functions well—at home, at school, or at work. The family experiences a major change in the way members relate to one another and to the outside world.

Stress and crisis are more frequent in industrial societies because change is more frequent. Also, guidelines for thinking, feeling, and behaving in new situations and changed social conditions are not as clear as they once were; and support from extended family members who live nearby is not as available as it once was.

Stages in Postindustrial Societies

The current number of stages that individuals and families go through, the timing of these stages, the average length of each stage, and the behavior during each stage varies depending on the time and place; on the type of society (developing, industrial, or postindustrial); and, within a particular society, on the ethnic origin and race, age and generation, and social class location of family members (Table 5.2).

In the United States today, working-class family members reach adulthood, middle age, and old age earlier, on the average, than upper-middle and upper-class families. They tend to finish school, take their first adult full-time jobs, marry and have children, become grandparents, retire, and die sooner than more educated, higher income people.[4]

Also, compared to the 1950s, many more couples in the United States today live together and don't marry, or they divorce, or they remarry and form stepfamilies. And, compared to the 1950s, more couples are deciding not to become parents, and there are more single parents and more same-sex couples—with or without children. Furthermore, more people are now remaining single, delaying or skipping stages, or starting all over again at older ages. And, finally, we have new stages that didn't exist in the agricultural and industrializing societies of the past.

TABLE 5.2   Life Stages in Postindustrial Societies

1. More life periods or stages. New stages: preadolescence, youth (postadolescence), middle age, young-old, and old-old
2. Older age before occupying adult economic, marital, and parent statuses, especially in the middle and upper classes
3. Blurring of boundaries between stages (more in-between stages, mixed stages, extension of stages)
4. More flexibility in timing of the change from one period to the next (more skipping of stages, returning to earlier stages)
5. Less conformity on the basis of age (cultural age norms—"act your age!"—are less binding) at any particular stage, especially among the middle and upper classes

---

New Stages

An example of a new stage is the *empty nest* stage, when all children are grown and have left home. In the early 1900s, the typical couple didn't survive or lived only a few years after their last child (typically the fifth) left home; there was no empty nest stage for most people.[5] Today, parents can expect to live an average of about 20 years in restored privacy and have less financial pressure after their last child leaves, provided that their adult children don't return home. Many adult children are returning home now—after a divorce (daughters with young children, usually), the loss of a job, the decision to go back to school, or simply to save money.

Another example of a stage that didn't exist in nonliterate and agricultural societies is adolescence. Adolescence as a separate and distinct stage between childhood and adulthood, beginning at puberty and ending at biological maturity, was not recognized. Industrial societies recognize not only adolescence, but additional stages called *preteens* (or *tweens*) and *youth*. Preteens are different from younger school-age children; sometime between the ages of 9 and 12, many more are beginning to behave in ways that were previously peculiar to adolescents. The youth stage is the period after girls and boys are physically mature but have not yet started their adult full-time jobs and become economically and socially independent.[6] This stage applies mainly to middle- and upper-class young people in college, graduate, or professional schools, who now spend years beyond adolescence training for more demanding adult occupations.

Other New Stages

Middle age begins somewhere between the ages of 45 and 64; the range depends, in part, on legal definitions, but also on social class differences in self-perception. Middle age was not recognized as a distinct stage in nonindustrial societies. And since life expectancy was much shorter, old age was not divided into stages. Now, in the United States, social scientists usually distinguish between the *young-old*, the *old-old*, and the *oldest old*. Originally, the young-old were people at any age over 65 who were healthy and functioning well; the old-old were people over 65 who were chronically ill and physically and/or mentally impaired.[7]

Recently, these terms have come to be tied more closely to chronological age, regardless of the state of health and functioning of older people. Now, for many researchers, young-old means somewhere between 65 and 74, old-old means 75 to 84, and oldest old means over 85. As life expectancy increases these boundaries expand, but self-image expands even more. On questionnaires, upper-middle-class and upper-class people in their early 80s, who are in good health and functioning well, still view themselves as "late" middle-aged.[8]

In industrializing societies, most young adults didn't have surviving grandparents; today, about 40 percent of grandparents in the United States are also great-grandparents.[9] Studies of four-generation families indicate a great deal of confusion about responsibilities and priorities in dealing with two generations who are old and very old.[10] In Japan, an increasing number of households of first-born sons contain two retired generations, each expecting the traditional support, deference, and veneration from younger members of their household and their society—which they continue to experience, more often than not.

Stages, Changes, and Roles

As usual, when dealing with humans, their relationships, and their surroundings, our categories and our stages are not neat and clear-cut. Especially in advanced industrial societies characterized by constant change and increased nonconformity, boundaries are difficult to establish. It becomes impossible to describe all families as proceeding through orderly, fixed, inevitable, and predictable stages; but all nuclear families, like individuals, do change over time. They experience a change in family roles as their circumstances change and as members come and go, no matter how the family was formed.[11] They go through major transitions as they age and they experience different *developmental tasks*, or new obligations and demands, at each new transition.

These stages are usually defined by getting married or moving in together, the birth of children, bringing up preschool, school-age, preteen, and teenage children, separating from children physically as well as emotionally as they age, relating to new in-laws, caring for older parents, retirement, and dying. Regardless of how these stages vary in timing and circumstances in different social locations, they tend to coincide with the aging of family members.

Family researchers usually focus on one or another of these stages in their studies; this is a convenient way to organize and explain changes such as marital satisfaction, conflicts, and the power of partners over time. Also, most family therapists use the developmental model when they try to understand at least some of the stresses of families who come to them for help. Young couples without children have different stresses and challenges than parents with preschoolers; and parents with adolescent children have the most stressful time of all.

In industrial societies, a major goal of adolescents is to become as independent of their parents as possible while continuing to maintain a close and cooperative relationship with them. Adolescents try to pull away, and parents have to let go, to some extent. This particular stage can precipitate a family crisis:

> Kim, a 15 year old adolescent, lived with her mother. Her father had died of stomach cancer when she was 9. Kim and her mother had become extremely close and dependent on each other after his death. Both worked very hard and successfully, Kim at school and her mother at work.
>
> Mother and daughter entered family therapy after Kim failed two courses when she was in the tenth grade. Kim had become very involved with a non-academically oriented clique at school and had withdrawn and become sullen in her attitude toward her mother. Her mother felt depressed and responsible for Kim's failure at school. She attributed Kim's problems to her shortcomings as a single parent.
>
> The therapist suggested that by failing her courses and having to repeat a grade at school, Kim might be postponing growing up out of loyalty to her mother, who, she believed, would have difficulty living alone, eventually. In time, Kim's mother developed more outside interests and Kim's work at school improved.[12]

Less Conformity

Another major trend in advanced industrial societies is the lessening of conformity in the thinking, feelings, and behavior of people in various life stages, especially in the upper classes. Not only is the timing of major status changes more variable than it was in previous generations, but age norms are more ambiguous, less binding, and more flexible and negotiable than in the past. Conceptions of the "right time" to do anything—finish school, get married, have children, become a grandparent, retire—are not as clear as they once were, and more people are likely to be "off time."[13]

My focus in the rest of the book will be on the typical changes and stages that most individuals and families go through during the course of their lives—especially in the United States but in other countries as well. The logical place to begin is with a discussion of love and attachment—the basis for forming most new families in urban, industrial societies.

Love and Attachment

Love becomes quite prominent in the fantasies, hopes, and desires of women and men in advanced industrialized societies. As I pointed out earlier, love was not the primary reason for choosing a marital partner in agricultural societies, nor was having someone to love a major reason for having children. Economic and political considerations were more important than emotional needs.

Changing Social Conditions

As the middle classes rose to increasing prominence in industrializing and industrialized countries, the status of individuals as separate from the family group rose, as did the prestige of individual women and children. This was reflected in changing images of men, women, and children in the popular culture—art, literature, and journalism—as well as in private sources, such as the diaries and letters of literate middle-class men and women.[14]

Paralleling this trend in industrial societies has been the increased employment of mothers with children from all social classes (not just the working class) in the nonfamily economy and changes in conceptions of masculinity and femininity. Especially since the 1960s in industrialized countries, men as well as women have been expected to express love and affection at home, and girls and women are encouraged to be successful achievers at school and in the marketplace. Also, in the United States, love relationships have become a legitimate subject of social scientific study. Up to the 1980s, social scientists rarely attempted to do research on love; love was a topic for poets, philosophers, and novelists. It wasn't a subject for objective, impersonal, scientific research. But scientists usually respond to human and societal needs in the topics they choose to investigate, and love is now a subject of intensified research.[15]

The modern emphasis on emotional gratification in marriage and the high divorce rate, especially in the United States, have precipitated a strong desire to understand what love is, where it comes from, what maintains it, and what destroys it. Research information on love can help people choose partners more wisely; it can point to realistic and unrealistic expectations in love relationships; and it can provide guidelines for improving the quality and stability of these relationships.

Love

Love is a strong, positive feeling toward others that is more difficult to define than emotions such as anger, hate, or fear. People love and are loved in different ways. What is "true" love? The different aspects of love—emotional closeness, physical attraction, commitment—are more or less strong, depending on the individual and the relationship. Some people can't love at all, especially if they did not experience consistent support and love in their relationships with parents or other caregivers when they were young and vulnerable.[16]

Some people experience great ambivalence, depending on what motivates their love. The experience of love changes with time. Psychologists contend that people get habituated to the physical aspects of love, just as they do to addictions; as time goes on, it usually takes more effort to feel physically stimulated. However, the loss of someone we love is the most painful of life's stresses. It may result in a withdrawal of interest in the outside world, fatigue, and profound sadness or depression, especially if the loss is unexpected.[17]

Aspects of Love

Recent attempts to study the various aspects of love seem to cover most, if not all, bases. This way of looking at love helps organize much of the research that has been done on love, and it enables us to distinguish different kinds of love. It can help clarify feelings, especially those that promote stability in love relationships; and it can help us understand why some love relationships break up, while others do not.

The question that is usually asked about love is "How do I know I'm in love?" A better question would be "What kind of love is this?" From this, we can proceed to the question "Is this what I want?" And that is, in part at least, a matter of values, which we can also clarify for ourselves.

The three aspects of love—intimacy, physical attraction, and commitment—involve different parts of the self: the biological (passion), the emotional (warmth and closeness), and the intellectual (commitment, or a conscious decision to maintain a relationship). They are all interrelated but they can be combined in different ways, and in any particular love relationship one or more may be absent. Depending on the relative strength of each of these three components, we can identify the kind of love we are feeling more clearly. Liking or friendship involves closeness and warmth (intimacy) without passion (as in friendships). Infatuation involves a strong physical attraction without closeness or commitment. Romantic love involves passion as well as closeness. Companionate love involves closeness and commitment without passion—and so on.[18]

The strength of each aspect of love may vary over time: Friends may become physically attracted to one another; partners who are close and passionate in their feelings may decide to try to maintain the relationship permanently by marrying or moving in together.

Intimacy

Intimacy is a feeling of deep attachment, bondedness, closeness, and warmth toward another person. The word intimacy comes from the Latin *intimas*, which means "innermost" or "deepest." Partners in intimate or close relationships enjoy being with each other and have fun doing things together. They identify and empathize with their partners, appreciate their good qualities, and accept their faults and failures because they feel the good qualities outweigh the bad. They are not martyrs; they strike a balance between *altruism*—a deep and sometimes costly concern for other people's needs—and *narcissism*—a lack of interest in the needs of others (selfishness) and a desire for gratification, whatever the cost to others.

Ideally, partners do not compete with one another; they share whatever they have with their partners, and they support one another. But they can also stand alone; they are *interdependent* but not *overdependent*. They talk to their partners freely and openly about their experiences and their deepest feelings; they trust each other; and they don't fear being abandoned or betrayed.[19] They are best friends.

Feelings of closeness or attachment develop gradually; they take time. There may be a strong feeling of physical attraction at first sight, but there is no closeness at first sight. Whether or not these feelings develop in a particular relationship depends on many things: previous experiences with love, similarities in interests, tastes, values, and goals, and self-confidence and self-esteem. People with low self-esteem have trouble trusting, empathizing, and giving. They avoid attachment, and they flee from the demands of close relationships. They fear dependence and they fear rejection; they have traveled that route before.

TYPES OF ATTACHMENT Researchers and therapists who use a Freudian or psychoanalytic perspective trace basic personality traits and the ability or inability to attach to other people in adulthood to an individual's earliest experiences with parents or other primary caregivers. They have identified three ways of attaching, or bonding, to others that are built up slowly during infancy, childhood, and adolescence: secure, ambivalent and anxious, or detached and avoidant (Table 5.3).[20] These ways of attaching tend to be repeated in adulthood and persist throughout the life history of individuals.

SECURE RELATIONSHIPS Individuals who have experienced warm, supportive, and approving relationships with parents or parent substitutes in childhood are secure in their adult relationships with others. They are confident and have high self-esteem. They are satisfied with themselves, their capabilities and their accomplishments and are happy, friendly, trusting, and accepting of others.

TABLE 5.3   Types of Attachment

Early Emotional Experiences	Adult Attachment Styles
Caregiver during infancy and childhood is available, responsive, supportive, helpful, encouraging	Secure—happy, friendly, trusting, supportive, accepting of others
Caregiver is inconsistent (warm, cold), unreliable—doesn't show up, disappoints	Anxious/ambivalent—emotional highs/lows; obsessional attractions; envious, jealous of others
Caregiver is detached, critical, rejecting	Avoidant—fear of closeness, commitment; emotional highs/lows; envious, jealous of others

ANXIOUS/AMBIVALENT RELATIONSHIPS   Those who experienced inconsistencies (encouragement as well as criticism, warmth as well as remoteness) or unreliability (unpredictable separations and absences, failure to appear as promised) in their early relationships with caregivers are anxious and ambivalent. They experience emotional ups and downs, obsessional sexual attractions (especially to people who are unavailable, such as celebrities, teachers, and other authority figures), and feelings of envy, jealousy, and mistrust.

AVOIDANT RELATIONSHIPS   Those who experienced the extremes of criticism, emotional unavailability, or rejection in their earliest family relationships defensively avoid attachment and closeness in future relationships. They are detached, and they fear and sabotage commitment, sometimes in very subtle ways; they can't tolerate the neediness of others. They, too, have emotional highs and lows, are envious, jealous, and suspicious, and fear betrayal and abandonment.

The psychoanalytic hypothesis that our earliest experiences with love affect our ability to love later in life is not accepted by some social scientists, but evidence in support of this point of view is accumulating. This evidence is more likely to come from therapists than from surveys, although survey researchers are becoming more sophisticated in measuring psychoanalytic principles. But it is very difficult to get valid answers on surveys that inquire into emotionally charged areas of life: People do not necessarily lie, but they may not be *aware* of what motivates them and how the present reflects the past.

DEFENSE MECHANISMS   This is another basic principle of the psychoanalytic perspective: the importance of unconscious impulses, feelings, and conflicts in motivating behavior and the role of mechanisms of defense such as denial, projection, and displacement in disguising these unconscious feelings. *Projection* involves accusing other people of unacceptable feelings or motives that are, in fact, one's own: "You're very competitive. You resent my success. You envy me." *Denial* is the blocking from conscious awareness of painful feelings about negative things that are happening: "It's true that Johnny wets his bed, has no friends, and keeps getting into trouble at school. But boys will be boys; he'll grow out of it." *Displacement* is the expression of inappropriate feelings, such as anger, toward someone who isn't to blame for one's problems. An example is the man who becomes enraged at his boss, comes home, and beats his wife or children instead; scapegoats are victims of displacement in families and in societies.

Both laboratory and survey research indicates that personal styles of attachment or detachment formed very early in life have a tendency to persist and are repeated in later love relationships. The degree of closeness in the peer relationships of adolescent girls, for example, tends to reflect the emotional closeness in their family relationships.[21]

Psychoanalysis as a method of treatment that involves re-creating early childhood experiences in the doctor-patient relationship is in decline now, partly because it is too costly and too time-consuming. But some of the basic insights of this approach to understanding human motivation and behavior have become part of the language and the culture in the United States and in European industrial societies. This is especially true of the concepts of denial, projection, and displacement; these are now common in the ordinary conversations of most educated people today.

PREVALENCE OF TYPES OF ATTACHMENT   In laboratory and survey research studies measuring attachment, most people report that they are able to form secure love relationships; they find it relatively easy to get close and stay close to others.[22] They can depend on others and be depended on, and they rarely worry about being abandoned. About one in five people in these studies avoids love, fears intimacy, and is unable to get close to others. They have difficulty trusting and depending on others; they often find themselves in situations where their partners are more committed to the relationship than they are.

About the same percentage of the population are anxious and ambivalent. They are intensely eager to fall in love (and they do, obsessively), but they are jealous, possessive, and overly dependent, and they expect too much from their partners. They have trouble believing that their partners *really* love them and worry about losing them. In fact, they *are* more likely to lose them, and they suffer more severe distress when they do.[23]

Physical Attraction

The second aspect of love, *physical attraction*, is a feeling of very strong passion toward another person. This is grounded, ultimately, on the biological sex drive and the need to gratify this drive. Males are more likely than females to experience this feeling of love "at first sight." When it is the major or only feeling in a love relationship, it is often labeled *puppy love*, a *crush*, *lovesickness*, or *infatuation*. This feeling does not last in its pure state. The love relationship ends if feelings of closeness, attachment, understanding, and empathy do not also develop. And if they do, it changes to a different kind of love that researchers usually label *companionate* or *mature* love.[24]

Feelings of physical attraction toward others occur in all known societies. But they are guarded against (by separating the sexes, secluding women, and arranging marriages) in cultures where physical attraction is not defined as an appropriate reason for marrying. These feelings become strongly intensified when sexual gratification is frustrated: when the object of one's affection is not available (a rock star, a teacher, a therapist, a faithfully married acquaintance, friend, or boss, or simply someone who doesn't return your love). Freud viewed this kind of love as a repetition of the erotic but frustrated love felt by children toward a parent of the opposite sex.[25]

Feelings of strong physical attraction that are gratified (because the person is available) tend to diminish in intensity over time as the novelty wears off and the uncertainties in the relationship decline. Psychologists have pointed out that intense physical arousal can also be a defensive response to negative feelings toward another person. These are feelings that we cannot accept or recognize. It is possible to feel intensely aroused by a person we are angry with, or by someone whom we actually dislike or disapprove of or who displays hostility to us.

Psychologists, in field or laboratory experiments, have also found that exposure to conditions of extreme fear and anxiety can result in a sudden feeling of sexual attraction toward people whom we barely know or whom we fear. In brutal prison situations, this may involve identifying with an oppressor. Given all the various reasons for the development of strong feelings of physical attraction toward others, most people experience a feeling of infatuation at some time or another. And it occurs at all ages—young, middle-aged, and old.[26]

Commitment

The third aspect of love, *commitment*, is a conscious decision to maintain a relationship temporarily or for life; it is the key to stability in love relationships. It may involve a personal dedication to the relationship for no other reason than love. Or it may involve internal or external constraints that keep people in relationships regardless of how they feel about their partners. Internal constraints are such things as unconscious needs, morals, and values (religious values, for example). External constraints are pressures from family or friends, the presence of children, joint possessions, and economic dependence (especially for women and, even more, for women with young children).

People who feel a strong need to keep a relationship going rarely think about the constraints that bind them.[27] They will do whatever they can for one another, spend as much time as possible together, make personal sacrifices when necessary, and confide good and bad feelings—this and more, without feelings of anger, deprivation, or guilt. They are loyal, and they defend each other in threatening situations. Deeply committed people *like* and respect one another; and usually this is because they have *similar* beliefs, goals, interests, and personality traits.

If opposites do attract (and this is not true for most people), this is not the kind of love relationship that is likely to last. Most people do, in fact, choose people with similar attitudes, values, and world views, and, except for dominance and submission, similar personality traits.[28]

Problems with Love

Most problems in establishing and maintaining love relationships stem from unrealistic expectations, difficulties in forming attachments, and differences in personality, background, and outlook. In some ways, the intentional breakup of a love relationship, especially a long-term one, can be more damaging than other kinds of losses (the death of a partner, for example). Death is unintentional, usually. But those who unwillingly lose someone they love by separation or divorce, and who don't initiate or want the breakup, usually experience a severe (but rarely permanent) blow to their self-esteem.

Unrealistic Expectations

Unrealistic expectations may be based on idealization of a partner's good traits. Warning signals of possible bad times to come—in the form of abusiveness, addictions of various kinds, passive aggression (seemingly helpful behavior that actually hurts or distresses a partner), or extreme jealousy and possessiveness, for example— are ignored because, as the old adage has it, "love is blind."

Problems also arise when two people have expectations such as sharing resources, confiding in one another, having children, or sharing work in the home that don't match and are never discussed in the relationship. And, finally, unrealistic expectations in love relationships arise because of differences in the capacities for passion, closeness, and commitment that are unrecognized or unacceptable by the partners in a love relationship.

IDEALIZATION   Idealization is strongest when infatuation and passion distort reality and are not corrected by the development of psychological closeness and mutual respect in the relationship.[29] This occurs, more often, for anxious, ambivalent people who have unfinished business from the past. Perhaps their parents were ill when they were very young or were not there because of other kinds of family problems. There was no healthy, continuous, bonding experience during the first years of life. They were left with separation anxiety: an almost desperate need for attachment and a strong fear of abandonment.

The hope is that *this* time the loved one will not disappoint. The adoring, accessible mother, the gentle father, the kindly uncle, the protective brother or sister, the loving grandparent (who never were) are there, finally, in one person; a tall order, too tall for most relationships. This is especially true because obsessive sexual attraction tends to focus on unavailable people. Available partners will not do because of the need to replay the ancient drama and make it come out right this time around.[30]

DISAPPOINTMENTS   A second major source of unrealistic expectations in love relationships stems from a failure to recognize and deal with basic differences in attitudes and values earlier in the relationship. Studies of disappointments in the love relationships of dating, newly married, and unhappily married couples indicate persisting differences in the expectations of men and women. These differences have been documented by sociologists for decades.[31] On surveys, women have reported being bothered most by the emotional reserve, neglect, thoughtlessness (unwillingness to be helpful), and condescension of their partners. Men have reported being bothered by the greater tendency of their partners to be preoccupied with feelings and emotions. Among unhappily married couples, not surprisingly, women are more likely to report that their partners are too demanding sexually, and men are more likely to report feeling sexually rejected.

In part, these differences are cultural in origin. Most women are still socialized to be more open in their expression of emotion, less aggressive sexually, and more committed in their love relationships. At a deeper personal level, and aside from the more obvious conflicts about money, childrearing, or relatives, gender differences in the expectations and disillusionments of men and women in love relationships persist. But this too is changing, especially among more educated middle-class women and men.[32]

Neither sex can realistically expect love relationships to fulfill certain needs completely, although they can help. It is unfair and burdensome to expect those we love (partners, parents, children) to give us our total and only sense of meaning, purpose, and identity in life: They can't guarantee that our futures will be safe, secure, and free of stress; they can't protect us from loss and separation; and they can't restore severely damaged self-esteem. Such neediness and dependency are too demanding, are bound to be frustrated, and are not found in secure love relationships.

Attachment Difficulties

Approximately the same percentages of women and men are secure, anxious and ambivalent, or distant and avoidant in their love relationships; researchers haven't found significant gender differences in these reactions.[33] But culture, socialization, and social location strongly affect how men and women experience and display the various aspects of love—passion, closeness, and especially commitment.

The *internal* need for commitment in love relationships may be the same for both sexes, for example, but *external* (situational) constraints are greater for women. These are such things as lower earning power, the greater dependence of children on mothers, the double standard of physical attractiveness and aging (women are judged more harshly than men as they age), and the surplus of available women at older ages (and at all ages in the African American subculture). The biological time limit on having children is an additional internal constraint for women who want to have a child. Men can and do father children when they are in their 80s; women's reproductive period is over in their 50s. Demography (the surplus of women in older age categories) is an external constraint.

Theoretically, people with matched loving styles should have similar expectations and experience the greatest satisfaction in their love relationships: two secure people, two avoidant people, two anxious and ambivalent people (they will at least be able to empathize with and accommodate each other's needs for closeness, distance, or both). But when anxious people who are very needy for love become attached to distant, aloof, emotionally unavailable people, we have the stuff of real-life (and Hollywood) tragedies and grist for the mills of countless women's magazine articles, romance novels, and "personal growth" books.

JEALOUSY Feelings of jealousy and possessiveness are usually interpreted as signs of love, but more often they are not. In their most extreme form, they are based on feelings of insecurity and inadequacy. Researchers have found that people with intense feelings of jealousy tend to have low self-esteem, impossible desires for support from their partners, and feelings of extreme dissatisfaction with who they are and what they have accomplished.[34]

There are two basic forms of jealousy: the fear of losing or being abandoned by a partner and feelings of envy and competitiveness with others. Neither set of feelings is easy to live with in a partner relationship, and both are intensified in individualistic, competitive, urban industrial societies where self-esteem is strongly affected by accomplishments and commitment. Jealous lovers resent their partner's interest in other people (children, relatives in the extended family, friends, former lovers, work associates) and in other things (work, hobbies, religious, or volunteer activities). They may resent their partner's accomplishments even if they share in the rewards. Possessiveness reflects excessive dependence: "Please stay home tonight; I hate being alone." "I feel left out when you take off with your friends."

In more traditional gender relationships, where women are subordinate, possessiveness is an aspect of male dominance and control. "Trust reflects a willingness to relinquish personal control, to put one's fate in the hands of another. . . . Control serves as a security operation, as a *substitute* for trust."[35]

Low Self-Esteem

A certain amount of jealousy about preserving a threatened relationship that one values is reasonable, and a secure, gratifying relationship promotes self-esteem, good health, and long life. But love, no matter how supportive, cannot cure the very low self-esteem and insecurities of an intensely jealous and possessive person; this situation is difficult to change without outside help.

Low self-esteem is sometimes difficult to recognize, especially when it is covered up by defensive arrogance and grandiosity. People with low self-esteem feel anxious and a lack of confidence when they are with strangers; they are embarrassed and do not accept compliments from others comfortably; they have difficulty recognizing and appreciating the accomplishments of others; they are difficult to please; and they can't tolerate a disagreement or a difference of opinion, which they interpret as a personal attack on their intelligence or judgment.

Personality Mismatches

Personality differences usually lead to the breakup of love relationships or to on-again, off-again relationships. The people involved feel they love each other, but they can't accept or live with their partner. They do not *like*, respect, or approve of their partners. Savers and spendthrifts, underachievers and overachievers, extroverts and introverts, uninhibited and controlled, orderly and messy partners may have great difficulty tolerating each other's differences.[36] These differences may not become apparent until after the romantic haze fades and partners have a chance to know one another better; and differences become more pronounced as people age, as do most personality traits.

People tend to be more tolerant, unobservant, on good behavior, or perhaps simply more hopeful in dating and living-together situations. Recognition may not come, unfortunately, until the commitment is sealed by marriage. Then expectations change, and mutual respect and acceptance, the basis of strong, lasting relationships, may be difficult to achieve.

> I love Harry, but he drives me crazy. I never buy anything unless it's on sale, and I shop only at discount or off-price stores. I check the supermarket sales and stock up on the specials. I save coupons. I hate going to expensive restaurants. I don't enjoy the food. I keep thinking of what I could buy that I *need* with the money I'm spending on the meal.
>
> I pay as I go. I can't stand owing people money and being in debt. I know exactly what I can afford and what I can't afford and I plan ahead.
>
> Harry is always in debt. He loves elegance. The food tastes better when it costs more and is served on table cloths by tuxedoed waiters. Clothes look better when they have a designer label and come from an expensive store.
>
> I save boxes from expensive stores and switch presents I buy for him at discount stores into these boxes. If he knew where they really came from, he wouldn't like them.
>
> Harry's always grabbing the check and finding a reason to treat people. He lends money to anyone who asks. He's an impulse buyer. Cost is no object as long as it's the top of the line. He's always buying love, from me, from friends, from his family. His self-worth bank balance is low and his checks keep bouncing. I couldn't live like that.
>
> I love him, but I think I'd be nuts to marry him. He's never going to change.[37]

Background Differences

Differences in social location, such as class, ethnic origin, age, and religion, strongly affect values, interests, tastes, and goals. Pollsters usually break down their results according to income, education, age, and gender because they tend to uncover significant differences in opinions when they do.

Most people meet, fall in love with, and marry people from similar backgrounds. It is easier to progress from physical attraction to understanding and closeness when two people have had similar experiences. But, increasingly, people don't make that kind of choice. In these situations, similarities in intelligence, personality, achievements, and interests may override differences in ethnic origin and class.

A national study of 5,039 couples, who were given a 125-item self-report test on marital satisfaction, indicates that social background factors are rated as much less important than relationship qualities in determining marital satisfaction. "Couples with good relationships were those with higher scores in the following categories: Communication, Conflict Resolution, Sexual Relationship, Leisure Activities, Egalitarian Roles, Religious Orientation, and Personality Compatibility."[38] On the other hand, social background factors usually have a strong effect on these relationship qualities.

The Sexual Revolution

In societies where love is the basis for choosing a partner, sexual attraction and gratification becomes a crucial aspect of this choice for all would-be partners. Economic changes and developments in medicine, science, and technology in industrial and postindustrial societies promote much freer sexual behavior—especially for women and for the middle social classes. Industrialization uproots people and encourages the movement to cities, where family, religious, and community control over sexual behavior is weaker; and the shorter work week in later stages of industrialization provides more leisure time for dating and sexual activity.[39]

The sexual revolution, when there was a widespread change toward more liberal sexual attitudes and freer sexual behavior, took place before, during, and after World War I (1914–1918) in the United States and Europe (Table 5.4).[40] It did not start during the 1960s, as is widely believed. *Public* morality during the period from about 1910 to 1929 required virginity before marriage and faithfulness after marriage. But *private* morality was different, especially for those who were planning to marry anyway. In the 1960s, private morality went public: People became more open about their sexual behavior, and nonmarital sexual activity continued to increase.

Developments in medicine, science, and technology provided more effective birth control techniques and better treatment for sexually transmitted diseases, easing fears and encouraging freer sexual behavior. At the same time, the automobile and mass transit took people away from farmhouses and crowded urban apartments. Commercial nonfamily places of entertainment (movies, bars, nightclubs) promoted nonfamily kinds of entertainment and facilitated the meeting of partners; the growth of hotels and motels increased the availability of private meeting places for sexual activity.

Even after the first case of AIDS was reported in the United States in 1981, premarital sexual activity continued to increase, although extramarital activity has been, and continues to be, less frequent in the United States than in other industrial countries. According to repeated national surveys, during the 1980s and 1990s, by the National Opinion Research Center, about nine out of ten married women and

---

TABLE 5.4   The Sexual Revolution

DEFINITION: A widespread change toward more liberal sexual attitudes and freer sexual behavior in the United States and Europe

WHO: Mainly the middle class; mainly women

WHEN: Before during, and after the *First World War* (1914–1918)—not the 1960s, which was a *second*, more *public* revolution

WHY:

1. Developments in medicine and science that provided more effective contraception and better control over sexually transmitted diseases
2. Technological developments that created more factory and service jobs (secretarial, selling) that drew workers from the farms to cities
3. Inventions of the automobile, mass transit, and dating
4. Shorter work week; more leisure time
5. Replacement of family recreation (church suppers, hoedowns, and barn raisings) by commercial, nonfamily entertainment (movies, bars, nightclubs, social clubs)
6. Spread of motels and hotels, increased availability of private meeting places for sexual activity

---

men reported having had only one partner the previous year, and a high percentage reported never being unfaithful to their spouses (about 85 percent of married women compared to about 75 percent of married men).[41] Even if some respondents were lying, married people are apparently more faithful to one another than images in the media and popular beliefs would have it. But unmarried couples who live together, African Americans, remarried people, urban residents, nonchurchgoers, and those with the lowest and highest levels of education have higher lifetime rates of extramarital sex.

Premarital sexual activity, however, did decline during the 1990s. In national surveys of high school students conducted every two years since the 1970s by the Centers for Disease Control and Prevention, the percentage of sexually active female students declined from 50.8 percent in 1991 to 47.7 percent in 1997; for male students the decline was from 57 percent in 1991 to 49 percent in 1997.[42] Researchers believe this decline is a result of greater efforts by parents, schools, and health professionals to educate young people about safe sex and the risks of pregnancy and sexually transmitted diseases such as AIDS.

We have seen that love and attachment are now considered essential in the choice of a partner in Western urban industrial societies. The road to love and marriage (or its alternatives) in these societies is an adventurous one marked by entrances and exits, detours, and sometimes costly tolls. In agricultural societies the way was usually paved by parents; now, meeting and establishing a close relationship with a partner is a gamble. Opportunity, choice, competition, skill, and luck are all part of the script. How do most people narrow their choices and find their partners—when they do?

Chapter 6
Finding a Partner

In the past, except in the upper classes, most people married someone they grew up with or who lived nearby. Parents and other members of the family guided, chaperoned, approved, and had the right to forbid the marriage if the choice was made without them and they disapproved. *Courting* did not require spending money on dates; men courted women by taking short walks together (within the parents' view), or by sitting in the parlor or porch in the presence of the woman's parents.[1] Women who were being courted had little to say; courtship was the pattern for choosing a partner when patriarchy defined the man–woman relationship.

Changing Social Conditions

As Western countries industrialized, adult children became more independent economically and psychologically; they were more mobile, socially and geographically, and dating and personal preference became the norm in determining who married whom. The geographic boundaries for finding a partner expanded, except for the poor and most of the working class. Lower-income people do not usually go away to college and do not get job offers from other cities, states, or countries; they are still most likely to marry or move in with the boy or girl next door.

Currently, for younger people living in urban areas in the United States, religion and ethnic origin are declining in importance as factors determining marital choice. But national surveys of class differences in marital choice since the 1930s indicate a trend toward increased matching in level of education between marital partners. A major reason for this trend is the rising educational and economic status of women in the United States, especially since the 1960s.[2] Today, when most married women with children earn independent income, it isn't as crucial for women to marry men with more education (and income) in order to guarantee a secure future for themselves and their children.[3]

The Emergence of Dating

In the United States, *dating* as the typical way of finding a marital partner, based on individual initiative and personal choice, emerged around the turn of the 20th century; it became widespread in Europe and in the United States during and after

World War I. Many young men and women had moved from rural areas to the cities, where job opportunities were expanding. Economic independence (especially for women), small city apartments that offered little privacy to young couples, mass transit, the automobile, and commercial entertainment (movies especially) all propelled young people out of the home and away from family control (but not influence) over marital choices.

Traditional Dating

Traditional dating (still prevalent in some areas of the United States) consists of a one-to-one relationship in which the cultural rules defining attitudes, feeling, and behavior are clear-cut and unambiguous—pretty much. The man phones to make the date. He picks up his date at her home at an agreed-upon time. He decides how they will spend the evening. They go out to dinner, a party, a movie, a sporting event, or some other form of commercial entertainment. The man pays. While both are bound by the norm of having fun, the woman usually talks more and is more likely to talk about her personal feelings.[4]

Toward the end of the evening, the man usually makes sexual advances of some kind, which the woman is less likely to accept on initial dates, especially now with the growing fear of sexually transmitted diseases. When the evening ends, the man escorts the woman home and either arranges for another date or says he will call.

From Dating to Marriage

If a traditional dating relationship develops into marriage, stages in the relationship tend to be public and relatively predictable. These stages are symbolized by traditional rituals: the couple starts *going steady*, which involves sexual exclusiveness (fidelity) and progressive commitment. This is usually followed by a formal *engagement* party, which is a public announcement to friends, family, and the community of the intention to marry. It is a time for making definite plans about the wedding and the future—about when and how they will be married, where and how they will live, how they will relate to in-laws and friends, and how they will present themselves as a couple.[5]

This is followed by a formal *wedding ceremony*, which publicly symbolizes and reinforces commitment to the relationship. In the United States, this ceremony is usually conducted by a member of the clergy and is usually paid for by the bride's parents. With the current delay in age at first marriage, however, adult children in well-paying occupations are now more likely to pay for their own weddings.

New Directions

The traditional dating pattern has been a way for adolescents and young adults to get to know one another, learn about their sexuality, and test out their desirability in the marriage marketplace. They also learn more about their standards for selecting a marital partner and their compatibility with various kinds of people. For younger adolescents, recreation, companionship, and having fun have been the primary goals in dating relationships.[6]

Spontaneous Pairing Off

Whatever the goal or goals, traditional dating is changing. This is not happening as much in certain areas of the United States (the South and Midwest) and among high school students as among college students.[7] But many young adults, especially in the larger cities, are shifting to an informal pattern that is more spontaneous, relaxed, and egalitarian. This involves informal, spontaneous socializing or *getting together*, as some researchers have called it: Young, unattached people go out in groups; they have a party, listen to music, study together, play group sports, attend sporting events together, and so on.[8]

If a particular couple is attracted to one another, they may pair off and meet informally for a coffee break or lunch (not dinner, at first). They share the expense and spend only a small amount of time together initially, and neither feels rejected, necessarily, if it doesn't work out.

This kind of meeting gives people a chance to get to know one another without being under the traditional cultural constraints that define gender roles in dating. It also tends to be less stressful. The male doesn't *have* to initiate, plan, and pay for the date and be the sexual aggressor; the female doesn't *have* to be flirtatious, alluring, conversationally adept, and sexually coy.

Spontaneous pairing off takes some of the fear of being rejected out of the dating situation, since the decision to pair off is gradual and mutual. It diminishes some of the potential exploitation and dishonest game playing of the traditional dating script. People are more likely to be themselves and less likely to feel they are auditioning for the job of steady companion, husband, or wife.

Getting together informally and gradually pairing off is less damaging to the self-esteem of those who have less to trade in terms of physical attractiveness, personality characteristics, and career or economic potential. Pressure and rejection are less likely, since the decision to pair off is spontaneous and mutual. Males, especially, don't have to put themselves on the line and experience being turned down when they ask for a date according to the traditional script. And since this kind of relationship is, basically, more egalitarian and mutual in terms of gender role attitudes and power, male violence, in the form of forced sex, is less likely to occur.

Older people who are never married, divorced, or widowed are also more comfortable in group situations that are not explicitly set up for matchmaking. Friends and family create a more relaxed situation when they don't inform the potential partners that a dinner party is designed especially for them to meet; this is less obvious when other guests are present.

High school dating guides generally continue to prescribe the traditional dating pattern. Revised etiquette books for adults, however, now say that it is quite acceptable for either sex to telephone or pay for a date. Splitting the bill gives the woman greater freedom to plan the date and end it (without guilt) if she wants to go home early—and alone. She need not feel obligated sexually. And it allows men with limited means to go out more. When, as is more common now in the United States, an older woman dates a younger man (who earns less), she can pay *his* way (not common, but acceptable until he catches up financially—if he does). Or she can scale down her leisure activities so that the man is able to share expenses: movies instead of the theater, camping vacations rather than trips abroad, home cooking instead of restaurants.[9]

The Public Announcement

With the shift from formal dating to more spontaneous pairing off, couples who decide to get married are now more likely to forgo the formal ritual of an engagement party. They simply announce their intention to marry and don't recognize a distinct stage of engagement. This is less binding in the event of a change of heart. In the past, a broken engagement after a formal engagement party could lead to a suit for breach of contract by the abandoned partner.

However it is marked, an announcement of the intention to marry, even if it isn't formally recognized by ritual or labeled an engagement, is a time for making certain changes in other relationships, especially with family and friends. The privacy of the courting couple may become secondary to the necessity to become incorporated into the partner's family (where this is considered important, possible, or necessary). Also, separate friends are consolidated—or dropped.

Informal Contacts

High school and college students have a built-in pool of potential dating partners. Later, most continue to meet through mutual friends. Blind dates are still fairly common, although they are often not particularly successful. The stereotype prevails that secure, outgoing, good-looking people can make their own social contacts. And low expectations (that the blind date will be a loser) tend to become self-fulfilling prophecies (people tend to get what they expect to get). Older adults—never married, divorced, or widowed—have a more difficult time meeting potential partners and, especially in large cities, are more likely to use commercial settings and services or on-line ways to connect with potential partners.

Meeting in Public Places

Once people leave high school or college, they can meet just about anywhere—in church, libraries, or bookstores, on the subway during rush hour, riding the bus, sharing a taxi or limo on the way to or from various destinations, or at the supermarket after work. Attitude and self-confidence are important. Those who are confident and are clear about who they are and what they want are good at sizing up opportunities, listening and talking, and moving from encounters, to dating, to closeness, to commitment.

For older adults, the office becomes the equivalent of the classroom. People can observe each other informally and get to know each other without the commitment of a date. But a teacher in an elementary school and people who work at home or in small firms have limited opportunities for meeting a potential partner. Even in large corporations, most people are married. Also, many companies still have an unwritten policy against employee dating (especially at the executive levels). Many firms will not employ members of the same family, and rules about sexual harassment in the workplace are becoming more stringent.

Making contact is easier in jobs that involve meeting the general public, although these contacts tend to be segmented and fleeting. Waiting tables (especially in restaurants with steady customers), selling big items that usually require a lot of discussion (cars, houses, insurance, investments), interior design, travel, political campaigning, journalism, photography, and interviewing are examples of jobs that promote meeting and getting to know people.

Actually, according to a personal interview survey of 459 women in the Detroit metropolitan area: "Dating activity that results eventually in marriage begins in a wide variety of settings. . . . Couples first meeting while in school is not the predominant pattern, nor is meeting at work. Personal introductions by third parties are the start of relationships that lead up to marriage more often than is generally recognized."[10]

Commercial Matching

Some older adults who delayed marriage, are too busy with their careers, or are single once again because of a breakup or a divorce are trying commercial matching for meeting people. Singles bars and nightclubs, where middle-class college graduates meet but rarely marry, and where good looks and fast talk are the price of admission, are declining in number (apparently because of the fear of crime and AIDS). Singles housing developments with common recreational facilities are expensive and exclude all but the very well off.

Increasingly, adults, mainly in their 30s and 40s, are using a variety of commercial methods for meeting potential partners, such as personal ads, matchmaking consultants, on-line e-mail and chat rooms, and commercial matchmaking Web sites. What these techniques all have in common is that the selection is made before the participants meet. This presumably cuts down on the importance of physical attractiveness in first encounters and, theoretically at least, promotes a more rational basis for meeting potential partners.

Dating services use the latest technologies, such as personal computers, modems, fax machines, videotapes, audiocassettes, and conference calls to arrange blind dates for consenting adults. Computer matching, based on filling out personality questionnaires, is old-fashioned by comparison. Dating services tend to be class ranked, age-graded, and ethnically segregated. The more exclusive ones charge the highest fees and handle very busy, high-status, financially successful men (business executives, bankers, doctors, lawyers) and very beautiful (younger) women.

On-line commercial matchmaking Web sites are booming.[11] More and more, single people who find just about everything else on the Internet are using it to find a partner. Busy professionals and business executives are looking for fast and efficient contacts that are inexpensive, appropriate, and safe. On the question of safety, the people who run matchmaking Web sites advise subscribers who decide to meet face-to-face to arrange the first meeting in a public place during the day. They should also tell a friend where they are going and when they expect to be back.

Effectiveness of Dating Services

We have no national follow-up studies on this topic, but commercial dating services do not seem to be particularly effective in promoting marriages, which is the ultimate goal of most of their clients. Age is an important factor here: Most men who use these services want younger women (in their 20s), but most women who use commercial services are older (in their 30s and 40s). Also, commercial matching often brings people together who like the same things but not each other. Love has rational and logical aspects; but it also has mysterious aspects that elude computers, cameras, consultants, and conversations—not to mention the lovers themselves.

Dating Violence

Researchers estimate that anywhere from one-third to one-half of all dating relationships in the United States involve forced sex, or *date rape*, as it is usually called.[12] This is probably too high an estimate, but they have also found that childhood experience with family violence is significantly related to dating violence; and people with avoidant or ambivalent/anxious attachment tendencies are most likely to be violent in close relationships before and after marriage.[13]

Despite violence during dating, many of these relationships lead to marriage. This is apparently because of the widespread tendency of people to idealize romantic partners, especially among adolescents and young adults, and the myth that marriage will change a partner in basic ways. But if a partner is violent during the courtship period, he or she is very likely to be violent *after* the marriage.[14] Courtship violence is often linked to serious personality problems such as compulsive gambling, alcoholism, compulsive infidelity, and drug abuse. These conditions are rarely cured by marriage or by any other change in status.

Most researchers have found that traditional patriarchal relationships, in which men are in absolute control and women are economically dependent and extremely unequal in prestige and privileges, promote physical violence and sexual exploitation. This occurs in all man–woman relationships—nonmarital, premarital, marital, and extramarital—in certain kinds of societies. Cross-cultural studies by anthropologists have found that wife beating is most frequent in societies where the inequality of women is extreme and male violence is regarded as evidence of virility and masculinity. In societies with little or no family violence, women and men share in decision making, marriage is monogamous, women have some control over economic resources, and divorce, while relatively infrequent, can be initiated by either sex (Table 6.1). "Family violence does not occur in societies where family life is characterized by cooperation, commitment, sharing, and equality."[15]

TABLE 6.1   Cross-Cultural Violence Between the Sexes

IN SOCIETIES WITH LITTLE VIOLENCE BETWEEN WOMEN AND MEN:

1. Men resolve conflicts with other men peacefully.
2. There is no premarital double standard: Boys and girls have equal freedom to be sexually active.
3. Women produce and maintain some control over family economic resources.
4. Marriage is monogamous.
5. Divorce is infrequent, and wives can divorce their husbands as easily as husbands can divorce their wives.
6. Husbands and wives share in family decision making; power differences between men and women are minimal.
7. Husbands and wives sleep together, not alone or with their children.
8. Communication between men and women is open and frequent.

Social Location and Dating Violence

Using a national representative sample of people between the ages of 18 and 30 who are dating, sociologists Jan Stets and Debra Henderson found significant differences in the amount of reported dating violence in different social locations.[16] On a number of surveys, including this one, women consistently reported being equally or more likely to be physically aggressive toward their partners. Most researchers attribute this to a greater likelihood on the part of women to report physical violence. Moreover, much of the physical aggression by women is defensive, and women experience more severe injuries in physically aggressive encounters with their partners.[17] Also, reported physical aggression in dating has been found to be more frequent among younger daters, among minorities, among those who are poor, and among those who live in the South.

Breaking Up

Love relationships that break up are rarely all bad, and breaking up is usually painful—even when both partners agree to the breakup. Ending unsatisfactory relationships is a problem that looms large in urban industrial societies, where people have more choices, take more chances, and risk more failures, especially with the newer psychological standards in love relationships.

Easing the Pain

Researchers and therapists have discovered certain techniques that can make breaking up less painful (Table 6.2).[18] They advise partners who are initiating a breakup to be sure that this is what they want. If they have doubts or start seesawing, they should write down the negative aspects of the relationship. This helps clarify the sit-

TABLE 6.2   Breaking Up

IF YOU DO THE BREAKING UP
1. Be sure that this is what you want. Write down the negative and positive aspects of the relationship; this helps clarify the situation and will reinforce the decision later, when the more destructive aspects of the relationship may have been repressed.
2. Make a clean break; off-and-on-again availability, if your partner does not want to end the relationship, will only increase the partner's feelings of loss, loneliness, and deprivation.
3. Do not vanish without notice or explanation, or break up in a letter or by telephone. Meet face-to-face in a new, neutral public place so that you can leave promptly afterward.
4. State your reasons for the breakup honestly in terms of *your* needs, values, and goals; do not criticize or blame your partner.
5. Choose the right time: not before a major holiday or when a partner is going through other stresses (job, family, health).

IF YOUR PARTNER BREAKS UP WITH YOU
1. Give yourself at least six months to recover. You are likely to go through a series of emotional stages similar to those of mourning: numbness; difficulty eating, sleeping, concentrating; denial (expecting the partner to come back); anger (at your partner or yourself for causing the breakup); and recovery (in due time).
2. Keep busy; go out, meet new people, find new interests and hobbies; avoid obsessional thinking about revenge or reconciliation; avoid rebound relationships in less than three months. (They are usually unrealistic, formed to compensate for a loss.)

uation and can reinforce the decision to end the relationship, especially later on, when they may not remember some of the more destructive things that were going on during the relationship.

They also advise making a clean break. It isn't wise to taper off a relationship that the other person doesn't want to end. Later, especially if both partners have gone on to other relationships, it may be possible (though not likely) to be friends, but not when one partner wants to continue the relationship and the other does not. The reluctant partner's on-and-off-again availability will simply intensify feelings of loss, loneliness, and deprivation in the other partner.

One should not simply disappear without notice or explanation, or announce an intention to break up by a letter or telephone call. Explanations should be made face-to-face in a neutral public place such as a quiet, unfamiliar restaurant (not one that they frequented as a couple). In this kind of public setting, the situation is less likely to get loud and out of hand, and the partner who wants to break up can leave promptly and alone after saying what has to be said. And this should be said honestly and in terms of his or her own needs, values, and goals, without criticizing or blaming the other partner. It is also important to choose the right time to make a break: not before a major holiday or if either partner is going through a major change or crisis, such as a death in the family, a job loss, or a health problem. This will intensify feelings of abandonment and isolation.

How does one recover from the loss of a partner? Psychologists point to emotional stages, similar to those of mourning, that most people go through: numbness and trouble eating, sleeping, and concentrating; then denial (the partner didn't mean it and will return); anger at the partner; self-blame (for provoking the breakup or being unlovable); and then, after six months or so, recovery—which is inevitable for most losses. Psychologists advise keeping busy with work, hobbies, and new or old interests, joining clubs, taking classes, and going to museums, parks, resorts, supermarkets, bookstores—whatever people are interested in and can afford to do that will distract them from obsessional thinking about reconciliation (or revenge).

Finding a new partner depends not only on motivation, but also on social location: age, class, and ethnic origin, especially, and the availability of eligible new partners. Intense new involvements (in less than three months) may be *rebound relationships* formed to compensate for the loss, not because of feelings of love, or even liking, for the new partner. These relationships are likely to break up also.

Gender Differences

Women are more likely to seek support by talking about a breakup to a close friend; men are more likely to seek distraction by quickly starting to date other women and by burying themselves in work or sports.[19] Reactions will differ, depending on personality; but gender differences tend to reflect surviving differences in the socialization experiences of men and women, despite the recent decline in these differences.

Getting Married

In industrial societies, the size of the never-married population varies at any particular time in response to various factors: changing values, standards of living, employment opportunities, sex ratios, gender roles, developments in science and technology, wars, and so on. Historically, the United States has had higher marriage rates than many countries of Europe, but this rate has always been closely tied to changes in the economy and to changing economic opportunities.[20] Since the 1960s, North America and western Europe have experienced quite similar trends in marriage and divorce rates, and for pretty much the same reasons.[21]

Delays in Marrying

The changing economic roles and attitudes of women in postindustrial societies have had a profound effect on marriage, divorce, and fertility rates. The slow but steady increase of unmarried women in the higher-status occupations of information economies has delayed marriage for many women; training for higher-level positions takes more time. And women (as well as men) in the middle classes are now taking the time to complete their training *before* marrying. They may live together, but they are less likely to marry at an early age.

At the same time, young adult men (working class or poor) who are high school dropouts, or who cannot find adequately paying blue-collar jobs in a deindustrializing economy, are also postponing marriage; they are most likely to be living with their partners.[22] These are some primary reasons why the median age at first marriage, for both men and women, has been rising in the United States.

Gender Differences

In finding someone to marry, women and men tend to have different priorities.[23] Women are usually more cautious about entering into love relationships and are more likely to end relationships that do not seem to be going anywhere. They are more pressed for time biologically (for childbearing), and demography and aging have favored men in the marriage lottery—at least until now. Women also tend to be more invested in the closeness and commitment aspects of love relationships. And they are likely to give more weight than men to ambition, industriousness, and the potential earning capacity of their suitors in choosing a marital partner. This is true in spite of the romantic love ideal, which, in the United States, is widely accepted as the only legitimate reason for getting married.

The economic fate of a woman's children, not to mention her own fate, still depends in large measure on her choice of a marital partner. In industrial societies, marriage tends to be a greater risk for women: Earning potential is more difficult to predict than in societies where opportunities to rise or fall in the social class structure are, or were, very limited. The tendency for women to be more practical economically in their choice of a husband is not peculiar to marriages in the United States. A cross-national survey research study conducted by psychologist David Buss has documented this gender difference in 33 industrializing and industrial societies located on six continents and on five islands.[24]

In all countries that were surveyed, men valued youth, good looks, and physical attraction more than women did in their marital choices. This emphasis was especially strong among older higher-status men. Older higher-status women, on the other hand, are now becoming more flexible about marrying up or down in terms of the age and socioeconomic status of the partners they choose. In the United States today, this trend is more prevalent in urban areas and among minority women in inner cities, but it is also increasing among upper-class white women.[25] Economically successful women can now afford to give personality, emotional support, and companionship as much or even more weight than economic support in their marital choices.

Narrowing the Choices

Good looks are important in initial encounters. They strongly affect who approaches whom at a party or anywhere else where people can meet and have brief exchanges. But here, too, people tend to seek their own level. Less attractive men will usually not approach very attractive women unless they have other assets to trade (high income and social status, power, kindness, understanding, intelligence). Looks are less important to women, older people, and people who have had a chance to get to know one another over a longer period of time—in school or work situations, for example.

In choosing a marriage partner, people also tend to sort themselves out according to factors other than background, personality, and outlook. Researchers have found similarities in the attractiveness, mental abilities, psychological problems, number of siblings, height, weight, and even eye color of marital partners.[26] All of these compatibilities have been found to affect marital satisfaction—except eye color (at least as far as we know at this point in social scientific research).

The Ultimate Mystery

But most adults have met dozens of people who, on every measure of personality, values, attitudes, and social location, would make suitable partners. Logically, they could have (and perhaps should have) loved any one of them. Yet most people have felt deeply attracted to only a few individuals, and, interestingly, these few were alike in many ways: They had similar personality traits, good and bad. Why does this happen? At the deepest personal level, why do we single out the particular people to whom we are most attracted?

The evidence is not all in, and it is based mainly on repeated observations by psychoanalytically oriented therapists. Their thesis is that we are attracted to people who have characteristics, positive and negative, similar to those of our parents or other primary caregivers.[27] Many people would deny this, and in some cases people look for partners who are dramatically *different* from their parents. But needs that partners may not be aware of do result in patterns in marital choice that seem to repeat themselves from generation to generation—statistically, if not inevitably, in any one particular family. In the social sciences, as I have said more than once, there are *probabilities* in predicting what will happen in human relationships, but there are no certainties.

Changing Attitudes and Values

Changes in attitudes and values have had important effects on when people marry for the first time. While divorce rates have declined, they remain high. Men and women are more cautious about investing in a situation that may not last. Women, especially, are increasingly concerned about developing their own interests, talents, and economic independence before they marry. The *displaced homemaker*, a woman who spent years as a full-time wife and mother, who suddenly becomes widowed or divorced in middle age and must return to the labor market with outdated or inadequate skills, is a specter that haunts mothers and daughters alike.

The traditional benefits of marriage are now more available to unmarried people of both sexes: sex for men and financial security (more or less) for women. Aside from childbearing and childrearing (a big aside), most other functions of the traditional household—cooking, baking, cleaning, laundry, sewing, repairing—can be bought in the marketplace. Why marry?

Furthermore, in the 1970s, on national surveys, married men and women were much more likely than unmarried people to report themselves as very happy. But by the 1980s the gap had closed considerably, especially for younger, never-married men aged 25 to 39, who were not too far from their married counterparts in describing themselves as very happy. And married women with young children reported less happiness than single women and were less well off physically and mentally than their husbands.[28] Answers to other questions on these surveys indicate that the decline in reported happiness of married women with children is related to the conflicting demands of marriage, work, child care, and housekeeping. Most working mothers feel torn by these demands, especially when their children are very young. Again, we can ask, why marry?

Why Marry?

Because of changes in gender roles, attitudes, values, and stresses in marriage, some social scientists are predicting a sharp increase in the number of people in the United States who will never marry. Certainly the stigma attached to being permanently single (especially for women, who are no longer called *spinsters* or *old maids*) has declined. Those who prefer this alternative, for whatever reasons, are freer than ever to pursue it, without pressure and without loss of self-esteem. And, in fact, for women at the very top educationally, occupationally, and financially, and for men at the very bottom economically and socially, getting married, later, or ever, is less likely, realistically.

Survey results indicating a decline in the personal happiness of married compared to unmarried people in the United States have to be interpreted cautiously, however. Expectations in family relationships are higher than they once were. Women are not as likely to settle for less as they were in the past. They are more aware of their sources of discontent and are more willing to talk about them and change them now, especially in the African American subculture. Most people, furthermore, still want close, caring, lasting relationships, at least ideally. These facts, and certain other trends in postindustrial societies, point to a more optimistic view of the future of marriage (and divorce), provided that the government and the economy provide necessary supports.[29]

Changing Sex Ratios

Changing sex ratios do not seem to point to huge numbers of permanently unmarried people in the future. The *sex ratio* is the number of males per 100 females in a society or in a particular geographic area. Alaska has a very high sex ratio; many more men than women move to Alaska to work on the pipelines and in the oil fields. Silicon Valley has the highest sex ratio in the continental United States; men far outnumber women in computer industries. Washington, D.C., and New York City have much lower sex ratios; more women than men work in the middle-level service occupations in government and business in these cities. Also, both cities contain a large number of African Americans, who have a very unbalanced sex ratio.

Biologically, the sex ratio at birth is 105. But male babies have a somewhat higher infant mortality rate. If not interfered with (by practices such as female infanticide, or by recently invented techniques for preselecting the sex of a child), the sex ratio tends to even out in most societies. Theoretically, then, all women and men could find marital partners; but values and traditions, as well as social conditions, have always intervened in the marriage lottery.

The Marriage Squeeze

As we have seen, in all contemporary societies that have been surveyed, women tend to marry men who are slightly older, richer, and more educated. Sociologists in the United States have called this tendency for women to marry up and men to marry down (slightly, on the average, and usually within the same class) the *marriage gradient*.[30] In terms of age differences, during times when the birth rate is increasing, younger women looking for older men are in a demographic squeeze: More women are looking for the fewer men who were born earlier, when birth rates were lower. But, except for temporary boomlets, birth rates have declined over the past 35 years. More men over 34 are now looking for fewer younger women in the United States (except in the African American subculture, where fewer males survive to adulthood).

Marrying Down

As for women who are between ages 35 and 44, most have postponed marriage but have not given up on it. Many have gone against the traditional norm by selecting slightly younger marital partners (by one to three years, usually) when the statistical odds were against them. In the Detroit metropolitan area study mentioned earlier, women were as likely to marry down as they were to marry up, although most women married men who were at the same status level. These figures are probably not representative of the total population, however, since the Detroit metropolitan area contains a large number of blacks.

The trend toward women marrying younger men will probably continue, regardless of what happens to the sex ratio. This has been a pattern in Europe for years—in France especially, where age has not disqualified older women from being sexually desirable to the extent that it has in the United States. The greatest imbalances in the sex ratio persist for older divorced and widowed women in the United States, but this, too, is beginning to change slightly as men live longer and are in better health. And, for most people, resources, personality, and attitude are becoming as important as demographic probabilities in affecting whether or not they marry.

Persistence and Change

The trend toward a marriage gradient reversal should persist as pressures on women to marry up continue to decline in postindustrial societies. Eventually, love may indeed conquer all—including higher levels of female income, education, and occupational prestige in love relationships. Even now, movies and women's magazines more often depict romantic attachments between female celebrities or professionals and male construction workers or storekeepers. The mass media are rarely in the forefront of cultural change because they need to appeal to large numbers of people in order to make money and can't afford to offend advertisers and audiences; but they do tend to reflect changing values and norms.

Why would a woman be attracted to someone with less education and lower occupational status? There are many possible reasons: She may have grown up in a working-class household and still feels more comfortable with men who remind her of her father or her brothers. She may still more strongly identify with certain values and interests of working-class people, regardless of her own change in status. She may believe that love, respect, and support are more important than clean fingernails and three-piece suits. Perhaps she needs to avoid competition or wants to hold the upper hand in a relationship. Or perhaps she needs the same kind of admiration and looking up to that most men look for in their romantic attachments. But regardless of the motives of those involved, people in marriages in which wives are more educated or earn more than their husbands report lower marital satisfaction; and these marriages are more likely to end in divorce.[31]

This conclusion is drawn from the responses of over 13,000 respondents in the first National Survey of Families and Households, conducted in the late 1980s and sponsored by the National Institutes of Health. The higher divorce rate of women in the United States who marry down is attributed by researchers to the "strong persistence of patriarchal values with respect to the traditional statuses and roles assigned to men and women."[32]

Predicting Lasting Marriages

Beginning with the pioneering work of sociologists Ernest Burgess and Paul Wallin in the 1940s, social scientists have tried to predict and explain which marriages will last, which will not, and why.[33] Psychologically, the factors that have been found to be most important in predicting lasting marriages include secure attachments to parents and to others; realistic expectations; compatible personalities; good communication skills; ability to resolve conflicts; healthy, secure children; a gratifying sexual relationship; and egalitarian relationships and roles in the household.[34]

Sociologists have been more likely to focus on social conditions and similarities in the social backgrounds, values, attitudes, and interests of partners in predicting lasting marriages (Table 6.3).[35] Other factors that are strongly associated with lasting marriages, some of which I have already mentioned, are older age at first marriage; higher socioeconomic status (higher levels of education, income, and occupational prestige); a long period of getting to know (and like) one another before marrying; and approval of the choice by friends and family.

Having reviewed what we know about finding a marital partner, we should also look at the increasing numbers of people who remain single or who move in with partners whom they do not marry.

TABLE 6.3   Predicting Lasting Marriages

THE ODDS OF STAYING MARRIED ARE BETTER:

1. If partners believe they come from happy families, believe themselves to be happy, and are able to experience the major aspects of love: passion, closeness, and commitment.
2. If partners have known each other for a long time; understand and *like* one another a great deal; and feel they are good friends.
3. If partners are older and have completed the education and training they need for their desired adult occupations. They will have less economic stress, and they will be less likely to grow apart psychologically as they continue to mature.
4. If partners are deeply religious and attend church regularly; they are more likely to value faithfulness and commitment.
5. If partners come from similar backgrounds, have similar levels of education, have the approval of and less conflict with family and friends about the marriage. They will be more likely to agree about values (familism, individualism, egalitarianism) and life goals (success, materialism, children); have similar tastes and interests; more likely to enjoy doing the same things together (hiking, camping, cruising, traveling, or staying home; going to action or art movies; listening to classical or pop music; living in the city or the suburbs; saving or spending).
6. If partners are not greatly mismatched in terms of personality dispositions: ambition/passivity; order/disorder; gregariousness/ reclusiveness, and so on.

Chapter 7
Other Options

Except for those who are celibate by choice, most young, unmarried people in the United States want to establish, or reestablish, a close and enduring attachment to a partner. The United States does not appear to be entering a "postmarital" stage, as some social critics and commentators have been predicting for some time. What evidence do we have on this issue?

In spite of reported declines in marital happiness in the United States in recent decades, on a 17-nation cross-national survey, divorced people were *least* likely to characterize themselves as very happy; the same is true for the United States.[1] Furthermore, marriage rates in the United States have declined only slightly over the past 20 years; remarriage rates continue to be quite high (three-quarters of all divorced men and two-thirds of all divorced women remarry). Also, the divorce rate leveled off in the late 1970s and has not increased since then. This "postmarital" stage is even less likely to happen if the economy remains relatively strong and employment rates remain high, especially among less educated workers.

The Couples Imperative

Ours is a couples society in which younger single people are pressured by family and friends in subtle, and sometimes not so subtle, ways to find a partner. Couples and their needs are favored when houses are sold, apartments are rented, tables at restaurants are reserved, loans are granted, and charge accounts are opened. Discounts for two are offered by airlines, railways, hotels, motels, cruise ships, and group travel operators. Also, men and women who become single after being divorced or widowed occupy an ambiguous status in our society; there are no clear-cut norms defining how they should think, feel, and behave.

How soon after meeting a new man should a divorced woman go to bed with him? Should she share her bedroom with him if she has small children living with her? Who pays when a formerly married woman goes out to dinner with old friends who are still married—especially if she has experienced a dramatic decline in income as a result of the divorce and can't really afford to pay her way?

Aside from the increased legal, economic, medical, and psychological security that marriage may provide, marriage holds out the promise of safe sex in an era of renewed danger from sexually transmitted diseases (and deadly danger from AIDS). But for those who don't want to or can't afford to marry, remaining single does not have the social stigma or the legal disadvantages it had in the past; quite the contrary—especially for women who are at the top in earnings and in entertainment, business, and professional careers. Many are divorced, with no desire to remarry; or they are remaining single because this is what they prefer.[2]

New Directions

Gone are the days when the dictionary defined women over 30 as spinsters with three options, as portrayed in popular novels: favorite aunt; humorless, hard-working grind devoid of all charm or grace; or bitter recluse, abandoned at the altar at a tender age. Now, gutsy, sexy, wisecracking career women are the heroines du jour—in currently best-selling short stories and novels (Melissa Bank's *The Girls' Guide to Hunting and Fishing*, Helen Fielding's *Bridget Jones's Diary*), TV shows (*Sex and the City, Providence, Judging Amy*), and movies with women who have beauty, brains, and brawn—in the same package.

Bachelors, in the past, were also stereotyped as love-'em-and-leave-'em swingers or lonely losers. Now, the stereotype has shifted to "commitment" or "attachment" problems. How valid is this popular image of the never-married man in the United States today? How many men (and women) actually prefer being single?

Remaining Single

According to a national poll conducted for *Time*/CNN in the year 2000, about two-thirds of the never-married women and men aged 18 to 44 would marry, but only if they find the right man or woman; and more than three-quarters of both the men and women were optimistic about eventually finding and marrying the "perfect" mate.[3] (This despite the peculiar wording of the question, using the descriptive word *perfect*. Who in this imperfect world is perfect?) As for those who have no desire to marry, almost equal percentages (8 percent of the women and 9 percent of the men) did not plan to marry ever. This figure is much lower (and more equal, incidentally) than it was in the early 1980s, when about 20 percent of the women and 33 percent of the men in a national survey reported no desire to ever marry.[4]

Postponing or Foregoing Marriage

Other national studies confirm this picture. Most never-married singles in the United States are postponing marriage; they have not voluntarily decided never to marry. Among all adults, about 90 percent of those who prefer being single are widowed or divorced; and many are not actually single, since they are living with partners whom they have not married and probably will not marry. Those who have live-in partners and report no desire to remarry say they don't want to risk another failure or that their children are strongly opposed to a remarriage. Many older widows who live alone claim they prefer remaining single because they fear having to nurse another disabled older man eventually—if they do remarry.[5]

Cross-National Comparisons

How does this picture vary in different countries and in the United States? Wars and immigration usually lower the sex ratio, as well as female marriage and fertility rates; poverty and economic recessions also lower female marriage and fertility rates, regardless of the sex ratio. After the breakup of the Soviet Union in 1991, unemployment surged, income deteriorated, government support services plummeted, and the marriage rate in Russia fell 30 percent compared to that in 1990. The divorce rate soared to a rate 60 percent higher than it was in 1990, and the fertility rate plunged from the highest to the lowest rate in Europe (from 1.89 to 1.17)—comparable to the historically low rates in Spain and Italy.[6]

On the effects of the sex ratio on marriage and fertility rates, sociologist Scott J. South, in a survey of 111 countries, found that in countries where there is an undersupply of marriageable women (usually because of female abortion and female infanticide practices), female marriage and fertility rates are higher.[7] (Contemporary China is an example of increased marriage rates for women, who are in short supply because of abortion of female fetuses.) Also, in countries where the sex ratio favors women, the average age at first marriage is lower and the divorce rate is low. Also, women in countries where these trends are most pronounced are not usually employed in the nonfamily economy.

As for subcultural differences in marriage rates in the United States, since ethnic minority males usually have less education and lower incomes, marriage rates are also lower among most minorities; and they are lower among low-income people generally, regardless of ethnic origin. The alternative of living together without marrying contributes significantly to this lower marriage rate.[8] Table 7.1 summarizes the conditions that lower marriage rates.

Living Together

Living together without marriage (called *cohabitation* by sociologists) is another option that can provide a sexually safe, economically practical, and—for increasing numbers of people, especially at older ages—emotionally satisfying alternative.

TABLE 7.1 Conditions That Lower Marriage Rates

1. Wars, massive immigration, plagues, and epidemics
2. Poverty, low income
3. Recessions and high unemployment rates
4. A surplus of women; a low sex ratio
5. Economic independence of women; employment in the nonfamily economy
6. Little or no government or private support for employed mothers
7. Growing up in highly conflicted or single-parent (divorced or never-married) households
8. Easy availability of nonfamily sources for satisfying basic needs: sex; prepared foods, laundries, dry cleaners; inexpensive, mass-produced clothing; hotels, motels, boarding houses, small apartments; commercial recreation

Who, When, and Where

As I pointed out earlier, nonmarital living together is on the increase almost everywhere. It is most frequent in industrialized countries and is less common, but also increasing rapidly, in Africa and Asia. In rural areas of China it is spreading among adolescents who are below the minimum legal age for marrying; in 1980, the Chinese government raised this age to 20 for women and 22 for men in an attempt to lower the birth rate.[9]

As for the United States, sociologists Larry L. Bumpass and James A. Sweet and others have analyzed data on unmarried living-together sexual relationships from responses to the two National Surveys of Families and Households. These surveys have yielded more complete information on unmarried couples who are living together in a sexual relationship than we have ever had—and a few surprises, too.[10]

Values and Family Background

Living-together couples in the United States are most likely to be city dwellers, living in the Northeast or Far West, not religious or churchgoing, less conventional in their behavior, and less traditional in their values. They are less familistic and less likely to stay in an unhappy relationship because they value duty, obligation, and commitment more than they value their own happiness or the freedom to pursue their own goals. Also, compared to married couples of similar class and ethnic origin, cohabitors are more likely to have parents who are divorced, to describe their parents' marriage as unhappy, and to report poorer relationships with their parents. And, finally, cohabitors are more likely to have the same level of education but are less likely to come from similar ethnic and racial backgrounds than married couples.[11]

African Americans are almost three times more likely than whites to be living in poverty, and they are about three times more likely to cohabit. African Americans now marry later than other minority populations, and although in earlier decades nearly 95 percent of black women eventually married, today about 30 percent are expected to remain single.[12] Historically, this seems to be grounded in changing economic opportunities in the United States. In Philadelphia, between 1880 and 1925, when employment opportunities for unskilled and semiskilled laborers were plentiful, African Americans were almost as likely as their European American counterparts to be legally married.[13]

This held true up until the first of the recurring recessions that started in the late 1960s in the United States. Beginning in the 1970s, intact black families who migrated from the South to deindustrializing inner cities in the North experienced increased rates of divorce over time; and during this same period, nonmarital living-together relationships increased steadily as well. From all available evidence that I have found, subcultural attitudes toward marrying have not been as important as changes in economic opportunities and economic security in affecting marriage and divorce rates in the United States—and in most other Western countries that have been surveyed as well.[14]

Number and Duration

The number of unmarried people in the United States who live together is continuing to increase, especially for people who marry more than once. About half of all living-together relationships end in less than a year; the couple either marries or breaks up. Most marry, since they had already set a date to be married before moving in together.[15]

Very few young couples stay in a living-together relationship permanently. Living together may postpone marriage, but it doesn't replace marriage, or remarriage, except for a small percentage of older people who are divorced or widowed. Older divorced women may choose a permanent living-together relationship because they would lose alimony or other benefits if they remarry. Also, as I pointed out earlier, older previously married men and women may live together because of strong pressures from adult children who oppose a remarriage. Less than 10 percent of living-together relationships last more than five years, and a majority of these couples, by far, are older and previously widowed or divorced people.[16]

Social Class and Ethnic Differences

People with low levels of education and income have always been most likely to enter a living-together relationship, and they still are. Historically, in the United States, these were known as *common-law* relationships if they lasted for several years. Common-law status came with certain legal benefits for women and children—for support, inheritance, and so on. But this is now a gray area legally, with widely different policies in various states.

Working-class men and women are still more likely than middle-class young adults to cohabit, and the gap is widening. There has been a recent turnabout in the willingness of younger college-educated women to enter a living-together relationship without setting a date to marry. Accumulating research information and publicity in the mass media about the possibly exploitive aspects of this relationship for women may be operating here. Living-together relationships are most likely to end in marriage for white and Asian Americans, less likely to do so for Hispanics, and least likely to do so for African Americans.[17]

Women tend to be more committed than their partners in living-together relationships.[18] They are under more pressure in terms of time, especially if they have completed their education and training, are successful, and want to have children before it's too late. They often contribute more than their partners economically, physically, and psychologically to the relationship, especially in the African American subculture. And they usually have less power in the relationship because they are more committed; they may give (and give in) more in order to keep the relationship going.

Gender Roles

Living-together couples are more likely than married couples to report an equal distribution of rights and responsibilities in their relationship. They are more likely to believe that both partners should work and that the man's career should not be given priority when choices have to be made (accepting a job offer in another city, for example). But research on the actual behavior of couples in these relationships indicates that while "cohabiting women spend less time than wives doing housework, their partners do not spend more time than husbands doing this kind of work. . . . It is apparently easier to endorse egalitarian ideas and philosophize about them than it is to successfully put them into practice."[19]

Power, Sex, and Violence

Young living-together couples are more likely than dating or married couples to be physically abusive to their partners. They are more likely to come from dissimilar social backgrounds, and they report lower levels of satisfaction with the relationship. Also, they are more likely than married couples to maintain their independence by keeping separate bank accounts; and while most are faithful to their partners, they have higher rates of infidelity than married couples. This is usually explained by their less conventional values, lower levels of commitment, and the fact that the partners they chose are different from those they end up marrying. Also, they have more frequent sex with their partners than either married or dating couples. And, like married couples, they are more likely to break up if the female is more educated, especially if she also earns more.[20]

Divorce Rates

One surprising research conclusion about living-together relationships is that couples who live together before getting married are *more* likely to divorce within the first ten years after they marry than those who do not. And this is also true in other postindustrial societies that have been surveyed—Sweden, Denmark, and Germany.[21]

Logically, we might expect that living together before marriage would make it easier to adjust after marriage. Couples would be used to the little frictions and frustrations that irritate many people who share living quarters, no matter what their legal status: leaving the toothpaste cap off, the toilet seat up, the milk out of the refrigerator; refusing to put laundry in the hamper, run the necessary errand, make the important telephone call; monopolizing the television set or playing the radio, record, or CD player too loudly—and so on, and on.

We would also think that couples who lived together before marrying would have worked out many of the more serious sources of potential conflict: finances and accounts; who does what inside and outside the home; sexual problems; contacts with friends and family; and incompatible needs for closeness, privacy, independence, or togetherness. They would have made the necessary compromises and concessions by the time they marry; and, if not, they would not have married.

But they do marry, perhaps because they believe that marriage will solve the problems they have with their partners, just as many people believe that having a child or moving to a new apartment, house, neighborhood, or region will solve their problems. But marriage does not usually accomplish these goals. For one thing, that little piece of paper—the marriage license—changes awareness, tolerance, and expectations. Living together is an extension of the dating relationship, and people tend to be on good behavior. Partners in a living-together relationship may tolerate certain behavior before they marry, such as infidelity, addictions, selfishness, or irresponsibility, that they are unwilling to tolerate after the marriage ceremony. It may be easier to start fresh than to try to renegotiate and change established patterns.

Another possible reason why couples who live together before marrying are more likely to get divorced is that these couples tend to be less religious and less familistic in their values. They may also have higher expectations for the relationship psychologically, and with less traditional values, they are unlikely to value commitment and loyalty at any cost.[22]

Some Common Problems

If the roles of wives and husbands are less clear and more ambiguous in rapidly changing societies, this is even more true of unmarried partners. Unmarried couples who live together tend to have the same problems that marriages have, but in more exaggerated form.[23]

Territoriality

In living-together relationships, one partner usually moves into the physical space of the other. This may be resented by those who have strong feelings of *territoriality* or possessiveness about their physical space. Guest and host have to redefine their status. Possessions may continue to be defined as "yours" or "mine" rather than "ours," especially if the future of the relationship is unclear. Married couples setting up their first household together usually bring in joint possessions (including wedding gifts) and joint purchases for the new space.

The boundaries between independence and togetherness are difficult to establish and maintain in marriage. They are even more blurred in living-together relationships, which have few legal supports and may have few familial or friendship supports.

Commitment

Except for couples who have set a date to marry and those who have agreed never to marry, many participants in unmarried-couple relationships are not equal in their degree of commitment.[24] Women are more likely to believe they will eventually marry their partner, and the balance of power in a relationship favors the one who is less dependent. It also favors those who have more resources—education, income, intelligence, psychological strength, and so on. And aside from issues of power, the less committed partner will usually not be as willing to confide and not as motivated to work out conflicts constructively.

Certain external clues point to the degree of commitment in a particular living-together relationship, regardless of what the participants may say. Among these, sexual exclusiveness and fidelity, giving up a previous desirable (rent-controlled) apartment, having both names on the answering machine, pooling economic resources and expenses (having a joint checking account for household expenses), and introducing the partner to family and friends are the most significant indications of commitment.

Role Conflict

Another problem that tends to be more severe in living-together relationships is a lack of mutual expectations about the relationship. *Role conflict*—feelings of strain or pressure in carrying out a role—will be stronger if partners disagree or are uncertain about their rights and obligations in the relationship. It will be more intense if the partners enter the relationship for different reasons or with different degrees of commitment; they will have different and usually incompatible expectations.[25]

Certain questions help pinpoint various kinds of living-together relationships and possible sources of conflict: Is the relationship a temporary one based on physical convenience or economic considerations, or is it meant to be permanent? Is it a trial relationship that may lead to marriage if it works out, or is it a head start before the marriage ceremony, scheduled for a particular date? Is it a desire for companionship without closeness or commitment, or is there closeness and companionship but a fear of commitment?

Do both partners agree on the definition of the situation, or is there a hidden agenda that they are not aware of or won't admit? Do both partners agree about who should pay for what, especially if one earns more? If there are children present, how should the live-in partner relate to them? If one partner gets a job in another area, will the other go along? Will they visit relatives together? How should they divide their time with relatives on Thanksgiving, Christmas, or other holidays? And how will relatives relate to the live-in partner: as family or intruder?

Which decisions should be made together, which should be made separately, whose business is it, and why? Who covers the medical costs of the uninsured partner? Who gets what if there is a breakup? If a partner dies and the house, apartment, or bank account is in his or her name, does the surviving live-in partner have any inheritance rights? What does this depend on: how long they have lived together, who contributed what to the relationship, or who sacrificed what for the relationship? How can this be proved? If unmarried parents separate, how much child support can the custodial parent demand and get? What are the visitation rights of the unmarried, noncustodial parent, not to mention the grandparents? The possibilities for conflicting expectations are almost endless.

Legal Ambiguities

Most laws are designed to protect the legally married, widowed, and divorced; laws reinforce expectations in relationships. In the absence of cultural norms that define cohabitors' legal rights, lawyers advise that living-together couples should be aware of how to protect their rights. If property and children are involved, they should probably draw up legal contracts; these contracts, including wills, should specify the sharing of earnings and property, inheritance, and child custody and support if the relationship ends, by separation or by death.[26]

This may not be very realistic, however, for most couples in living-together relationships, especially those who are young, are just beginning the relationship, and are uncertain about its future. It certainly would be irrelevant for those who have little or no property or earnings and no children. And it might be defined as crass and expedient by people caught up in the fervor of a romantic attachment. But for well-off, established, older people, especially those with children from previous marriages or relationships, it makes sense.

Roles, boundaries, and legalities are even more unclear in living-together relationships than in marriages. It could be argued that conflicts are less severe because the living-together relationship is less committed, usually temporary, and more easily ended legally. But it would also seem to depend very much on who is less committed and who is more interested in ending the relationship. And here, too, we get some interesting gender differences.

Breaking Up

Women tend to be more reluctant to enter a living-together relationship, they report more problems in the relationship, and they are more likely to end living-together relationships that seem to be going nowhere.[27] According to research information, this is probably because women tend to be more committed and emotionally invested in the relationship, more likely to be dissatisfied with the unequal sharing of household and economic responsibilities, and under more pressure to marry, especially if they are older and want children before it is too late. The ultimatum "Either we get married or I leave" may work, but it may also boomerang.

Reasons for Breaking Up

Living-together couples who break up most often cite emotional immaturity, "growing apart," unequal commitment, differences in values and interests that are too great to overcome, and external pressures and transitions in explaining the breakup.[28] Transitions are such things as the loss or relocation of a job, graduation from college, and temporary physical separations, for whatever reasons. Outside pressures that may destroy living-together relationships are negative reactions from family members—from parents of younger cohabitors and from adolescent or adult children of older cohabitors.

Is the experience of loss or separation less painful than it is for married couples who divorce? Again, it depends on the reasons for the relationship. Unmarried couples in short-term relationships that break up will not feel the guilt, loss of self-esteem, and sense of failure of those who divorce. And they will have fewer legal problems, usually. But those who have had an intense emotional involvement over a longer period of time may experience the same sequence of feelings and stresses as those who divorce: denial, anger, grief, and a gradual redefinition of the self as a single person, with all that this implies. Table 7.2 summarizes the comparisons of married and unmarried partners who live together.

TABLE 7.2   Married and Unmarried Partners

COMPARED TO MARRIED PARTNERS, UNMARRIED PARTNERS WHO LIVE TOGETHER:

1. Are less committed to the relationship; women are usually more committed than their partners.
2. Do less housework than married husbands and wives.
3. Are more violent than married or dating couples.
4. Are more likely to divorce if they do marry.
5. Tend to be more equal in education and less similar in social background (ethnic origin, race, religion).
6. Have few or no cultural or legal guidelines defining the rights and responsibilities of partners.
7. Women are more reluctant to enter the relationship and are more likely to end relationships that seem to be going nowhere.

Note: These conditions do not apply to couples who move in together after they have set a date to be married or to older couples who have been previously married and do not plan to ever remarry.

Same-Sex Living-Together Relationships

Individuals who are sexually attracted to members of the same sex are called *homosexuals*. This label is disliked by most people who have a same-sex sexual orientation; they prefer the terms *lesbian* (for same-sex female relationships) or *gay* (for same-sex male relationships). Others use the term *gay* to refer to all same-sex sexual relationships. The situation is further complicated by the distinction between a lifelong gay or lesbian sexual orientation and a bisexual orientation. Individuals with a bisexual orientation shift back and forth between a heterosexual and a same-sex orientation. Or, after years of being identified as heterosexual, they suddenly change their public identity. *Coming out* is the public announcement of a same-sex sexual orientation by an individual.

Demographics

In the past, estimates of the actual extent of homosexuality in the population of the United States differed only slightly. Most researchers set this figure at about 10 percent, which is similar to the figure in nonliterate societies of the past and in most contemporary societies that have been surveyed.[29] More recent surveys, especially a national survey by the National Opinion Research Center (NORC) in the early 1990s, set this figure at about half of the 10 percent figure.[30] But most studies are based on self-reports, and a major question about the results is whether respondents are being truthful. Also, the NORC survey did not include the homeless, college students, and people in prisons, the military, and other institutions. The large concentrations of homosexuals in specific neighborhoods, near college campuses and in large cities such as San Francisco, Los Angeles, and New York, were also undercounted.

Origins of Homosexuality

We have no evidence from academic or clinical researchers that points unquestionably to genetics, specific childrearing practices, or specific parent-child relationships in the formation of a gay or lesbian identity. What is clear is that homosexuality occurs in all known societies, it is more tolerated in some cultures than others, and it has even been highly respected in some cultures.[31]

Since similar rates of homosexuality are found in all known societies, some researchers believe there is a genetic predisposition in certain individuals that environmental factors may or may not bring out. But a majority of the children who might seem to have this predisposition because they behave like "sissies" or "tomboys" during childhood do not grow up to be gay or lesbian as adults. And if there is a strong genetic predisposition, we can't explain why homosexual or bisexual parents, with children from a previous heterosexual relationship or from artificial insemination (about 20 percent of all lesbian and gay family households), are not more likely than heterosexual parents to bring up children who are homosexual.[32]

Those who have never felt physically attracted to a member of the opposite sex probably do have a strong genetic inclination to be gay or lesbian, but those who become gay or lesbian in adulthood have often experienced a profound disappointment in their relationship with an opposite-sex partner. The specific environmental factors that reinforce or extinguish a genetic tendency (if it does exist) are still at issue. Research, on this and other related issues, has to be read carefully; most conclusions do not meet the scientific standards of validity and reliability.[33]

Whatever the answer, the question of why certain people become homosexual while others do not is no longer considered as important as it once was, since homosexuality is no longer defined as a mental disorder in the United States. Only individuals who are deeply troubled by their gay or lesbian identity, and want to change it, are now defined as having a psychological problem. On the other hand, if researchers could establish an overriding genetic factor in the homosexual behavior of some individuals, this would mean that they didn't *choose* and can't *change* their sexual identity, just as people can't change their ethnic ancestry or the color of their skin. If this is the case, their behavior might gain greater acceptance by the public and by policy makers.

Community and Family Reactions

Legally, same-sex couples are single and experience the same legal disadvantages as heterosexual living-together couples. But in 1989, a landmark decision of the highest court in the state of New York ruled that same-sex couples can be defined as a family on the grounds of long-term "emotional and financial commitment and interdependence."[34] This decision applied only to the right of the survivor of a ten-year gay relationship to remain in the rent-controlled apartment the couple had occupied before the death of one of the partners. Since then, this standard has been extended in New York and in a number of other states with large homosexual populations. It now includes other legal rights for *domestic partners*, such as family medical insurance coverage and the right to visit a partner who is in intensive care in a hospital. Obituary columns in the *New York Times* now routinely list long-term "companions" of gay men as survivors, along with parents, brothers, and sisters.

Public Opinion

Reported tolerance of homosexual behavior is increasing in the United States, but a majority of the public does not approve of this behavior, and does not believe that marriages between homosexual couples should be recognized by law or that homosexual couples should be allowed to adopt children. But most people do believe that being gay should not keep someone from holding a public job: as a teacher, police officer, judge, city government official, or member of Congress. And a majority believe that homosexual couples should be allowed to inherit each other's property and be permitted to receive medical and life insurance benefits from their partners.[35]

Eventually, the legal definition of a family will probably be extended to include gay and heterosexual domestic partners. This is likely to happen because it reflects and reinforces the traditional obligation of married couples to care for each other in sickness and in health and to share financial benefits and burdens. The family diversity movement in the United States is growing in numbers and support. Its primary goal is to gain legal recognition for all unmarried couples who define themselves as a family, regardless of their sexual preferences.

Parental Reactions

According to recent research studies, most parents react with shock, denial ("This is just a phase; it won't last"), guilt, and rejection when they first learn about their son's or daughter's gay or lesbian sexual orientation.[36] Mothers are usually the first to be told, and their reactions are not predictable; mothers who are deeply religious are most likely to disapprove. Fathers, regardless of their religious persuasion, are more likely to cut off all contact with their gay or lesbian child, especially their male child. Norms defining what is masculine and what is feminine, remember, are more binding and less negotiable for males than for females, both culturally and psychologically.

In the more benign situations, the relationship between the generations is simply cut off. But sometimes more extreme or forceful solutions are pursued by parents: kidnapping (of lesbians, usually) and attempts at deprogramming; threats to cut them off financially (especially if the son or daughter is a college student); attempts to force them into psychotherapy; or attempts to take away grandchildren who were born during a previous heterosexual relationship.

The Gay and Lesbian Subculture

Since same-sex couples experience greater disapproval from family, community, and church than heterosexual couples (married or unmarried), they are much more likely to voluntarily segregate themselves geographically. They are drawn to gay and lesbian communities in large cities or near college campuses, where they are less isolated socially and can find a wide variety of activities and organizations that cater to their special interests and needs.[37]

Gay and Lesbian Neighborhoods

In gay and lesbian neighborhoods, inhabitants find newspapers, bookstores, theaters, restaurants, clothing stores, therapists, lawyers, doctors, dentists, and others who cater exclusively to gays and lesbians. Also, they now have their own Website with news and information about services available and issues that concern gays and lesbians. Gay bars are losing ground to the Internet as a source for meeting and dating potential partners. But anonymity tends to strip away accountability; lies and other kinds of subterfuge on the part of potential partners are common, as they are on heterosexual Internet dating services.

As residents of a gay and lesbian territory and subculture, with its special values and customs, newcomers find new reference groups and develop more positive feelings about themselves. They find approval, acceptance, and reassurance from like-minded people in the new community, and perhaps for the first time in their lives, they may experience the feeling of being like everyone else in the new world they have found.

Leisure Activities

Since gay and lesbian households do not usually contain children, leisure activities are less likely to be home-based, and going out is very important in this subculture. Gay bars have declined since the advent of AIDS, but gay rights organizations and the Metropolitan Community Church (an interdenominational church for lesbians and gays) are thriving. They sponsor picnics, dances, lectures, nonfamily Thanksgiving and Christmas dinners, and other social events that keep their members from feeling isolated. Economically, however, especially in meccas such as San Francisco, a large-scale influx of gays and lesbians has resulted in higher rates of unemployment or underemployment for this particular wave of migrants from less hospitable places, despite their higher levels of education and occupational skills compared to the rest of the population of the United States.

Roles and Relationships

Individuals who identify themselves as gay or lesbian do not usually conform to popular stereotypes in their speech, behavior, or body language. Most gay males are not effeminate, and most lesbian females are not masculine in appearance or behavior; they are not easily recognizable as gay or lesbian. And most do not play butch and femme roles in the kitchen or in the bedroom. Roles depend on talents, tastes, and interests.

Power

Power imbalances exist among gay and lesbian couples and are related to differences in education and income. But these power differences are less extreme in gay and lesbian households, usually. In heterosexual households, power is reinforced by differences in income, age, and gender. But gay couples are of the same sex and usually have similar incomes and education; despite popular stereotypes, "kept boys" are actually not common in this subculture.

Women, generally, whatever their sexual orientation, are less likely than men to value power in their close relationships. They tend to form intimate friendship relationships more easily, and they are also less likely than men to equate their self-worth with their earned income. Lesbian women reflect these gender differences in their relationships. Women in lesbian relationships report greater intimacy and equality and more equal sharing of household responsibilities than men in gay or heterosexual relationships. And compared to married heterosexual partners, both gay and lesbian partners report more autonomy, fewer barriers to leaving, and more frequent breaking up of their relationships.[38]

Another aspect of heterosexual gender socialization that carries over into gay and lesbian relationships is the difference in the value placed on commitment and sexual loyalty: Lesbian relationships, in the past, were more often permanent and monogamous; gay men were more likely to be involved in casual sex (but not serious affairs) outside of their long-term partner relationships. Lesbians very rarely engaged in casual sex, and an outside affair usually represented a desire to leave their partner. Now, gay males are also more likely to be exclusive and monogamous in their sexual liaisons as the AIDS epidemic continues—although recent increases in gay male casual sex have been reported.

Gay and Lesbian Parents

Most gay and lesbian couples were raised in heterosexual nuclear families and, as parents, they experience childrearing challenges that are similar to those of heterosexual parents. But they also have to contend with unique issues and problems that are difficult for people who are not in their situation to empathize with and understand.[39] Gay and lesbian parents are usually disowned by their own parents, and their children lack a sometimes crucial source of economic and emotional support from grandparents and other relatives. Those who have children from a previous heterosexual relationship live in constant dread that they will lose custody or visiting rights should the courts discover their new sexual orientation. They are rarely given custody if their same-sex orientation is known at the time of the divorce proceedings.

They are highly vulnerable to discovery if they attempt to establish a new family situation in secrecy in heterosexual neighborhoods: How do they introduce their same-sex partner (to teachers at parent-teacher conferences, to their children's friends, to local storekeepers and doctors) in small-town or suburban communities? A same-sex friend would be suspect; some have bestowed more plausible statuses on their same-sex partners: sister, brother, or godparent. How much guilt and discomfort does this pretense cause—for the parent, for the child? What happens when they are discovered (and most are sooner or later)?

If there is no biological opposite-sex parent or grandparent waiting to take away the child (or children), they can live in a gay and lesbian community and enjoy the luxury of living without sham, pretense, or rejection. And this is where most gay and lesbian couples, with children conceived by artificial insemination, do in fact live.

How do the children of gay and lesbian parents fare in terms of gender identity, sexual orientation (gay or heterosexual), personality development, functioning, and self-esteem? In a review of research studies on this topic for the American Psychological Association by psychologist Barbara F. Achene in 1995, the author concludes: there is "virtually unanimous agreement that there are no significant differences between the children of homosexual and heterosexual parents on any dimension of personality functioning or personality development."[40] Parental attitudes, behavior, and childrearing styles are similar in middle-class families, regardless of sexual orientation.

The Oldest Generation

In the late 1960s, the first generation of gay and lesbian couples came out in large numbers—declaring their sexual orientation openly. Now, this first generation is middle-aged or older. Since most do not have children or relatives who will help them in their old age, many have been concerned about getting the care they will need in an accepting and tolerant environment when they are old and more dependent on others. To meet this need, developers around the country, many of whom are gay and share the same concerns, are now building retirement communities and assisted-living and nursing complexes for gays and lesbians. This enables them to age and die among people with similar life histories, who will be their neighbors, friends, and surrogate families.[41]

Getting Help

For those who have difficulty establishing or maintaining partner relationships, psychotherapy is an increasingly accepted option in postindustrial societies. The stigma attached to getting help from professional therapists is declining, although strong gender differences persist. Therapy is increasingly accepted even among poor, severely stressed families who, traditionally, did not seek professional help voluntarily and did not fare well with talking cures. They preferred family support, drugs, and specific expert directives from therapists. Many still do, but therapists now prescribe drugs for all social classes. Marriage and family therapy is also booming, and practically every college campus in the United States now has a psychological counseling center.

Changing Values

In an age of wonder drugs, miracle cures, quick fixes, and small consolations, getting short-term, effective treatment for school, work, or relationship problems is becoming the norm. In the middle social classes especially, young couples who have postponed marrying and are having problems with commitment are going to therapists for premarital counseling. Young married partners are there to keep floundering marriages afloat; middle-aged and older couples are coming in to revitalize empty relationships.

Books that describe the devastating effects and lasting wounds of divorce on women, men, and children are best-sellers.[42] People seem to be trying harder to stay together, and they want faster, more effective help for their problems.

Changing Therapies

The current national trend is toward short-term therapy, or *brief therapy*, as practitioners call it.[43] The goal is to provide more focused, direct help for an immediate problem. These therapies emerged from crisis-oriented therapy in which people are treated for severe reactions to traumas such as divorce, death, serious illness, loss of a job, failure at school, and so on.

Varying Techniques

Most practitioners of brief therapy use the same techniques as longer-term therapists. Psychoanalytically oriented brief therapists focus on destructive early childhood experiences and their reappearance later in life, but they avoid lengthy discussions of lost childhood memories, hidden meanings, or parental shortcomings. Behavioral therapists focus on specific symptoms such as a fear of flying or of heights; they try to reinforce positive behavior and extinguish disabling emotions and behavior in the people they work with. Cognitive therapists try to change conscious beliefs and perceptions that are inaccurate. They teach people with *thinking problems* to correct their false ideas by *testing reality*, that is, by looking for objective evidence that confirms or disconfirms their beliefs.[44]

The following is an example of how cognitive therapists work: Women who are orthodox in their religious beliefs find it hard to cope with infertility; they blame themselves for their inability to bear children and tend to interpret their situation as a punishment from God. A cognitive therapist would try to substitute their belief about infertility with a medically established belief.

> When a woman who had suffered recurrent miscarriages said God was punishing her, Dr. Demeure replied, "So, God kills babies?" The shocked patient said, "Oh, no, God would never do that!" Only after logic replaced her fear could the woman see infertility as a physiological problem.[45]

College Counseling

College counseling is now defined as a distinct subspecialty among therapists. College students have special problems. Aside from problems with love and sex, those who go away to college must separate from their families and learn to live with peers. All students (commuter and residential) must cope with academic pressures and decide on an adult identity and career.[46]

According to yearly national surveys of entering first-year college students conducted by the Department of Education at the University of California at Los Angeles since 1990, students are experiencing record levels of stress: Competition for college admission and completion is higher than ever; record numbers of students engage in paid employment (almost one-third work full time and one-half work an average of 25 hours a week to help pay for their education); record numbers report taking remedial classes in high school; and more report feeling bored in the classroom than ever before. The dot.com generation is entertained by interacting with screens; teachers who do not use an interactive teaching style are considered boring.[47]

These surveys also reveal a significant gender gap in the amount of stress experienced by students. Female students are almost twice as likely as males to report high levels of stress: They spend more time studying, doing volunteer work, and participating in clubs; male students report spending more hours exercising, watching television, partying, and playing video games.

Nationally, a majority of the college students who come to psychological counseling centers for help stay for only a few sessions. Most are relieved to know that what they are going through is typical; what they need, basically, is reassurance that they are not alone and are not deeply disturbed.

Marriage Counseling

Marriage counseling is also booming. Therapists working with troubled couples try to change destructive thoughts and behavior, reduce conflict, improve communication skills, help marital partners become more aware of their anger, and teach them to cope with anxiety more effectively.[48]

At the prevention level, premarital counseling is also burgeoning. A new state law in Florida offers marriage-license discounts ($32.50 off on the $88.00 license) to couples who take a four-hour marital education course. Other states are urging clergy to recommend minimal counseling requirements before entering into marriage; giving tax credits for taking marital education courses; requiring completion of high school courses in marital skills before graduation; and providing emergency funds to train teachers and researchers in premarital and marital counseling. These new programs are being pushed by state governors who are concerned about high divorce rates in their state. In the words of the current governor of California: "Tell me the sense of a system where it is easier to get a marriage license than it is to get a hunting or a driver's license . . . easier to get out of a marriage with children than it is to get out of a Tupperware contract. Ours is an effort to encourage families to appreciate the lifetime commitment of a marriage contract, to recognize that a marriage that can be saved, should be saved."[49]

The Role of Therapists

Therapists can be helpful in ways that friends and family can't be because friends and family are not impartial. They tend to take sides; furthermore, they will be blamed if their advice doesn't work. Also, family and friends may be subsidizing, or even promoting (*enabling*), personality and relationship problems in ways they aren't aware of. When relationships are severely destructive, outside professional help may be the only recourse for building up (or restoring) self-esteem and the ability to function. But whatever the problems of those who need help, and however different the approach of various therapists, brief therapies work best for basically secure people: people who relate fairly well to others, are highly motivated to confront their difficulties, and come in with a specific pressing problem that needs immediate attention.

We turn now to what researchers have discovered about relationships between husbands and wives in the early years of marriage. After people have traveled one or another of the various routes to finding a partner and have settled on a choice, what happens next? What are the usual stages, or transitions, that most people go through after they marry? What are the changing demands, stresses, satisfactions, and rewards they experience as they carry on from day to day and year to year?

Chapter 8
Partner Relationships

Marriage is a major transition that involves new decisions, new conflicts, and new compromises, even if the partners are strongly attached and committed and in-laws and friends are approving and enthusiastic about the marriage. Getting married requires two people to decide things together that they previously decided as individuals: who will be their friends, what to do with leisure time, how to use space, time, and money. They will also have to redefine their previous relationships with parents, siblings, friends, and co-workers; the needs and wishes of the new husband or wife now have to be taken into account in making plans and relating to others.

Issues

Newly married couples bring long-established habits and baggage into the marriage. Arguments and disagreements usually center on the same age-old issues: money, work, sex, in-laws, infidelity, and physical or psychological abuse. But conflicts are more likely under certain circumstances.

Background Differences

Great differences in age and family background (social class, ethnic origin, race, and religion, especially) can create problems because of persisting differences in attitudes and values. Problems also arise if personalities are extremely mismatched or birth order is strongly incompatible. How can birth order affect partner relationships? An example is two first-born children who were both responsible for the care of younger siblings; they may each tend to give orders in their new family. Two youngest children, who were indulged by older siblings, may expect to be taken care of by their new partners.[1]

Poor relationships with parents and siblings, an unhappy childhood and adolescence, divorced parents, or coming from a violent or highly conflicted home are also associated with marital problems. At this point, though, we have good evidence from national longitudinal studies that children who grow up in strongly conflicted households have fewer behavior problems and are better off emotionally, in the long run, if their parents divorce rather than stay together.[2]

If a couple marries before the age of 20, economic problems are usually more pressing, an established identity is less likely, interests and values are likely to change, and the couple is more prone to growing apart as time goes on. Also, if the marriage is impulsive, after partners know each other only a short time, it may be a rebound reaction; if they marry after a long engagement, one or both partners may have a commitment problem. Other signs of possible trouble to come are elopements—not always, but specifically when family and friends are not invited to the wedding because they disapprove of the relationship. Also, if the wife becomes pregnant before or within the first year after marrying, the partners may not have enough time to build a strong relationship as a couple; for most people, this takes at least three years.

Unrealistic Expectations

Marital problems are also more likely if one of the partners marries shortly after a major loss or change in status that the marriage is expected to compensate for. This may involve a major disappointment at work, a divorce, or the death, desertion, or chronic illness of a parent, partner, sister, or brother. Problems in a marital relationship will also be more severe if a partner marries to escape an unpleasant home situation and does not know enough about the new partner, or hasn't developed enough positive feeling about the new relationship, to anticipate and surmount the usual hurdles that come up during the early years of marriage.

Illusions

A major source of arguments and disputes in the early years, especially in the United States, is illusion: a delusion or false belief that is based on a wish rather than reality. And the grand illusion, as I mentioned earlier, is that a partner's basic personality can be changed after marriage by persuasion or example. A reserved partner will not suddenly become warm, open, and outgoing, nor will a passive person become assertive and ambitious. A depressed partner will not become cheerful and bubbly, any more than a violent partner will become forever kind and gentle. Hasty marriages based on overwhelming physical attraction and idealization of a partner may bring disillusionment and disenchantment as daily routines unfold and reality sets in.[3]

Boundary Problems

Couples who live close to their relatives may have boundary problems. What was previously viewed as permissible "dropping in" by members of the extended family may come to be defined as an intrusion by the new husband or wife. Parental expectations for weekly visits or daily calls may be opposed by new sons- and daughters-in-law. Expensive gifts to a married daughter may be viewed by a new husband as an attempt to discredit him as a provider. If the independence issue with parents has not been resolved, it will carry over into the new relationship.[4] Couples who are isolated or estranged from their extended families lack an important source of support during transitions or crises, and they may expect too much from their partners. Also, problems about who has the ultimate say in making major decisions may arise if the couple is dependent on either extended family—financially, physically, or emotionally—especially when parents feel that their help buys them the right to exercise control over the young couple's decisions.

Still, regardless of new challenges and adjustments, most newly married couples who stay married report the highest levels of satisfaction with their relationship during the early years of marriage, before the birth of a first child.[5] And, in advanced industrial countries, this satisfaction is closely tied to the ease with which partners can talk to one another.

Communication

In industrial societies, problems in communicating during the early years of marriage (and in the later years as well) usually reflect other problems in the relationship. Communication involves sending verbal and nonverbal messages to others about our thoughts, feelings, motives, and needs. Talking to a partner about problems and dissatisfactions in the relationship is now considered essential for settling disputes and strengthening relationships.[6] This is particularly true in advanced industrial countries, where friendship, closeness, and emotional support in partner and parent–child relationships are believed to be the most important aspects of family life.

Difficulties

In these societies, communication difficulties are now recognized as a major symptom of marital unhappiness and a good predictor of potential marital breakup. This is true not only in the United States, but also in England, France, the Netherlands, and other industrialized countries that have been surveyed.[7] Sociologists have focused mainly on cultural and subcultural values as these affect communication: *how* family members talk to one another (giving orders, suggesting ways to handle things, discussing and providing necessary information for making mutual decisions); *how much* they talk to one another (freely and openly, only when necessary, hardly at all); *to whom* they talk (the immediate family, other relatives, friends, hired helpers); and *what* they talk about (feelings, problems, needs, goals, or inconsequential small talk).

Self-Disclosure

An important aspect of family communication is what social scientists call *self-disclosure*. How willing are family members to *confide* in each other—to talk about and reveal their problems, their worries, and other unpleasant feelings? How does this vary in major types of societies and in the different classes, ethnic populations, and generations in the United States today? How does this vary among males and females? Sociologists have found, for example, that older working-class women, especially if they grew up in an agricultural environment, in this country or abroad, are more likely to confide in their sisters or children than in their husbands; and older working-class white males are not likely to confide in anyone, regardless of where they grew up.[8]

Verbal and Nonverbal Messages

A major discovery of communication researchers is that people in troubled families distort or misinterpret what they hear and what they see. What they see, incidentally, are nonverbal cues: body language such as facial expressions, eye contact, tone of voice, posture, touch, dress, and gestures.[9] And what they see is more revealing than what they hear, as in the cliché "One picture is worth a thousand words." Visual messages provide clues about what people are *really* thinking and feeling, regardless of what they say: *Susan*: "How are you?" *Peter* (unsmiling, eyes downcast, barely audible voice, shoulders slumped): "Fine, thanks." *Susan*: "What's wrong, Peter?"

Silent Thoughts

People in troubled relationships have negative and often untrue *silent thoughts* that they are unable or unwilling to talk about: "Where was he? His explanation doesn't make sense. He must be having an affair."[10] Or "She would rather go out with her friends than stay home with me. She doesn't like being with me." These thoughts about a partner's motives or behavior may be untrue and the resulting feelings of anger or depression unwarranted. But the only way to test reality in this situation is to talk about these silent thoughts and listen to the partner's explanation—which isn't easy in troubled relationships:

> Melanie cut Martin off when he was speaking to a group of friends. His automatic thoughts were: "She doesn't think I have anything to say. She's putting me down." Later, when he asked Melanie why she had interrupted him, she explained that she changed the subject because she knew something that he didn't know: the topic was a very sensitive one for one of the people at the gathering.[11]

Power and Communication

Couples who feel strongly attached and very close are not concerned about who has power in the relationship. They are more likely to sit or stand close to one another. They touch and look at one another more, smile and laugh together more, and understand each other better. They accept their partners as they are, not as they think their partner should or could be. And they talk to each other more freely and easily because differences in the amount and kind of communication are highly correlated with differences in power in human relationships. Bosses are usually not effusive about their personal problems when talking to employees. This is a major reason why powerful men are less likely than women to confide in others: Confiding is viewed as a sign of weakness.[12]

Psychological Abuse

Aside from willingness to confide, another type of communicating that reflects power differences in relationships is psychological abuse. Hostile jokes, ridicule, teasing, nagging, or criticism of a partner's problems or weaknesses are verbal assaults on personality and self-esteem; they make it easier to dominate the person who is being attacked. More serious threats, to injure the partner or to destroy the

TABLE 8.1   Strong Partner Relationships

PARTNERS IN STRONG RELATIONSHIPS

1. Feelings: Feel close to one another, warm and affectionate, accepting, approving, liking
2. Communication: Talk openly, honestly, freely about almost anything, including their relationship
3. Support: Encourage and help one another in whatever way they can
4. Conflict: Settle arguments, disagreements, and disputes by talking and compromising so that both can accept the solution
5. Power: Make decisions on the basis of interest, knowledge, and skills—not because of tradition or status
6. Flexibility: Can change roles and adapt to transitions, new situations, losses, and unexpected stresses without going into crisis
7. Enjoyment: Have fun being with one another and doing things together
8. Balance: Achieve a comfortable balance between family and personal needs and goals

Note: All of the above apply in strong partnerships and in strong families—but not all of the time.

partner's property, are most likely to lead to physical violence. Also, people who are less powerful, or more dependent and vulnerable (women and children, usually), tend to be more sensitive to psychological abuse (as well as to nonverbal cues).[13]

When family members talk to each other openly, freely, and frequently, they are a strong family; they have satisfying physical, emotional, and verbal connections. They feel close, and they are *flexible*: highly resourceful if things change and they need to change their role in the family. Strong families manage change, resolve conflicts, and settle disagreements by talking, negotiating, and compromising. They respect one another; they feel free to talk about what they want, need, don't want, or object to; they provide strong emotional support when needed; and, on surveys, they report the highest amounts of marital satisfaction and feelings of psychological well-being (Table 8.1).[14]

Getting close and remaining close to other human beings is one of the most difficult challenges of our time, especially now when computer technologies and increased geographic mobility tend to draw people away from face-to-face contact with family and old friends. Almost inevitably, geographic distance leads to some degree of psychological distancing as time goes by. "Reaching out" by telephone or e-mail makes it easier and less expensive to send messages to distant family members and friends than in the past, but reaching out is not touching. Electronic technology cannot provide the nonverbal physical and emotional messages that accompany close encounters: the loving look, the tender smile, the comforting touch, the affectionate hug or kiss.

Gender Differences

In agricultural societies, emotional closeness in human relationships was not a cultural norm for males; in postindustrial societies, it becomes a cultural ideal and a psychological necessity for both sexes (Table 8.2). In the United States, those who avoid or evade closeness are now likely to be labeled reserved, cold, or, at the extreme, psychologically disturbed. Sociolinguist Deborah Tannen claims that gender differences in communicating tend to persist, regardless of social location. She

TABLE 8.2   Gender Differences in Communicating

COMPARED TO MEN, WOMEN TEND TO BE:

1. More sensitive to nonverbal cues and body language.
2. Unlikely to interrupt others to correct what they are saying; usurp the conversation; change the topic.
3. Less likely to lecture or monopolize conversations.
4. More likely to talk about their problems and weaknesses; ask for help; ask for information.
5. Use communication to achieve closeness and connection rather than to achieve or maintain power.
6. Less likely to boast about their accomplishments.
7. Less likely to demand what they want.

Note: These differences in communicating styles are declining among younger, more educated, achieving women.

finds that women are more likely to value closeness and connection than men; are usually more willing to talk about their feelings, worries, and personal experiences; and tend to talk in ways that reflect their lower prestige and lesser need for power.[15]

According to Tannen and other researchers who have studied gender differences in communication, men are more likely to use communication to assert power and to validate their superior status: They tend to talk more in public and less in private; are less likely to talk about their troubles; are reluctant to ask for help or information (if they are lost, for example); and are more likely to lecture, give orders, interrupt, and take over conversations. Women, even when they know more, are more likely to apologize, hedge, or name their sources.

I should point out, however, that these gender differences in communicating are declining now, especially among younger, more educated generations of women and men in advanced industrial societies. Men cry in public now; women in top leadership positions are unlikely to hedge or apologize, although they may name their sources if pressed. At this point in time, the similarities between women and men in similar social statuses are greater than the differences.[16]

Gender differences are stronger or less strong in different cultures and subcultures as a result of different socialization experiences. In the United States, less educated working-class men and women, especially those who are recent immigrants from agricultural or industrializing societies, are more likely to have difficulty talking to one another freely and honestly. They are also more likely to display power and prestige differences in communicating. This is not true in the African American subculture, however, where women have long had higher prestige and more power in their relationships with men.[17]

Some Cautions

While truthful and open communication is essential in maintaining close relationships in modern societies, total honesty can be self-indulgent, destructive, and cruel. People should be told things they have every right to know. But there is little to be gained in a relationship by telling people they have bad taste, are bad cooks, are tone deaf, or are uninformed. It takes as much effort to cook a bad meal as it takes to cook a good one. One can praise the effort without judging the end product and thereby avoid the kind of lie that leaves the truth teller feeling compromised, embarrassed, or guilty.

Secrets

In partner relationships, it is not wise to talk about first loves or lost loves (who tend to be idealized in any case). Discussions of previous affairs, attraction to other people, or the flirting behavior of others does not strengthen a relationship. Further, revealing a guilty secret about something that can't be changed or undone serves no constructive purpose and invites rejection. It may unnecessarily lower the confidence and self-esteem of an innocent member of the family, and it may reduce the bargaining power of the guilty family member in future conflicts. Guilt makes people more vulnerable in power struggles in family relationships.[18]

Relationship Messages

Talking about problems in a relationship is the most difficult and painful kind of talking and truth telling; unwelcome feelings and impulses are likely to be denied. People tend to avoid this kind of communication because of what they don't know, or what they suspect but would rather not know about the relationship—such as differences in attachment or commitment. The partner who is more committed to a relationship may fear losing the other person and hesitate to point out evasive, hostile, or even destructive behavior; the one who is less committed may not be willing to express mixed feelings or dissatisfaction for expedient reasons.

Improving Communication

Researchers can now point to a number of highly effective techniques for improving communication. Many of these techniques are also useful ways to resolve conflicts.[19]

Choosing a Time and Place

To begin with, when the need to talk to a partner about a situation or a disagreement is urgent, it is important to choose the right time and place. Going for a walk together, for an automobile ride, or out to dinner at a quiet restaurant is helpful. This may be the only way to find the privacy, the time, and the freedom from distraction that are necessary to discuss a personal problem. Bringing up a stressful issue when your partner is late for work, or is exhausted and trying to fall asleep, is not helpful.

Listening

It is also important to listen carefully and give *feedback*—frequent signals that indicate your interest and attention. Silence is threatening. It may mean contentment, comfort, security, and love; or where there is strong conflict in the relationship, it may mean avoidance, anxiety, mistrust, or anger. Whatever the situation, silence is usually interpreted negatively. Constructive feedback—a nod, a "Yes" or "Go on"—is an active response that indicates one is listening. Asking a question about something your partner says that doesn't make sense, or repeating a significant phrase or part of what was said, usually encourages further conversation. (Repeating the *entire* sentence is unwise; in the heat of an argument, you may be accused of being stupid or hard of hearing.)

Evidence

One should also avoid distorted assumptions about how a partner is thinking or feeling. Assumptions—that a partner is angry, hurt, or hostile—should be checked out by asking how your partner feels, or asking for clarification if the emotion seems mixed or unclear. Guessing and mind reading are necessary with young infants who can't tell you what they need or want, but language eliminates the necessity for this kind of behavior in humans. It is a tool for intelligent problem solving.

Compromising

One should not interrupt a partner who is talking. Interrupting implies superior ability to tell a story or answer a question. This may be true, but telling the story better or providing the correct answer is hardly worth offending one's partner. It is also helpful to avoid monopolizing the conversation. Long, droning monologues are boring and often infuriating. In situations of conflict, possible solutions to the problem should be discussed, and the decision reached should be mutually acceptable, one that doesn't impose a zero-sum, win-lose solution on a partner: "Why don't we go to Rino's for dinner? They have steak (which you want) as well as seafood (which I want)."

In arguments, it is crucial to avoid exaggerating. Very few human beings "always" or "never" think, feel, or act in certain ways: "You *never* listen to me!" or "You're *always* late!" Open-ended questions, which can't be answered with a simple "Yes" or "No," help promote further conversation: "Tell me about what happened when you talked to your boss at work today" rather than "Did you have a good day at work?"

I, You, and We

When a partner's behavior offends, it helps to talk about one's *own* feelings and reactions rather than the offensive behavior: "I am a neat person, and I find dirty laundry and piled-up old papers and magazines in every room of the house very upsetting" rather than "You are a world-class saver and litterer. You never throw out anything or put your dirty laundry in the hamper." "I feel upset" is less likely to draw defensive replies than accusing, critical "You are . . ." statements.

"We" statements focus on the *relationship* and its problems.[20] Leveling with a partner about feelings and what one really wants and needs, especially when the partner is likely to disagree or disapprove, may be difficult, but it is a highly effective way to reduce tension. Being agreeable and saying "Yes" when one would rather say "No" results in resentment and anger. It isn't necessary to be cruel or tactless, but it is important to reveal your preferences. A direct request, even if refused, will cause less frustration and anger than lying, pretending, or manipulating.

It also helps to focus on what is right rather than what is wrong with what a partner is saying. This reframes the picture in a more positive way and makes for more constructive solutions: "I agree with you, basically, but I feel we should do it a little differently."

Fixed Perimeters

Discussing one issue at a time is also important: "Let's not bring up the past; it's irrelevant. For now, let's take first things first. We should agree about where we want to go given the money we have to spend. Then we can discuss whether or not to bring the children along." *Issue hopping*—changing the subject and shifting from one issue to another in quick succession—resolves nothing and increases a partner's frustration and resentment. Also, *gunnysacking*, or hitting a partner over the head with a number of stored-up resentments that are irrelevant to the present situation, should be avoided. Bringing up past issues that have not been resolved and are still sore spots is gunnysacking. This increases tension and is more likely to fuel the argument, disagreement, or conflict rather than resolve it.[21]

Aside from difficulties is communication, another problem that is more frequent during the early years of marriage and declines as family members age is psychological abuse and physical violence. Researchers have asked: How and why do rates of abuse and violence vary among families in various social locations in the United States? Are these rates increasing or declining? Why? They have also tried to trace the reasons for violence and, at the psychological level, to determine how power, abuse, and violence are interrelated.

Power, Abuse, and Violence

Power, as I pointed out earlier, is the ability to get what one wants despite resistance (and *especially* against resistance).[22] Having power involves three things: It is the ability of individuals, groups, and countries to increase their resources and rewards (financial, physical, psychological); it is the capacity to win in a dispute; and it is the skill to control (dictate) or change the thoughts, feelings, and behavior of other people.

The Resource Theory of Power

For over 40 years, since a landmark study by sociologists Robert Blood and Donald Wolfe, we have measured power in families by determining who makes certain decisions in the household. These researchers asked who has the final say on decisions such as what car to buy, whether or when to have children, what house or apartment to take, whether either partner should take or quit a job, and how much money to spend on household necessities.[23]

Blood and Wolfe, and many researchers since then, have related the balance of power in a relationship to the relative amounts of personal or economic resources each partner has—an approach known as the *resource theory of power.* The basic assumption of this approach is that the person with the most resources—economic (income, property), educational, physical (size, strength, good health), and psychological (intelligence, self-esteem, self-confidence)—will have more power in a relationship.

We have seen how women's role in producing and controlling economic resources affects their power in nonindustrial societies. In industrial and industrializing societies, a woman's level of education also becomes a major factor affecting her power. In Mexico, for example, women with higher levels of education are more likely to have an equal say in family decision making, are more likely to be satisfied with their role in decision making, and are less likely to be victims of marital violence than less educated women.[24]

The important thing to remember about the question of who has the power in a family is that it applies when there is a disagreement about what to do or how to think and feel. It is not the decision about which bill to pay first, but rather what to do with extra money that comes in, such as a bonus, an increase in salary, or a windfall from the stock market. For example: It is summertime, and the father wants to use an unexpected bonus to rent a vacation house on a lake so that he can fish; the mother would rather send the children to camp and escape housekeeping and childcare responsibilities. Whoever wins has power in that particular relationship. In situations where disagreements or conflicts are resolved cooperatively and by compromise, everyone is satisfied, more or less, and nobody wins or loses: The parents go to a resort on a lake that provides meals and has day-care facilities for children.

Where cooperation and compromise are typical in family relationships, power in families is situational and egalitarian. It varies according to the issue, the interests, and the abilities of those involved and is, in fact, irrelevant in most day-to-day encounters between family members.

Exceptions

In any specific partner relationship, we can't predict who will have power simply on the basis of income or other personal resources such as intelligence, education, income, or physical and emotional strength and health. Certain factors undermine the effect of personal resources in the exercise of power, no matter what these resources are.

Manipulation

Good health is a resource that affects power. A partner (or older parent) who has a heart attack, or develops some other kind of life-threatening, chronic illness, usually becomes more dependent and loses power in a close relationship. But sometimes the illness is used to control a partner or an adult child indirectly by manipulation. The sick person can become more powerful than ever: "I'm too sick; I can't do what you want me to do" or "You can't leave me alone; I might need you."

Cultural Values

Strong traditional values, such as patriarchy or familism, can also override personal resources in determining the power of husbands and wives.[25] But resources do have some effect. Historically, in Italy, wives were permitted to keep their dowries (land, livestock) in their own name after they married. Male dominance was not as strong there as in countries such as India or China, where the husband and the husband's family became owners of the dowry after a marriage.

Commitment

Another circumstance that affects power in a relationship is a difference in the degree of commitment. People who love more and are more committed to a relationship will be anxious to please; they will be more likely to give, give in, and give up, regardless of their personal resources. Long ago, sociologist Willard Waller referred to this as the *principle of least interest*: The person who has less interest in maintaining a relationship will have more power in that relationship.[26] And this applies not only to husbands, wives, and unmarried partners, but to parents and their adult children as well.

If grandparents are more familistic than their adult children and grandchildren and more eager to maintain contact, they may give up in an argument even if they know they are right. Or they may give money and gifts they can't really afford in an attempt to buy good will or maintain the relationship.[27] Another example, but one that involves manipulation rather than giving in, involves a divorced or separated mother who was abandoned by the father of their child. She may use the child to maintain contact with the father: "Emily fell and needs to go to the emergency room; would you please come over and take her? I'm too upset." Divorce ends a marriage; it does not end a relationship, especially when children and shared custody are involved.

Psychological Factors

Low self-esteem and a feeling of guilt can also lead people to give in unnecessarily. Some researchers feel that by defining love as a greater need for women than for men, women have been encouraged to feel more dependent, more needy, and more committed in love relationships. And, as a result, they have tended to exert less power in these relationships: "Men's dependency on women remains covert and repressed, while women's dependency on men is overt and exaggerated. . . . In fact, evidence on the higher death rates of unmarried men implies that men need love at least as much as women."[28]

For these various reasons, we can't assume an exact exchange between resources and power. Surveys that ask more revealing questions about conflicts and disagreements do not find a direct, absolute, one-to-one connection between income and power in families: "Wives who have relatively high incomes, compared to other women and even to their husbands, do not have that much more power in their marriages than women who do not have such economic clout."[29] This is especially true of women in the African American subculture, where eligible, highly educated middle-class men are not abundant.

Sociologist Martin King Whyte and his associates at the Michigan Survey Research Center explain seeming exceptions to the resource theory of power in terms of the greater importance of individual experiences and circumstances now than in the past. And they explain this, in turn, as a trend in the United States toward less conformity to traditional norms and values, especially among younger generations. According to these authors, traditional values generally, and religious, ethnic, and subcultural values in particular, now have a weaker effect on family relationships than they had in the past.[30]

Ethnic Differences

This shift may be true, generally. But we can't ignore the persisting influence of ethnic origin and other social locations on power in family relationships. Social class does tend to override subcultural ethnic differences over the generations. But dozens of studies have revealed significant differences between whites and ethnic minorities in family roles, values, power, and conflicts, regardless of socioeconomic status. In the middle social classes, for example, black women are less likely than white women to experience physical and verbal abuse in their marriages; black husbands and wives report more stress and have higher divorce rates than whites; black wives are less likely to pool their earnings in a joint bank account with their husbands; and, compared to whites, black wives value having a good income somewhat more and marital fidelity less as important qualities of a good marriage.[31]

Ethnic subcultures in the United States today are converging in some ways: Younger members tend to identify with the same national heroes and share the same tastes and fashions in dress, food, music, movies, and sports. Fashions come and go with dizzying speed in the media-drenched United States. But differences in the values and roles of women, men, and children in ethnic families change more slowly, especially now, when the celebration of ethnic differences and multiculturalism is becoming a cultural norm. Also, power in families appears to be more resistant to change than other aspects of family life. Among families who immigrate from strongly patriarchal countries, changes in the power of husbands and wives and parents and children may occur quite slowly—among succeeding generations rather than among the first generation of immigrants.[32]

Violence in Families

Power is not something we are necessarily aware of in family relationships. Family members are supposed to cooperate, not compete; support, not frustrate. But the uses of power can be quite subtle. The person who is being manipulated may feel hurt, anxious, or uneasy without knowing exactly why. Or the exercise of power can be more obvious—an attempt to dominate by the use of force and violence. Physical force is the ultimate basis of power—when influence, negotiation, and all else fails (in societies as well as in families).

Physical and Psychological Aggression

Aggression is hostile speech or behavior that hurts another person physically or psychologically. Physical harm is obvious, but abuse can be damaging in more subtle ways. Examples are "malnutrition, failure to thrive, sexual exploitation, educational neglect, medical neglect and emotional abuse."[33]

Aggression may be used to give vent to strong feelings of frustration, anger, or stress, or it may be used to control others. Long-term victims of severe psychological abuse tend to become convinced they are worthless; they come to believe that practically everything they do, think, feel, and want is wrong.[34] They are usually unaware of the power aspects of the emotional abuse they have experienced; they don't trust their judgment in arguments, and they are afraid to express their opinions and ask for what they want. They tend to feel depressed, guilty, and responsible for whatever failures or disappointments their partners experience.

Victims are usually afraid of their partners; they never know what will set off another attack. Psychological abusers attack their partner's friends and relatives also: They try to prevent or destroy their partner's relationships with others so that their victim will be deprived of outside support that might bolster self-esteem and encourage fighting back.[35]

Physical Violence

Like other survivors of repeated and unpredictable traumas and abuse, battered women tend to deny the psychological effects of the assault, although they usually have little difficulty remembering the physical effects. They may not react with severe depression or emotional collapse for weeks, months, or even years—like war veterans suffering from a posttraumatic stress disorder. They feel isolated, trapped, helpless, and powerless to change their situation, especially if they are financially dependent on their partners. But, at some level, they may be aware that their partner's emotional dependence is more intense than their own: "Many battered women believe that they are the sole support of the batterer's emotional stability and sanity, the one link their men have to the real world. Sensing the batterer's isolation and despair, they feel responsible for his well-being."[36]

Passive Aggression

Passive aggression is another aspect of power (indirect winning or getting even) that, like psychological abuse, usually goes unrecognized. It is behavior that seems to be helpful and well intended but actually hurts another person: A reluctant husband may agree to do the laundry but ruin the wife's new blouse by using too much bleach; he may agree to do the dishes but chip her treasured platter or plate. Or he may agree to go to the grocery but buy the wrong brand, the wrong amount, or the wrong thing (because, he explains, he "misread" the item on the shopping list or they didn't have what was on the list).

An employed wife, irritated by homemaking obligations, especially when she comes home after a long day's work, may forget to turn off the oven and burn the dinner. She may forget to pick up her husband's suit at the cleaners (one that he needs for an important meeting the next morning). Or she may accidentally throw out an important piece of mail while straightening up his desk. Passive aggressors, incidentally, are usually unaware of the hostility in their behavior and will strongly deny bad intentions if they are accused of being hostile or destructive.[37]

In families and societies, politics is the struggle to obtain or maintain power. In families (and friendship groups) power struggles are not as obvious as in executive suites or electoral campaigns. In talking, there are indirect or deceptive ways to maintain control, win, or put down others, some of which I have already mentioned: Interrupting or correcting a partner, refusing to discuss certain things, changing the subject, monopolizing the conversation, remaining silent, or mumbling, so that the partner can't hear, and feels frustrated and tense are examples. An even more sophisticated technique is leaving out an important piece of information in a discussion, so that the partner feels confused (or stupid). Physical violence, on the other hand, is neither subtle nor deceptive.

The United States has the highest rate of family violence of any industrialized country in the world, and more than two-thirds of murders in families are committed with guns. Also, "People are more likely to be killed, physically assaulted, hit, beaten up, slapped, or spanked in their own homes by other family members than anywhere else, or by anyone else."[38] Why is this so?

Reasons for Family Violence

Involuntary Membership

To begin with, membership in a family group is involuntary; we don't choose our families any more than we choose other statuses we are born with and can't change (our age, gender, and ethnic origin, for example). Also, the degree of emotional involvement is more intense in families than in other groups.

Intense Relationships

Moreover, in the early and middle years of family life, we usually spend more time and do more things with family members than with others, and conflicts are more likely to arise. And, finally, unlike other small groups, families include members of both sexes and different generations with different amounts of power and different needs and desires.

Arbitrary Authority

Historically, authority in families has been based on age and gender rather than the interests, needs, and abilities of family members. This, too, makes for more potential conflict, especially when conflicts are played out as win-lose, zero-sum games with no compromises. Examples are a wife who unwillingly gives up her career to take care of her husband and young children because this is what her husband wants or a child who is forced to give up a toy to a brother or sister (who is the younger child, the favorite child, or the sick child).

Change and Stress

Other reasons for violence in families are change and stress; both are common in modern times, and stress is contagious. Parents react to troubled children; children respond to distressed parents. This is what social scientists have called the *family systems perspective*. The trouble starts somewhere but it may be hard to tell where, since family groups are like other systems—in the body, in a society, or in the universe. Whatever affects one part of the nervous system, the economic system, or the solar system affects other parts of the system and sets off reactions throughout the system.[39]

Dependence and Interdependence

One member of a family may precipitate a crisis or a major change by leaving, having an affair, becoming a drug addict, entering adolescence, moving back home, losing a job, or retiring. Other members react by changing their behavior to cope with the change or defuse the crisis: If the father or mother leaves, children take over some of the housekeeping chores and may become the confidant or the principal source of emotional support of the remaining parent; drug abuse by an adolescent child may enable parents to avoid confronting their own problems by blaming the child for their distress; if the father of preschool children loses his job and the mother works full time, he becomes the primary caregiver.[40]

Vulnerability

Finally, the more we know about our parents and brothers and sisters, the more we can help them. But this same knowledge makes them more vulnerable; it can be used to attack them if the relationship has been hostile or disappointing. An example is tell-all, "mommy dearest" memoirs written by vengeful children who feel they were wronged by their famous parent or parents.

Social Location and Family Violence

With this information, we can now shed some light on a controversy about family violence in the United States: Is it increasing or decreasing? Sociologists Murray Straus and Richard Gelles and their associates compared family violence reported in two National Family Violence Surveys conducted in 1975 and 1985.

They distinguish between "minor" and "severe" physical violence: throwing something at a family member, pushing, grabbing, shoving, slapping, and spanking are minor; kicking, biting, punching, choking, and using or threatening to use a knife or a gun is severe. Severe violence against children also includes burning and scalding.[41]

Changing Economic Conditions

Strauss and Gelles conclude that family violence is declining in the United States. Reports of family violence have increased, but they believe this is due to the increased publicity about violence and a greater willingness by family members (mainly women) to report violence to the police. Also, they link the down trend in violence to a decline in male dominance and the improved economic and social status of women in the United States since the 1970s. They also point out that rates of family violence go down when economies improve. Unemployment and inflation declined slightly during the period from 1975 to 1985 (though actual purchasing power also declined for most families during that period).

Recently, in the United States, unemployment rates have been at their lowest in 25 years and, according to national statistics collected by the Department of Justice, wife and child abuse has also been at a similar low.[42] And this is happening despite an epidemic of violent images in the media: the spread of these images from the tabloids to more prestigious newspapers and magazines; to network television; from "B" and "C" movies to "A" movies; from television to the Internet and e-mail. In market economies, sensationalism sells products and creates instant millionaires and celebrities; public confessions, exhibitionism, and voyeurism thrive; and privacy diminishes.

Violence Against Children

When does the use of physical punishment become abuse? The line between the two can be thin, but researchers make a distinction between the use of physical force to control a child's behavior and behavior that deliberately injures a child—the legal definition of child abuse. Sexual abuse and physical and emotional neglect come under the rubric of psychological injury to a child. Child abuse has declined in advanced industrial societies and in the United States even as conflicts between work and family obligations have increased among the current generation of two- and three-job families. Why? Because in some ways, bringing up children is less stressful now: "Individuals are getting married later in life, having children later, having fewer children and having fewer unwanted children. All these factors are consistent with a lower risk of child abuse."[43]

The decline in most kinds of family violence has important consequences for individuals, families, and societies. When abuse in families declines, violence in societies declines. Historically, the most war-prone societies have used the most severely abusive forms of physical punishment in their childrearing practices.[44] Also, we now have mounting evidence that children who witness habitual physical violence between their parents, and who experience severe physical punishment and abuse during childhood, are more likely to assault nonfamily members during adolescence and adulthood.[45] They are more likely to have uncontrollable temper tantrums; to have trouble making friends; to fail in school; to commit property crimes (vandalism and theft); and to assault their own partners and children when they become adults.

National surveys indicate that about 90 percent of parents in the United States use physical punishment at times to discipline their children.[46] This is a higher rate than in most advanced industrial countries; and on psychological tests, children in the United States reveal more aggressive emotions than children in Sweden, Germany, and other countries that have been surveyed.[47] In the United States, spanking is more acceptable in some ethnic subcultures—among African Americans, for example—but nonabusive physical punishment does not seem to be emotionally damaging if the parent is perceived as warm and loving.

Gender Differences

The reasons for and consequences of wife or husband abuse have been subjects of controversy in the social sciences.[48] For decades, national surveys on violence have consistently reported that wives are more likely than husbands to start violent fights, and in the 1970s the idea of the *battered husband* was born. Studies since then have tried to get clearer information about the *reasons* for marital violence (intimidation, self-defense, frustration, displacement, or abandonment), and the seriousness of injuries to women, compared to men, and gender differences in willingness to report violence.[49] Domestic violence may be declining generally, but death rates for white women who are killed by former or current boyfriends and husbands are, in fact, increasing.

We now know that whatever the reasons for marital violence and no matter who starts it, wives are far more likely than husbands to be seriously injured or killed, since most husbands are bigger and stronger than their wives. Women more often throw things and use whatever is at hand; men use their hands or fists and are more likely to use lethal weapons such as guns and knives. Also, men tend to deny the seriousness of their acts of violence.

In 1998, younger white women in the United States were almost as likely to die as a result of an attack by a current or former husband or lover (about one-third of all deaths of white women aged 14 to 44) as they were to die of cancer, heart disease, and strokes—the major causes of death in the United States and in most advanced European countries today.[50] Further, while violent death rates for white women have not declined, rates among black women have been declining steadily and dramatically since the 1970s.[51]

How do criminologists, demographers, and other experts explain this fact? Most lethal attacks on women occur after a woman has left, or threatens to leave, an abusive partner—who then decides, "If I can't have her, nobody will." As for differences in black–white violent death rates among women, black women have long achieved higher average levels of education than black men and, since the 1970s, have more easily found jobs that enable them to be independent and leave a dangerous relationship.

White women have only recently begun to catch up, educationally and occupationally, with their partners. They are leaving abusive relationships more frequently now than in the past, and they are more likely to be attacked by their abandoned husbands and lovers. Recent changes in the criminal justice system give women more protection, but the new laws have not been particularly effective in bringing down domestic death rates for white women. Abusive men usually kill during an uncontrollable fit of rage or jealousy; legal sanctions do not seem to be particularly effective in deterring this kind of behavior.

Psychologists find that abusive men usually have low self-esteem and feel inadequate at work and at home. Their violence is an attempt to assert their manliness when they feel rejected, harassed by fellow employees or their boss, or threatened by a wife or partner who is more successful at work or stronger in other ways (physically, emotionally, or intellectually). Men who are violent toward their partners are often deeply disappointed with their lives and their accomplishments.

Social Class Differences

Family violence occurs in all social classes—among the wealthy, the poor, and those in the middle. But violence is most frequent among the poor: They experience the greatest amount of physical, economic, and psychological frustration, they tend to be angrier, and they more often displace their anger onto family members.[52] Also, low-income families live in more crowded quarters; neighbors are more likely to hear what is going on and call the police. And, like underreported white-collar crimes (shoplifting, price fixing, income tax evasion), middle- and upper-class violence is less likely to be reported to the police by doctors and hospitals. Still, it is important to bear in mind that most low-income men and women do not abuse their partners or their children—even in the United States, which has the highest rate of family violence of any advanced industrial society.

Stage in Family Life History

The tendency to physically abuse a partner declines with age; young adult couples (in their 20s) are most prone to family violence. Conflicts decline among older families, in part, because the most violently conflicted couples are more likely to have separated or divorced. On a later survey, they would no longer be included in a national sample of married couples.[53]

Marital Status

Couples who live together without marrying have a higher rate of violence than dating or married couples. Cohabitators tend to value independence, autonomy, and control more than traditional married couples; they are more likely to fight about rights and responsibilities. Dating couples are slightly more likely to be violent than married couples, but they can simply break up the relationship if violence does occur; if they don't, the violence is quite likely to reappear in the marriage.[54]

Married couples have the most to lose legally, materially, and perhaps psychologically if the relationship ends because of violence. This keeps rates of marital violence lower. But researchers have also pointed to the importance of the traditional cultural definition of wife beating as an acceptable way for husbands to exercise power. Traditional women (and men) usually believe in the right of men to be violent. This, plus the economic dependence of women with children and the belief in a partner's promises to reform, are major reasons why traditional women remain in these relationships. Female victims with a traditional outlook (in dating as well as marital relationships) have been likely to interpret violence as a sign of love, to believe that they as well as their partners are responsible for the violence, or to blame themselves ("I asked for it").[55]

But these beliefs, too, are changing. Like other traditional attitudes and beliefs, they are most likely to be found among older women, less educated women, and those who have recently immigrated to the United States from more patriarchal cultures. Increasingly now, among educated, economically independent women, the decision to stay or leave is based on the answers to two questions: "Will I be better off?" and, even more practically, "Can I do it?"[56] The answers to these questions are now more likely to depend on a woman's degree of commitment to the violent relationship and her resources for establishing a financially independent existence rather than arbitrary conformity to cultural or religious traditions.

If a couple successfully manages to settle the usual issues that arise when people marry or move in together and they do not separate (most separations occur during the first three years of marriage), the next major change, for most people who marry (and for some who do not), is the transition to parenthood.

Chapter 9
Parents and Children

How does reality change for most couples who become new parents in the United States today, and how does this reality change as their children grow—from infancy, through childhood and adolescence, to adulthood and beyond? In what ways do the problems and pleasures of bringing up children depend on who the parents are, how much they own and earn, how educated they are, where they live, and how things are changing in the world they live in? Before we get to these questions, given the recent increase in single-parent households and in unmarried women who are starting new families, I'll start with what we know about these types of families.

Single Parents

Single parents have different reasons for being single. When they are very young, they are more likely to be never married; later, they are more likely to be separated or divorced; and still later, they are more likely to be widowed or voluntarily single. Their ethnic origin and race, their financial circumstances, and their individual physical and psychological resources (their health, energy, ability, education, confidence, and self-esteem) also differ. But one thing most researchers would agree about is that bringing up a child without the help of a partner is far more difficult, especially when the children are young and extremely dependent. This is true regardless of individual differences in resources and the age of the single mother or father.[1]

Older, more educated, single fathers (usually divorced; rarely widowed, as was common in the past) are fewer in number than single mothers and, in some ways, have an easier time: They usually have more income than single mothers and are better able to pay for housekeepers, day care, and other amenities. On the other hand, older, well-educated women who become single parents by choice manage better than single mothers in less advantaged circumstances, and they tend to produce highly successful children (girls especially).[2] But whatever the social context, the boundless need for love and emotional support that young children have, and the daily challenges they present, are easier to deal with when both parents are around.[3]

Definitions

Since 1970, the percentage of children living in one-parent families has almost tripled. The percentage living in father-only families is also increasing, but still, more than eight out of ten single-parent households are mother-only households. Adopted children in single-parent families tend to be better off economically, especially now that the number of newborn children has dwindled and the cost of adopting newborns has skyrocketed. Furthermore, higher-income couples who are not married (same sex as well as heterosexual couples in many states) are now permitted to adopt children legally. In the past, the census defined these couples as single parents because they were not married.[4] The 2000 census was revised to include an "unmarried partner" response in its questions about household composition, but we still don't know if this partner is the father of the children who live in the household. To avoid confusion, when I use the term *single parent*, I mean mother-only or father-only households, with no partner living in the household.

Poverty

Contrary to stereotypes in the media, a majority of single mothers are divorced, not never married. They are white, and they do not live in high-poverty inner-city neighborhoods. Moreover, many divorced single mothers who are poor were not poor before their divorce. The average income of fathers increases by about 10 percent after a divorce; divorced mothers usually experience a drop in income of at least 25 percent after they leave, or are left by, their husbands.[5] Single mothers fare better in European countries because of more adequate government-sponsored child-care facilities and income supports.

In the United States, younger mother-only families are poor for a number of reasons. The mothers are likely to have low earning capacity because most have less education, training, and job experience than other women.[6] If they go out to work, as welfare mothers in the United States are now required to do, they must find day care for their children, and this usually costs more than a quarter of what they earn.[7] Grandmothers are less available than they were in the past because they too are now more likely to be employed. Nationally, only about 2 percent of children live exclusively with a grandparent, without a parent in the household; about 5 percent live in households that are maintained by grandparents.[8] These children are usually preschool children whose single mother or father is physically or mentally ill, drug-addicted, imprisoned, or has abused, neglected, or abandoned them. Many low-income minority grandmothers, who are most likely to be in this situation, are now paid (as foster parents) to care for their grandchildren, since they need the income.

Subcultural Differences

Ethnic families continue to show differences in mother-only households largely because of differences in economic conditions (the availability of jobs), political conditions (government policy), and human conditions (tolerance or discrimination). Subcultural values (attitudes toward marriage that survive from the past and those that are a reaction to changing social conditions) are also a factor, but according to mounting evidence from dozens of studies, attitudes are not as important as objective social conditions in explaining the increase in mother-only families.[9]

African Americans

Nationally, African Americans have higher rates of mother-only families than Latinos and Asian Americans for many reasons, some of which I cited earlier. A very unbalanced sex ratio of marriageable men resulting from the high death, imprisonment, and unemployment rates of black males is the major reason according to national surveys.[10] Attitudes toward marriage are less important but not unimportant: Most black women prefer being married and some marry down, but others do not. Many older, highly educated, high-income black women fear losing what they have worked so hard to achieve to a less successful male partner.[11]

Middle-class black women tend to prefer a middle-class partner who has similar values, tastes, and goals. But given the surplus of black women in all social classes, black middle-class men tend to seek out (and find) more attractive, less independent, and less assertive women. Then too, at all social class levels, compared to whites, black males are less secure financially; this makes marriage a riskier undertaking. Further, since African Americans now have the highest national rates of never-married, divorced, or separated mother-only households, both women and men in this subculture tend to be more hesitant about making the commitment to marrying up, down, or at all.[12]

Latinos

As for single parents in various other ethnic subcultures today, national statistics can be misleading. While African Americans have the highest rate of single-parent households nationally, in New York City the teenage pregnancy rate of black women is now actually lower than the Latino rate. Black teenagers in New York are more likely than young Catholic Latina women to use birth control, especially newer, long-lasting injected Dopo-Provera or implanted Norplant patches. Also, Latinos are more likely than blacks to live in three-generation households, and these households are not counted as single-parent households by the census. Moreover, Latina single mothers, who do not live with their parents, are more likely than blacks to be supported by, or living with, the unmarried fathers of their children—a widespread pattern in Latin America.[13]

Middle-class white researchers in the United States have tended to be highly critical of the machismo tradition among immigrant Latino males, focusing mainly on the male dominance, sexual conquest, and infidelity aspects of this tradition. But machismo norms also require Latino males to protect and provide for their wives and children, in nonmarital as well as marital relationships, and most do—especially in the middle class.[14]

Asian Americans

Compared to other ethnic minorities, Asian Americans have the lowest fertility rate and the lowest rate of nonmarital childbirth. And, incidentally, they also have the lowest rates of divorce, separation, and drug addiction and the highest percentage of three-generation extended family households. They are more likely than native-born whites to have BAs and graduate degrees and to be employed in managerial or professional occupations. But Asian Americans also have the highest rate of racial intermarriage in the United States, and women outnumber men in marrying out by far. This is usually explained as a desire by women in this diverse ethnic subculture to escape the strong surviving traditions of patriarchy among many Asian American males.[15] The more extreme patriarchal traditions of the Asian continent are also reflected in the higher rates of violence toward women among low-income, less educated Asian American families.

Psychological Stresses

Aside from greater economic insecurity, more stressful work–family conflicts, and increased tolls on energy and health, mother-only families are also more likely to experience a loss in social status, the stress of moving, and less social support from former relatives and friends, especially after a divorce.[16] For children, a move usually means starting a new school, finding new friends, adjusting to a new neighborhood, and sometimes losing contact with favorite relatives. These changes can be disastrous, especially for adolescents. Moreover, young widowed mothers usually remain in touch with and receive help from supportive in-laws; divorced mothers more often do not; and younger never-married mothers are less likely to have close relatives who can afford to help. Furthermore, when parents do help, they tend to feel they have the right to criticize the single mother's way of dealing with her child and her life situation.

Loneliness

The term *intimate strangers* refers to the fact that it is quite possible to be lonely in a supposedly close relationship; and we are well aware of the loneliness that people can feel in crowds. Loneliness is a feeling of sadness that occurs when social relationships do not measure up to an individual's need or desire for contact and connection with other people. It is a subjective feeling and is not necessarily the same as actual social isolation. Most single parents report strong feelings of loneliness.[17]

Generally, people who are not married report more frequent feelings of loneliness than married people. Psychological tests indicate that the tendency to feel lonely is associated with depression, low self-esteem, and anxiety. And in terms of the individual life cycle, feelings of loneliness are usually most intense during adolescence, even with the unrelenting presence of the peer group. Loneliness peaks again in old age, especially after the age of 80, when many family members and old friends have died and going to wakes, funerals, and memorial services becomes almost routine.[18]

Women are more likely than men to admit feeling lonely on surveys, but unmarried, successful career women report less loneliness. The more refined psychological tests that are now available, however (tests that measure physiological responses to questions asked), find no significant gender differences in these feelings. In case studies, divorced single fathers who have custody of their preschool children report amounts of loneliness, role conflict, and role overload (too many demands on their time and energy) similar to those of single mothers. But higher-status divorced fathers are better able to hold on to their previous socioeconomic status than their divorced wives; they are also more likely to remain in their community and to retain friends they had as a couple after a divorce.[19]

Effects on Children

In the 1950s and 1960s, studies of the effects on children of single parenting were based primarily on children who were receiving psychological treatment in clinics or were living in correctional institutions. Most researchers traced behavior problems in children to psychological factors, such as neglect and harsh or inconsistent discipline by less available single mothers. Since the 1970s, the emphasis has shifted to income differences and the negative effects of poverty on children in mother-only families. We now have a number of large, nationally representative, longitudinal studies that provide more accurate answers to questions about the short-term and long-term effects on children in mother-only families.[20]

Compared to two-parent households, children in mother-only families are five times more likely to be living in poverty; more likely to drop out of school; less likely to go to college; more likely to commit antisocial acts; and more likely to use drugs and alcohol. At school, boys act out more (fighting, failing, and skipping classes); girls are more likely to become depressed, sexually active at an early age, and more likely to become single parents like their mothers. As adults, both women and men from mother-only families are more likely to marry early, have children early, and divorce. These effects are more frequent in mother-only families regardless of income and ethnic origin, but they are most frequent among the lowest-income, mother-only, ethnic and racial minority families living in segregated ethnic communities.[21]

We don't know how much weight to give to various factors in predicting the future of an individual child in any specific family. How important are neighborhoods, income differences, and differences in parental love, values, expectations, and childrearing practices, relatively, in determining the fate of children in mother-only families? The reality of these situations is complex (Table 9.1). And even against all odds, in the highest-risk situations of poverty and high-crime neighborhoods where asthma, AIDS, father absence, and homelessness are endemic, there are individual cases of strong, loving, supportive single mothers and their confident, well-functioning, cheerful children.[22] Still, economic security, emotional support from family and friends, and, when necessary, helpful information and guidance from empathic, service-oriented professionals are also crucial.

TABLE 9.1 **Effects of Mother-Only Households on Children**

CHILDREN IN MOTHER-ONLY HOUSEHOLDS:

1. Are more likely to be living in poverty.
2. Have more short- and long-term psychological problems.
3. Achieve lower levels of education: more likely to drop out of high school and less likely to go to college.
4. Boys are more negatively affected academically than girls.
5. Both boys and girls are more likely to marry early, have children early, and divorce.
6. Girls are more likely to become single mothers as a result of divorce or nonmarital childbearing.
7. Both boys and girls are at higher risk of addiction to drugs and alcohol, and are more likely to commit antisocial acts.
8. These disadvantages apply to mother-only families, regardless of social class and ethnic origin, but they are more prevalent among impoverished mother-only minority families.

Note: Children of middle- and upper-class European American women who voluntarily become single mothers do not show these disadvantages.

Married Parents

Becoming a parent differs in certain ways from other major life transitions, such as getting married or starting a first adult full-time job or career.[23] For one thing, there is less preparation for the new parent role, despite the current boom in child-care classes among middle-class parents-to-be. Also, the new status of mother or father is sudden, and restricts freedom to come and go and do what one pleases far more than does getting married or taking a first full-time job. Responsible parents can't divorce or quit a child; nor can most new parents shift to a consulting role: instructing nannies or other hired helpers on how to bring up their children. Finally, in industrial societies, there are conflicting rules, guidelines, and standards for defining good parenting. But one thing most new parents do is renew old contacts, or make new contacts, with people who can help.

Social Networks

Networks are the number and kind of direct or indirect contacts people have with other people, and the birth of a first child usually leads to certain changes in the family and friendship networks of new parents. Contact with middle-aged or older parents tends to increase, regardless of whether or not they live nearby. Renewed contact with old friends who have young children also increases, as does finding new friends who have children of the same age. Help from grandparents is at a peak at this time and declines in later years. In the middle classes, financial help is most common during the early years, especially from the wife's family, who is usually in closer contact and provides more help. Working-class grandparents are more likely to provide help in the form of services (doing housework, cooking, running errands, babysitting) if they can. The flow of help is from grandparents to their children and grandchildren; it is not usually reciprocal at this stage in family life histories. Most grandparents want only friendship and love in return.[24]

Mothers and Fathers

Another change that occurs after a first child is born is a shift to more traditional roles within the home. The new mother is more likely to resent this change if household responsibilities were previously shared and her current expectations for help are ignored. But the greatest amount of conflict and dissatisfaction occurs when parents retain traditional gender role attitudes and are forced to play nontraditional roles (the employed mother who would rather be at home, or the unemployed or underemployed husband who would rather be the sole provider). The most important factor for new mothers (and, increasingly, for new fathers as well) is choice: being able to stay at home or continue working outside of the home if this is what they prefer and enjoy most.[25]

Marital Satisfaction

Social scientific research has focused mainly on the decline in marital satisfaction after the birth of a first child. Researchers have pointed to the increased psychological stress that results from the sudden restriction in the freedom to pursue personal interests (work, hobbies, friendships, recreation) and the decline in privacy, companionship, and communication between the parents of newborns. The physical and emotional demands of caring for an infant are boundless, especially if the mother is not well, the infant has a low birth weight, or the mother has had a multiple birth.

More recent research on marital satisfaction after the birth of a first child has taken a more positive turn. Couples who like and respect one another, who were satisfied with their relationship before they became parents, and who planned and looked forward to having their first child continue to feel satisfied after they become parents.[26] In fact, these couples adapt better to all family transitions and are more likely to stay together, for better and worse and for life. In situations where the couple has not established a close, mutually confiding and supportive relationship, the birth of a first child (especially if the pregnancy was not planned) may precipitate a nuclear family triangle. One parent (usually the mother) may develop a compensatory bond with the child, while the other parent becomes increasingly resentful, distant, and detached.[27]

Creating Time and Space

Another challenge for new parents is finding time and space for the new baby, both of which are in short supply for most families with young children in the United States today. Adequate space has become a major problem for low-income families since the 1980s, as affordable rentals in the private sector and subsidized housing in the public sector have steadily declined. The greatest increase in the homeless (and the hungry) since then has been among mothers with dependent children, who now outnumber the previous mainstays of homeless society: single men and women who are drug addicted, alcoholic, or psychotic.[28]

Work–Family Conflicts

The topic of work–family conflict is discussed in this chapter because this kind of conflict is most intense after the birth of a child and when there are very young children in the family. Work is any activity that has economic value and is not, like hobbies, done primarily for pleasure. Employees in more prestigious occupations usually enjoy their work more, but paid work is not a hobby; it is a necessity for most people, everywhere, economically and psychologically. Work produces goods or provides services, and in industrial societies, this kind of activity takes place in offices, factories, and stores, as well as in the fields and in the home. But wherever it takes place, it earns money, or it would cost money to hire someone else to do the work (cook, clean, sew, launder, care for and transport children to various destinations, and run the countless errands that modern housekeeping requires).

Financial Stress

Financial stress usually increases after the birth of a first child, especially if the new mother shifts to part-time work or takes an unpaid leave from her job. The United States is one of the few industrialized countries that does not provide paid maternity leave for new mothers.[29] Currently, in Sweden, both mothers and fathers can receive up to 80 percent of their salary for 18 months after the birth of a child, though fathers rarely take paternity leave. In the United States at this time, the Family and Medical Leave Act allows up to 12 weeks of unpaid job-protected leave, during any 12 month period, for the birth or adoption of a child, the care of a sick relative, or a serious illness. But the law applies only to employees of firms with 50 or more employees that provide benefits such as paid vacation time and sick leave for their employees; younger, poorer, less educated women working in low-pay, low-status, insecure jobs (in child care, domestic work, and small, nonunionized manufacturing businesses) usually can't afford to take unpaid leave. This is true also in Denmark, France, and other European countries that have been surveyed.[30]

Most mothers of newborns in the United States do cut back on their jobs; their income declines, as does their independence and authority in the marriage.[31] Career-oriented women who continue to work full time after giving birth do not experience these changes typically. But regardless of the hours spent in paid work and the degree of commitment to jobs or careers, on national surveys women report the greatest stress from increased time pressures after becoming a mother; men report having to work longer hours to support the new child as their major source of stress.[32]

Caring and Sharing

Until the early 1970s, most researchers emphasized the negative effects of wives' employment on the marriage relationship, especially the threat to men as providers. Researchers also focused on the unpaid contributions of middle-class women to the career advancement of their husbands in what came to be known as the *two-person career*.[33] Wives entertained their husband's important business associates; they attended parties and other events connected with their husband's job; they made important business contacts for him through their volunteer work in the community; they provided free secretarial services such as bookkeeping, typing, and editing; and they followed him wherever he moved or was transferred.

Satisfaction

Attitudes (and the economy) have changed greatly since then. Movement out of the home into paid employment is now the norm for mothers in almost all social circumstances, and the largest increases have taken place among mothers with children under six. Higher income reduces the stress of work–family role conflict because business executives and professionals can afford to hire more and better household and child-care help. Marital satisfaction is also higher.[34] It is highest among employed mothers who have high levels of education, are working out of choice, are working part time, and share household chores and child care with their husbands. As for ethnic subcultural differences in work at home by husbands, according to the National Survey of Families and Households, black and Latino men spend more time on housework and child care than do white men.[35] This may be because they have higher rates of unemployment or underemployment than white men.

Work and Leisure

Women have always had less leisure time than men, and in the United States today, working mothers have less leisure time than fathers, since they continue to have primary responsibility for homemaking and child care.[36] But there have been some changes: Men are doing more housework (especially the kind that involves using mechanical equipment), and fathers are caring for their young infants rather than waiting until the children are older, as they did in the past. (Women's rest rooms come equipped with diaper-changing tables; newer rest rooms for men, in public places such as airports, museums, supermarkets, and department stores, are now similarly equipped.) But husbands in two-earner households are more willing to help out in the home if they earn more money than their wives and are secure about their masculine identity; they are less likely to feel threatened by doing what has been traditionally defined as "women's work."[37]

Two-Career Marriages

Two-earner families are those in which both fathers and mothers have jobs or careers. But a career, in contrast to a job, requires more education, more time, and more commitment. It is not a powerless, routine, low-prestige, nine-to-five job; it usually involves promotions and increased authority, responsibility, and earnings over time. Workers earn yearly salaries rather than hourly wages. And for those who are happy with their choice, a career is a major source of identity, self-esteem, and enjoyment.

Roles and Stability

Two-career marriages are most likely to be equal-partner marriages, especially if the earned income of the partners is equal or nearly equal.[38] But two-career marriages have higher divorce rates if the wife works in the same occupation, is in a demanding, high-paying occupation traditionally sex-typed for men (medicine, law, architecture, and engineering), and if she earns more than her husband. Husbands tend to feel threatened in these situations, and competition and power struggles between husband and wife are more frequent.[39]

Why, then, do some two-career marriages last while others don't? Attitudes and values are most important: Does the husband approve of his wife's career? Is he sensitive to the increased pressures she experiences? Does he try to relieve these pressures as much as he can? Is he secure about his own achievements? Is he open to his wife's ideas? The most important factors in successful two-career marriages (those with high reported marital satisfaction) are understanding, empathy, and support. Also, in two-career marriages that last, "the exercise of power as an expression of dominance and submission is not a part of these interpersonal relationships."[40]

Commuter Marriages

Moves related to job conditions or opportunities affect women more than men. This is changing, but still, women are more likely than men to move in response to a husband's transfer or a husband's new job offer. Compared to employed married women who do not move, those who move are more likely to be unemployed, working part time, and earning a lower salary. But commuter marriages are becoming more frequent, especially in upper-middle-class and new-upper-class, two-career families. In these marriages, as I mentioned earlier, partners work in different geographic areas; the partners travel to either home, or to where children are (if there are children), as often and as regularly as possible.

According to research studies, these marriages have higher divorce rates, but they do best under certain conditions: when the jobs of husband and wife are located near each other (in San Francisco and Los Angeles rather than in bicoastal locations such as Los Angeles and New York); when commuting separations are temporary (lasting only a year or two) rather than permanent; when at least one partner is established in a career and can afford to compromise more; and when couples in commuter marriages are older, married longer, and have no dependent children at home.[41]

Effects on Children

How does having an employed mother affect the emotional, intellectual, and physical development of children? Are the children of working mothers more likely to be disturbed, delinquent, or deficient in some way? Do they feel more emotionally deprived than the children of mothers who are at home full time? According to research studies conducted over a period of more than 20 years, there is no hard evidence of specific and inevitable child development problems if mothers return to paid work.[42] Children raised in day-care centers tend to be more outgoing and somewhat slower in developing language skills (they have less exclusive, one-to-one contact with adults), but they catch up. Warmth, acceptance, and emotional support by dependable caregivers, whoever they are and wherever they are, is now believed to be the most important factor in child development.

Maternal Availability

Studies based on large national samples have found that employed mothers spend almost as much time in actual hands-on activities with their children as full-time homemakers.[43] Their children are as likely to be psychologically secure; and, in fact, children of employed mothers (especially girls) are more likely to be independent, resourceful, and academically successful.[44] (Employed mothers are less likely to be overinvolved with and overprotective of their children.) Most important in affecting the mother–child relationship of employed mothers are the mother's willingness to work, helpful conditions at work (flexible hours if needed, minimal travel demands, empathic and cooperative attitudes of employers and co-workers), dependable high-quality day care for their children, and constructive help and support from husbands, relatives, and friends.[45]

Working at Home

Working at home (an age-old custom among low-income mothers, who took in laundry, sewing, infants, and boarders, and prepared homemade food to sell in marketplaces and stores) is becoming increasingly popular today in advanced industrial societies; in the United States, it is increasing among parents of both sexes and all social classes. More than half of the workers in the newest electronically connected cottage industries are self-employed; the rest are telecommuters who do paid work at home for businesses, government, and private agencies. They are connected to their offices by personal computers, modems, faxes, direct-link telephones, cellular phones, videophones (the virtual equivalent of face-to-face conferences and encounters at the water cooler), beepers, and other wonders of modern technology. Large corporations such as Sears, Bankers Trust, and American Express long ago established telecommuting programs; others are joining them daily.[46]

Demographics

The typical home worker (self-employed, wage, or salaried) is white, married, between the ages of 25 and 54, and has at least some college education. Almost one-half of all home workers are women, as are one-third of those who are self-employed. On surveys, employers list a number of advantages to telecommuting: greater employee productivity because of fewer interruptions by co-workers, less absenteeism, lower turnover rates, and higher morale; lower overhead expense for office and parking spaces; and fewer air quality problems with environmental agencies, which are now requiring corporations employing more than 200 people to cut back on employee automobile commuting.[47]

Motivation of Home Workers

Home-based workers list savings in time and money for transportation, business clothes, and lunches as somewhat important. But having more control over their work situation is most important for men (second to family responsibilities); women list "coordinating work schedule with personal and family needs" first and foremost.[48]

Complaints

Complaints center on the need for self-discipline in structuring their time and work; a feeling of isolation; interruptions by neighbors and children; telephone calls from friends and family; and inadequate supervision over their work (for those at lower skill levels). Another complaint, especially among women, is that they are not taken as seriously or given the respect that workers in offices get. They may also experience resentment from co-workers who do not have the option of working at home. And they are often asked by employed friends, neighbors, and relatives who do not work at home to run errands or keep an eye on their children when their children are home sick, have no after-school supervision, or are dismissed from school because of bad weather.[49]

While working at home can help reduce work–family conflicts, it is not without problems: Young children do not understand the idea of work the way adults or older children do. No amount of reasoning can persuade them that it is more important for their parents to spend time doing something else (talking on the telephone or working on the computer) than taking care of them. They compete with the telephone, clients, customers, and computers for their parent's attention. Older children do better (they are at school), but even they have trouble when only a door separates them from a working parent. Starting a home-based business in order to spend more time with children also has its disadvantages. Many women who try this end up spending *less* time with their children, at least initially, because of the effort it takes to get a new small business going.

Reducing Work–Family Role Conflict

Compared to other industrial countries, workers in the United States work longer hours, have much shorter paid vacations (one or two weeks at most, compared to one month in France, Italy, Germany, and the Scandinavian countries), earn less per hour on the average, are more likely to work at two or three jobs, and are more sleep deprived.[50] Three-quarters of all workers in the United States get less than eight hours of sleep on work nights (almost one-half get six hours or less), and two-thirds, if they had a choice, would opt for more time off rather than higher earnings.[51]

Furthermore, less than one-third of all employees in the United States now have the standard work shift: 35 to 40 hours a week, during the day, Monday through Friday. And, according to sociologist Harriet Presser's projections, based on data from the National Survey of Families and Households, the largest job growth rate between 1992 and 2005 will be among people working evenings, nights, and weekends. What is the significance of this trend? Among other things, men who work nonstandard shifts, who have young children, and who are married for less than five years are almost six times more likely to separate or divorce than fathers who work a standard shift.[52]

Class and Nonstandard Work Hours

Less educated women with children are most likely to be working nonstandard hours as cashiers, waitresses, sales clerks, nurse's aides, and cleaning help in offices, hospitals, and other buildings. They work these hours because their jobs require it; businesses are staying open later and longer to accommodate customers and clients who have more varied work schedules (or who live in different time zones nationally and internationally). But off-hours child care (for single mothers who work the night shift, for example) is rarely available to mothers of young children; fathers and grandparents are now providing most of this care, in addition to their own job commitments.[53]

The increase in work–family conflicts that results from changing economic and political conditions in the wider society is not easily resolved by individual family members. But certain techniques are known to be effective in reducing this particular source of stress.[54]

Values and Priorities

First, parents need to be clear about their values and priorities. If a child is most important, certain compromises will have to be made. Lowering impossibly high standards at work, at home, or in child care and asking for or insisting on more help (paid or unpaid) are essential. Talking to others with similar work–family conflicts (family, friends, support groups) helps. Making out a list of specific sources of stress—inadequate income, too much debt, too demanding a job or boss, little or no support from a partner, inadequate child care, unrealistic standards—can also be helpful. At the least, this can reduce chaos and point to the specific work–family problems that need to be tackled.

Taking Action

Taking action of any kind, or even drawing up a plan of action, reduces feelings of stress. Cutting back, especially when standards are impossibly high, helps: keeping the house less clean; cooking simpler, quicker meals; washing clothes less often. More difficult but also effective are keeping work and family activities and problems separate. Setting up a schedule and sticking to it, limiting leisure activities, and taking young children along on leisure or work activities, if possible, are other ways to cope.

Finding New Reference Groups

Seeking out other people who have similar work–family problems (family, friends, support groups), no matter what these problems are, can also be constructive. It is comforting to know that we are not alone—that other people have similar problems; furthermore, their solutions may be worth trying. Men tend to have more difficulty admitting to a need for support and reaching out to families and friends, but this need is not limited to the female of the species.

New Trends and Choices

Advances in modern medicine, birth control, and reproductive technologies provide much more control over childbearing and childrearing now than in the past (Table 9.2). Most parents are spared the death of a child, a common experience in agricultural and industrializing societies, where infections and other diseases for which there was no treatment or cure were rampant. Also, most parents in advanced industrial countries can maintain a standard of living today that only the very wealthy could achieve in less technologically advanced societies. Technological improvements that we take for granted (indoor plumbing, central heating, air conditioning) promote better health, longer life, and greater comfort; these conveniences were not available even to the wealthiest families until well into the 20th century in some industrial societies.

New Fertility Technologies

On a national survey of women aged 14 to 44, about 10 percent reported some sort of problem bearing children.[55] The inability to conceive occurs almost equally among men and women; about half of all couples who are infertile do conceive eventually—with or without medical help. In the past, in strongly patriarchal societies, infertility or the inability to produce a male child was devastating, especially for women. Now, if they can afford it (most insurance companies in the United States do not cover infertility procedures), infertile couples who want a child can get

TABLE 9.2 New Choices and Challenges for Parents

COMPARED TO AGRICULTURAL SOCIETIES, PARENTS IN ADVANCED INDUSTRIAL SOCIETIES:

1. Are spared the death of a child, a common experience in agricultural and industrializing societies of the past because of infectious and other incurable childhood diseases that can now be successfully treated.
2. Have more control over the reproduction process: more effective birth control techniques and more effective techniques for promoting fertility.
3. Have a higher standard of living (access to food, shelter, clothing), even among the poorest members of advanced industrial societies.
4. Do not have the certainty and the clear-cut, unquestioned norms and values for childrearing that were prevalent in simpler, less rapidly changing societies.
5. Must maintain higher standards of cleanliness, nutrition, and health in childrearing, which requires more work and more information.
6. Face competition from experts (teachers, social workers, psychologists), the mass media (messages of sex and violence), and peers (especially among adolescents) to confident childrearing.

effective medical help to achieve their goal; those who specifically want a male or a female child can even preselect the sex of their child—again, if they can afford it.

Controversial Issues

The new medical technologies have raised a number of ethical, legal, and medical issues.[56] Controversy centers on issues such as interfering with biological safeguards by using a younger woman's eggs to impregnate older women who are past menopause; commercializing reproduction by treating eggs, sperm, embryos, and uteruses as salable products; promoting unwilling fertility by the use of frozen embryos to impregnate women whose husbands have divorced them; and obscuring the issue of parental rights (and responsibilities) in the case of artificial insemination.

Most states now have laws that grant parental rights to the husbands and wives who take custody of the child rather than to egg or sperm donors in cases of artificial insemination.[57] But frustrated or disappointed donors (and surrogates), though few in number, sometimes find loopholes in the laws and sue for parental rights. The issue can be quite complicated: Who has parental rights over a child created with an egg or a sperm donor, a gestational surrogate mother, and a contracting husband and wife?

As for the use of fertility drugs and other techniques to "rewind the biological clock" by permitting older women to bear children, one issue here is that the genetic quality and viability of eggs diminish with age, and the chances of having a child who is disabled increase greatly for middle-aged women.[58] Eventually, young women may be able to freeze their eggs for future use; but, at the present time, the technique for doing this is still quite primitive. Regardless of growing opposition from researchers to the sale of human embryos, eggs, and sperm, as well as commercial surrogacy, newspapers across the country now routinely carry ads for egg and sperm donors.

Ads in Ivy League college newspapers offer as much as $50,000 to egg donors with outstanding Scholastic Aptitude Test (SAT) scores and other desirable endowments.[59] Many of the 100 or so sperm banks operating in the United States today offer catalogues with background information on available donors, and thousands of additional choices, with profiles, are available online. From a sociological point of view, the new reproductive technologies raise social class and inequality issues: Most donors are relatively poor, and most recipients are well off; donors usually sell their eggs or sperm or rent out their wombs because they need or want the money.

Regardless of the issues raised by new inventions and discoveries, however, the demand for rational (more effective and efficient) solutions to medical problems has been unrelenting historically; pragmatism tends to override ethical, legal, and medical obstacles over time, especially in technologically advanced postindustrial societies. The new assisted reproductive technologies are costly, and the odds against success, especially for preselecting the sex of a child, are still high. But chances are improving almost daily as fierce competition for fame, fortune, or both among government, academic, and commercially based scientists intensifies the pace of new scientific, medical, and technological advances.[60]

Multiple Births

During the 1970s and 1980s in the United States, medical inventions such as fertility drugs, in vitro fertilization, embryo transplants, and artificial insemination, as well as improvements in public health, resulted in a striking decline in infertility rates. But rates are going up again now, mainly because middle-class women are delaying marriage and motherhood until they finish college and are economically independent.[61] Women in their late 30s and early 40s are more likely to have multiple births (triplets or more) naturally, but the increased use of fertility drugs is the major reason why some women in this age category are having more children than they hoped for or expected. In the 1930s, the first quintuplets were received with spectacular fanfare: They were feted, followed, photographed, and exploited throughout every stage of their development, from infancy through adulthood. The current record holders in the multiple-birth league, octuplets, made headlines for a few days and were then quietly relegated to a footnote in the history of childbearing.

Since 1970, multiple births, though not common (about 150 per 100,000 live births), have resulted in an increase in low-birth-weight, preterm babies who are at much higher risk of dying or being born with developmental disabilities such as brain damage and cerebral palsy.[62] Children born as a result of in vitro fertilization are twice as likely as children who are naturally conceived to have major congenital abnormalities. In the United States, reproductive endocrinologists typically transfer up to four embryos during an in vitro fertilization procedure; the United Kingdom now has a law limiting the number of embryos that can be transferred to two. If three or more embryos are detected on an early sonogram, couples are given the option of *selective reduction*, that is, destroying one or more of the fetuses. But most couples, for ethical or religious reasons, or because they have been through years of previously unsuccessful costly treatments, opt to have their triplets or quadruplets.

Voluntary Childlessness

Couples who choose not to have children are more open about their decision now. The stigma of childlessness and pressure from parents and friends to bear children have declined somewhat, especially among very ambitious, well-educated, successful two-career couples. Women are more likely than men to make this choice, especially if they are highly successful, an only child, or a first-born child who needed to take care of younger brothers and sisters in a hard-pressed low-income family. Their husbands more often do want children, and this is becoming a new source of conflict in two-career marriages.[63]

Reasons

On surveys, couples who decide against having children give freedom from childrearing responsibility, a desire for a closer partner relationship, and career commitments as primary reasons for their decision.[64] They also report greater marital satisfaction than couples with children: They have less work–family conflict, fewer bills, more time for one another, and fewer stressful daily events. They do not have to contend with children who come home in a bad mood; refusals to do homework; calls from the principal's office about a child's poor work, bad behavior, lateness, or truancy; refereeing quarrels between brothers and sisters; loud music, spills, breakages, or lost prized possessions; and so on, and on.[65]

But childless couples with marital problems are more likely to divorce than couples who have young children, and these couples would not show up on surveys of marital satisfaction. The presence of younger children acts as a brake on divorce, especially now with the changing values of our marriage-counseling culture. For parents, the suffering of their children is the most important barrier to divorce; for fathers, losing their children is next in importance.[66]

Adopting Children

Less than 4 percent of family households in the United States contain adopted children, and the number of infants available for adoption has declined sharply in recent years: Teenagers are delaying becoming sexually active or opting for sexual abstinence; the use of contraceptives is more widespread; abortion is legal, although not easy to obtain; and unmarried mothers are now more likely to keep their infants. (Only about 3 percent of unmarried white mothers and about 1 percent of black mothers give up their infants for adoption.[67])

Since the demand exceeds the supply, potential adoptive parents are now paying more for their infants through private sources; turning to other countries for infants; or trying to adopt children who are more difficult to place: nonwhite, older, or disabled children. Despite a federal law prohibiting race as a factor in placing children, adoption agencies in the United States have tended to discourage interracial adoptions, assuming that children in these situations would have identity problems. Most interracial adoptees in the United States have been unwanted girls from Asia—mainly from China and Korea—and we have no good information, that I know of, on the identity problems of these children. Meanwhile, growing numbers of native-born ethnic minority children are in foster care, and most of these children will never be adopted.

As for adopting older and disabled children, we do have evidence on this topic: Generally, the older the child at the time of adoption, the more likely it is that the child will be returned to the sponsoring agency.[68] Why? To begin with, older children who are adopted, with or without physical disabilities, are more likely to have experienced emotional and physical abuse from their biological or foster parents. They have usually experienced a lack of attachment, or a series of separations from biological or foster parents, and are less able to become attached to adoptive parents—or to anyone else for that matter.[69] Children born of drug- or alcohol-addicted parents or of human immunodeficiency virus (HIV)-positive mothers are developmentally impaired as well. Given the demands of bringing up any child, adopting an older child can become impossibly stressful even for the most patient, altruistic, and resourceful adoptive parents.

A current issue in adopting children is whether adoptions should be *open* (biological and adoptive parents are in direct contact) or *closed* (biological and adoptive parents have no contact and don't know one another). In the past, adoptions were almost always closed; today they are more often open. Secrecy in adoptions becomes less important as the stigma attached to nonmarital childbearing declines, and the identity of biological parents becomes more important as scientific knowledge about genetic factors in disease increases. Also, in closed adoptions, adult adopted children are now more likely than in the past to search for their unknown biological parents. Reunions, however, have sometimes turned out to be disappointing, ambivalent, or even traumatic for all concerned.[70]

Adults who are happy with themselves and their adoptive parents are less likely to look for their biological parents:

> Placing a child that you have carried for nine months in the arms of another family has to be the most gut-wrenching decision one can make. To then have this person walk back into your life opens a Pandora's box of problems. As a healthy, happy adopted child myself, I see absolutely no need to disrupt the lives of people who have already made one of the toughest choices of their lives.[71]

Parenting Challenges

Relationships between parents and children vary, typically, during the different maturational (biologically based) stages of child development. And, once again, the boundaries of the various stages are not exact: Individual children vary a great deal, and new stages are being added as advances in medicine and nutritional science affect biological maturation at both ends: enhancing growth among the young and slowing the biological declines of old age. A focus on stages in child development has a long history in the social sciences, with parallel contributions from the fields of philosophy, sociology, psychology, and psychiatry.[72]

Infants

Infancy is the period from birth until a child learns to crawl or walk—from eight months to one year, usually. Newborn infants need to be fed when they are hungry and held and comforted when they cry. They cry not to annoy but because they are hungry, in pain, or need human contact. If these needs are satisfied during the first months of life, infants will feel good about themselves and their world; they will develop a basic trust in other people that tends to persist throughout their lives.[73]

Newborn infants must learn to conform to certain basic rules in any culture: They must learn to sleep through the night, and they must regulate their hunger drive so that they eat at specific times and only during the day. Some infants will take these hurdles easily; others are difficult. Infants are born with biologically grounded differences in temperament that are obvious from the day they are born. *Temperament* refers to emotional intensity, energy level (passive, active), and ability to tolerate frustration (thirst, hunger, pain). Temperament has a great deal to do with how easy or difficult parenting is, especially if the parent's and the infant's temperaments are not compatible.[74]

As for the major challenges that infants must cope with, sleeping through the night usually comes when the infant can eat enough to last through the night. Getting up and feeding the infant when it cries during the night appeases hunger; playing with the infant rewards wakefulness. The infant will wake up more frequently, stay awake longer, and turn night into day. As for eating three meals a day, if the food is put before the child and a refusal to eat is ignored by the parent, the child will eventually eat. Nature is on the parent's side: Children get hungry, especially if they are not given snacks between meals; but they will not eat if eating becomes an attention-getting mechanism or a power struggle between parent and child.

Toddlers

Infants enter the toddler stage of human development when they become mobile—crawling or walking. This stage ends when children are about three years of age. At around this age, toddlers make the transition from baby to child and achieve a slightly greater ability to reason and to compromise. For parents, the first year of the toddler stage is usually a more difficult stage than infancy because toddlers are enormously curious about anything they can reach, touch, see, or get to, especially if this involves a dangerous climb. Toddlers have huge amounts of energy—overwhelming amounts by older parent and grandparent standards.

Toddlers must be watched at all times; gone are the days when the caregiver can do anything without interruption when a toddler is awake and in motion. Silence from the other room usually means the toddler is doing something that is dangerous or will require a great deal of cleaning up. The major challenge during this stage, for parents and toddlers, is getting through the potential hazards of toddler explorations with affection, good humor, and minimum damage to parent, child, and household.

Babyproofing the household by removing dangerous, breakable, and treasured objects from the reach of the toddler is essential. Also, it isn't wise to take toddlers visiting in households that haven't been babyproofed; it is an unfair test of friends who have no toddlers or have forgotten what toddlers are like. A stimulating environment in which "no" is kept to a minimum and toddlers are encouraged to explore and to satisfy their tremendous curiosity safely promotes confidence during this stage and creativity in later life.

The second year of the toddler stage, sometimes called the *terrible twos*, is a time of conflict between independence and dependence for parent and child. On the one hand, two-year-olds display their independence by saying "no" automatically to almost anything they are asked to do; on the other hand, they shift back and forth from "yes" to "no." This is an important time during which they try to establish an identity: to discover who they are and what they want. It is a growth period when the child's rebelliousness and negativism can try parents' patience almost beyond endurance.

Probably the most important principles to follow during this period are *firmness* and *consistency*: "You stand your ground and do whatever is necessary, within reason, to see to it that the child knows when you say something, you mean it."[75] In spite of the negativism of two-year-olds, parents usually absorb some of the boundless enthusiasm and excitement that confident, cheerful children have about the world and its enchantments. This enthusiasm is contagious and can be extraordinarily gratifying to parents.

From Three to Six

Children alternate between being cooperative and reasonable and defiant and negativistic during the years from three to six. Three-year-olds tend to be relatively calm and reasonable; they can be delightful. Four-year-olds tend to be turbulent as well as delightful. If parents or other caregivers have not set clear and consistent rules that they enforce, or if they reward crying and whining by giving in, children of this age can be trying. A major developmental challenge for children during the preschool years is learning to give and take in relationships with peers. Since children are more oriented toward peers at age three, the feeling of rivalry toward a newborn sibling tends to be less severe if children are spaced at least three years apart. Other important developmental challenges during the preschool years are learning to separate from the parent or caregiver (at preschool, for example) and developing a sense of morality.

From Six to Twelve

The first part of this stage, up to the age of about nine or ten, is sometimes called *middle childhood*. It is characterized by comparative tranquility. This relatively calm period is sandwiched in between the turbulent ups and downs of the preschool years and preadolescence, which begins anywhere from age nine to twelve in individual children. The family shares much more of the child's energies, loyalties, and concerns in school and with peers during middle childhood. One major challenge to parents during preadolescence is to begin the process of letting go gracefully. Parents can't let go entirely; children still need them, even if they aren't likely to admit it. And they must know where to draw the line between support and overprotection. Parents must also support their children's need to cope with what is demanded of them at school and in their relationships with peers.

Preadolescence

From a period of relative stability and reason, children are likely to turn into unrecognizable monsters somewhere between the ages of nine and twelve. This is the period between childhood and adolescence labeled *preteens* or *tweens* in the popular press. Girls mature about two years faster than boys during the period of middle childhood; they usually reach the preadolescent stage sooner. This stage is easily recognized by parents and caregivers: simple, polite requests—please take out the garbage, set the table, wear a sweater because it's cold outside, go to bed because it's past your bedtime—are met with outrage and sarcasm. These demands were greeted with no comment or a mild grumble in the past; suddenly, and with no warning, they result in defiance and endless arguments.

This kind of preadolescent behavior is more frequent in middle-class, democratic households; children in these settings are more likely to feel and to express their anger. In the upper social classes, parents usually send unruly preadolescents to boarding school; middle-class parents send them to their room. In the working class and among the poor, children may not have a room of their own, and defiant behavior is usually greeted with a slap.

Preadolescents are extraordinarily adept at knowing where parents are most vulnerable. If parents are conservative about sexual activity, they will start acting out sexually. Children who act out, incidentally, express their anger or hostility toward a parent (or anyone else) indirectly: by smashing up the parent's car or setting the house on fire instead of directly attacking the parent or other offenders. If parents value academic achievement, their child's grades may suddenly drop; if they value strict obedience, the child may spend as much time as possible away from home, with friends whose parents are more lenient. If parents value neatness and cleanliness, the child's room becomes impenetrable, and not simply because the door is locked. But this too passes—as does the next stage: full-blown, identity-experimenting, risk-taking, authority-testing adolescence.

Adolescence

The status of *adolescent* did not have a name, nor did adolescents as a separate and distinct subculture exist until the beginning of the 20th century. The term was coined by psychologist Stanley H. Hall in 1904; it refers to the period that begins at puberty and ends when physical growth is completed.[76] Today, this period corresponds roughly to the teenage years, and for increasing numbers of children, it begins during the preteen years (ages 10 to 12); it continues until physical growth is completed at age 19 (or even earlier now). Puberty is a period of speeded-up biological change during which females develop breasts and begin to menstruate and males develop a deeper voice, body hair, and ejaculatory capacity. Both sexes must adjust to new and powerful hormonal changes, to sexual urges, and to bodies that are very different from their childhood bodies.

In postindustrial societies, adolescents achieve legal adulthood in various spheres of life at different times, and for most adolescents, adult rights lag behind physical maturity. Inconsistencies in the legal recognition of adulthood in the United States can be quite frustrating to older adolescents who are adults physically. Eighteen-year-olds can legally sign contracts, join the army, vote, drive, and be tried as adults for crimes; but they can't legally drink, smoke, rent a car, and, in some states, marry without the consent of their parents. Time passes slowly for adolescents, much more slowly than for older people who are running out of this particular resource, and it passes too slowly for many adolescents as well as their parents. Religious, philosophical, artistic, and literary images of the turbulence, impulsivity, negativism, and grandiosity of middle-class adolescents abound in the cultural heritage of Western societies.[77]

Delayed Home Leaving

Today, young people in postindustrial societies do not become completely independent financially until they finish their training and take their first full-time job in their field. It is hardly appropriate to refer to college students and graduate students as adolescents. And yet they are not usually defined as adults, especially by their parents, until they have completed their training and are economically self-sufficient—more or less. The major difference between youths in agricultural and industrial societies is that in industrial societies most young people live at home until they become self-supporting adults; in the past, children aged ten, or even younger, were sent off to serve apprenticeships or to serve in other people's homes until they reached adulthood.

Today, in Europe as well as in the United States, the number of young people in their 20s who delay leaving home (especially boys) is increasing steadily as training requirements for functioning in the information economy expand. But national surveys indicate that southern European countries (Greece, Spain, and Italy) are experiencing much larger increases in delayed home leaving than central and western European countries (France, Germany, and the United Kingdom). Increases in the latter countries and in the United States are almost identical.[78]

A major reason for these differences is the higher rate of young adult unemployment in southern European countries. Grown children are not remaining at home as they get more training and build up their qualifications for better jobs; they are "parked" at home because they have no jobs. The current delay in the median age at first marriage (to the middle to late 20s) in the United States, incidentally, coincides with the age when most young people in agricultural societies completed their apprenticeships and got married—if they married at all.[79]

Gender Differences

Studies of families with adolescent or grown children at home point to certain conditions that favor the early departure from home of children of both sexes: poverty, crowded living quarters, violence between parents, and single-parent or stepparent families.[80] But even among middle-class, two-parent traditional families, either immigrant or native-born, girls are more likely to leave home, and to leave home sooner, than boys. How do we explain this curious fact, given the stronger emotional ties to family, traditionally, of girls and women? The most important reason why women leave home earlier is that they tend to marry at younger ages than do men.[81]

Sexual and other forms of abuse by stepfathers or live-in male friends of single mothers is a primary reason why very young working-class girls run away from home. Other reasons why girls leave sooner are the tendency of parents to allow more freedom to come and go to grown sons who live at home than to grown daughters, and their tendency to make more demands for help with cooking, cleaning, laundry, and other household chores on daughters than on sons. Finally, daughters now are more likely to be high school and college graduates and are better able to find self-supporting entry-level jobs in the service economy.

Consequences of Delayed Home Leaving

Young people who remain at home longer achieve higher levels of education at every level—from high school to college to professional school. Relationships with parents are more positive if the parents view the child as making progress toward independence—when the child is in school or is employed. If not, contact with parents is avoided (eating separately and communicating through notes on the refrigerator), and children report a lack of trust and respect from their parents.[82] As for adult children who return home after having left, parents are usually quite supportive, regardless of their own circumstances, since these returns are often temporary and for good reasons. According to the National Longitudinal Surveys of Mature Women, during the period 1969 to 1984 "between one-fourth and one-third of white middle-aged women lived in extended-family households for some time over the 15-year period, and approximately two-thirds of black women experienced this household form for at least a part of their middle years."[83]

For most young adults, living in an extended family household means returning to the parental home temporarily during a period of emotional crisis (separation, divorce, widowhood) and/or financial need (job loss, or job income that has not kept up with rising costs of housing, food, and clothing). Legally, parenting ends after a child reaches adulthood (18 to 21 years of age); but, in some ways and for many, it never ends. When "boomerang kids" return, major challenges that parents face are deciding how much help to extend (or expect) from their grown children and what rules to insist on. Only a small number of parents ask their children to pay room and board.[84]

Independence–Dependence Conflicts

The major conflict and challenge of adolescents in industrial societies is to become as emotionally independent of parents as possible; the contradictory urge, or conflict, is to remain a dependent child, safe and secure—as in the past. The easiest way for adolescents to diminish their emotional attachment to parents is to disagree and find fault with them and to distance themselves from their parents physically. In early adolescence especially, the peer group usually provides the needed support to make this change.

The price that is exacted by peers is conformity—in dress, speech, behavior, tastes in entertainment and in professed values, especially if these disagree with parental values. But situational sources of storm and stress during adolescence have been declining in the United States since the late 1990s. In the current economy, parental unemployment, and underemployment rates are relatively low, as is teenage idleness (teens who are school dropouts and are not working). Also declining are nonmarital teenage pregnancies, delinquency rates, and teenage deaths by accident, homicide, or suicide.[85] Another aspect of parent–adolescent conflict is less obvious.

This is the need for adolescents to adapt to changes in the availability, authority, and independence of mothers (especially), who return to full-time work or to other outside interests they had put aside when their children were younger. Parents at this stage, especially in the middle social classes, are likely to reassert their need for privacy and their desire to pursue their own work or leisure activities; and adolescents, like their parents, also need to let go.[86]

Ideals and Reality

Most parents of young children try to be loving, patient, supportive, and encouraging; they do the best they can. And most succeed, especially when personal resources are supplemented by good information and support from partners, relatives, friends, employers, and governments. Contrary to reports on confessional talk shows, most people on repeated national surveys report fond memories of their childhood and their relationship with their parents.[87]

But social location, especially social class, strongly affects the possibility of fulfilling childrearing goals. A pileup of unpaid bills can drive patience, tolerance, and support, not to mention love, out the window. Severe financial problems make it hard for parents to provide consistent love, involvement, nurturance, empathy, and discipline.[88] Also, parents' own childhood experiences may influence them in ways they are not aware of. Still, even if a father or mother had an unhappy childhood, the next generation suffers less, usually. Parents try hard to avoid repeating the mistakes they feel their parents made, and strong, supportive relationships with a partner, extended family, or friends can help prevent the passing on of destructive patterns to the next generation.

We now turn to other transitions that families go through as they age—some expected and some unexpected. We start with divorce, a transition that is usually unexpected but, from all available evidence, is the second most stressful life event that married people in the United States experience—next to the death of a spouse.[89]

Chapter 10
Divorce and Remarriage

Divorce is widespread in industrial societies—in fact and in fantasy. All known societies have some form of marriage, and all provide ways for unhappy couples to separate or dissolve their marriages. Even in societies that have been most restrictive about ending marriages, people have managed to find ingenious ways to circumvent family, religious, legal, and moral barriers to separation and divorce. In any society, the divorce rate is a sensitive barometer of cultural values, the status of women, and experiences of attachment and detachment in that society.

Divorce

Divorce rates are higher, generally, in societies in which women's status is higher and their economic independence greater. In patrilineal horticultural societies, where descent is traced through the male line, divorce rates are low; in matrilineal societies, in which descent is traced through the female line, the status of women is higher and divorce rates are higher. In agricultural societies, divorce rates are usually low; in industrial societies, where marriage is based on personal choice and where marital happiness and the emotional tie between husband and wife are more highly valued, rates are usually higher.[1]

But in the late 19th century, divorce rates were higher in certain agricultural societies, such as Japan, Egypt, and Algeria, than they are in the United States today.[2] And currently Japan has a low divorce rate, despite a high level of industrialization. Given current life expectancies, however, if we take into account all causes of nuclear family breakdown (death and desertion as well as divorce), more marriages in the United States and in other advanced industrial countries are now remaining intact for longer periods of time than ever before.[3]

The Social Context of Divorce

Divorce rates in the United States have been increasing gradually for more than 100 years. The rate declines during severe economic downturns and during wars, and it increases sharply when wars come to an end: The highest short-term increase in divorce rates in the history of the United States occurred after the end of the Second World War, when husbands returned home from military service.[4]

In fact, the period immediately following all wars since the Civil War (when divorce rates were first measured) has been characterized by a temporary peak in divorce rates. Why? Divorce is considered unpatriotic while a war is still on. Also, people tend to marry impulsively during wartime; they experience long separations; infidelity is more likely; and values change. When the war ends, differences that did not exist, or were previously denied, become more obvious and the divorce rate surges.

During the 1950s in the United States, an atypical decade in some respects, divorce rates dipped and larger families became more popular, especially in the middle social classes. This is believed by some researchers to be a reaction to family losses and other stresses experienced during the Second World War. But from the mid-1960s to the mid-1970s, the divorce rate doubled and divorce came to be viewed as a new start, a second chance, and a release or reprieve from a bad choice.[5] It was a time when the new women's movement had its greatest appeal and married women's participation in the labor force surged as new jobs in the service sector multiplied. But by 1977, after a series of recurring (worldwide) recessions and increased financial pressures, attitudes and values began to change once again; the divorce rate leveled off (at the highest level ever) and began a slight decline that continues to this day.

Reasons for Higher Rates

Why has the divorce rate increased gradually, with short-term exceptions, for over 100 years in the United States? And why are divorce rates increasing now in industrializing societies in almost all parts of the world?[6]

Unrealistic Expectations

I have mentioned unrealistic expectations (that marriage can change the basic personality of a partner, solve severe personal problems, satisfy all basic needs, and eliminate the feelings of loneliness and despair) as a factor in high divorce rates, especially in the United States, where expectations tend to be more unrealistic than in other industrial societies.

More Alternatives

Other reasons for higher divorce rates are the increased availability of alternative ways to satisfy physical needs; the diminishing control of family, religion, and community; the changing status and economic roles of men and women; and medical advances, especially in birth control and control over venereal diseases (pre-AIDS) that help subsidize alternative lifestyles.

Increasing numbers of married women earn independent income that they can keep in industrial societies and especially in postindustrial societies. This promotes the possibility of divorce for women in unhappy marriages, since it diminishes their economic dependence. Men also have more alternatives in industrial societies. They can buy the housekeeping services that wives or other family members provided in the past: cooked food, sewing, laundry, ironing, cleaning. And for both sexes, sexual gratification outside of the marital bond is more available now, even with the fear of AIDS.

Diminishing Social Control

As social, psychological, and geographic mobility increase in industrial societies, family influence becomes less imperious, community norms less binding, and religious conviction less effective in maintaining conformity to the traditional norms of duty and obligation in family relationships. Rising levels of education and greater economic independence also open up new horizons and options and promote less conformity to cultural traditions.

Changing Values

At the same time, divorce loses much of its stigma, as does remaining single. The increased emphasis on the self and on individualism diminishes the value placed on self-sacrifice in family relationships. This general trend varies according to social location (in the United States, for example, Jewish and Italian Americans tend to be more familistic and have lower divorce rates than other ethnic populations). It also varies according to the specific parent–child relationships in the families people come from. Closely attached, or highly ambivalent, or detached and rejecting relationships with parents during childhood and adolescence tend to persist (though not always or inevitably) in the parallel life histories of individuals and their families.

New Standards

The newer standards for judging the quality of marriages in industrial societies (emotional support, friendship, companionship, open communication, personal fulfillment, and equality in decision making) also increase divorce rates. These needs, as I described earlier, are more demanding psychologically and less binding materially than the economic and physical trade-offs and dependencies of the past. Changes in the reasons people give for getting a divorce reflect the increased value placed on personal needs and goals in recent decades.

In the 1950s, when familistic values were stronger, the most frequent reasons women gave for divorcing their husbands were clear and concrete: nonsupport, infidelity, drinking, gambling, physical abuse. Now, "the reasons given in more recent studies more often involve personal incompatibility and personal growth issues."[7] This reflects changing standards in judging partner relationships and the increased value placed on emotional support in contemporary marriages.

Individualism

Individual needs and desires are given more weight now in determining the costs, rewards, and exchanges in marital relationships and in deciding whether to stay in or leave a relationship. The concept of *irreconcilable differences* in no-fault divorce laws reflects this trend; it eliminates the need to assign guilt in marital breakups. Some researchers and social critics feel the new standards promote self-ishness and narcissism in family relationships; others take a more positive view, emphasizing the new freedoms and greater possibilities for personal fulfillment in modern marriages.[8]

Given these changed social conditions and newer standards, how stable are marriages in the United States today? What is the actual divorce rate? Who divorces whom and why, and what are the consequences of divorce for men, women, and children?

Demographics of Divorce

About one-third of all divorces occur within five years after marrying; two-thirds occur within ten years; and only about 1 percent take place after 25 years of mar-riage, although there is a slight increase in the divorce rate after the last child has left home. These figures are from an analysis by sociologist Theodore N. Greenstein of a national, longitudinal study of over 5,000 women who were married in 1968 and were interviewed almost every year thereafter for the next 15 years.[9]

The Actual Divorce Rate

In the Greenstein study, 20.5 percent were separated or divorced after 15 years. This is probably a more accurate predictor of future marital breakups than the usual pre-dictions of 50 percent, or more, that are common in the media and even among aca-demic researchers. The one in five figure is particularly impressive, since the Greenstein study continued over a period of 15 years, and most separations and divorces occur within the first ten years of marriage. Also, separation and divorce rates were increasing rapidly during the early years of this study and are declining now, as more people delay getting married for first time and are more financially secure and psychologically mature when they do get married.

Sociologist Norval D. Glenn reached an almost identical conclusion about the *actual* divorce rate in the United States. Professor Glenn analyzed yearly data from the General Social Survey conducted by the National Opinion Research Center over the period from 1973 to 1988. He also found that about one-fifth of all first-time marriages ended in separation or divorce over a period of 9 to 29 years from the date the marriage began.[10]

To predict that one in five marriages will end in separation or divorce seems to be more realistic than the one in two predictions that have become a cliché in the media. We need more longitudinal studies on this topic (that are now on the way), but the recent decline in the divorce rate seems to support a more optimistic pre-diction about future divorce rates. As for now, however, do *any* marriages have a 50 percent rate of separation and divorce? If we break down the data according to *age* at first marriage, we find that teenage first marriages do have a 50 percent (or more) rate of separation or divorce and, in fact, are twice as likely to break up as marriages by people who marry in their early 20s.[11] Statistical chances of separation and

TABLE 10.1   Predicting Divorce

A COUPLE IS MORE LIKELY TO DIVORCE IF:

1. One or both partners are teenagers or middle-aged (45 or older) at the time of the first marriage.
2. The marriage is impulsive—takes place a few days, a few weeks, or even a few months after the couple meets for the first time.
3. The couple has very low income—the husband or wife is underemployed, unemployed, or employed at the minimum wage.
4. The social backgrounds of the husband and wife are very different—class, ethnic origin, race, religion, nationality.
5. The ages of the husband and wife are very different—a difference of 20 years or more.
6. The marriage is the second (or more) marriage for the husband or wife; the divorce rate is higher if there are children from a previous marriage.
7. Neither the husband nor the wife is religious; they do not attend church regularly.
8. The husband or wife has a history of violence, drug addiction, mental illness, or criminal behavior.
9. The husband or wife had parents who divorced.
10. Family and friends disapprove of the husband or wife.

Note: Values and a strong commitment to the partner may mediate and prevent divorce regardless of these circumstances.

divorce tend to decline with every year that young people wait to get married for the *first* time.

But those who wait until their mid-40s or later before marrying for the first time are more likely to get divorced. People who are much older than the usual age for marrying for the first time seem to be less tolerant of differences in the behavior and the values of their partners, differences that become more obvious after the marriage. Also, the prospect of living alone for people who marry for the first time when they are that much older is not especially frightening; they've done that, and doing it again is not inconceivable. Table 10.1 summarizes the factors that are associated with divorce.

Women in Divorce

Sociologists Liana C. Sayer and Suzanne M. Bianchi analyzed two sets of data collected from over 13,000 households interviewed in 1987 and again in 1992 on the National Survey of Families and Households.[12] They looked specifically at how the employment of women affects divorce rates. They found that women with the highest divorce rates had no premarital work experience; were under the age of 18 when they married; gave birth before they married or were pregnant at the time of the marriage; had no children or no male children; had parents who were divorced by the time they were 14; and were more likely to live in rented apartments than in private homes.

How did the wife's employment affect the likelihood of divorce? Married women with the lowest earnings (waitresses, cashiers, domestic workers) were twice as likely as those with higher incomes (college graduates, business managers) to separate or get a divorce. Women who worked 35–40 hours a week were four times more likely to separate or divorce than were women who averaged 20 hours or less a week. But the added income of employed wives did not destroy *happy* marriages: Especially at lower income levels, it was more likely to preserve than to threaten a marriage. Mainly, the independent income of employed married women was used to escape bad marriages, where marital satisfaction steadily declined as the years went by and the feeling of commitment also declined.

Social Location and Divorce

How do separation and divorce rates differ in the various subcultures of class, ethnic origin, race, and region in the United States today? Given publicity in the mass media, one might think celebrities and other old- or new-upper-class people have the highest divorce rates in the country. They do not. The poor have the highest *legal* divorce rate (with help from Legal Aid agencies). Separation is no longer the "poor man's divorce," though both are certainly more frequent among low-income families.[13]

Social Class

With the exception of the new upper class, divorce rates tend to go down as socioeconomic status goes up; old-upper-class people have the lowest divorce rate. More educated people have lower divorce rates, generally, as do people with higher incomes and higher occupational prestige. Why? For one thing, money doesn't buy marital happiness, but it helps. Stress levels and physical and mental illness also decline as socioeconomic status goes up. Then too, more educated people marry later and have more access to help from a larger number and variety of sources—family, friends, therapists, courses, books, magazines, and online information services.[14]

Female college professors, doctors, and lawyers (especially lawyers) are an exception: They are less likely to marry (although this is changing now), are more likely to divorce if they do marry, and are less likely to remarry if they divorce. Career–family conflicts are more intense among higher-level professional women than among nine-to-five female workers, and they are more likely to outearn their husbands. In fact, many of the highest-earning female doctors and lawyers, who are married, cut back to part-time employment to lessen the conflict, especially when their children are young.[15]

Region

In the United States, divorce rates have been higher in the West and lower in the East. Differences in the rate, which was 50 percent higher in California in the 1970s, are narrowing and are barely significant now, however.[16] The higher divorce rates in California are usually attributed to more liberal divorce laws in that state; the first no-fault divorce law in the country was passed in California in 1970. The fact that more liberal divorce laws originated in California is usually explained by the stronger subcultural emphasis on individualism and self-fulfillment in that state. This, in turn, is attributed to the "frontier atmosphere" and the greater independence, social tolerance, and nonconformity of California residents. Compared to other states, California has the highest percentage of uprooted native-born migrants from other parts of the country; and migrants are less constrained by the more traditional controls of extended family, neighborhood, and the religion they grew up with.

Ethnic Origin

Blacks, Latinos, and English-speaking women from the Caribbean have higher divorce rates than whites at all social class levels; and these rates are increasing in spite of the recent decline in divorce rates generally. The fact that rates are higher among lower-income groups may explain some of this difference, since minorities have lower median incomes than whites. But why does this difference in the divorce rate persist even in the middle social classes? Here, the higher average levels of education among women relative to men in these subcultures and their higher earnings, or more steady incomes, are major factors.

In the African American subculture, wives earn about 90 percent of the income earned by their husbands, on the average; married white women who are employed full time earn an average of 40 percent of family income.[17] This could theoretically make for more power conflicts between husbands and wives in black households, although, as I said before, emotional support from the partner and overall marital satisfaction are now more important than the relative incomes of husbands and wives in predicting divorce.

Another factor that is often cited in explaining the higher divorce rates of middle-class African Americans is the greater tendency of black middle-class women to marry down compared to white women. Black middle-class (and new-upper-class) women have been less likely than white women to pool their economic resources with their husbands (in joint checking and savings accounts and jointly owned property)—although this trend is now becoming increasingly common among white women.[18]

Consequences of Divorce

A couple's resources—psychological, financial, and social (support from family, friends, and community)—strongly affects how divorce is experienced by divorcing couples. Confidence, optimism, and resourcefulness are major psychological strengths. With these resources, individuals can cope more effectively even with the most difficult objective reality. Educational level and job skills are also important personal resources. High levels of both are associated with higher income, less perceived stress, and stronger commitment to and enjoyment of the work situation—which helps when a marital relationship breaks down.[19]

Effects on Children

Cooperation and closeness in the parent–child relationship and willingness to change (adaptability, flexibility) are as crucial in a divorce situation as they are in other stressful family transitions. Studies of the effects of divorce on children have found that the most important factor in determining the adjustment of a child to a divorce is the relationship of the divorcing parents: whether the relationship is friendly and amiable or angry and vengeful.[20]

Reactions of Children

Children may react to a divorce with no obvious and dramatic change in behavior and mood (as most children do); with a drop in functioning at school; with withdrawal and depression (girls, more likely); or with increased aggressive behavior (boys, more often).[21] But aside from cooperative relationships between the divorced parents, a continuing supportive relationship with both parents—especially from fathers, who usually see much less of their children after a divorce—is also crucial. Children who do well after a divorce also have good, continuing, supportive relationships with grandparents, stepparents, sisters and brothers, aunts and uncles, and mentors (classroom teachers especially).[22]

Cooperative Parents

A cooperative relationship on the part of divorced parents seems to be more important for positive long-term effects on children than the specific details of the divorce, custody, or child-support agreements. An example is joint custody: Joint custody works best if *both* parents want it; it does not work well when it is imposed by the court on unwilling parents, who are forced to cooperate. The child often becomes the tale bearer and the pawn in the continuing conflicts of the parents.[23]

Gender and Custody

Currently, more fathers are successfully suing for custody of their children. But they are successful in less than 10 percent of all custody awards, and mainly when the child is older and a male.[24] Usually fathers who win custody have high social status (upper class or upper middle class), and they often win on the grounds that the mother is psychologically disturbed or otherwise unfit for the parenting role.

But sometimes in these situations there is an enormous amount of anger in the relationship between the divorcing parents, and the father may be more interested in revenge against the mother and depriving her of their children than he is in having them for himself. This is true also of biological fathers who kidnap their children. Recently enacted laws in most states now recognize out-of-state custody decrees, and the federal and local governments are doing more to locate and extradite fathers who abduct their children.[25] But, given the values of most judges and jurors, if the mother takes off and leaves her children behind, she has almost no chance of *ever* obtaining custody of her children should she decide to sue for custody at a later time.

What else do we know about the short- or long-term effects of divorce on children from case studies and from national surveys?[26] The purpose of this overview, incidentally, is to increase understanding of, and control over, the possible negative effects of divorce. Also, I need to point out, once again, the inadequacy of U.S. government policies, compared to those of other industrial countries, in supporting divorced parents and their children. This shows up most dramatically in studies of working mothers with dependent children, who do not have the high-quality, reasonable, and dependable day care for their children that is taken for granted by mothers in most industrialized countries today.[27]

Psychological Problems

Children whose parents have divorced are more likely to be in treatment with mental health professionals, and they are more likely to be described as having psychological problems by custodial parents, by teachers, and by the children themselves. Also, children from divorced single-parent families report more psychological problems than children from other types of single-parent households (widowed, separated, never married). Researchers have also found that children who experience the greatest difficulties after a divorce were in serious trouble psychologically before their parents divorced.[28] But I should emphasize, once again, that the great majority of children, on various surveys, seem to make a successful adjustment to their changed circumstances; they continue functioning pretty much as they did before, and they neither seek nor receive professional help.

Gender Differences

Since boys are more likely to behave aggressively and impulsively with antisocial acts (fighting, stealing, disruptive behavior in class) after their parents divorce, they have been characterized as having a more difficult time emotionally than girls. The typical reactions of girls, such as depression and withdrawal, are less measurable and less disruptive to others, but this doesn't mean that they suffer less. At this point, most researchers conclude that boys have a *different* time, typically, but not necessarily a more difficult one.[29]

Other gender differences that have been reported have to do with educational and occupational achievement and sexual behavior. Boys, especially, tend to do less well in school after a divorce. They have lower grades, are more likely to drop out of school, and are less likely to go to college. These differences in educational achievement persist regardless of social class, although they are more extreme among the poor. Girls whose parents have divorced tend to start sexual activity at an earlier age, are more active sexually, and are more likely to enter a living-together relationship when they are older; and again, this is true in all social classes.

Children of divorce tend to grow up faster. They usually have to assume new practical and emotional responsibilities—providing more household help and emotional support to their single custodial parent, for example. And in the higher social classes, they may experience overindulgence after a divorce, especially from an absent parent who feels guilty about not being around more. But in all social classes, custodial mothers report having more difficulty disciplining their children after a divorce (especially their sons) in the absence of fathers.[30]

Age Differences

How do children at different ages react to their parents' divorce? Children under the age of three at the time of the divorce seem to make the best long-term adjustment. Adolescents are hardest hit: They lose a parent at a time of great biological and psychological change, when the need for stability and consistent, dependable emotional support and discipline is very strong.[31]

But children who are adults at the time of parental divorce also experience stress—the stress of having no place to go home to, for example, especially if parents have remarried and the adult child has not been able to establish a good relationship with the new stepparent. As adults, they see both parents less often and give (and receive) less help and emotional support from their parents. Moreover, they are more likely to experience a divorce of their own if they marry; this is true regardless of their social class and ethnic origin. They are also more likely to report being unhappy, having poorer health, and being less satisfied with family, friends, work, and their lives in general.[32]

In some ways, the consequences of divorce for children are more serious than they are for parents. Children are more dependent economically and emotionally, and they have fewer alternatives available to them to compensate for the loss of a parent. Moreover, the decision to divorce (or remarry) is made by the parent, with or without advance notice to the child, and children tend to feel guilty and responsible for their parents' divorce. But, again, as I pointed out earlier, mounting and indisputable evidence from national longitudinal surveys indicates that children in highly conflicted or extremely violent and abusive households do better, in the long run, if their parents do separate or divorce.[33]

Consequences for Parents

The financial consequences of divorce are almost always more serious for women than for men, but men are more likely to lose their children.[34] Furthermore, the psychological consequences of divorce seem to be more distressing for men, especially in the working class. Distress is also greater for the one who does not want the separation if the decision to divorce was not mutual. In the working and lower middle classes, where the greatest number of divorces take place, wives are now more likely than husbands to initiate a divorce, especially if the husband has not been as successful as the wife wanted or expected him to be. In two-career families, the decision to divorce is more likely to be mutual.[35]

Gender Differences

Most mothers do not have the job skills and earning capacity to support themselves and their children comfortably after a divorce. The discrepancy in the standard of living between divorced mothers and fathers usually increases with time and, in the middle class, is a major source of conflict between parents after a divorce. No-fault divorce on the grounds of irreconcilable differences avoids blame and alimony payments. No one is guilty in the case of desertion, infidelity, violence, or psychotic behavior, let alone milder transgressions. No one can ask for support on the grounds of gender, goodness, or need—not the young, unskilled woman with preschool children to take care of, or the older displaced homemaker, divorced after many years of full-time housekeeping, with outdated or no job skills, no medical insurance, and no job pension to rely on in the future.

As sociologist Lenore Weitzman has pointed out, the law falsely assumes that men and women are equal in their ability to earn income, and that divorced mothers can support their children financially as well as fathers can.[36] Then too, the United States government does not provide as much support to divorced mothers (for child care, income maintenance, subsidized housing, and health care) as other advanced industrial countries provide. This often results in the additional upheaval of having to move to less expensive housing and leaving friends, schools, neighbors, and neighborhood behind.

But, in contrast to the past, laws requiring automatic wage withholding for child support and severe penalties for nonsupport are now universal in the United States. More than 80 percent of noncustodial divorced fathers (but not never-married fathers) do pay child support unless they have disappeared or are unemployed or underemployed.[37] On the other hand, these payments usually amount to less than half of a child's expenses.

The stress of a divorce usually reduces the energy available to take care of children, sometimes permanently if psychological problems become severe. And in more extreme cases of parental grief, anger, or need for revenge, children may be used to control or get back at the other partner: "You forgot to sign the support check! Johnnie has a cough. You can't take him out today." Or children may be used to maintain contact with a partner by asking for advice or support: "Johnnie just fell and broke a front tooth. I can't get him to stop crying. Would you please come over as soon as you can?" Some feelings, such as anger, hurt, or humiliation, can last for years, especially if the mother becomes a single parent with inadequate financial resources and little outside support of any kind.

This tends to be true also of older women and men who are divorced after many years of marriage: "Older men and women coming out of long-term marriages are alone and unhappy, facing old age with rising anxiety. They lean on their children, with mixed feelings, for support and companionship, ten and fifteen years after divorce. Opportunities for work, play, sex, and marriage decline rapidly with age, especially for women."[38]

But this is changing now. Most young unmarried middle-class women in the United States today are optimistic about the divorce rate in the future; they are preparing for economic partnership in future relationships. Only a small minority value a successful career more than a happy marriage; and most married men with young children report a greater investment in family relationships than in achievements at work.[39] This is quite a change from the attitude of the 1950s "organization man," who ranked work obligations above everything else in his life.[40]

Since women are now more likely than men to get four-year undergraduate college degrees, the much publicized displaced homemaker will be rare in future generations. Many middle-class women, who married for life in the 1940s and 1950s, did not anticipate the winds of change; now, younger, college-educated, middle-class women are better prepared to support themselves in the future—whatever happens.

Emotional Distress

Evidence from survey research, clinical data, and depth-interview studies indicates that after a divorce, most men experience greater psychological distress (depression, anxiety, physical complaints, obsessions, paranoid ideas) than women—in spite of the well-documented tendency of men to deny feelings of vulnerability, anxiety, and need.[41] Men appear to be more likely than women to apply achievement standards to their marriage and to view a divorce as a personal failure, especially if they did not want the divorce. Furthermore, single middle-aged men (aged 45 to 64) are more than twice as likely as married men of the same age to die in the ten years following a divorce (or the death of a wife). This is usually explained in terms of weaker friendship and extended family ties among men and poorer eating and health-care habits. Divorced single women aged 45 to 64 also have double the death rate of their married counterparts, but this is usually attributed to the stress of being the single head of a low-income household.

For women who leave dangerous or otherwise destructive marriages that are impossible to change, the consequences of divorce can be quite positive; second marriages are happier for those who learned from their previous experience. Women, especially those who leave highly abusive husbands, often show a dramatic increase in competence and self-esteem after divorce.[42] Women are more likely than men to emphasize the positive psychological aspects of their divorce. This includes increased freedom to do what they want to do and relief from domination and abuse. As for their outlook, this depends to a large extent on education and financial security, the presence or absence of children, and age at the time of the divorce. These factors strongly affect values and the realistic alternatives available to women and men after a divorce.

Separation and Recovery

Of loneliness after a divorce we have no good measure. Men usually become more involved in formal, job-related, or community activities; women become more involved with extended family and long-time intimate women friends, especially those who are also divorced.[43] Married friends may be helpful at first, but they usually become less empathic with their divorced friend as time goes on; the differences in life circumstances become too uncomfortable for all involved. Then, too, we tend to shift reference groups when we experience a major change in status; we seek out and are more comfortable with people who are in similar life circumstances.

> It's interesting how we have changed friends since we got married. I was 33 and Steve was 57. My friends were all my age, or younger, before I married and Steve's friends were all in their mid-or-late 50s. We tried keeping both sets of friends. We would invite

them at separate times. But it didn't work out too well. One of my friends once said, "You know, Steve is the same age as my *father*!" Now, I see women friends who are my age, alone—for lunch or shopping, usually. Steve doesn't have much in common with their husbands. As a couple, we see mainly Steve's friends, and four out of five of these old friends, incidentally, are divorced older men who married much younger women.[44]

An unexpected separation is probably the most painful of all separations because of feelings of betrayal or abandonment of the deserted partner. An extramarital relationship by the one who is leaving may help bridge the gap for that partner, but most of these relationships don't last.[45] And recovery from the severe distress following a divorce usually takes anywhere from one to three years—again depending on personal and situational stresses and resources.[46]

Married and Divorced Individuals

How do divorced people compare to those who are married? Generally, those who are divorced report more unhappy life experiences, greater social isolation, more depression, lower self-esteem, less satisfying sex lives, more financial difficulties (mainly women), poorer health, and have higher death rates than individuals who are married.[47] The pattern is similar in all industrial societies that have been surveyed.[48] Also, compared to married fathers, divorced fathers report more difficulty relating to and disciplining their children, and more conflict with their former wives about childrearing techniques and goals.

The question here is: Which is the cause and which is the effect? Are divorced individuals more troubled psychologically to begin with and consequently more prone to divorce? Or does the experience of divorce have serious negative consequences for the psyche? The answer is, both. The evidence from before-and-after longitudinal studies points to predisposing psychological traits among some individuals who divorce, particularly in cases of severe psychological disturbance; but longitudinal studies also indicate that happiness, self-esteem, and functioning decline after a divorce, slightly more so among women.[49]

From all the research and information that we now have about divorce, how would we answer the question of whether divorce is beneficial or destructive, liberating or disastrous for individuals? As usual, the answer is: It depends on the person and the situation. "Divorce benefits some individuals, leads others to experience temporary decrements in well-being, and forces others on a downward cycle from which they might never fully recover."[50]

Remarriage

Remarriage is quite common in the United States today.[51] In the mid-1980s, about 60 percent of all marriages were remarriages for at least one partner. More recently, about 45 percent of all marriages involve a remarriage for at least one of the partners. Given the record high divorce rate from the mid-1960s to the late 1970s and the leveling off of this rate since then, this decline is not surprising. But another important reason for the decline in remarriages is the large increase in living-together relationships as an alternative to marriage, especially among older divorced women and men.[52]

Who, When, and Why?

Who remarries, when do they remarry, and for what reasons do they remarry? About 75 percent of divorced people remarry, which is similar to the rate of remarriage in the 19th century. The big difference now is that people remarry primarily because of divorce rather than death; widows and widowers are less likely to remarry, especially at older ages.[53]

Gender Differences

Most remarriages occur within a period of three years after a divorce becomes final. Men are more likely to remarry, and they remarry sooner than women. Age is an important factor here, especially for women: Most women who divorce before the age of 25 remarry, but less than a third of women who are over 40 at the time of their divorce remarry.[54]

Women with children are less likely to remarry than women without children, but this also has to do with age. In the past, higher-status men, with more income, occupational prestige, and education, were more likely than higher-status women to remarry. But this is changing now. College-educated women are now more likely than high school graduates or dropouts to remarry; apparently, their higher potential earnings are now viewed as a resource rather than a threat.

Ethnic and Regional Differences

The remarriage rate for African Americans is less than half the rate for whites but only slightly lower than that of Latinos. Here, again, since minorities are concentrated at lower median income levels, they are more likely to cohabit after a divorce than to remarry. Also, rates of remarriage in the South and Midwest are higher than in the Northeast, and probably for the same reason: Living-together rates are higher in the Northeast.[55]

Divorce Rates

While many husbands and wives in remarriages do not report less satisfaction in their new marriage (especially if there are no stepchildren present), second marriages do have a higher divorce rate than first marriages—except among African Americans. Remarriages in the African American subculture are more frequent in the middle class than among the poor or the working class; these remarriages are, therefore, more likely to be stable than first marriages. For the rest of the population, the higher divorce rate in second marriages is usually explained in terms of the psychological problems of those who divorce, their values, or greater differences in interests and outlook, especially since remarriages are more likely to involve people from different class, ethnic, and religious backgrounds.[56]

Some people are impossible to live with, and this isn't likely to change in a new marriage. As for values, divorce does not seem as ominous to one who has been through it before; there are fewer "stayers" in second marriages, fewer people who value loyalty above other, more personal needs.[57]

On reasons people give for remarrying, surveys consistently find that romantic love is not as important as other, more practical considerations.[58] The need for a father or (less often) a mother for their children and financial considerations tend to outweigh romantic love as the primary reason for remarrying, especially for divorced women with small children. And, in fact, remarriage does pull many divorced women with children out of stressful financial circumstances. Also, some men are attracted to the nurturing qualities that women with small children are more likely to have.

Stepchildren

The amount of conflict in remarriages seems to be strongly associated with the presence of stepchildren in the home and the age and sex of these stepchildren. On most surveys, adolescent stepchildren report more conflict with stepparents than do adolescents in first-marriage families; and younger stepchildren report more willingness than adolescents to accept the authority of a stepparent.[59] Also, as with other kinds of conflict, low-income families seem to be more vulnerable than middle-class stepfamilies to serious conflicts between stepparents and stepchildren.

Another conclusion about stepchildren that most researchers agree on is that stepchildren do not do as well in school as children in first-marriage families.[60] They have lower grades and higher dropout rates; they are more likely to run away from home (especially girls living with stepfathers) or enter into cohabiting relationships.[61] Compared to children in intact first-marriage families, stepchildren are also more likely to report being depressed and to use drugs and alcohol. But, again, as is true of children in single-parent households, differences in behavior and mood, when compared to those of children in intact first-marriage households, are not overwhelming; and a secure attachment to a loving, supportive, confident parent or caregiver can overcome even the worst of times.[62]

How do remarriages differ from first marriages (Table 10.2)? To begin with, partners in remarriages differ in the extent to which they have been able to resolve feelings of loss, grief, or anger from their previous marriage, especially if they did not want the divorce in their first marriage.

Residual Scars

Traumatic emotional leftovers from conflicts in the previous marriage may result in hostilities and trusting difficulties in the new relationships. This is intensified when young children are present and continued contact with a former partner is underwritten by custody agreements. Then too, a previous marriage usually serves as a

TABLE 10.2 Marriages and Remarriages

COMPARED TO FIRST MARRIAGES, IN REMARRIAGES:

1. Partners carry with them memories of the first marriage, which serves as a basis for comparison—good or bad.
2. Partners may have unresolved feelings of grief, anger, or loss from the previous relationship.
3. Partners are more mature, have different expectations—less romantic usually, but not always more realistic.

IF CHILDREN ARE PRESENT IN THE REMARRIAGE:

1. *Instant Families*—Often created before children and stepparents get to know, like, and accept one another.
2. *Absence of Norms*—Ambiguous or no cultural rules defining rights of and obligations to stepchildren.
3. *Vulnerable Boundaries*—Former husbands and wives and former in-laws continue their relationships with children; independence of the new unit may be difficult to achieve.
4. *Mixed Loyalties and Allegiances*—Who is responsible for what and for whom, given the competing needs of stepchildren, new biological children, and noncustodial biological children?
5. *Unwillling Members*—Stepchildren usually prefer the old life with both parents or with a more available single parent.
6. *Generational Mixups*—Stepchildren may be too close in age for the new stepparent (stepmother usually) to establish authority.

basis for comparison; this may result in feelings of greater or less satisfaction that might not otherwise exist.

> If he had stayed married to Eileen, he'd have a very good combined income, now. She earns over 90 thousand dollars a year! Instead, he has to pay for me to go back to school and he has to help support my parents until I'm finished with my training and can go back to work. This makes me feel a little insecure at times.[63]

People are also more mature when they remarry, and they usually have different (but not necessarily more realistic) expectations than in a first marriage. Previous ways of doing things may not work in the new relationship. New, less traditional roles may be unacceptable to an older man who remarries a much younger woman, for example, although older men in remarriages usually do more household work and are more emotionally involved with children who are born in the new marriage. Also, an older man in a second marriage may have less patience with a much younger wife who is now experiencing things he went through many years ago. Even more differences between a first marriage and a remarriage show up when children from a previous marriage come and go or live in the new household.[64]

Instant Families

In remarriages, where there are children from one or both previous marriages, instant families are created, children and all, usually without adequate time for children and stepparents to get to know, accept, and like one another. There may be generational mixups: Stepmothers, particularly, may find it difficult to relate in an authoritative way to older stepchildren who may be members of the same generation. There may be mixed loyalties and allegiances: Who is responsible for what and for whom, especially if time and money are scarce? What demands should be made of stepchildren, new biological children, and noncustodial biological children?

Stepchildren come with the package, but they may be unwilling participants who prefer the old life to the new; and the new marriage usually ends fantasies, common among children whose parents are divorced, that biological parents may reconcile someday. It also competes with the strong parent–child defensive bond that is often formed after a divorce, mainly between divorced single mothers and their daughters. And children, especially adolescents, who disapprove of a stepparent can ignore, defy, and humiliate their perceived oppressor in unimaginably clever ways.[65]

Boundaries

Boundaries are more vulnerable in remarriages. Privacy and independence are more difficult to achieve when former husbands and wives or grandparents exert their legitimate claim to continue their relationship with the children after a remarriage. Stepparents and stepchildren, not infrequently, are left off the list when children or adults are asked, "Who is a member of your family?" What, then, are the boundaries of these particular families? What if husbands and wives in a new marriage disagree about boundaries (the husband wants to include his nonresident child from a previous marriage in a family vacation and the new wife does not)?

Role Ambiguities

The rules in remarriages are much more ambiguous, especially with respect to discipline, finances, and conflicting marital–parenting obligations. This is a major source of role conflict in remarried families where stepchildren are present. Money, time, space, and affection tend to become problems in second marriages, especially if they are in short supply. If a stepchild is receiving money from a biological father who is not present, should this money be pooled with other income? If a father works full time or more during the week, how much time can he give on weekends to the child or children of a previous marriage without stirring up the resentment of children in his current marriage? If five people from two separate households merge into one household, who should be required to share space?

If the biological mother and the stepmother have different values and standards for disciplining children, whose rules should be enforced when the child is in the noncustodial stepmother's home? How much household help can the stepmother ask from the visiting stepchild? How much time should the visiting stepchild be allowed to watch television? How much independence should the stepchild be granted? (Should the visiting child be left at home alone, or be subject to a curfew, if these rules are different in the child's custodial home?) How much visiting time should biological parents and stepgrandparents be permitted? Should visiting stepgrandchildren as well as biological grandchildren be given gifts, or be taken along on outings, when grandparents come to visit? The possibilities for uncertainty, confusion, and doubt about rules and roles are almost endless.[66]

Satisfaction

Whatever the expectations in a remarriage, they rarely coincide perfectly with reality. Living together before remarrying does not make for greater satisfaction in remarriages, any more than it does in first marriages. Almost all studies agree, furthermore, that marital satisfaction is slightly lower in second marriages and that women tend to be more dissatisfied than men.[67] Since women are usually more involved in caring for children in remarriages (their own and their husband's children), this is not surprising. Regardless of whether or not there are children present, however, satisfaction in a remarriage also depends to some extent on who initiated the divorce in the first marriage.

Remarriage is another example of how little we can anticipate the effects of a major change in status until we are actually in the new situation. No matter how much we see, hear, and read, remarriages almost always involve unexpected consequences and relationship conflicts. A major reason for this is that most remarrying couples do not discuss certain important issues (other than stepchildren and finances) *before* they remarry. Topics such as the continuing relationship with a former husband or wife, doubts about the present relationship, where and how to live in the future, career or work commitments, and the sharing of household work are rarely talked about before a remarriage.

Nevertheless, and regardless of the special challenges in remarriages, strong remarriages are quite similar to strong first marriages: Family members are able to talk freely about how they feel; they are honest and explicit about what they want and expect in the new relationships; they are flexible about making necessary changes; and they cooperate and compromise in resolving disputes so that there are no winners and no losers.[68]

Chapter 11
The Middle and Later Years

Especially for people in the middle and upper social classes, the middle years, beginning anywhere from age 35 to 45 and ending legally at age 65, are the peak time: for living, loving, health, earnings, and accomplishment. By that time, major decisions about work, family, and identity have long been made; family stresses are handled better (for families that have remained intact); and while some transitions may be highly stressful, experience helps and most people manage quite well.[1] Midlife crises are usually less trying than the pressures many young people in industrial societies experience as they try out and decide on a lifetime occupation, look for a partner (also for life, hopefully), and come to terms with their family—if their adolescence was exceptionally stormy.[2]

Midlife Myths

Given the emphasis on youth in the United States (declining but still strong), we have a number of negative stereotypes about middle-aged people and about family relationships in the middle years that are not true. It is important to dispel these myths so that they do not become self-fulfilling prophecies. If people in their middle (and older) years expect crisis, decline, and loss, they may be more likely to experience these misfortunes.

A dramatic example of a stereotype that has become a self-fulfilling prophecy is the belief in the United States that older people experience a decline in intelligence and memory. Psychologists Becca Levy and Ellen Langer tested performance on four memory tasks among young people (ages 15 to 30) and older people (ages 59 to 91) in Beijing, China, and in the United States.[3] Older Chinese men and women outperformed older subjects tested in the United States; their memory scores, furthermore, did not differ significantly from those of the younger Chinese men and women who were tested. They also reported more positive attitudes toward aging than did the older people tested in the United States. The Chinese culture attributes great wisdom to older people, and this attitude strongly affects the self-image and behavior of those who are older (Table 11.1).

Necessary and Unnecessary Losses

Certain losses are common during the middle years, such as the loss of elderly parents and other close relatives and the loss of shorter-lived friends. There is also some loss of physical energy and strength, a slowing of the reflexes and metabolic

TABLE 11.1 Stereotypes About Older People

1. Older people experience a decline in intelligence and creativity. *Fact*: This is not true even of people in their 80s and 90s who are in good health physically and psychologically.
2. They are less productive on their jobs. *Fact*: Their work is slower but steadier. There is less absenteeism among older employees, more job satisfaction, and greater loyalty to employers.
3. Their sexuality disappears. *Fact*: It declines but continues for those who have been sexually active and are in good health.
4. Women experience a decline in well-being after menopause. *Fact*: This is not typical, necessary, or inevitable.
5. Older people are a financial burden to children. *Fact*: Up to age 85 and older, on national surveys, parents help children economically more than the reverse.
6. Older people are cranky, irritable, and demanding. *Fact*: There are no new changes in personality with aging among healthy individuals. Previous personality traits do tend to become more pronounced.
7. Older people fear death and have an insatiable desire to cling to life, regardless of the cost to society and to their families. *Fact*: Their reference groups are friends and family members who have already died, usually at a younger age. They die quietly and with dignity—if they are allowed to.

rate (weight control becomes harder), and a decline in the functioning of the five senses (sight and hearing, especially).[4] There may also be a loss of excellent or even good health. Chronic but not immediately life-threatening diseases such as arthritis and adult-onset diabetes are more frequent, and vulnerability to infections and cancer also increase: The thymus, a gland that plays a key role in the immune system, shrinks by 90 to 95 percent. Most people start shrinking because of bone loss, changes in posture, and compression of the spongy disks that cushion the vertebrae.

Mythical Losses

But the current generation of middle-aged people is in better health generally (except for obesity) than any previous generation, and the baby boom generation will be even healthier as it proceeds through middle and old age. Other presumed losses in middle age are mythical: In the absence of disease, sexual desire, activity, and pleasure continue, and, in fact, improve for many people (postmenopausal women, especially).[5] Tested intelligence does not decline, and actually increases in areas that involve verbal skills (which improve with age). Most people with mental health problems remain stable or get better, given the new and more effective medications now available. Basic personality does not change, but certain tendencies (anger, depression, reclusiveness, ambition, passivity) tend to become more pronounced in the later years; irritable, demanding 80-year-olds were irritable, demanding 40-year-olds. But self-confidence, openness, and flexibility also tend to increase and, in fact, are at a peak during the middle years, especially among college-educated middle-class women and men.[6]

Midlife Crisis

There is no evidence of a *universal* midlife crisis, at home or at work, for middle-aged people in the United States or in other countries that have been surveyed.[7] Whether the midlife transition is viewed as a positive challenge or a disaster depends in part on individual psychological strengths and resources; but social location is quite important here, also. The notion of a midlife crisis was based on research by psychologists on men who were upper middle class and middle-aged in the 1960s and 1970s. It may be that a specific economically deprived generation, which was born or grew up during the Depression in the United States, was particularly prone to experiencing a crisis in midlife. This generation was more likely to have certain highly stressful or unrealistic expectations (of men as ultra-high achievers and of women as contented full-time homemakers for life).[8] But this was not universal even then, and it is certainly not universal now.

In the area of work and achievement, given current economic needs in the United States, most college-educated older workers are at the height of their earnings, job prestige, and job satisfaction. At the moment, they are thriving in a tight job market fueled by lower birth rates in recent decades and fewer available young adults (ages 20 to 34) to take jobs in high-tech and higher-level service sectors (banking, finance, investment, advertising, public relations, marketing, sales, and so on). Large companies (and schools) are now offering bonuses and unprecedented perks to educated young people who will come aboard.

But they are also turning to the over-50 pool of talented workers who, just a few years ago, were considered expendable: They were too expensive to employ, slow, burned out, unmotivated, too set in their ways.[9] Recruiting firms that do executive searches are also pursuing experienced middle-aged workers. And myths about older workers are fading: They are now seen as experienced, hard-working, disciplined, patient, loyal, and well connected (very important to sales and investment firms). Some older workers are intimidated by the newer, more sophisticated advances in computer technology, but most manage quite well to retool and keep up with technological changes on the job.[10]

Extended Family Relationships

Some middle-aged people are parents of still-dependent older children and, at the same time, they are the children of aging parents—with obligations toward both generations. For this reason, they have been described as caught in the middle and dubbed the *sandwich generation* by some researchers.[11]

Caregivers

In the working class, since life transitions take place earlier, middle-aged parents may be caring for grandchildren, their own adolescent or young adult children who are still living at home, and their older parents (who are more likely to need physical care than middle-class parents) at the same time. Caregivers are almost always daughters (much less often sons or daughters-in-law), except among Asian American families, where the first-born son may carry on the cultural tradition of caring for parents in their old age.[12]

Daughters provide care regardless of time pressures, conflicts, feelings, and finances. Sons of dependent older people usually get involved as care managers (hiring help, managing finances) but rarely as hands-on physical care providers (unless they have remained unmarried and have never left home). Among married couples, wives care for husbands who become ill and husbands care for their wives—taking over cooking, cleaning, shopping, and other chores even if they have never done these things in the past.[13] But since most women outlive men and two-thirds of women over 75 are widowed, women who are ill or disabled are more likely to get help from children, nieces, nephews, and friends than from husbands.

Role Reversal

Some women spend more time taking care of aging parents than they spend caring for their own still-dependent children. According to a survey sponsored by the American Association of Retired Persons, the average length of home care for a severely disabled person over 70 is five or six years.[14] Aside from time, energy, and money for expenses not covered by Medicare or Medicaid, there is also the psychological shock of a role reversal. The child becomes the parent symbolically and effectively; the frail, dependent mother or father can no longer be a source of comfort and support.

The Sandwich Generation

Caregiving can be a serious problem for some middle-aged women who work full time, especially if they have a very demanding job. But actually, less than 10 percent of women in their 40s and an even smaller percentage in their 50s and 60s are combining full-time work, active parenting, and caregiving to older parents.[15] The sandwich generation concept doesn't apply to most women. And daughters who are employed usually provide the same amount of physical care as full-time homemaker daughters, but they are more likely to delegate some of this care to paid help (that they pay for out of their salaries). Middle-class women in the most demanding jobs usually earn more and have little difficulty paying for caregiving help.

Attitudes Toward Caregiving

Some researchers have found that adult children who did not have a warm, secure relationship with their parents during childhood are likely to report ambivalent feelings about caring for their parents.[16] But on national surveys, most adults report a strong feeling of obligation to both younger and older dependent generations, regardless of past histories and social circumstance.[17]

Stresses and Rewards

The amount of stress experienced by caregivers seems to depend mainly on three factors: the previous relationship with the mother or father (high or low levels of closeness and communication), the severity of the parent's illness (mental or physical), and the economic resources available to pay for outside help.[18]

After they themselves become mothers, daughters usually feel closer to their mothers than they did during adolescence; they are better able to empathize with their mothers and appreciate the stresses and rewards of bringing up children. But in families characterized by strong conflicts and abuse, a bitter divorce, or extreme differences in generational values and lifestyles, caregiving can be a highly ambivalent experience. And while most older parents in the United States try to maintain their autonomy and independence as much as possible, they may become more controlling toward a caregiver to compensate for their loss of control over their own bodies and their own lives.[19]

On the positive side, caring for an older parent can be a valuable time for reminiscence and life review, for reestablishing old feelings of closeness and attachment, for resolving ancient conflicts, and for answering or getting answers to questions that were never asked:

> My mother was a warm, loving person, but I grew up feeling angry with her most of the time. When I was three years old, and my twin brothers were infants, I came down with scarlet fever. This was before antibiotics, and scarlet fever was a deadly disease at that time. I was shipped off to a glass-enclosed charity ward for six weeks, and my mother never came to visit. When she was dying, I finally asked her *why* she sent me away and *why* she didn't visit me. She explained that she had to send me away because the doctor told her that the twins, who were born prematurely, would die if they caught the disease. As for visiting me, the first time she came, I got very upset and kept screaming and crying and pounding on the glass window to get to her. The nurses told her that she could come again, but she would have to hide behind a pillar so that I wouldn't know she was there. Which is what she did, only I never knew it.[20]

When adult children are geographically distant, they may feel enormously guilty about not being able to do more for a parent who is ill and needs help. Other problems arise when brothers and sisters quarrel about sharing the responsibility of caring for older parents or when sons- and daughters-in-law resent the demands of their dependent in-laws.

Current Trends

In the United States, only about 6 percent of the over-65 population is in a nursing home at any particular time, and this percentage hasn't changed much in decades.[21] What has changed is that nursing home residents are now mainly over 85 rather than younger. Millions of people in their middle years are postponing decline and disability by eating better, taking vitamins, exercising, not smoking, keeping alcohol consumption down, handling stress better, and remaining active socially. The results have been dramatic, since with few exceptions, genes account for less than one-third of the physical or mental problems that come with aging.[22]

Future Prospects

In the future, as the older population continues to expand, and even if the federal government continues to contract, new medical technologies to replace defective genes and destroyed cells will have a remarkable effect on banishing disabilities at all ages. Lower-risk and less expensive treatments will become widely available for the mental and physical problems associated with aging: drugs to unclog fatty deposits in arteries, in contrast to enormously expensive coronary bypass surgery; natural compounds with fewer side effects to replace costly synthetic drugs; and less invasive and disabling laser surgery to treat diseased tissues and speed recovery.[23]

There will also be continuing progress in the diagnosis, prevention, and treatment of Alzheimer's disease and other dementias; in preventing the declines of the immune, endocrine, and neurotransmitter systems, so that there will be less susceptibility to acute and chronic illnesses; and in identifying and treating the factors that cause sleep disorders in older people, so that physical recovery during sleep will improve. The future has never looked better for controlling the normal disabilities of aging. The popular *Life Begins at Forty* books, which go back to the 1920s in the United States, were prophetic but premature; today, their message approaches reality.

Contact Between the Generations

On repeated national surveys, most adult children report that they keep in close touch with their parents, live not too far away, and visit frequently.[24] But independence is strongly valued in the United States; only about 5 percent of older parents and their grown children share a home (almost always the parent's home), and only because of economic necessity, extreme physical disability, or the unwillingness of an adult child ever to leave home. A major factor in the amount of visiting between parents and their adult children is the number of children in the family. Parents with four or more children see less of any one adult child, but spend much more time with their adult children than do parents who have one or two children.[25]

Also, mothers with four or more children are more likely to receive help with housework, transportation, and repairs to their homes and cars; and they are more likely to view a child as available in emergencies and as a source they can turn to for money or advice. But social class and ethnic subcultural values are quite important here—more so, perhaps, than the number of children mothers have. Since the 1950s, few native-born middle-class white women have had four children; less help may mean less need for help from children.

As for financial help, up to age 75 or 80, money flows from parents to adult children and grandchildren, with no expectations for repayment; after that age, cash gifts from parents tend to disappear.[26] Divorced or widowed mothers see their middle-aged children more often.[27] Low-income mothers over 80 are most likely to receive financial and other kinds of help from their adult children. Black, Latino, and Asian American parents of all ages are much more likely to visit, live in two- or three-generation households, live nearby, and help their adult children with money, caregiving, babysitting, housework, cooking, and other services.[28] But second-generation adolescent children of immigrants report more conflict with their parents, since they are torn not only between two cultures, but also between their parents and their peers.[29]

Fictional "brothers" and "sisters" (usually fellow church members) provide help of all kinds in the African American subculture, and "comadres" and "copadres" do the same among Latinos.[30] And relationships between real brothers and sisters are warmer and closer in these subcultures. Asian American elders are the longest-lived of all minorities and, surprisingly, new ultramodern Asian American homes for the aged are popping up in large cities on both coasts (and in urban areas of mainland China), with huge waiting lists for potential occupants. In the Asian American subculture, communal living is highly valued, and living with peers is becoming preferable to the obligatory and sometimes ambivalent care and companionship of first-born sons and their families. An example is older Korean Americans who do not follow their adult sons and their grandchildren from areas of initial settlement in the city out to the suburbs; they prefer staying in place and living in senior residences with their peers.[31]

Contact Between Brothers and Sisters

Sibling relationships last longer than any other kind of human relationship; parents die and friends come and go, but siblings are for life, or for as long as they live. About eight out of ten adults in the United States have living sisters or brothers; only a small (but growing) number of adults are only children (about 10 percent of all children).[32] The study of relationships between sisters and brothers becomes more important in advanced industrial societies because in the absence of children, siblings, nieces, and nephews become an important source of support for many middle-aged and older people. A question here is: Why do some brothers and sisters grow up to be friends, while others don't? Most brothers and sisters love, help, and are loyal to one another; and yet sibling violence is the most frequent form of family violence (though less destructive, usually, than violence between husbands and wive and rarely fatal).[33]

Sibling rivalry and hostility in adulthood are open and obvious among very few brothers and sisters (less than 10 percent) and seem to be strongly related to the feeling of having been unfairly treated by parents during childhood.[34] A younger child, for example, may have been given more privileges and freedom by parents who were more experienced and relaxed than they were with their first-born child. Or parents may have given more praise, support, and encouragement to a brother or sister who was physically, emotionally, or intellectually less strong (and more needy) or more gifted and talented. Prolonged, irrational, bitter squabbling over an inheritance is usually a symptom of surviving feelings of parental unfairness and hostility toward a more favored brother or sister. But most brothers and sisters are close and cooperative as they live out their lives, especially if their values and achievements do not turn out to be insurmountably different and incompatible.

Adult contact and closeness are strongest between sisters, between men and their sisters (rather than between brothers), and between siblings who are closely spaced in age. (Twins are almost always close, even if sometimes competitive.) Contact with brothers and sisters is also more frequent and more important for those who never married, are divorced or widowed, or are married but have no children. Contact declines during the middle years, when siblings are more heavily involved with their own nuclear family responsibilities. It picks up again in old age: Leisure time increases (especially after retirement); chronic and acute illnesses also increase, as does awareness of mortality; and many alternative relationships with friends and work associates have been severed by death or retirement. Since women are more likely to be responsible for maintaining family ties (calling, sending cards, setting up family get-togethers), contact with the wife's relatives is usually more frequent.[35]

Feeling emotionally close to a brother or sister is more important than a feeling of obligation or living nearby in determining the amount of voluntary contact between brothers and sisters (friendly visiting on nonholiday and nonceremonial occasions, letters, phone calls, Internet chatting, and e-mail messages). Feelings of closeness are cemented by memories of warm and loving relationships with parents (one or both), shared childhood experiences (good and bad), built-up feelings of trust and empathy over the years, and enjoyment in being together.[36]

The Later Years

How do we regard our oldest people and our oldest families, and how do these attitudes compare with those of other societies, historically and today?

The Social Status of Older People

The overall prestige of the oldest people in human societies has varied in major societies according to their personal qualities, their wealth and property (in horticultural, agricultural, and industrial societies), and their usefulness to the society.[37] Generally, their social status has been lower in the simplest societies if living conditions are extremely harsh, especially if they became frail or disabled. Assisted suicide for incapacitated or terminally ill people is common in hunting and gathering societies; the incapacitated are expected to depart voluntarily from a world they can no longer keep up with comfortably and with dignity. The prestige of the oldest citizens is also lower in most industrial societies; it is highest in horticultural and agricultural societies, especially if older people maintain control over their property.

On the other hand, the knowledge and wisdom of older people are highly valued in nonliterate societies.[38] Their accumulated lifelong memories and experiences are useful in societies that don't change much and don't have a written language: The old are essential as teachers who pass on oral traditions and folklore to younger generations.

The prestige of the oldest citizens is highest in economically stratified (with rich and poor families) horticultural and agricultural societies that practice religions involving ancestor worship. Cultural values such as authoritarianism and familism that prescribe respect for authority and for older people are strongest in East Asian societies such as China and Japan. But these values have been declining among younger generations in these societies.[39]

The prestige of the oldest people is usually low in postindustrial societies; their labor isn't needed, and their skills are likely to be out of date in constantly changing economies. Nevertheless, historically and throughout the world today, individ-

TABLE 11.2   Factors Affecting the Social Status of Older People

SOCIOCULTURAL PATTERN: Social status is generally lower in hunting and gathering societies characterized by harsh living conditions and in postindustrial societies. It is highest in horticultural and agricultural societies. The factors that affect the social status of older people in particular societies are:

1. Climatic conditions and economic resources of the society; harsh conditions lower the status of older people.
2. Importance of experience and wisdom—usefulness of advice.
3. Importance of their functions—economic, familial, educational, cultural (passing on of oral traditions and folklore in nonliterate societies).
4. Personal resources such as control over property, knowledge, skills, physical health, and psychological strength.
5. Survival of prestige from previous statuses.
6. Cultural values—traditional values emphasizing familism, authoritarianism, and religiosity (ancestor worship, especially) are associated with higher status.

ual differences in wealth, intelligence, psychological strength, and physical and mental health have offset the effects of changes in the culture and in economic and political conditions in the society. Extreme disability, however, spells a loss in social status for individuals in all societies. Table 11.2 summarizes the factors affecting the social status of older people.

Older Families

In the later years of marriage, when childrearing is over and the last child has left home, most men and women face four major challenges: They must adapt to normal biological aging, adjust to retirement, recover from the loss of a husband, wife, or live-in partner, and come to terms with their own ultimate death.[40] Also, most parents are grandparents (a status that is also being delayed, but that more people in minority and working-class households still enter when they are in their 40s and 50s). I'll start with a brief description of the biological changes that people in their 60s, 70s, and 80s face typically, because these underlie other changes in individual and family realities during this period. For individuals, self-image and outlook change; for families, caregiving and mortality begin to loom large.

Normal Biological Aging

When people enter their 60s, high-frequency hearing usually deteriorates further, especially for men. With hearing aids, people will hear conversations, but the meaning of what is being said may be unclear, since consonants, which anchor the meaning of speech, are high-frequency sounds. The pancreas, which processes sugar, works less efficiently, the blood sugar level rises, and adult-onset diabetes flourishes; also, with continued wear and tear on the cartilage that cushions joints, getting out of bed in the morning may become a challenge, as knees, hips, and spine become stiff when not in use; and running, jumping, and dancing become nostalgic memories.

In the 70s, blood pressure is about 25 percent higher than in the 20s; short-term memory (for the names of people, places, things, and recent insignificant events) declines; more than half of all men have symptoms of coronary artery disease; and sweat glands shrink or stop working, which increases vulnerability to heat stroke (but saves money on deodorants). In the 80s and beyond, women are more likely to fall and fracture their hips (having lost considerable bone mass in their hips and thighs); about half of all men and women over 85 have symptoms of Alzheimer's disease or stroke-induced dementias; the heartbeat slows down; lung capacity declines and breathing becomes more labored, even for nonsmokers.[41] This all sounds pretty grim, but identifying with similarly situated peers, optimism, a sense of humor, and activities that maintain health or at least stave off decline can soften the never-ending blows.

Grandparents

Most parents report a brief honeymoon effect after their last child has left home. Marital happiness increases, but overall life satisfaction and feelings of well-being are highest when parents also have frequent contact with one or more of their departed adult children. Older parents have a high stake in maintaining these relationships, higher perhaps than their children, whose primary loyalties are transferred to their own new families. But one way to maintain relationships with grown children is through grandchildren. Less than 10 percent of grandparents have grandchildren living with them or provide day care for them. But more than three-quarters of grandparents in the United States live within one hour's drive of at least one grandchild, and about 40 percent see their grandchildren weekly or speak to them on the telephone weekly.[42]

How do these relationships differ from the past? In a national study of grandparents conducted some years ago, sociologists Andrew Cherlin and Frank Furstenberg profiled the "new American grandparent." They found that relationships between grandparents and their grandchildren were now more likely to be based on love, friendship, and companionship rather than the authoritarian control (underwritten by economic interdependence) that was (and still is) widespread in agricultural societies.[43]

They identified three kinds of relationships between grandparents and their grandchildren: remote, companionate, and involved. Grandparents whose relationship was remote rarely saw their grandchildren except at Thanksgiving, at Christmas, or on other ceremonial occasions such as christenings, landmark birthdays, and school graduations. This kind of relationship was most often a result of geographic separation: Their adult children had moved to another part of the country, usually in pursuit of a job offer. Disapproval of or a poor relationship with daughters-in-law were other, less frequent reasons for emotional distance.

But most grandparents had a relaxed, friendly, loving relationship with grandchildren, seeing them regularly (but not daily) and enjoying their company. They were available to help in emergencies, but did not make or enforce disciplinary rules for their grandchildren. The biggest challenge here, as anthropologist Margaret Mead noted long ago, was in knowing when and how "not to interfere, not to spoil, not to insist, not to intrude."[44] Grandparents (usually minority and low-income grandmothers) who were actively involved in raising their grandchildren disciplined them and assumed primary responsibility for their behavior and their physical, emotional, and intellectual development. This usually happened in situations where the mother was an unmarried adolescent, was divorced or separated from the children's father, worked full time outside of the home, or was unavailable because of physical or mental illness. The biggest problems here were overinvolvement and physical, emotional, and financial exhaustion.

For most men and women today, being a grandparent is uniquely gratifying: Grandchildren are their ode to immortality. They are a source of love that is usually less ambivalent than in parent–child relationships; the relationship involves less guilt since the grandparent, unlike the parent, is not responsible for the child's development and behavior. Moreover, for most grandparents the relationship is not a daily obligation, but a pleasurable (and temporary) diversion from other responsibilities. Grandparents can take off or call the parent if a child becomes unmanageable; parents don't usually have these options. The central value in the grandparent–grandchild relationship is friendship; most grandparents, especially in the more educated middle social classes, have no desire or interest in being substitute parents.[45]

Social Location

Aside from geographic distance, the age and personality of grandparents, their ethnic origin, and their social class are important in affecting relationships with grandchildren. Physically or emotionally fragile older grandparents may try to maintain a degree of emotional reserve from their grandchildren to protect themselves from conflicts and demands they can't deal with. Younger grandparents are usually more playful (they are more agile) and more openly affectionate and companionate. But relationships depend largely on their social circumstances and their past relationship with their own grandparents (especially in rural areas) and their own children.[46] As sociologist Lillian E. Troll describes it: "Grandparenting is a contingent process. This means that grandparenthood can be either a gift or a curse, a reward or punishment for what one has done or been earlier."[47] True, but social location is an underlying factor that is also crucial.

In the middle and upper classes, grandparents help out with smaller expenses when their grandchildren are small (clothing, dental bills, sports equipment, books, video games) and larger expenses when grandchildren are grown (college tuition, cars, weddings, down payments on houses).[48] Newer immigrants from industrializing countries are more likely to be involved in actively taking care of grandchildren; they value living in the same neighborhood and the same household (in an emergency) more than native-born blacks and whites.[49] Young African American grandmothers (low-income and in their late 20s or 30s) are very likely to be caught in the middle, actively caring for younger and older generations; and they are usually less satisfied with the grandparenting role than on-time (and higher-income) African American grandmothers in their 40s and 50s.[50]

Studies so far of great-grandparents point to their importance as symbols of personal and family renewal and continuity. The role is emotionally important to them, usually, as it is to grandparents; but their relationships with great-grandchildren tend to be more remote. There are two generations in between, and divorce, remarriage, ethnic intermarriage, and cohabitation among younger generations may strain relationships. Contact is usually limited to holidays and other ceremonial occasions.[51]

Retirement

Retirement is a voluntary or involuntary withdrawal from paid employment. Retirement is common in advanced industrial societies. In labor-intensive agricultural societies, most people worked until they died; they had no choice.

Demographics

In the United States today, eight out of ten men over age 65 are retired. A majority (especially those in routine, boring, low-level jobs) take early retirement (at age 62 and even earlier) and look forward to retirement; professionals don't usually retire unless they are ill and have no choice. "Those who have unfinished agendas at work, have high job satisfaction, perceive retirement as financially unfeasible, and retain their health are least likely to anticipate retirement favorably."[52] Those who continue working past the age of 65 are mainly in high-prestige occupations, where they have a great deal of authority and autonomy (self-employed doctors and lawyers, for example), but they usually cut down on the number of hours they work.

Satisfaction with Retirement

Most retired people report satisfaction with their lives if their retirement was voluntary; unexpected (forced) retirement is associated with increased death rates after two or three years. But those who die shortly after retirement were usually forced to retire because they were in poor health. If retirement is voluntary, it does not usually result in a loss of identity, low self-esteem, or an earlier death.

Good health, adequate income, hobbies, and frequent contact with relatives and friends are most important in determining psychological well-being and overall life satisfaction during this time of life. Ethnic minorities, especially if they are poor, report lower satisfaction in retirement; they may have frequent contact with relatives, but they are less likely than whites to be in good health, to have adequate pensions or other sources of income, and to have hobbies or other absorbing interests to replace work routines.[53]

Husbands and Wives in Retirement

Husbands and wives claim to have greater satisfaction when both are retired than when wives continue to be employed after their (older) husbands have retired. Husbands may help out more in the home after they retire. But if the wife continues to work outside of the home, most arguments center on the wife's unavailability to do things together or the husband's unwillingness to take over more errands and do more work in the home. These arguments are less heated, however, among couples who are strongly attached to the marriage and to one another; and those who have spent decades together do tend to show greater tolerance and affection toward one another than many younger couples.[54]

The Future of Retirement

The baby boomers are a huge bulge moving up the age pyramid. A major political issue now is: Who will support the baby boomers when they retire? Throughout the Western world, birth rates are declining, life expectancy is increasing, and the *dependency ratio*—the number of older people (and children) who are not employed and who are supported, in part, by the payments of younger workers into pensions and into the Social Security systems—is also climbing. A political issue, by definition, means differences of opinion, and on this issue, too, attitudes are split: Pessimists are predicting the bankruptcy of pension plans and the Social Security system; optimists point to a number of trends that are likely to ease the situation.

Those who are confident about a solution to the problems of an aging population point to the fact that those who are over 65 are healthier than ever; fewer people are disabled, unable to work, and in need of care. Also, they point out that attitudes toward retirement seem to be changing. In the past, retirement was viewed as an earthly paradise inhabited by people in their "golden years."

But disenchantment about retirement appears to be growing, aided probably by negative images of retirees who have been depicted as "greedy geezers" or "crocks" in the popular culture.[55] An additional incentive to the postponement of retirement is the increased willingness of employers to hire older workers, especially in service jobs. Also, in 1999, Social Security regulations were changed so that retired workers aged 65 to 69 did not have to return part of their earnings to the federal government (in addition to paying income tax). Given these changes and others, it is not surprising that according to a 1998 national survey conducted by the American Association of Retired Persons, 80 percent of baby boomers, born between 1946 and 1964, plan to continue working past the age of 65.[56]

Widows and Widowers

The last stage in the family life history of a specific generation (among couples who have remained together) is marked by the death of both partners. As family members approach the end of their lives, circumstances change and, in some ways, become more like those of the historical past; but in other ways, they are far, far different. As in the past, more people are dying at home now rather than in hospitals and nursing homes, but they are dying at much older ages.

In advanced industrial societies most of the time, death is relegated to old age; it is not a daily part of living, highly visible and undeniable, affecting young and old without prejudice, as in the past. But death is becoming more visible once again now—in the media, if not at first hand. Another difference is that dying is much slower now than it was in the past (medical advances keep people alive longer); and for increasing numbers of those who are terminally ill, it is too slow. Hospices for the terminally ill are multiplying throughout the country, as are signed requests by patients that no "heroic" measures be used to keep them alive if they are near death. Husbands, wives, and live-in partners who are caring for their dying mates now spend more hours and more years at this task than ever before in history; and this care is unlikely to be delegated to others, since most caregivers can't afford to hire outside help, and extended family members are not as available to help as they once were.[57]

Women tend to outlive men in almost all contemporary societies, but the life-expectancy gap between women and men is slowly closing; childbed fever no longer dispatches women who give birth, but cancer and heart disease are becoming more egalitarian in killing women as well as men. In the United States in the 1970s, widows outnumbered widowers by a ratio of almost five to one; today the ratio is almost four to one. This is happening not only because older men are more likely to remarry and are no longer counted as widowers, but also because differences in the higher death rates of men are being reduced by the new life-preserving medical technologies now available.

For now, though, among those who are over 85 (the fastest-growing age category in the United States today), about half of all men have wives to take care of them if they become seriously ill or disabled; but only one in five women at this age are married and have husbands to rely on if they need physical care. Moreover, in contrast to divorce, grieving usually lasts longer in the case of death; there is a tendency to idealize the dead partner. Divorced husbands and wives, if they maintain contact with their former partners through their children, can more easily correct for distorted memories and idealization than can widows and widowers, who take longer to recover.[58]

Dependency Differences

Older widowers almost always marry younger women, especially if they have assets other than youth to offer; those who don't remarry tend to be more isolated socially than older widows.[59] In agricultural and industrializing societies (especially in Asia and the Middle East), the extended family has been more available, usually, to provide daily contact, companionship, and physical care, but this is changing.[60] And it is changing more rapidly in Europe, even in countries such as Italy, where the traditional value of familism has been strong.[61] In the United States, as I pointed out earlier, older immigrant women and low-income minority women continue to experience high levels of social, economic, and physical support from their families, although this too is changing.[62]

In the past, having many children guaranteed economic support and physical care in old age. But this can no longer be taken for granted, especially as young people in rural areas migrate to the cities and middle-class children in urban areas migrate to other parts of the country. Governments in agricultural or industrializing countries do not usually assume responsibility for the care of their older citizens; relatively few people in these societies receive pensions from government or private industry. But while older widowers in most societies are less likely than widows to have financial problems, they are more likely to die or develop serious illnesses after becoming widowed. The death rate within six months after being widowed is much higher for widowers than for other men of the same age who are not widowed; and most die from heart disease, the "broken heart syndrome." This is true also in other industrial societies that have been surveyed.[63]

The catchall phrase for the sudden, mysterious, unsuspicious deaths of many older men shortly after their wives die is *natural causes*. But advances in medical science and technology (bypass and laser surgery, pacemakers, transplants, magnetic force and ultrasound diagnosis, more effective drugs for high blood pressure, heart attacks, and strokes) and healthier trends in eating, exercise, and smoking habits will continue to lower the death rate from heart disease in the 21st century. Up to now, men aged 55 to 74 have been much more likely than women to die of heart disease; but women are catching up.[64]

Historically, among mortals, a new scourge usually comes along to partially undo medical advances and reprieves. Currently, scientists are anticipating that cancer will replace heart disease as the leading cause of death among older men; and if the cancer rate among men does not increase dramatically as heart disease declines, the ratio of older men to women should be more balanced in the future. Also, if infectious diseases make a comeback as newer and more resistant strains of bacteria and viruses evolve, death will no longer favor men over women, since germs are equal-opportunity scourges.

Other equalizing factors will also diminish the differences in the fate and fortune of older men and women: More older women will be better educated than ever before; more will be economically independent and better off financially; more will be involved in outside nonfamily activities and interests that provide identity and promote friendships; and more will be able to buy caregiving services, regardless of the availability of relatives and government support.

Social Location and Widowhood

Many currently widowed women and men feel stressed about the vagueness and ambiguities of their new status. Some have identity problems, especially traditional women, who may continue to use their husband's name on credit cards and in the telephone directory for years after his death. Traditional men are more likely to miss their only confidant and best friend; friends do not compensate for the loss of a wife. Older widows tend to regard their status as normal; they can easily find other widowed friends for companionship, unlike young widows, who are off time. Middle-class widows usually have a more secure income, higher levels of education, better occupational and money-managing skills, more friends and associates, and a less traditional conception of gender roles. They tend to adapt to widowhood better than working-class widows, who may have more support during bereavement but are more likely to report loneliness, financial pressures, and isolation—in the long run.[65]

Having looked at how family realities in the United States change as family members age, come and go, live and love, prosper or decline, we turn now, in Chapter 12, to the future of families—in the United States and everywhere else. As with other predictions about humans and their prospects, those who try to predict family life in the future divide along two lines: optimists or pessimists. Optimists see a rose garden; pessimists see a wasteland. And reality is somewhere in between.

Chapter 12
Yesterday, Today, and Tomorrow

If we take the long view of human history, going back to the earliest known human societies, what have been the major effects on family realities as advances in scientific knowledge and technological skills have provided more control over human environments and more understanding of human nature? What are some of the lessons we can draw from the social sciences about curbing human destructiveness and greed, preventing war, and promoting the greatest good for the greatest number of families in all societies everywhere?

To begin with, many destructive social conditions that we might think are inevitable in human social life—organized group warfare, intense greed, extreme economic inequality, and exorbitant differences in the power of political and religious leaders and followers, employers and employees, women and men, parents and children, teachers and students—are a matter of time and place; they are socially located. These conditions were unknown in the earliest known human settlements and for 99 percent of human history until the invention of planting. The ability to produce more goods than people needed or could use created rich and poor families and societies.

Over time, developments in science and technology provided greatly increased economic resources in human societies, and greed, competition, and conflict over these resources flourished—not because these economic goods were scarce, but because they were very unequally distributed.

Also over the centuries, communication and connections within and between societies increased and less advantaged people, especially the educated and more connected urban middle classes, became more aware and less accepting of their social circumstances. Mainly, it is the more educated and more successful people (but not those at the top in prestige, power, and wealth) who have led the successful reform and revolutionary movements of human history, backed up by the more deprived elements of the population.

Awareness of other people's situations in other societies increased as technological advances provided easier, faster, and cheaper means of transportation, and migration and immigration to other countries intensified. At the same time, advances in electronics led to improvements in communications (movies, television, satellites), and a feeling of relative deprivation increased, as did rising expectations, among the masses of people.

Mass education, especially higher education, was (and is) the foundation of this heightened awareness, aided and abetted by information and motivating ideas and images in books, newspapers, magazines, movies, and the Internet. Long ago, sociologists demonstrated that as much as 50 years after graduating from college (and beyond, if not arrested by the development of Alzheimer's disease or other mentally debilitating diseases of old age), those who had graduated from college were far more informed about world events and more critical of attempts at propaganda by government leaders than were people of the same age who had never gone to college. The effects of higher education are permanent and enduring.

Fatalism and authoritarianism decline in human societies as the need for higher levels of formal education to function in more complex economies becomes essential. The effects of higher education, the need to be well informed, and the ability to think critically become more widespread as higher education spreads to more and more segments of the population. Education is the crucial resource in promoting equality between the powerful and the powerless, the haves and the have-nots, and the accepted and the rejected, in all areas of life.

How do all of these trends affect family realities? The current generation of college-educated people in the United States are healthier, more secure financially, more likely to be egalitarian in their partner relationships, and more democratic in disciplining their children than poorer, less educated parents. They are taking longer to marry or move in together, to have children, and to find meaning and direction in their lives. The older they are, the less likely they are to make impulsive, irrational choices and to experience unnecessary disappointments and losses. They are more committed to their partners and their children than their parents were, and they are more likely to fight rather than flee when they and their families are in trouble.

Children who grow up in loving, supportive, nonpunitive environments are less likely to be prejudiced and intolerant of those who are different physically and culturally. They are not destructive to themselves and to others, and they are less tolerant of destructiveness in others—by anyone, anywhere. They grow up with the ability to identify with, empathize with, and show compassion for other people. If they succeed in rising above impoverished and unfortunate circumstances, they do not look back in anger at those who were left behind; they do what they can to bring others up also. Those who did not find acceptance by the most important people in their lives as they were growing up lack this empathy; they can only look to themselves; they can only work to promote their own increased gain and glory—in areas of life outside of their families.

Warmer, more accepting, egalitarian qualities in partner and parent–child relationships are becoming the norm among educated people in advanced industrial countries in all parts of the world; and this is a harbinger of things to come in developing nations. Greed and inequality are poor substitutes for love and compassion. Change will take longer in rigidly authoritarian, patriarchal, militaristic countries; but even there, things are moving: Cruel, corrupt oligarchies are falling from grace, speeded on their way by more educated, more aware, less fatalistic citizens.

Cultural values help or hinder social change, but scientific and technological developments and new economic imperatives have a way of undermining even the most cherished and sacred traditional values in human societies. As the world comes closer and becomes less mysterious, the need to change this world seems less daunting; and the essential humanity of all people in all countries, everywhere, becomes clearer.

Notes

Chapter 1 Sociological Reality

1. German sociologist Max Weber described this method at the beginning of the 20th century and used it to understand historical changes in major aspects of human social life—economics, politics, and religion especially. See his pathbreaking work *The Methodology of the Social Sciences* (Glencoe, IL: Free Press, 1949 [1903]), translated and edited by Edward A. Shils and Henry A. Fitch.

2. For some examples of experimental projects carried out in urban neighborhoods during the 1990s, see Linda M. Burton and Robin I. Jarrett, "In the Mix, Yet on the Margins: The Place of Families in Urban Neighborhood and Child Development Research." *Journal of Marriage and the Family*, 2000, Vol. 62, pp. 1114–1145.

3. Emile Durkheim, the first professor of sociology in France, after sociology became a separate field of study at the end of the 19th century, used the comparative cross-cultural research method in his classic studies of religion, economic life, education, and suicide rates. See his *The Rules of the Sociological Method*, 8th ed. (Chicago: University of Chicago Press, 1938 [1895]), translated by George E. G. Catlin.

4. See Margaret Mead's classic description of rejecting mothering among the Mundugumoor tribe of New Guinea in *Sex and Temperament in Three Primitive Societies* (New York: William Morrow, 1935).

5. On the pervasiveness of child abuse in agricultural societies, see Lloyd de Mause, *The History of Childhood* (New York: Psychohistory Press, 1974). For a cross-cultural review of social conditions associated with domestic violence in 90 small-scale societies located in all major regions of the world, see David Levinson, *Family Violence in Cross-Cultural Perspective* (Newbury Park, CA: Sage, 1989).

6. For a recent analysis by sociologists who believe biological factors should be given more weight than learning and experience in determining human behavior, see Joseph Lopreato and Timothy Crippen, *Crisis in Sociology: The Need for Darwin* (New Brunswick, NJ: Transaction Publishers, 1999). For a review of how recent scientific and technological breakthroughs have promoted new research and renewed controversy on this topic, see Alan Booth, Karen Carver, and Douglas A. Granger, "Biosocial Perspectives on the Family." *Journal of Marriage and the Family*, 2000, Vol. 62, pp. 1018–1034. For a clear, highly readable account of the implications of recent biogenetic discoveries for the future well-being of individuals and families, see Matt Ridley, *Genome* (New York: HarperCollins, 2000).

7. Stephanie Coontz, *The Way We Never Were: American Families and the Nostalgia Trap* (New York: Basic Books, 1992), pp. 183–185.

8. See Gerhard Lenski, *Power and Privilege* (New York: McGraw-Hill, 1966), for an early review of anthropological research on this topic; also Betty Yorburg, *Sexual Identity: Sex Roles and Social Change* (New York: Wiley, 1974); and, more recently, Rae Lesser

Blumberg, ed., *Gender, Family, and the Economy* (Newbury Park, CA: Sage, 1991). A classic source on the economic factor as this affects the status of women in human societies (though based on much less adequate anthropological evidence than is now available) is Friedrich Engels, *The Origin of the Family, Private Property, and the State* (New York: International Universities Press, 1942 [1884]).

9. See Shahin Gerami, *Women and Fundamentalism: Islam and Christianity* (New York: Garland, 1996).

10. For examples of how social science research and projections of future public needs can provide a foundation for public policy, see Mary Jo Bane and David T. Ellwood, *Welfare Realities: From Rhetoric to Reform* (Cambridge, MA: Harvard University Press, 1994); and Theda Skocpol, *Social Policy in the United States: Future Possibilities in Historical Perspective* (Princeton, NJ: Princeton University Press, 1995).

11. For an original and still valid definition of culture, see Edward B. Tylor, *Primitive Culture* (London: Murray, 1871), p. 1.

12. A good source on research methods in the social sciences is Earl Babbie's *The Practice of Social Research*, 8th ed. (Belmont, CA: Wadsworth, 1998).

13. A good interdisciplinary source on this topic, written by two sociologists, is Patrick Nolan and Gerhard Lenski's *Human Societies*, 8th ed. (New York: McGraw-Hill, 1999).

14. This is an area where research is booming, especially in recent years, as immigration to the United States from non-European countries has accelerated and become a political issue. A monumental source, especially on the history of immigration, is Stephan Thernstrom, ed., *Harvard Encyclopedia of American Ethnic Groups* (Cambridge, MA: Belknap Press/Harvard, 1980). For the current picture, with up-to-date statistics on the huge growth in non-European immigration to the United States since 1965, see Philip Martin and Elizabeth Midgley, "Immigration to the United States." *Population Bulletin*, 1999, Vol. 54, pp. 1–41.

15. A brief, well-written, and informative account of changes in the experiences of different waves of immigrants to the New World since the 16th century is Roger Daniels, *Coming to America* (New York: HarperCollins, 1990).

16. Two pathbreaking research studies, the first by a sociologist and the second by a demographer, on how membership in a specific generation affects opportunities, values, and behavior, are Glenn H. Elder, Jr., *Children of the Great Depression* (Chicago: University of Chicago Press, 1974) and Richard A. Esterlin, *Birth and Fortune* (Thousand Oaks, CA: Sage, 1987).

17. This approach to doing research on families began in the 1930s. See Charles P. Loomis and Horace H. Hamilton, "Family Life Cycle Analysis." *Social Forces*, 1936, Vol. 15, pp. 225–231. Other landmark publications describing or applying this model are Paul C. Glick, "The Family Cycle." *American Sociological Review*, 1947, Vol. 12, pp. 164–174; Evelyn Mills Duvall, *Family Development* (Philadelphia: Lippincott, 1957); Evelyn Mills Duvall, "Family Development's First Forty Years." *Family Relations*, 1988, Vol. 37, pp. 127–139; and David M. Klein and Joan Aldous, eds., *Social Stress and Family Development* (New York: Guilford Press, 1988).

18. David Olson, Hamilton I. McCubbin, and Associates, *Families: What Makes Them Work*, 2d ed. (Newbury Park, CA: Sage, 1989), p. 123; see also Thomas N. Bradbury, Frank D. Fincham, and Steven R. H. Beach, "Research on the Nature and Determinants of Marital Satisfaction: A Decade in Review." *Journal of Marriage and the Family*, 2000, Vol. 62, pp. 964–980.

19. For a problem-oriented source on becoming a parent and its consequences in the United States today, see Terry Arendell, ed., *Contemporary Parenting: Challenges and Issues*

(Thousand Oaks, CA: Sage, 1997). For reviews of recent trends in the sharing of house-keeping chores by husbands and wives, see Linda W. Waite, "The Family as a Social Organization: Key Ideas for the Twenty-First Century." *Contemporary Sociology*, 2000, Vol. 29, pp. 463–469; and Scott Coltrane, "Research on Household Labor: Modeling and Measuring the Social Embeddedness of Routine Family Work." *Journal of Marriage and the Family*, 2000. Vol. 62, pp. 1208–1233.

20. Monica Morris, *Last Chance Children: Growing Up with Older Parents* (New York: Columbia University Press, 1988). On the effects on fathers of being an older first-time parent, see D. Terry Heath, "The Impact of Delayed Fatherhood on the Father-Child Relationship." *Journal of Genetic Psychology*, 1994, Vol. 155, pp. 511–530.

21. Joan Aldous and Rodney F. Ganey, "Family Life and the Pursuit of Happiness." *Journal of Family Issues*, 1999, Vol. 20, pp. 155–180. On national differences in reported feelings of well-being, see Steven Stack and J. Ross Eshleman, "Marital Status and Happiness: A 17 Nation Study." *Journal of Marriage and the Family*, 1998, Vol. 60, pp. 527–536.

22. On the increase in the number of life cycle stages in industrial societies, see Bernice L. Neugarten, "Age Groups in American Society and the Rise of the Young-Old." *Annals of the American Academy of Political and Social Science*, 1974, Vol. 415, pp. 187–198. On the decline in conformity to age norms, see Bernice L. Neugarten and Dale A. Neugarten, "The Changing Meanings of Age." *Psychology Today*, May 1987, pp. 29–33; and on the "stretching" or lengthening of age categories with increased life expectancy, see Theodore Roszak, *America the Wise: The Longevity Revolution and the True Wealth of Nations* (Boston: Houghton Mifflin, 1998).

23. Hiromi Ono, "Husbands' and Wives' Resources and Marital Dissolution," *Journal of Marriage and the Family*, 1998, Vol. 60, pp. 674–689.

24. For brief narrative descriptions of major types of human societies, see V. Gordon Childe, *Man Makes Himself* (New York: Mentor, 1951) and *What Happened in History*, rev. ed. (Baltimore: Penguin, 1964). For more recent anthropological accounts, also written in a clear, accessible style, see Marvin Harris, *Cannibals and Kings* (New York: Random House, 1977) and *Our Kind: Who We Are, Where We Came From, Where We Are Going* (New York: Harper and Row, 1989).

25. Among the first sociologists to describe the distinguishing features of this type of society is Daniel Bell. See his *The Coming of Post-Industrial Society: A Venture in Social Forecasting* (New York: Basic Books, 1973).

26. William F. Ogburn, *Social Change* (New York: Viking, 1922).

27. *United Nations World Development Report 2000* (New York: Oxford University Press, 2000).

28. Hung-Chao Tai, *Confucianism and Economic Development* (Washington, DC: Washington Institute Press, 1989).

29. Demographers at the Population Reference Bureau have collected some awesome statistics on recent declines in the material quality of life, especially for women and children in nonindustrial societies. See *The World of Child Six Billion* (Washington, DC: Population Reference Bureau, 1999).

30. Edward H. Spicer, "American Indians." Pp. 58–114 in Stephan Thernstrom, ed., *Harvard Encyclopedia of American Ethnic Groups* (Cambridge, MA: Belknap Press/Harvard, 1980), p. 58.

31. Anthropologists were the first to define and make significant contributions to understanding the concepts of culture, status, role, and socialization—the process by which humans learn to become functioning members of their societies. Major contributions to

this topic historically are Edward B. Tylor, *Primitive Culture* (London: Murray, 1871) and Ralph Linton, *The Study of Man* (Englewood Cliffs, NJ: Prentice Hall, 1936). Classics in the field of sociology are William Graham Sumner, *Folkways* (Boston: Ginn, 1906); Charles Horton Cooley, *Human Nature and the Social Order* (New York: Scribners, 1902); and *Social Organization* (New York: Scribners, 1909); and George Herbert Mead, *Mind, Self, and Society* (Chicago: University of Chicago Press, 1934), edited by Charles W. Norris. Mead was actually a professor of philosophy.

32. Patricia L. East, "Racial and Ethnic Differences in Girls' Sexual, Marital, and Birth Expectations." *Journal of Marriage and the Family*, 1998, Vol. 60, pp. 150–162.

33. Marlise Simons, "Dutch Becoming First Nation to Legalize Assisted Suicide." *New York Times*, November 29, 2000, p. Al.

34. For reviews of persisting differences in the socialization experiences of girls and boys and men and women, see Jerome Kagan, *Galen's Prophecy* (New York: Basic Books, 1994); Eleanor S. Maccoby, *The Two Sexes: Growing Up Apart, Coming Together* (Cambridge, MA: Belknap Press/Harvard, 1998); and Scott Coltrane, *Gender and Families* (Thousand Oaks, CA: Pine Forge Press, 1998).

35. For early descriptions of this change in marital values, see Ernest W. Burgess and Harvey J. Locke, *The Family: From Institution to Companionship* (New York: American Book Co., 1945); and William F. Ogburn and Meyer F. Nimkoff, *Technology and the Changing Family* (Boston: Houghton Mifflin, 1955).

36. See Susan F. Mayer, *What Money Can't Buy: Family Income and Children's Life Chances* (Cambridge, MA: Harvard University Press, 1997); Greg J. Duncan, W. Jean Yeung, Jeanne Brooks-Gunn, and Judith R. Smith, "How Much Does Childhood Poverty Affect the Life Chances of Children?" *American Sociological Review*, 1998, Vol. 63, pp. 406–423; and Glenn H. Elder, Jr., and Rand D. Conger, *Children of the Land: Adversity and Success in Rural America* (Chicago: University of Chicago Press, 2000).

37. On sibling relationships and rivalries with parents and with each other, see Gerald Handel, "Beyond Sibling Rivalry: An Empirically Grounded Theory of Sibling Relationships." Pp. 105–2 in Patricia A. Adler and Peter Adler, eds., *Sociological Studies of Child Development*, Vol. 1 (Greenwich, CT: JAI Press, 1986); Thomas R. Lee, Jay A. Mancini, and Joseph W. Maxwell, "Sibling Relationships in Adulthood: Contact Patterns and Motivations." *Journal of Marriage and the Family*, 1990, Vol. 52, pp. 431–440; and Ingrid Arnet Connidis and Lori D. Campbell, "Closeness, Confiding, and Contact Among Siblings in Middle and Late Adulthood." *Journal of Family Issues*, 1995, Vol. 16, pp. 722–745.

38. Given the increased diversity of ethnic subcultures in the United States, we have a growing number of research studies on this topic. A good source on 17 different ethnic and religious (Amish, Mormon, and Jewish American) family subcultures in the United States is Charles H. Mindel, Robert W. Habenstein, and Roosevelt Wright, Jr., eds., *Ethnic Families in America* (Upper Saddle River, NJ: Prentice Hall, 1998); see also David H. Demo, Katherine R. Allen, and Mark A. Fine, eds., *Handbook of Family Diversity* (New York: Oxford University Press, 2000), pp. 232–292.

39. On the new nonterritorial virtual communities, see Joel Kotkin, *The New Geography* (New York: Random House, 2000).

40. For traditional anthropological definitions of the family, see Bronislaw Malinowsky, *A Scientific Theory of Culture* (Chapel Hill, NC: University of North Carolina Press, 1944); and George Peter Murdock, *Social Structure* (Glencoe, IL: Free Press, 1949). For earlier, more traditional definitions by sociologists, see Talcott Parsons and Robert F. Bales, *Family, Socialization, and Interaction Process* (Glencoe, IL: Free Press, 1955); and,

more recently, David Popenoe, *Disturbing the Nest: Family Decline in Modern Societies* (New York: Aldine de Gruyter, 1989), p. 1.

41. Harriet Engel Gross, "Dual-Career Couples Who Live Apart: Two Types." *Journal of Marriage and the Family*, 1980, vol. 42, pp. 567–576; Frank E. Winfield, *Commuter Marriage: Living Together, Apart* (New York: Columbia University Press, 1985); and Elaine A. Anderson and Jean W. Spruill, "The Dual-Career Commuter Family: A Lifestyle on the Move." *Marriage and Family Review*, 1993, Vol. 19, pp. 121–147.

42. On extending the definition of families to include all groups that define themselves as families, see Catherine S. Chilman, Elam W. Nunnally, and Fred M. Cox, eds., *Variant Family Forms* (Newbury Park, CA: Sage, 1988), p. 11; John Scanzoni, Karen Polonko, Jay Teachman, and Linda Thompson, *The Sexual Bond* (Newbury Park, CA: Sage, 1989), p. 270; and Katherine R. Allen, "A Conscious and Inclusive Family Studies." *Journal of Marriage and the Family*, 2000, Vol. 62, pp. 4–17.

Chapter 2 The Language of Family Change

1. Two classic articles on changing family forms in industrial societies are Marvin B. Sussman, "The Isolated Nuclear Family: Fact or Fiction." *Social Problems*, 1959, Vol. 6, pp. 333–340; and Eugene Litwak and Stephen Kulis, "Technology, Proximity, and Measures of Kin Support." *Journal of Marriage and the Family*, 1987, Vol. 49, pp. 649–661.

2. For this definition of extended families, see Betty Yorburg, "The Nuclear and the Extended Family: An Area of Conceptual Confusion." *Journal of Comparative Family Studies*, 1975, Vol. 6, pp. 1–14.

3. Anne R. Roschelle, *No More Kin: Exploring Race, Class, and Gender in Family Networks* (Thousand Oaks, CA: Sage, 1997), p. 200.

4. For ethnic differences in help from extended families, see Yean-Ju Lee and Isik A. Aytac, "Intergenerational Financial Support Among Whites, African Americans, and Latinos." *Journal of Marriage and the Family*, 1998, Vol. 60, pp. 426–441. On help from "fictive" (make-believe) kin and from godparents among minority families, see Bonnie Thornton Dill, "Fictive Kin, Paper Sons, and Compadrazco: Women of Color and the Struggle for Family Survival." Pp. 2–19 in Stephanie Coontz, ed., with Maya Parson and Gabrielle Raley, *American Families* (New York: Routledge, 1999).

5. An early analysis of this type of family that is still valid is Marvin B. Sussman's "The Isolated Nuclear Family: Fact or Fiction?" *Social Problems*, 1959, Vol. 6, pp. 333–340.

6. See Ronald L. Taylor, ed., *Minority Families in the United States,* 2d ed. (Upper Saddle River, NJ: Prentice Hall, 1998), Part III; Jennifer E. Glick, Frank D. Bean, and Jennifer V. W. Van Hook, "Immigration and Changing Patterns of Extended Family Household Structure in the United States." *Journal of Marriage and the Family*, 1997, Vol. 59, pp. 177–191; and Jay D. Teachman, "Diversity of Family Structure: Economic and Social Influences." Pp. 32–58 in David H. Demo, Katherine R. Allen, and Mark A. Fine, eds., *Handbook of Family Diversity* (New York: Oxford University Press, 2000).

7. Yean-Ju Lee and Isik A. Aytec, 1998, p. 440; and Jay D. Teachman, 2000, p. 54.

8. Rubye W. Beck and Scott H. Beck, "The Incidence of Extended Family Households Among Middle-Aged Black and White Women." *Journal of Family Issues*, 1989, Vol. 10, pp. 147–168. For a more recent picture, see Andrew J. Cherlin, Eugenia Scabini, and Giovanna Rossi, "Still in the Nest: Delayed Home Leaving in Europe and the United States." *Journal of Family Issues*, 1997, Vol. 18, pp. 572–575; and Frances Goldscheider, "Recent Changes in U.S. Young Adult Living Arrangements in Comparative Perspective." *Journal of Family Issues*, 1997, Vol. 18, pp. 708–724.

9. On current practices of polygamy in various parts of the world, see Irwin Altman and Joseph Ginat, *Polygamous Families in Contemporary Society* (New York: Cambridge University Press, 1996). On polyandry, see William N. Stephens, *The Family in Cross-Cultural Perspective* (New York: Holt, Rinehart, and Winston, 1963), pp. 39–49; and Margaret L. Cassidy and Gary R. Lee, "The Study of Polyandry: A Critique and Synthesis." *Journal of Comparative Family Studies*, 1989, Vol. 20, pp. 1–11.

10. This term was introduced by sociologists Constance Ahrons and Roy Rodgers in *Divorced Families: A Multidisciplinary View* (New York: W. W. Norton, 1987).

11. U.S. Department of Commerce, *Statistical Abstract of the United States*, (Washington, DC: U.S. Government Printing Office, 1999), Table 100, p. 80; also see Jay D. Teachman, 2000, p. 43.

12. An edited volume with articles on this controversy by well-known sociologists, lawyers, theologians, and employees of various research institutes is David Popenoe, Jean Bethke Elshtain, and David Blankenhorn, eds., *Promises to Keep* (Lanham, MD: Rowman and Littlefield, 1996).

13. Edward L. Kain, *The Myth of Family Decline* (Lexington, MA: Lexington Books, 1990); and Stephanie Coontz, *The Way We Never Were: American Families and the Nostalgia Trap* (New York: Basic Books, 1992); also her follow-up study, *The Way We Really Are: Coming to Terms with America's Changing Families* (New York: Basic Books, 1997). Sociologist Judith Stacy in *In the Name of the Family: Rethinking Family Values in the Postmodern Age* (Boston: Beacon Press, 1996) argues that, for women, in fact, recent changes in family values and roles are an improvement, rather than a decline, in their life situations.

14. Lynne M. Casper and Martin O'Connell, "Work, Income, the Economy, and Married Fathers as Child-Care Providers." *Demography*, 1998, Vol. 35, pp. 243–250.

15. On increased commitment to family responsibilities among the baby boom generation (compared to that of their parents), see Stacy J. Rogers and Paul R. Amato, "Is Marital Quality Declining? The Evidence from Two Generations." *Social Forces*, 1997, Vol. 75, pp. 1089–1100; also see Paul R. Amato and Alan Booth, *A Generation at Risk: Growing Up in an Era of Family Upheaval* (Cambridge, MA: Harvard University Press, 1997).

16. See William F. Ogburn, *Social Change* (New York: Viking, 1922); and William F. Ogburn and Meyer Nimkoff, *Technology and the Changing Family* (Boston: Houghton Mifflin, 1955).

17. Many historians have documented this trend. See, for example, Edward Shorter, *The Making of the Modern Family* (New York: Basic Books, 1975); also John Demos, *A Little Commonwealth* (New York: Basic Books, 1970); Stephanie Coontz, *The Social Origins of Private Life* (New York: Verso, 1988); and Stephen Mintz and Susan Kellog, *Domestic Revolutions* (New York: Free Press, 1988).

18. See Lloyd de Mause, *The History of Childhood* (New York: Psychohistory Press, 1974), for more details on this difference between agricultural and industrial societies generally. On the historical treatment of women in the United States compared to other countries, see Elise Boulding, *The Underside of History*, rev. ed., 2 vols. (Newbury Park, CA: Sage, 1992), Vol. 1 especially.

19. Norval D. Glenn and Charles N. Weaver, "The Changing Relation of Marital Status to Reported Happiness." *Journal of Marriage and the Family*, 1988, Vol. 50, pp. 317–324; also Walter R. Gove, Carolyn Briggs Style, and Michael Hughes, "The Effect of Marriage on the Well-Being of Adults." *Journal of Family Issues*, 1990, Vol. 11, pp. 4–35.

20. See, for example, Frank F. Furstenberg, Jr., and Graham Spanier, *Recycling the Family: Remarriage After Divorce*, rev. ed. (Thousand Oaks, CA: Sage, 1987); also Andrew J. Cherlin, *Marriage, Divorce, Remarriage* (Cambridge, MA: Harvard University Press,

1992); David R. Johnson and Alan Booth, "Marital Quality: A Product of the Dyadic Environment or Individual Factors?" *Social Forces*, 1998, Vol. 76, pp. 883–905.

21. See, for example, Arlene Skolnick, *Embattled Paradise* (New York: Basic Books, 1991).

22. For a classic formulation of this theory, see John Bowlby, *Attachment and Loss*, Vol. 1, *Attachment* (New York: Basic Books, 1969).

23. Alice S. Rossi and Peter H. Rossi, *Of Human Bonding* (Hawthorne, NY: Aldine de Gruyter, 1990); also Vern L. Bengtson, Timothy J. Biblarz, and Robert E. L. Roberts, *Kin, Career, and Values: Intergenerational Transmissions and Social Change* (in press).

24. The shift from traditional rural to modern urban values as societies industrialize has been documented in a number of studies. An excellent source is the massive cross-national survey research project conducted by Alex Inkeles and his associates in the late 1960s and early 1970s. See Alex Inkeles and David H. Smith, *Becoming Modern: Individual Change in Six Developing Countries* (Cambridge, MA: Harvard University Press, 1974); also Alex Inkeles, *Exploring Individual Modernity* (New York: Columbia University Press, 1983).

25. In sociology, the pioneering research on this topic was done by Melvin L. Kohn. See his "Social Class and Parental Values." *American Journal of Sociology*, 1959, Vol. 63, pp. 337–351, and *Class and Conformity* (Homewood, IL: Dorsey, 1969). From the field of psychology, see Diana Baumrind, "Authoritarian versus Authoritative Parental Control." *Adolescence*, 1968, Vol. 3, pp. 255–272. See also Jay Belsky, "Parental and Nonparental Child Care and Children's Socioemotional Development: A Decade in Review." *Journal of Marrriage and the Family*, 1991, Vol. 52, pp. 885–903.

26. Reuben Hill, *Families Under Stress* (Westport, CT: Greenwood Press, 1971 [1949]).

27. On familistic values among African Americans, Mexican Americans, and Asian Americans, see the essays by Ronald L. Taylor, Maxine Baca Zinn, Barbara Wells, and Masako Ishi-Kuntz in Demo, Allen, and Fine, 2000, pp. 232–292.

28. Steven Mintz and Susan Kellog, 1988, pp. 113–131; also Rozsika Parker, *Mother Hate/Mother Love* (New York: Basic Books, 1996).

29. Sigmund Freud, "The Future of an Illusion." Pp. 5–56 in James Strachey, ed., *The Standard Edition of the Complete Psychological Works of Sigmund Freud* (London: Hogarth Press, 1961 [1927]), Vol. 21, p. 31; see also John F. Crosby, *Illusion and Disillusion: The Self in Love and Marriage*, 5th ed. (Belmont, CA: Wadsworth, 1995).

30. Robert Waelder, *Basic Theory of Psychoanalysis* (New York: Schocken Books, 1960), p. 48.

31. On the implications of individualism in the United States for political democracy and other aspects of daily life, see Herbert J. Gans, *Middle-American Individualism* (New York: Free Press, 1988).

32. Edward H. Spicer, "American Indians." Pp. 58–114 in Stephan Thernstrom, ed., *Harvard Encyclopedia of American Ethnic Groups* (Cambridge, MA: Belknap Press/Harvard, 1980).

33. James R. Kluegel, "Trends in Whites' Explanations of the Black-White Gap in Socioeconomic Status." *American Sociological Review*, 1990, Vol. 55, pp 512–525; also Howard Newman and Maria Krysan, "A Historical Note on Whites' Beliefs About Racial Inequality." *American Sociological Review*, 1999, Vol. 64, pp. 847–855. On individualism and the failure of leftist reform movements in the United States, see Betty Yorburg, "The Failure of Socialism in America." Pp. 3–23 in John H. M. Laslett and Seymour Martin Lipset, *Failure of a Dream? Essays in the History of Socialism* (New York: Doubleday, 1974).

34. Katherine S. Newman, *Falling from Grace: The Experience of Downward Mobility in the American Middle Class* (New York: Free Press, 1988), p. 229, and *No Shame in My Game* (New York: Alfred A. Knopf/Russell Sage Foundation, 1999).

35. John B. Schwartz, *Illusions of Opportunity: The American Dream in Question* (New York: W. W. Norton, 1997); also Timothy Smeeding, "The International Evidence on Income Distribution." Pp. 79–103 in Jon Neill, ed., *Poverty and Inequality: The Political Economy of Redistribution* (Kalamazoo, MI: Upjohn Institute for Employment Research, 1997); also Andrew Hacker, *Money: Who Has How Much and Why* (New York: Scribners, 1997).

36. Valerie S. Mannis, "Single Mothers by Choice." *Family Relations*, 1999, Vol. 48, p. 126.

37. U.S. Department of Commerce, *Statistical Abstract of the United States*, Table 130, p. 95; Table 137, p. 99 (Washington, DC: U.S. Government Printing Office, 1999).

38. For a report on the latest thinking of researchers on the actual prevalence of depression among men and gender differences in the experience and expression of depressive symptoms, see Nancy Wartik, "Depression Comes Out of Hiding." *New York Times*, June 23, 2000, Section 16, pp. 1, 5. On violence against women, see U.S. Department of Justice Statistics, "Violence by Intimates: Analysis of Data on Crimes by Current or Former Spouses, Boyfriends, and Girlfriends" (Washington, DC: Office of Justice Programs, March 1998).

39. For a psychiatric view of gender differences in suicide rates conceptualized in terms of differences in guilt, denial, and depression, see Kay Redfield Jamison, *Night Falls Fast* (New York: Knopf, 1999).

40. On the increased emphasis on activism in socializing children in the United States, see Duane F. Alwin, "Cohort Replacement and Changes in Socialization Values." *Journal of Marriage and the Family*, 1990, Vol. 52, pp. 347–360.

41. For this conception of rationalism, see Max Weber, *The Theory of Social and Economic Organization* (New York: Oxford University Press, 1947), p. 91, translated and edited by A. M. Henderson and Talcott Parsons.

42. Betty Yorburg, *Sexual Identity: Sex Roles and Social Change* (New York: Wiley, 1974), p. 25, 141, 182.

43. On the primary importance of education in transforming values, see the work of Alex Inkeles and his associates, cited above. On the links between education, income, power, and the fertility rates of women in various countries, see Nancy Riley, "Gender, Power, and Population Change." *Population Bulletin*, May 1997, Vol. 52, No. 5. For an analysis of the persistence of certain traditional value—religious and patriarchal values especially—regardless of the effects of industrialization and economic development in major geographic areas of the world, see Ronald Inglehart and Wayne E. Baker, "Modernization, Cultural Change, and the Persistence of Traditional Values." *American Sociological Review*, 2000, Vol. 65, pp. 19–51.

44. Stephanie Coontz, *The Way We Really Are* (New York: Basic Books, 1997), pp. 83–84.

45. The concept of a *reference group* originated in a massive World War II study of morale in the United States military. Some major contributions on this topic were described by Robert K. Merton and Alice S. Kitt (née Rossi) in "Contributions to the Theory of Reference Group Behavior." Pp. 40–105 in Robert K. Merton and Paul F. Lazarsfeld, eds., *Continuities in Social Research: Studies in the Scope and Method of "The American Soldier"* (Glencoe, IL: Free Press, 1950); see also Herbert A. Hyman and Eleanor D. Singer, eds., *Readings in Reference Group Theory* (Glencoe, IL: Free Press, 1968).

46. Daniel Lerner, *The Passing of Traditional Society: Modernizing the Middle East* (Glencoe, IL: Free Press, 1958), pp. 157–158.

Chapter 3 Families in Time and Place

1. See Betty Yorburg, *Families and Societies* (New York: Columbia University Press, 1983) for documentation of many of the generalizations in this section.
2. Among the first sociologists to document this relationship were Meyer F. Nimkoff and Russell Middleton in "Types of Family and Types of Economy." *American Journal of Sociology*, 1966, Vol. 71, pp. 215–225; also Rae Lesser Blumberg and Robert F. Winch, "Societal Complexity and Familial Complexity: Evidence for the Curvilinear Hypothesis." *American Journal of Sociology*, 1972, Vol. 77, pp. 898–920.
3. See Betty Yorburg, 1983, pp. 123–163, for a more extended discussion of these similarities.
4. William H. Frey, "Black Migration to the South Reaches Record Highs in the 1990s." *Population Today*, February 1999, Vol. 27, No. 2, pp. 1–3.
5. M. Belinda Tucker and Claudia Mitchel-Kernan, "New Trends in Black American Interracial Marriage: The Social Structural Context." *Journal of Marriage and the Family*, 1990, Vol. 52, pp. 209–218 and "Interracial Dating and Marriage in Southern California." *Journal of Social and Personal Relationships*, 1995, Vol. 12, pp. 341–361.
6. Gary R. Lee, "Marital Structure and Economic Systems." *Journal of Marriage and the Family*, 1979, Vol. 41, pp. 701–714; also Linda Stone, *Kinship and Gender* (New York: Westview Press, 1998). The classic source on types of economies and family relationships, but dated now that we have better anthropological information, is Frederick Engels, *The Origin of the Family, Private Property, and the State* (Chicago: Charles H. Kerr, 1902 [1884]).
7. Betty Yorburg, *Sexual Identity: Sex Roles and Social Change* (New York: Wiley, 1974), pp. 62–63.
8. For persisting psychological differences between men and women, especially the need for power and control in work and in parenting situations, see Eleanor S. Maccoby, *The Two Sexes: Growing Up Apart, Coming Together* (Cambridge, MA: Belknap Press/Harvard, 1998); also on this topic, see Scott Coltrane, *Gender and Families* (Thousand Oaks, CA: Pine Forge Press, 1998).
9. Arlie Hochschild with Anne Machung, *The Second Shift* (New York: Viking, 1989); also Alan C. Acock and David H. Demo, *Family Diversity and Well-Being* (Thousand Oaks, CA: Sage, 1994), Table 4.1, p. 77; also Laura Sanchez and Elizabeth Thomson, "Becoming Mothers and Fathers: Parenthood, Gender, and the Division of Labor." *Gender and Society*, 1997, Vol. 11, pp. 747–772; Francine M. Deutch, *Halving It All* (Cambridge, MA: Harvard University Press, 1999); Maureen Perry-Jenkins, Rena L. Repetti, and Ann C. Crouter, "Work and Family in the 1990s." *Journal of Marriage and the Family*, 2000, Vol. 62, pp. 981–998.
10. Margaret O'Brien, "The Place of Men in Gender Sensitive Therapy." Pp. 195–208 in Rosine J. Perelberg and Ann C. Miller, eds., *Gender and Power in Families* (New York: Routledge, 1990); also Richard L. Meth and Robert S. Pasick, *Men in Therapy* (New York: Guilford Press, 1992).
11. Lawrence H. Ganong and Marilyn Coleman, *Remarried Family Relationships* (Thousand Oaks, CA: Sage, 1994), pp. 77–82; also Irene Levin and Marvin B. Sussman, eds., *Stepfamilies: History, Research, and Policy* (New York: Haworth Press, 1997).
12. Clellan S. Ford and Frank A. Beach, *Patterns of Sexual Behavior* (New York: Harper and Row, 1972 [1951]).
13. A concise, clearly written source that includes historical as well as contemporary information on this topic is Pepper Schwartz and Virginia Rutter, *The Gender of Sexuality* (Thousand Oaks, CA: Pine Forge Press, 1998).

14. Edward O. Laumann, John H. Gagnon, Robert T. Michael, and Stuart Michaels, *The Social Organization of Sexuality* (Chicago: University of Chicago Press, 1994).

15. Douglas Jehl, "Arab Honor's Price: A Woman's Blood." *New York Times*, June 20, 1999, pp. A1, A8.

16. Clellan S. Ford and Frank A. Beach, *Patterns of Sexual Behavior*, pp. 113-115. For information about the current situation, see Kate Chalkley, "Female Genital Mutilation: New Laws, Programs Try to End the Practice." *Population Today*, November 1997, Vol. 25, No. 11, pp. 4–5; Megan McKenna, "A Centuries-old Practice, a Deadly Tradition." *Thursday's Child* (New York: U.S. Committee for UNICEF, 1998), pp. 14–18; James Dakar, "Female Genital Mutilation: Is It a Crime or Culture?" *The Economist*, February 13, 1999, pp. 46–47; and Claudia Dreifus, "A Life Devoted to Stopping the Suffering of Mutilation." *New York Times*, July 11, 2000, p. F7.

17. E. A. Wrigley, *Population and History* (London: University Library, 1969).

18. U.S. Bureau of the Census, *Statistical Abstract of the United States*, 118th ed. (Washington, DC: U.S. Government Printing Office, 1998), Table 67, p. 60.

19. Susan Heitler, *From Conflict to Resolution* (New York: W. W. Norton, 1990).

20. David McClelland, *Power: The Inner Experience* (New York: Irvington, 1975).

21. Rae Lesser Blumberg, ed., "Gender Stratification, Economy, and the Family." *Journal of Family Issues*, 1988, Vol. 9, No. 6, entire issue. On generational changes in the power of women over three generations after immigration, see Jaffa A. Schlessinger, *An Interview with My Grandparent* (New York: McGraw-Hill, 1998); and Merrill Silverstein and Xuan Chen, "The Impact of Acculturation in Mexican American Families on the Quality of Adult Grandchild-Grandparent Relationships." *Journal of Marriage and the Familly*, 1999, Vol. 61, pp. 188–198.

22. Olive Banks, *Faces of Feminism: A Study of Feminism as a Social Movement* (New York: Blackwell, 1986).

23. Nancy J. Davis and Robert V. Robinson, "Men's and Women's Consciousness of Gender Inequality: Austria, West Germany, Great Britain, and the United States." *American Sociological Review*, 1991, Vol. 53, pp. 72–84. On gender inequality in post-Soviet Union Russia, see Linda Racioppi and Katherine O'Sullivan, *Women's Activism in Contemporary Russia* (Philadelphia: Temple University Press, 1997).

24. Diana Baumrind, "Authoritarian versus Authoritative Control." *Adolescence*, 1968, Vol. 3, pp. 255–272; also Diana Baumrind, "Reciprocal Rights and Obligations in Parent-Child Relations." *Journal of Social Issues*, 1978, Vol. 34, pp. 179–195; Diana Baumrind, "The Discipline Controversy Revisited." *Family Relations*, 1996, Vol. 45, pp. 405–414.

25. National Research Council, *Losing Generations: Adolescents in High-Risk Settings* (Washington, DC: National Academy Press, 1993).

26. A classic research study on this topic is Theodore W. Adorno, Else Frankel-Brunswik, Daniel J. Levinson, and R. Nevitt Sanford, *The Authoritarian Personality* (New York: Wiley, 1950).

27. William J. Goode, *World Revolution and Family Patterns* (New York: Free Press, 1963).

28. Quoted in Fergus M. Bordewich, *Killing the White Man's Indian* (New York: Anchor Books, 1999), p. 49.

29. Steven Mintz and Susan Kellog, *Domestic Revolutions* (New York: Free Press, 1988), pp. 54, 55.

30. Children's Defense Fund, *The State of America's Children, Yearbook 2000* (Washington, DC: Children's Defense Fund, 2000), p. 3; also John E. Schwartz, *Illusions of Opportunity: The American Dream in Question* (New York: W. W. Norton, 1997);

Timothy Smeeding, "The International Evidence on Income Distribution." Pp. 110–116 in Jon Neill, ed., *Poverty and Inequality: The Political Economy of Income Redistribution* (Kalamazoo, MI: Upjohn Institute for Employment Research, 1997); Andrew Hacker, *Money: Who Has How Much and Why?* (New York: Scribners, 1997).

31. See, for example, Helen Ware, "Polygyny: Women's Views in a Traditional Society, Nigeria 1975." *Journal of Marriage and the Family*, 1979, Vol. 41, pp. 188–196.

32. Anastasia J. Gege-Brandon, "The Polygyny-Divorce Relationship: A Case Study of Nigeria." *Journal of Marriage and the Family*, 1992, Vol. 54, pp. 285–292.

33. For more specific statistics on global trends, see Judith Bruce, Cynthia B. Lloyd, and Ann Leonard, with Patrice L. Engle and Niev Duffy, *Families in Focus* (New York: The Population Council, 1995).

34. Naomi Neft and Ann D. Levine, *Where Women Stand*, An International Report on the Status of Women in Over 140 Countries (New York: Random House, 1997).

35. John Bogaarts, "Demographic Consequences of Declining Fertility." *Science*, October 8, 1998, Vol. 282, pp. 419–420; also United Nations Children's Fund, *The State of the World's Children: 1998* (New York: Oxford University Press, 1998); Sharon K. Housknecht and Jaya Sastry, "Family 'Decline' and Child Well-Being." *Journal of Marriage and the Family*, 1996, Vol. 58, pp. 726–739.

36. The tremendous decline in the birth rate in Mexico and its consequences has been documented by demographers in Mexico. For a report on this trend, see Sam Dillon, "Smaller Families to Bring Big Change in Mexico." *New York Times*, June 8, 1999, pp. A1, A12.

37. Jorge del Pinal and Audry Singer, "Generations of Diversity." *Population Bulletin*, October 1997, Vol. 52, No. 3, p. 7.

38. For a review of the beginnings of this controversy, see Joan Aldous and Wilfried Dumon, "Family Policy in the 1980s: Controversy and Consensus." *Journal of Marriage and the Family*, 1990, Vol. 52, pp. 1136–1151.

39. See Charles Deverics, "Is Welfare Reform Reforming Welfare?" *Population Today*, October 1999, Vol. 27, No. 10, pp. 1–2; also "Welfare Caseloads: Families and Recipients, 1960–1998" (Washington, DC: U.S. Department of Health and Human Services, 1999); Kathryn Edin, Kathleen Mullan Harris, and Gary D. Sandefur, *Welfare to Work: Opportunities and Pitfalls* (Washington, DC: American Sociological Association, 1998).

40. Adapted from an interview with Indian women's rights activist Pramila Dandavate reported in the *New York Times*, January 15, 1989, p. A10.

41. Yolanda T. Moses, "Female Status, the Family, and Male Dominance in a West Indian Community." in B. Bunster, et al., eds., *Women and National Development: The Complexion of Change* (Chicago: University of Chicago Press, 1977). Cited in Judith Bruce et al., 1995, p. 30.

42. U.S. Bureau of the Census, *Current Population Reports*, P20–496 (Washington, DC: U.S. Government Printing Office, 1998).

43. On gender differences in the use of earnings to pay for household expenses, see Lawrence Haddad, John Hoddinot, and Harold Alderman, eds., *Intrahousehold Resource Allocation in Developing Countries: Methods, Models, and Policy* (Baltimore: Johns Hopkins University Press, 1996). On the destructive effects on marital relationships of long separations as a result of imprisonment or military service, see Ronald R. Rindfuss and Elizabeth Hervey Stephen, "Marital Noncohabitation: Separation Does Not Make the Heart Grow Fonder." *Journal of Marriage and the Family*, 1990, Vol. 52, pp. 259–270.

44. United Nations Development and Human Rights Section, "Women at a Glance" (New York: United Nations Department of Public Information, 1997).

45. On the increased gap in women's earnings compared to men in the same occupations, see Naomi Neft and Ann D. Levine, 1997, p. 391. For United Nations data on the increase in prostitution in former Communist countries (in Russia, Eastern Europe, and Asia), see Alison Smale, "After the Fall, Traffic in Flesh, Not Dreams," *New York Times*, June 11, 2000, p. wk6.

Chapter 4 U.S. Families in Time and Place

1. A brief but comprehensive source on this topic is Dennis Gilbert and Joseph H. Kahl, *The American Class Structure* (Belmont, CA: Wadsworth, 1993).

2. A classic source on the old upper class by a member of this class is E. Digby Baltzell, *The Protestant Establishment* (New Haven, CT: Yale University Press, 1987 [1964]). For an updated account, see Howard G. Schneiderman, "The Protestant Establishment—Its History, Its Legacy—Its Future?" Pp. 141–151 in Silvia Pedraza and Ruben G. Rumbaut, eds., *Origins and Destinies* (Belmont, CA: Wadsworth, 1996).

3. See, for example, James Collard, "Blimy! New Yorkers to the Manners Born." *New York Times*, June 27, 1999, pp. ST1, St5.

4. Susan Ostrander, *Women of the Upper Class* (Philadelphia: Temple University Press, 1984); and Arlene Kaplan Daniels, *Invisible Careers: Women Civic Leaders from the Volunteer World* (Chicago: University of Chicago Press, 1988).

5. David Spain and Susan M. Bianchi, *Balancing Act: Motherhood, Marriage, and Employment Among American Women* (New York: Russell Sage Foundation, 1996).

6. Melvin Kohn, "Social Class and Parent-Child Relationships: An Interpretation." *American Journal of Sociology*, 1968, Vol. 68, pp. 471–480; and Melvin Kohn, *Class and Conformity* (Homewood, IL: Dorsey, 1969). For similar results on surveys of child-rearing practices in other industrial countries, see Maja Dekovic and Jan R. M. Gerris, "Parental Reasoning Complexity, Social Class, and Child-rearing Behaviors." *Journal of Marriage and the Family*, 1992, Vol. 54, pp. 675–685.

7. For a more sympathetic portrait of this social class, see Herbert J. Gans, *The Urban Villagers* (New York: Free Press, 1962) and *Middle American Individualism* (New York: Free Press, 1998).

8. A classic on this topic is Mirra Komarovsky, *Blue Collar Marriage* (New York: Random House, 1962). For a more recent picture, see Lillian B. Rubin, *Families on the Fault Line: America's Working Class Speaks About the Family, the Economy, Race, and Ethnicity* (New York: HarperCollins, 1994).

9. U.S. Bureau of the Census, *Current Population Reports*, Series P60–201, "Poverty in the United States: 1998" (Washington, DC: U.S. Government Printing Office, 1999); also Jorge del Pinal and Audrey Singer, "Generations of Diversity: Latinos in the United States." *Population Bulletin*, October 1997, Vol. 52, No. 3, pp. 15, 32.

10. Randall Collins, "Women and Men in the Class Structure," *Journal of Family Issues*, 1988, Vol. 9, pp. 27–50; also Ida Harper Simpson, David Stark, and Robert A. Jackson, "Class Identification Processes of Married, Working Men and Women." *American Sociological Review*, 1988, Vol. 53, pp. 284–293; and Nancy J. Davis and Robert V. Robinson, "Do Wives Matter? Class Identities of Wives and Husbands in the United States, 1974–1994." *Social Forces*, 1998, Vol. 76, pp. 163–168.

11. The most comprehensive source on this topic, especially on the history of immigration to the United States, is Stephan Thernstrom, ed., *Harvard Encyclopedia of American Ethnic Groups* (Cambridge, MA: Belknap Press/Harvard, 1980). For a more recent pic-

ture, see Silvia Pedraza and Ruben G. Rumbaut, eds., *Origins and Destinies* (Belmont, CA: Wadsworth, 1996); and Robert Aponte, with Bruce A. Beal and Michelle E. Jiles, "Ethnic Variation in the Family: The Elusive Trend Toward Convergence." Pp. 111–141 in Marvin B. Sussman, Suzanne K. Steinmetz, and Gary W. Peterson, eds., *Handbook of Marriage and the Family*, 2d ed. (New York: Kluwer Academic/Plenum, 1999).

12. Luigi Luca Cavalli-Sforza, *Genes, Peoples, and Languages* (Boston: North Point Press, 2000); also Elliot Marshall, "DNA Studies Challenge the Meaning of Race." *Science*, October 23, 1998, pp. 654–655; Scott L. Malcomson, *One Drop of Blood* (New York: Farrar, Strauss, and Giroux, 2000).

13. Louis Wirth, "The Problem of Minority Groups." Pp. 347–372 in Ralph Linton, ed., *The Science of Man in the World Crisis* (New York: Columbia University Press, 1945), p. 347.

14. Betty Yorburg, *Sociological Reality* (New York: McGraw-Hill, 1995), pp. 260–265.

15. Ellen Somers Horgan, "The Irish-American Family." Pp. 39–67 in Charles H. Mindel, Robert W. Habenstein, and Roosevelt Wright, Jr., eds., *Ethnic Families in the United States* (Upper Saddle River, NJ: Prentice Hall, 1998).

16. Matthew Frye Jacobson, *Whiteness of a Different Color: European Immigrants and the Alchemy of Race* (Cambridge, MA: Harvard University Press, 1998).

17. Sylvia Pedraza, "Cuba's Refugees: Manifold Migrations." Pp. 263–279 in Silvia Pedraza and Ruben G. Rumbaut, eds., 1996.

18. The contrasting picture for Mexican Americans, especially in rates of nonmarital sexual activity and pregnancy among second-generation teenagers, is described in Patricia L. East, "Racial and Ethnic Differences in Girls' Sexual, Marital, and Birth Expectations." *Journal of Marriage and the Family*, 1998, Vol. 60, pp. 150–162.

19. Monica McGoldrick, "Ethnicity and the Family Life Cycle." Pp. 69–90 in Betty Carter and Monica McGoldrick, eds., *The Changing Family Life Cycle* (Needham Heights, MA: Allyn and Bacon, 1989).

20. For these differences, see Alan Booth, Ann C. Crouter, and Nancy Landale, eds., *Immigration and the Family* (Mahwah, NJ: Erlbaum, 1997).

21. D. Ann Squiers and Jill Quadagno, "The Italian American Family." Pp. 102–127 in Charles H. Mindell, Robert W. Habenstein, and Roosevelt Wright, Jr., eds., *Ethnic Families in America*, 4th ed. (Upper Saddle River, NJ: Prentice Hall, 1998).

22. On Asian Americans, a good source is Sharon M. Lee's "Asian Americans: Diverse and Growing." *Population Bulletin*, June 1998, Vol. 53, No. 2, pp. 1–40.

23. On differences in values, roles, and conflicts among various ethnic minority families, including Asian Americans, see Beth B. Hess, Elizabeth W. Markson, and Peter J. Stein, "Racial and Ethnic Minorities: An Overview." Pp. 258–270 in Paula S. Rothenberg, ed., *Race, Class, and Gender in the United States* (New York: St. Martin's Press, 1998).

24. Robert Staples, "Patterns of Change in the Postindustrial Black Family." Pp. 281–290 in Robert Staples, ed., *The Black Family*, 6th ed. (Belmont, CA: Wadsworth, 1999).

25. Beth Anne Shelton and Daphne John, "Ethnicity, Race, and Difference: A Comparison of White, Black, and Hispanic Men's Household Labor Time." Pp. 144–155 in Jane C. Wood, ed., *Men, Work, and Family* (Thousand Oaks, CA: Sage, 1993).

26. Joan Aldous and Rodney F. Ganey, "Family Life and the Pursuit of Happiness." *Journal of Family Issues*, 1999, Vol. 20, pp. 155–180.

27. On discrimination experienced by middle-class blacks, see Maurice Berger, *White Lies: Race and the Myths of Whiteness* (New York: Farrar, Straus, and Giroux, 1999). On the reactions of middle-class blacks to this behavior, see Ellis Cose, *The Rage of a Privileged Class* (New York: HarperCollins, 1994). For a vivid community study of differences

between the white and black middle class, see Mary Pattillo-McCoy, *Black Picket Fences* (Chicago: University of Chicago Press, 1999).

28. Ramona Marotz-Baden, Charles B. Hennon, and Timothy H. Brubaker, eds., *Families in Rural America: Stress, Adaptation, and Revitalization* (St. Paul, MN: National Council on Family Relations, 1988), p. 3; Cynthia B. Struthers and Janet L. Bokemeier, "Myths and Realities of Raising Children and Creating Family Life in a Rural County." *Journal of Family Issues*, 2000, Vol. 21, pp. 17–26; Glenn H. Elder, Jr., and Rand D. Conger, *Children of the Land: Adversity and Success in Rural America* (Chicago: University of Chicago Press, 2000).

29. Janette K. Newhause and William J McCauley, "Use of Informal In-Home Care by Rural Elders." Pp. 233–242 in Ramona Marotz-Baden, Charles B. Hennon, and Timothy Brubaker, eds., *Families in Rural America* (St. Paul, MN: National Council of Family Relations, 1988). On middle-class "white flight" from the cities and suburbs to rural areas, see Kenneth M. Johnson, "The Rural Rebound." *Reports on America*, September 1999, Vol. 1, No. 3, pp. 1–19.

30. Stephen M. Golant, "The Metropolitanization and Suburbanization of the U.S. Elderly Population: 1970–1988." *The Gerontologist*, February 1990, Vol. 30, pp. 80–95; also Nina Glasgow, "Rural/Urban Patterns of Aging and Caregiving in the United States." *Journal of Family Issues*, 2000, Vol. 21, pp. 611–631.

31. Judith M. Stillion and Eugene E. McDowell, *Suicide Across the Life Span* (Washington, DC: Taylor and Francis, 1997). For the cross-national picture and gender differences in suicide rates, see Fred C. Pampel, "Nation, Social Change, and Sex Differences in Suicide Rates." *American Sociological Review*, 1998, Vol. 63, pp. 744–758.

32. Peer Scheepers and Frans van der Silk, "Religion and Attitudes on Moral Issues: Effects of Individual, Spouse, and Parental Characteristics." *The Journal for the Scientific Study of Religion*, 1998, Vol. 37, pp. 678–688.

33. Martie P. Thompson and Paula J. Vardaman, "The Role of Religion in Coping with the Loss of a Family Member to Homicide." *The Journal for the Scientific Study of Religion*, 1997, Vol. 36, pp. 44–52.

34. On the better health, longer lives, and greater feeling of emotional well-being of people who attend church regularly, see the following unpublished papers presented at the annual meetings of the American Sociological Association, Chicago, August 1999: Linda K. George, "Religion and Physical Health"; Christopher E. Ellison, "Religion and Emotional Well-Being"; David R. Williams, "Health and Well-Being and the Black Church"; and Benjamin Zablocki, "Health and Well-Being and New Religious Movements."

35. Jay D. Teachman, Kristin Paasch, and Karen Price Carver, "Social Capital and the Generation of Human Capital." *Social Forces*, 1997, Vol. 75, pp. 1343–1359; also Brent B. Benda and Robert Flynn Corwyn, "Religion and Delinquency: The Relationship After Considering Family and Peer Influences." *The Journal for the Scientific Study of Religion*, 1997, Vol. 36, pp. 81–93.

36. Robert Joseph Taylor, Linda M. Chatters, and Vicki M. Mays, "Parents, Children, Siblings, In-Laws, and Non-Kin as Sources of Assistance to Black Americans." *Family Relations*, 1988, Vol. 37, pp. 298–304; also Christopher G. Ellison, "Religious Involvement and the Subjective Quality of Family Life Among African Americans." Pp. 117–131 in Robert Joseph Taylor, James S. Jackson, and Linda M. Chatters, eds., *Family Life in Black America* (Thousand Oaks, CA: Sage, 1997).

37. Mirra Komarovsky, *Women in College* (New York: Basic Books, 1985).

38. Christopher G. Ellison, John P. Bartkowsky, and Kristin L. Anderson, "Are There Religious Variations in Domestic Violence?" *Journal of Family Issues*, 1999, Vol. 20, pp. 87–113.

39. A classic study documenting historical differences in family relationships among Catholics, Protestants, and Jews is Gerhard Lenski's *The Religious Factor* (Garden City, NY: Doubleday, 1961).

40. For evidence of converging religious beliefs in the United States since 1900, especially the belief in life after death among people from different religions, see Andrew M. Greeley and Michael Hout, "Americans' Increasing Belief in Life After Death: Religious Competition and Acculturation." *American Sociological Review*, 1999, Vol. 64, pp. 813–835; also Don S. Browning, Bonnie Miller-McLemore, Pamela Couture, K. Brynoll Lyon, and Robert Franklin, *From Culture Wars to Common Ground: Religion and the American Family Debate* (Louisville: Westminster/Knox, 1997).

41. Reported in the *New York Times Magazine*, "Spirituality." May 7, 2000, p. 84.

42. Lynn Davidman, *Tradition in a Rootless World: Women Turn to Orthodox Judaism* (Berkeley: University of California Press, 1993); also Shahin Gerami, *Women and Fundamentalism: Islam and Christianity* (New York: Garland, 1996); Jen'nan Ghazai Read and John P. Bartkowski, "To Veil or Not to Veil? A Case Study of Identity Negotiation Among Muslim Women in Austin, Texas." Paper presented at the annual meeting of the American Sociological Association, Chicago, Illinois, August 1999.

43. Duane F. Alwin, "From Obedience to Autonomy: Changes in Traits Desired in Children." *Public Opinion Quarterly*, 1988, Vol. 52, pp. 33–52.

44. W. Bradford Wilcox, "Conservative Protestant Childrearing: Authoritarian or Authoritative?" *American Sociological Review*, 1998, Vol. 63, pp. 796–809.

45. Maude McCleod, "I Did Not Join the Hebrew Faith—I Returned." *New York Times Magazine*, September 26, 1999, Section 6, p. 116.

Chapter 5 Love and Attachment

1. Some classic publications using or describing this approach are Robert Rountree, *Poverty: A Study of Town Life* (London: Macmillan, 1906); Charles P. Loomis and Horace H. Hamilton, "Family Life Cycle Analysis." *Social Forces*, 1936, Vol. 15, pp. 225–231; Paul C. Glick, "The Family Cycle." *American Sociological Review*, 1947, Vol. 12, pp. 164–174; Evelyn Mills Duvall, *Family Development* (Philadelphia: Lippincott, 1957), and "Family Development's First Forty Years." *Family Relations*, 1988, Vol. 37, pp. 127–139; Joan Aldous, *Family Careers: Rethinking the Family Development Perspective* (Thousand Oaks, CA: Sage, 1996).

2. David M. Klein and Joan Aldous, eds., *Social Stress and Family Development* (New York: Guilford Press, 1988).

3. Pauline Boss, *Family Stress Management* (Thousand Oaks, CA: Sage, 1988).

4. David L. Gutmann, *The Human Elder in Nature, Culture, and Society* (Boulder, CO: Westview Press, 1977) and *Reclaimed Powers: Toward a New Psychology of Men and Women in Later Life* (New York: Basic Books, 1987).

5. Michael Gordon, *The American Family* (New York: Random House, 1978); and Edward L. Kain, *The Myth of Family Decline* (Lexington, MA: Lexington Books, 1990).

6. Child psychiatrist Kenneth Keniston was among the first to describe this new stage in advanced industrial societies. See *Youth and Dissent* (New York: Harcourt Brace Jovanovich, 1971).

7. This distinction first appeared in Bernice Neugarten's "Age Groups in American Society and the Rise of the Young-Old." *Annals of the American Academy of Political and Social Science*, 1974, Vol. 415, pp. 187–198.

8. Jeanne Brooks-Gunn amd Barbara Kirsh, "Life Events and Boundaries for Women," cited in Ski Hunter and Martin Sundel, eds., *Midlife Myths* (Newbury Park, CA: Sage, 1989), p. 10.

9. Andrew J. Cherlin and Frank F. Furstenberg, Jr., *The New American Grandparent* (New York: Basic Books, 1986).

10. Gunhild Hagestad, "Demographic Changes and the Life Course: Some Emerging Trends in the Family Realm." *Family Relations*, 1988, Vol. 37, pp. 405–410.

11. Reuben Hill, "Life Cycle Stages for Types of Single-Parent Families." *Family Relations*, 1986, Vol. 35, pp. 19–29; also Paulette Moore Hines, "The Family Life Cycle of Poor Black Families." Pp. 513–544 in Betty Carter and Monica McGoldreick, eds., *The Changing Family Life Cycle* (Needham, MA: Allyn and Bacon, 1989).

12. Tom Large, "Some Aspects of Loneliness in Families." *Family Process*, 1989, Vol. 28, pp. 25–35, p. 32.

13. Bernice L. Neugarten and Dale A. Neugarten, "The Changing Meanings of Age." *Psychology Today*, May 1987, pp. 29–33; also Douglas E. Crews, "Cultural Lags in Social Perceptions of the Aged." *Generations*, Spring-Summer 1993, pp. 29–34.

14. John D'Emilio and Estelle B. Freedman, *Intimate Matters* (New York: Harper and Row, 1988).

15. Zick Rubin, Preface, pp. vii-xii in Robert J. Sternberg and Michael L. Barnes, eds., *The Psychology of Love* (New York: Yale University Press, 1988).

16. Philip Shaver, Cindy Hazan, and Donna Bradshaw, "Love as Attachment." Pp. 68–99 in Robert J. Sternberg and Michael L. Barnes, eds., *The Psychology of Love*.

17. Sigmund Freud, "Mourning and Melancholia." Pp. 243–258 in James Strachey, ed., *The Standard Edition of the Complete Psychological Works of Sigmund Freud*, Vol. 14 (London: Hogarth Press, 1957 [1917]).

18. Robert J. Sternberg, "The Triangular Theory of Love." *Psychological Review*, 1987, Vol. 93, pp. 119–135.

19. Steve Duck, ed., *Personal Relationships* (Thousand Oaks, CA: Sage, 1990).

20. John Bowlby, *Attachment and Loss*, Vol. 1, *Attachment* (New York: Basic Books, 1969), also Vol. 2, *Separation* (New York: Basic Books, 1973), and Vol 3, *Loss* (New York: Basic Books, 1979).

21. Linda G. Bell, Connie S. Cornwell, and David G. Bell, "Peer Relationships of Adolescent Daughters: A Reflection of Family Relationship Patterns." *Family Relations*, 1988, Vol. 37, pp. 171–174.

22. The classic experiments on this topic were done by psychologist Mary D. Salter Ainsworth. See her "Infant-Mother Attachment." *American Psychologist*, 1979, Vol. 34, pp. 932–937, and "Attachment Beyond Infancy." *American Psychologist*, 1989, Vol. 44, pp. 709–716. See also Mary D. Salter Ainsworth and John Bowlby, "An Ethological Approach to Personality Development." *American Psychologist*, 1991, Vol. 46, pp. 333–341.

23. Ellen Berscheid, Mark Snyder, and Allen M. Omato, "Issues in Studying Close Relationships." Pp. 63–91 in Clyde Hendricks, ed., *Close Relationships* (Newbury Park, CA: Sage, 1989).

24. Elaine Hatfield, "Passionate and Companionate Love." Pp. 191–217 in Robert J. Sternberg and Michael L. Barnes, eds., *The Psychology of Love*.

25. Sigmund Freud, "Group Psychology and the Analysis of the Ego." Pp. 67–144 in James Strachey, ed., *The Standard Edition of the Complete Psychological Works of Sigmund Freud*, Vol. 18 (London: Hogarth Press, 1955 [1921]).

26. Kris A. Bulcroft and M. O'Conner-Roden, "Never Too Late." *Psychology Today*, June 1987, Vol. 20, pp. 66–69; also David Heller, "A Meditation on Lost Love." *Psychology Today*, March 1987, Vol. 20, pp. 74–75.

27. Jeanette Lauer and Robert Lauer, *'Till Death Do Us Part: How Couples Stay Together* (New York: Haworth Press, 1988).

28. David M. Buss, "Human Mate Selection." *American Scientist*, January-February 1985, Vol. 73, pp. 47–51.
29. Robin Norwood, *Women Who Love Too Much* (New York: Pocket Books, 1985).
30. Augustus Y. Napier, *The Fragile Bond* (New York: Harper and Row, 1988).
31. David M. Buss, "Conflict Between the Sexes." *Journal of Personality and Social Psychology*, 1989, Vol. 56, pp. 735–747.
32. Francesca M. Cancian, *Love in America* (New York: Cambridge University Press, 1987); also Roger E. Lamb, ed., *Love Analyzed* (Boulder, CO: Westview Press, 1997).
33. Judith A. Feeney and Patricia Noller, *Adult Attachment* (Thousand Oaks, CA: Sage, 1996).
34. Sandra S. Brehm, *Intimate Relationships*, 2d ed. (New York: McGraw-Hill, 1992); also Peter Salovey and Judith Rodin, "Envy and Jealousy in Close Relationships." Pp. 221–246 in Clyde Hendrick, 1989.
35. John C. Holmes and John K. Rempel, "Trust in Close Relationships." Pp. 187–220 in Clyde Hendrick, 1989, pp. 199–200.
36. Arnold H. Buss, *Personality: Matches and Mismatches*. Unpublished manuscript.
37. Melissa Sands, *Look Before You Leap* (New York: St. Martin's Press, 1988), p. 61.
38. David H. Olson, "Marriage in Perspective." Pp. 402–419 in Frank D. Fincham and Thomas N. Bradbury, eds., *The Psychology of Marriage* (New York: Guilford Press, 1990), p. 407.
39. John D'Emilio and Estelle B. Freedman, *Intimate Matters* (New York: Harper and Row, 1988).
40. Ira L. Reiss and Gary R. Lee, *Family Systems in America* (New York: Holt, Rinehart & Winston, 1988); Martin King Whyte, *Dating, Mating, and Marriage* (New York: Aldine de Gruyter, 1990); and Stephanie Coontz, *The Way We Never Were: American Families and the Nostalgia Trap* (New York: Basic Books, 1992), pp. 193–196.
41. Similar findings on extramarital behavior from various national surveys have been reported by Andrew M. Greeley in his analysis of the General Social Surveys of the National Opinion Research Center between 1972 to 1989 in *Faithful Attraction: Discovering Intimacy, Love, Fidelity in American Marriage* (New York: Tom Doherty,); Edward O. Laumann, John H. Gagnon, Robert T. Michael, and Stuart Michaels, *The Social Organization of Sexuality: Sexual Practices in the U.S.* (Chicago: University of Chicago Press, 1994); and Michael W. Wiederman, "Extramarital Sex: Prevalence and Correlates in a National Survey." *The Journal of Sex Research*, 1997, Vol. 36, pp. 59–66.
42. Centers for Disease Control and Prevention, "Trends in Sexual Risk Behaviors Among High School Students—United States, 1991–1997." *Morbidity and Mortality*, September 18, 1998, Vol. 47, pp. 749–751.

Chapter 6 Finding a Partner

1. Barbara L. Bailey, *From Front Porch to Back Seat* (Baltimore: Johns Hopkins University Press, 1988).
2. Robert D. Mare, "Five Decades of Educational Assortative Mating." *American Sociological Review*, 1991, Vol. 56, pp. 15–32.
3. Robert D. Mare, 1991, p. 31.
4. Bernard L. Murstein, *Paths to Marriage* (Beverly Hills, CA: Sage, 1986).
5. Frederic S. Wamboldt and David Reiss, "Defining a New Family Heritage and a New Relationship Identity: Two Central Tasks in the Making of a Marriage." *Family Process*, 1989, Vol. 28, pp. 317–336.
6. Bernard R. Murstein, 1986, p. 87.

7. Suzanna Rose and Irene Hanson Frieze, "Young Singles' Scripts for a First Date." *Gender and Society*, 1989, Vol. 3, pp. 258–268; Mary Liege Laner and Nicole A. Ventrone, "Egalitarian Daters/Traditional Dates." *Journal of Family Issues*, 1998, Vol. 19, pp. 468–477.

8. Martin King Whyte, *Dating, Mating, and Marriage* (Hawthorne, NY: Aldine de Gruyter, 1990), and "Choosing Mates—The American Way." *Society*, March-April 1992, Vol. 29, pp. 71–77.

9. Mary Liege Laner and Nicole A. Ventrone, "Dating Scripts Revisited." *Journal of Family Issues*, 2000, Vol. 21, pp. 488–500.

10. Martin King Whyte, 1990, p. 243.

11. See Bonnie Rothman Morris, "Seeking Love on Line." *New York Times*, August 16, 1999, pp. B1, B7.

12. Sally A. Lloyd, "The Dark Side of Courtship: Violence and Sexual Exploitation." *Family Relations*, 1991, Vol. 40, pp. 14–20; Jan E. Stets and Debra A. Henderson, "Contextual Factors Surrounding Conflict Resolution While Dating: Results from a National Study." *Family Relations*, 1991, Vol. 40, pp. 29–36; Jan E. Stets, "Interactive Processes in Dating Aggression: A National Study." *Journal of Marriage and the Family*, 1992, Vol. 54, pp. 165–177; B. P. Marx, V. Van Wie, and A. M. Gross, "Date Rape Risk Factors: A Review and Methodological Critique of the Literature." *Aggression and Violent Behavior*, 1996, Vol. 1, pp. 27–45.

13. Ronald L. Simons, Kuei-Hsiu Lin, and Leslie C. Gordon, "Socialization in the Family of Origin and Male Dating Violence: A Prospective Study." *Journal of Marriage and the Family*, 1998, Vol. 60, pp. 467–478. On attachment difficulties and dating violence, see Mary D. Salter Ainsworth, "Attachment Beyond Infancy." *American Psychology*, 1989, Vol. 44, pp. 709–716.

14. Ofra Mayseless, "Adult Attachment Patterns and Courtship Violence." *Family Relations*, 1991, Vol. 40, pp. 21–28.

15. David Levinson, *Family Violence in Cross-Cultural Perspective* (Newbury Park, CA: Sage, 1989), p. 104; also Nancy E. Riley, "Gender, Power, and Population Change." *Population Bulletin*, May 1997, Vol. 52, No. 2, pp. 1–45.

16. Jan E. Stets and Debra A. Henderson, 1991, p. 35.

17. Jan E. Stets and Murray A. Straus, "Gender Differences in Reporting Marital Violence and Its Medical and Psychological Consequences" and "The Marriage License as a Hitting License." Pp. 151–165 and 224–227 in Murray A. Straus and Richard J. Gelles, eds., *Physical Violence in American Families* (Newbury Park, CA: Sage, 1990).

18. There have been literally hundreds of trade books, magazine articles, and newspaper articles published on this topic. A popular trade book is Stephen Gullo and Connie Church, *Loveshock* (New York: Simon and Schuster, 1998). Some good academic sources are Diane Felmlee, Susan Sprecher, and Edward Bassin, "The Dissolution of Intimate Relationships: A Hazard Model." *Social Psychology Quarterly*, 1990, Vol. 53, pp. 13–30; and Thomas B. Holman and Bing Dao Li, "Premarital Factors Influencing Perceived Readiness for Marriage." *Journal of Family Issues*, 1997, Vol. 18, pp. 124–144.

19. On gender differences in coping with breaking up, see Kelly A. Sorenson, Shauna M. Russell, Daniel J. Harkness, and John H. Harvey, "Account-Making, Confiding, and Coping with the Ending of a Close Relationship." *Journal of Social Behavior and Personality*, 1993, Vol. 8, pp. 73–86.

20. For a discussion of the relationship between generational marriage rates and changing economic factors, see Richard Esterlin, *Birth and Fortune*, 2d ed. (Chicago: University of Chicago Press, 1987). For the overall historical pattern in the United States, see Stephanie

Coontz, *The Way We Never Were* (New York: Basic Books, 1992), pp. 42–67; for the pattern in the 20th century, see Theresa M. Cooney and Dennis P. Hogan, "Marriage in an Institutionalized Life Course: First Marriage Among American Men in the Twentieth Century." *Journal of Marriage and the Family*, 1991, Vol. 53, pp. 178–190.

21. For cross-national comparisons of marriage rates and other family patterns in Europe and the United States since the 1960s, see Andrew J. Cherlin and Frank F. Furstenberg, Jr., "The Changing European Family." *Journal of Family Issues*, 1988, Vol. 9, pp. 291–297.

22. Larry L. Bumpass and James A. Sweet, "National Estimates of Cohabitation." *Demography*, 1989, Vol. 26, pp. 615–625.

23. David M. Buss, "International Preferences in Selecting Mates." *Journal of Cross-Cultural Psychology*, 1990, Vol. 21, pp. 5–47.

24. David M. Buss, 1990, p. 47.

25. Martin King Whyte, 1992, p. 77.

26. Renate M. Houts, Elliot Robins, and Ted L. Huston, "Compatibility and the Development of Premarital Relationships." *Journal of Marriage and the Family*, 1996, Vol. 58, pp. 7–20; Michael D. Botwin, David M. Buss, and Todd K. Shackelford, "Personality and Mate Preferences." *Journal of Personality*, 1997, Vol. 65, pp. 107–136; Jennifer Hahn and Thomas Blass, "Dating Partner Preferences." *Journal of Social Behavior and Personality*, 1997, Vol. 12, pp. 595–610.

27. Harville Hendrix, *Getting the Love You Want: A Guide for Couples* (New York: Henry Holt, 1988).

28. Norvel D. Glenn and Charles N. Weaver, "The Changing Relation of Marital Status to Reported Happiness." *Journal of Marriage and the Family*, 1988, Vol. 50, pp. 317–324; also Steven L. Nock, *Marriage in Men's Lives* (New York: Oxford University Press, 1998).

29. See Edward L. Kain, *The Myth of Family Decline* (Lexington, MA: Lexington Books, 1990); also Frank F. Furstenberg, Jr. "The Future of Marriage." *American Demographics*, 1999, Vol. 22, pp. 620–628.

30. Jessie Bernard, *The Future of Marriage*, 2d ed. (New Haven, CT: Yale University Press, 1982).

31. Larry L. Bumpass, Teresa Castro Martin, and James A. Sweet, "The Impact of Family Background and Early Marital Factors on Marital Disruption." *Journal of Family Issues*, 1991, Vol. 12, pp. 12–42; also Veronica J. Tichenor, "Status and Income as Gendered Resources: The Case of Marital Power." *Journal of Marriage and the Family*, 1999, Vol. 61, pp. 638–650.

32. Larry L. Bumpass, Teresa Castro Martin, and James A. Sweet, 1991, p. 39.

33. Ernest W. Burgess and Paul Wallin, *Engagement and Marriage* (Philadelphia: Lippincott, 1953).

34. An example of more recent research that builds upon and confirms Burgess and Wallin's generalizations about marriages that last is Blaine J. Fowers, "Predicting Marital Success for Premarital Couple Types Based on PREPARE Scores." *Journal of Marital and Family Therapy*, 1996, Vol. 22, pp. 103–119.

35. Jeffry H. Larson and Thomas B. Holman, "Premarital Predictors of Marital Quality and Stability." *Family Relations*, 1994, Vol. 43, pp. 428–437.

Chapter 7 Other Options

1. Steven Stack and J. Ross Eshelman, "Marital Status and Happiness: A 17 Nation Study." *Journal of Marriage and the Family*, 1998, Vol. 60, pp. 527–536; for the picture in the

United States, see Joan Aldous and Rodney F. Ganey, "Family Life and the Pursuit of Happiness." *Journal of Family Issues*, 1999, Vol. 20, pp. 155–180.

2. See the results of a national poll conducted by Yankelovich Partners for *Time/*CNN on August 9–10, 2000, reported by Tamala M. Edwards in "Flying Solo." *Time*, August 28, 2000, pp. 47–53.

3. Tamala M. Edwards, 2000, p. 48.

4. Jacqueline Simenauer and David Carroll, *Singles: The New Americans* (New York: Simon and Schuster, 1982).

5. On the overwhelming predominance of divorced or widowed people among those who do not plan to ever marry, and the reasons for this preference, see Patricia Frazier, Nancy Arikian, Sonja Benson, and Ann Losoff, "Desire for Marriage and Life Satisfaction Among Heterosexual Adults." *Journal of Social and Personal Relationships*, 1996, Vol. 13, pp. 225–239.

6. Michael Wines, "For All Russia, Biological Clock Is Running Out." *New York Times*, December 28, 2000, p. A1, A10.

7. Scott J. South, "Sex Ratios, Economic Power, and Women's Roles: A Theoretical Extension and Empirical Test." *Journal of Marriage and the Family*, 1988, Vol. 50, pp. 19–31.

8. Scott J. South, "Racial and Ethnic Differences in the Desire to Marry." *Journal of Marriage and the Family*, 1993, Vol. 55, pp. 357–370; and Peter D. Brandon and Larry Bumpass, "Children's Living Arrangements, Coresidence of Unmarried Fathers, and Welfare Receipt." *Journal of Family Issues*, 2001, Vol. 22, pp. 3–26.

9. Naomi Neft and Ann D. Levine, *Where Women Stand*, An International Report of the Status of Women in 140 Countries (New York: Random House, 1997), p. 244.

10. Larry L. Bumpass and James A. Sweet, "National Estimates of Cohabitation." *Demography*, 1989, Vol. 26, pp. 615–625; also Larry L. Bumpass, R. Kelly Raley, and James A. Sweet, "The Changing Character of Stepfamilies: Implications of Cohabitation and Nonmarital Childbearing." *Demography*, 1995, Vol. 32, pp. 425–436.

11. On the social backgrounds of cohabitors, see Bram B. Buunk and Barry van Driel, *Variant Lifestyles and Relationships* (Newbury Park, CA: Sage, 1989), p. 56; also Arland Thornton, "The Influence of the Marital History of Parents on the Marital and Cohabitational Experiences of Children." *American Journal of Sociology*, 1991, Vol. 96, pp. 868–894. On the greater educational similarity and lesser tendency toward ethnic and racial matching among cohabiting couples, see Debra L. Blackwell and Daniel T. Lichter, "Mate Selection Among Married and Cohabiting Couples." *Journal of Family Issues*, 2000, Vol. 21, pp. 275–302.

12. M. Belinda Tucker and Claudia Mitchell-Kernan, "African American Marital Trends in Context: Toward a Synthesis." Pp. 345–362 in M. Belinda Tucker and Claudia Mitchell-Kernan, eds., *The Decline in Marriage Among African Americans* (New York: Russell Sage, 1995).

13. Frank F. Furstenberg, Jr., Theodore Hershberg, and John Modell, "The Origins of the Female-Headed Black Family: The Impact of the Urban Experience." *Journal of Interdisciplinary History*, 1975, Vol. 5, pp. 211–233.

14. Stewart E. Tolnay and Kyle D. Crowder, "Regional Origin and Family Stability in Northern Cities: The Role of Context." *American Sociological Review*, 1999, Vol. 64, pp. 97–112; also Sharon Sassler and Robert Schoen, "The Effect of Attitudes and Economic Activity on Marriage." *Journal of Marriage and the Family*, 1999, Vol. 61, pp. 147–159.

15. For trend data on the duration of living-together relationships from the two National Surveys of Families and Households, see Larry L. Bumpass and Hsien-Hen Lu, "Trends

in Cohabitation and Implications for Children's Family Contexts in the United States." *Population Studies*, 2000, Vol. 54, pp. 29–41.

16. Judith A. Seltzer, "Families Formed Outside of Marriage." *Journal of Marriage and the Family*, 2000, Vol. 62, pp. 1247–1268.
17. Wendy D. Manning and Pamela J. Smock, "Why Marry? Race and the Transition to Marriage Among Cohabitants." *Demography*, 1995, Vol. 32, pp. 509–520.
18. Eleanor D. Macklin, "Heterosexual Couples Who Cohabit Nonmaritally: Some Common Problems and Issues." Pp. 56–72 in Catherine S. Chilman, Elam W. Nunnally, and Fred M. Cox, eds., *Variant Family Forms* (Newbury Park, CA: Sage, 1988).
19. Bram B. Buunk and Barry van Driel, 1989, p. 62; also Scott J. Smith and Glenna Spitz, "Housework in Marital and Nonmarital Households." *American Sociological Review*, 1994, Vol. 59, pp. 227–247.
20. Stephen L. Nock, "A Comparison of Marriages and Cohabiting Relationships." *Journal of Family Issues*, 1995, Vol. 16, pp. 53–76; also Julie Brines and Kara Joyner, "The Ties That Bind: Principles of Cohesion in Cohabitation and Marriage." *American Sociological Review*, 1999, Vol. 64, pp. 333–355; and Judith Treas and Deirdre Giesen, "Sexual Infidelity Among Married and Cohabiting Americans." *Journal of Marriage and the Family*, 2000, Vol. 62, pp. 48–60.
21. Neal G. Bennett, Ann Klimas Blanc, and David E. Bloom, "Commitment amd the Modern Union: Assessing the Link Between Premarital Cohabitation and Subsequent Marital Stability." *American Sociological Review*, 1988, Vol. 53, pp. 127–138; Elizabeth Thomson and Ugo Colella, "Cohabitation and Marital Stability: Quality or Commitment?" *Journal of Marriage and the Family*, 1992, Vol. 54, pp. 259–267; and Lee A. Lillard, Michael J. Brein, and Linda J. Waite, "Premarital Cohabitation and Subsequent Marital Dissolution: Is It Self-Selection?" *Demography*, 1995, Vol. 32, pp. 437–457.
22. Stephen L. Nock, 1995, p. 75.
23. On problems that are more extreme among cohabitors than among married couples, see the previously cited article by Eleanor D. Macklin, 1988. See also Susan L. Brown and Alan Booth, "Cohabitation versus Marriage: A Comparison of Relationship Quality." *Journal of Marriage and the Family*, 1996, Vol. 58, pp. 668–678.
24. On gender differences in commitment among living-together couples, see Neal G. Bennett, Ann Klimas Blanc, and David E. Bloom, 1988.
25. On role conflict, see Betty Yorburg, *Sociological Reality* (New York: McGraw-Hill, 1995), pp. 115–121.
26. Monica Seff, "Cohabitation and the Law." *Marriage and Family Review*, 1995, Vol. 21, pp. 141–168.
27. Patricia Choo, Timothy Levine, and Elaine Hatfield, "Gender, Love Schemas, and Reactions to Romantic Breakups." *Journal of Social Behavior and Personality*, 1996, Vol. 5, pp. 143–160.
28. Stephen L. Nock, 1995, p. 76.
29. Barbara Sherman Heyl, "Homosexuality: A Social Phenomenon." Pp. 321–349 in Kathleen McKinney and Susan Sprecher, eds., *Human Sexuality: The Societal and Interpersonal Context* (Norwood, NJ: Ablex, 1989).
30. Edward O. Laumann, John H. Gagnon, Robert T. Michael, and Stuart Michaels, *The Social Organization of Sexuality* (Chicago: University of Chicago Press, 1994). For a condensed, more popular account written with a *New York Times* science reporter, see Robert T. Michael, John H. Gagnon, Edward O. Laumann, and Gina Kolata, *Sex in America* (Boston: Little, Brown, 1994). For a description of myths about sexual behav-

ior that have been exposed by social scientific research, see Pepper Schwartz, *Everything You Know About Sex Is Wrong* (New York: Putnam, 2000).

31. Clellan S. Ford and Frank A. Beach, *Patterns of Sexual Behavior* (New York: Harper and Row, 1972 [1951]).

32. Katherine R. Allen and David H. Demo, "The Families of Lesbians and Gay Men: A New Frontier in Family Research." *Journal of Marriage and the Family*, 1995, Vol. 57, pp. 111–127; Mike Allen and Nancy Burrell, "Comparing the Impact of Homosexual and Heterosexual Parents on Children: Meta-Analysis of Existing Research." *Journal of Homosexuality*, 1996, Vol. 32, pp. 19–35; Katherine R. Allen, "Lesbian and Gay Families." Pp. 196–218 in Terry Arendall, ed., *Contemporary Parenting: Challenges and Issues* (Thousand Oaks, CA: Sage, 1997); and Ritch G. Savin-Williams and Kristin E. Esterberg, "Lesbian, Gay, and Bisexual Families." Pp. 197–215 in David H. Demo, Katherine R. Allen, and Mark A. Fine, eds., *Handbook of Family Diversity* (New York: Oxford University Press, 2000).

33. On this and other issues, including problems in doing unbiased research on homosexuality, see Francis Mark Mondimore, *A Natural History of Homosexuality* (Baltimore: Johns Hopkins University Press, 1996); also Timothy F. Murphy, *Gay Science: The Ethics of Sexual Orientation Research* (New York: Columbia University Press, 1997); and Simon LeVay, *Queer Science: The Use and Abuse of Research on Homosexuality* (Cambridge, MA: MIT Press, 1996).

34. Reported in the *New York Times*, July 7, 1989, p. A1.

35. National surveys conducted by Princeton Survey Research Associates and reported by John Leland and Mark Miller in "Can Gays Convert?" *Newsweek*, August 17, 1998, pp. 46–51.

36. Pepper Schwartz and Virginia Rutter, *The Gender of Sexuality* (Thousand Oaks, CA: Pine Forge Press, 1998); also Ritch C. Savin-Williams and Kristin G. Esterberg, 2000, p. 200.

37. Danielle Julien, Elise Chartrand, and Jean Begin, "Social Networks, Structural Interdependence, and Conjugal Adjustment in Heterosexual, Gay, and Lesbian Couples." *Journal of Marriage and the Family*, 1999, Vol. 61, pp. 516–530.

38. Mayta A. Caldwell and Letitia Anne Peplau, "The Balance of Power in Lesbian Relationships." Pp. 204–215 in Christopher Carlson, ed., *Perspectives on the Family: History, Class, and Feminism* (Belmont, CA: Wadsworth, 1990).

39. Lawrence A. Kurdek, "Relationship Outcomes and Their Predictors: Longitudinal Evidence from Heterosexual Married, Gay Cohabiting, and Lesbian Cohabiting Couples." *Journal of Marriage and the Family*, 1998, Vol. 60, pp. 553–568.

40. Barbara F. Okun, *Understanding Diverse Families: What Practitioners Need to Know* (New York: Guilford Press, 1996), p. 133.

41. Rick Bragg, "Fearing Isolation in Old Age, Gay Generation Seeks Haven." *New York Times*, October 21, 1999, pp. A1, A16.

42. See, for example, Judith Wallerstein and Sandra Blakeslee, *Second Chances: Men, Women, and Children a Decade After Divorce* (New York: Ticknor and Fields, 1990).

43. Tori De Angelis, "More Than McTherapy." *Psychology Today*, March 1996, pp. 20–21.

44. Cognitive therapy was founded by the psychiatrist Aaron T. Beck. For a good description of this approach and its use in dealing with a wide range of problems, see Brad A. Alford and Aaron T. Beck, *The Integrative Power of Cognitive Therapy* (New York: Guilford Press, 1997).

45. Brad A. Alford and Aaron T. Beck, 1997, p. 127.

46. Paul Grayson and Kate Cauley, eds., *College Psychotherapy* (New York: Guilford Press, 1989).

47. These research results were reported in the *New York Times*. See Jodi Wilgoren, "More Than Ever, First-Year Students Feeling the Stress of College." *New York Times*, January 24, 2000, p. A18.

48. For a good treatment of this topic, see Nadine J. Koslow, Florence W. Kaslow, and Eugene W. Farber, "Theories and Techniques of Marital and Family Therapy." Pp. 767–792 in Marvin B. Sussman, Suzanne K. Steinmets, and Gary W. Peterson, eds., *Handbook of Marriage and the Family*, 2d ed. (New York: Plenum, 1999).

49. Quoted in Pam Belluck, "States Declare War on Divorce Rates, Before Any 'I Dos'." *New York Times*, April 21, 2000, P. A1.

Chapter 8 Partner Relationships

1. Betty Carter and Monica McGoldrick, eds., *The Changing Family Life Cycle* (Needham Heights, MA: Allyn and Bacon, 1989), Part I; also John M. Gottman, James Coan, Sybil Carrere, and Catherine Swanson, "Predicting Marital Happiness and Stability from Newlywed Interactions." *Journal of Marriage and the Family*, 1998, Vol. 60, pp. 5–22.

2. Donna Ruane Morrison and Mary Jo Coiro, "Parental Conflict and Marital Disruption: Do Children Benefit When High-Conflict Marriages Are Dissolved?" *Journal of Marriage and the Family*, 1999, Vol. 61, pp. 626–627.

3. John F. Crosby, *Illusion and Disillusion: The Self in Love and Marriage*, 4th ed. (Belmont, CA: Wadsworth, 1991).

4. David H. Olson, Hamilton I. McCubbin, and Associates, *Families: What Makes Them Work*, 2d ed. (Newbury Park, CA: Sage, 1989), p. 123; also David R. Johnson and Alan Booth, "Marital Quality: A Product of the Dyadic Environment or Individual Factors?" *Social Forces*, 1998, Vol. 76, pp. 883–904.

5. David Olson, Hamilton I. McCubbin, and Associates, 1989, p. 122, p. 181; John M. Gottman et al., 1998, p. 20; also David R. Johnson and Alan Booth, 1998, p. 903.

6. Patricia Noller and Mary Anne Fitzpatrick, "Marital Communication in the Eighties." *Journal of Marriage and the Family*, 1990, Vol. 52, pp. 832–843.

7. Kim W. Halford, Kurt Hahlweg, and Michael Dunne, "The Cross-Cultural Consistency Associated with Marital Distress." *Journal of Marriage and the Family*, 1992, Vol. 52, pp. 487–500.

8. A classic study on this topic is Mirra Komarovsky's *Blue Collar Marriage* (New York: Vintage, 1966). On persisting class and ethnic differences in family communication, see Lillian Rubin, *Intimate Strangers* (New York: Harper and Row, 1983) and *Families on the Fault Line: America's Working Class Speaks About Family, the Economy, Race, and Ethnicity* (New York: HarperCollins, 1994).

9. On male-female differences in the willingness to confide, see Joseph H. Pleck, "Prisoners of Manliness." Pp. 98–107 in Michael S. Kimmel and Michael A. Messner, eds., *Men's Lives* (New York: Macmillan, 1992); and Valerian J. Derlega, Sandra Metts, Sandra Petronio, and Stephen T. Margulis, *Self-Disclosure* (Thousand Oaks, CA: Sage, 1993).

10. See Felix Berardo, "Trends and Directions in Family Research in the 1980s." *Journal of Marriage and the Family*, 1990, Vol. 52, pp. 809–817. On nonverbal communication, a classic source is anthropologist Edward T. Hall's *The Silent Language* (New York: Doubleday, 1959); also Sherod Miller, Daniel Wackman, Elam Nunnally, and Phyllis Miller, *Connecting with Self and Others* (Littleton, CO: Interpersonal Communications Programs, 1988).

11. Aaron T. Beck, *Love Is Never Enough* (New York: Harper and Row, 1988), p. 145.

12. Mary Anne Fitzpatrick, *Between Husbands and Wives: Communication in Marriage* (Newbury Park, CA: Sage, 1988).

13. On psychological abuse, see Sherry L. Hamby and David B. Sugarman, "Acts of Psychological Aggression Against a Partner and Their Relation to Physical Abuse." *Journal of Marriage and the Family*, 1999, Vol. 61, pp. 959–970. For a review of evidence on the greater sensitivity of women and children to psychological abuse, see Patricia Noller and Mary Anne Fitzpatrick, 1990, p. 132–140.

14. David H. Olson, Hamilton J. McCubbin, and Associates, 1989, p. 271. On the importance of communication in settling arguments and disputes, see Susan Heitler, *From Conflict to Resolution* (New York: W. W. Norton, 1990). For studies that confirm the high degree of communication and support in egalitarian partnerships, see Susan C. Rosenbluth, Janice M. Steil, and Juliet Whitcomb, "Marital Equality: What Does It Mean?" *Journal of Family Issues*, 1998, Vol. 19, pp. 227–244; Barbara J. Risman and Danette Johnson-Summerford, "Doing It Fairly: A Study of Postgender Marriages." *Journal of Marriage and the Family*, 1998, Vol. 60, pp. 23–40; and Jane R. Wilkie, Myra Marx Ferree, and Katherine S. Ratcliff, "Gender and Fairness: Marital Satisfaction in Two-Earner Couples." *Journal of Marriage and the Family*, 1998, Vol. 60, pp. 574–594.

15. See Deborah Tannen's best-selling books *You Just Don't Understand: Women and Men in Conversation* (New York: William Morrow, 1990) and *Talking from Nine to Five* (New York: William Morrow, 1993); also psychologist Mary Crawford's *Talking Difference: On Gender and Language* (Thousand Oaks, CA: Sage, 1995).

16. For this view, see sociologist Sandra L. Bem's *The Lenses of Gender: Transforming the Debate on Sexual Inequality* (New Haven, CT: Yale University Press, 1993); also psychologist Michael S. Kimmel's *The Gendered Society* (New York: Oxford University Press, 2000). On myths about the "weaker sex" and explanations of the greater longevity and physical resistance to disease of women (and of females throughout the animal kingdom), see Ashley Montagu, *The Natural Superiority of Women*, 2d. ed. (New York: Macmillan, 1999).

17. For a historical and cross-cultural picture of learned gender differences in communicating and how these differences reinforce female inequality, especially in agricultural societies, see sociolinguist Suzanne Romaine's *Communicating Gender* (Mahwah, NJ: Erlbaum, 1999).

18. H. G. Lerner, *The Dance of Deception: Pretending and Truth-Telling in Women's Lives* (New York: HarperCollins, 1993); also Evan Imber-Black, *The Secret Life of Families* (New York: Doubleday/Bantam, 1998).

19. Adapted from Sherod Miller and Phyllis A. Miller, *Core Communication: Skills and Processes* (Boulder, CO: Interpersonal Communication Programs, 1997). This is a highly useful guide for improving communication skills and resolving conflicts.

20. Wesley R. Burr, "Beyond 'I' Statements in Family Communication." *Family Relations*, 1990, Vol. 39, pp. 266–273.

21. For more details and illustrations of gunnysacking, see John F. Crosby, 1991, p. 177.

22. For this definition of power, see Max Weber, *The Theory of Social and Economic Organization* (New York: Free Press, 1947 [1925]), translated by A. M. Henderson and Talcott Parsons, p. 152.

23. Robert O. Blood and Donald M. Wolfe, *Husbands and Wives* (New York: Free Press, 1960).

24. See Bron B. Ingoldsby, "Poverty and Patriarchy in Latin America." Pp. 335–351 in Bron B. Ingoldsby and Suzanna Smith, eds. *Families in Multicultural Perspective* (New York: Guilford Press, 1995).

25. Hyman Rodman, "Marital Power and the Theory of Resources in Cultural Context." *Journal of Comparative Family Studies*, 1972, Vol. 3, pp. 50–67.

26. Willard Waller with Reubin Hill, *The Family: A Dynamic Interpretation*, rev. ed. (New York: Dryden Press, 1951), p. 275.

27. Vern L. Bengtson, "Diversity and Symbolism in Grandparent Roles." Pp. 11–25 in Vern L. Bengtson and Joan F. Robertson, eds., *Grandparenthood* (Newbury Park, CA: 1985).

28. Francesca M. Cancian, *Love in America* (New York: Cambridge University Press, 1987), p. 78.

29. Martin King Whyte, *Dating, Mating, and Marriage* (Hawthorne, NY: Aldine de Gruyter, 1990), p. 244.

30. Martin King Whyte, 1990, p. 246.

31. See Ronald L. Taylor, "Black American Families." Pp. 19–45 in Ronald L. Taylor, *Minority Families in the United States*, 2d ed. (Upper Saddle River, NJ: Prentice Hall, 1998); also M. Belinda Tucker, "Marital Values and Expectations in Context: Results from a 21–City Survey." Pp. 166–187 in Linda J. Waite, ed., *The Ties That Bind* (Hawthorne, NY: Aldine de Gruyter, 2000).

32. See, for example, Yen Le Espiritu, *Asian American Women and Men* (Thousand Oaks, CA: Sage, 1997).

33. Richard Gelles and Claire Pedrick Cornell, *Intimate Violence in Families*, 2d ed. (Newbury Park, CA: Sage, 1990), p. 11.

34. Jan E. Stets, "Verbal and Physical Aggression in Marriage." *Journal of Marriage and the Family*, 1990, Vol. 52, pp. 501–514; also Murray A. Straus and Stephen Sweet, "Verbal/Symbolic Aggression in Couples: Incidence Rates and Relationship to Personal Characteristics." *Journal of Marriage and the Family*, 1992, Vol. 54, pp. 346–357.

35. Sherry L. Hamby and David B. Sugarman, "Acts of Psychological Aggression Against a Partner and Their Relation to Physical Assault and Gender." *Journal of Marriage and the Family*, 1999, Vol. 61, pp. 959–970.

36. Lenore Walker, *Terrifying Love* (New York: Harper and Row, 1989), p. 45; also Elizbeth Kandel Englander, *Understanding Violence* (Mahwah, NJ: Erlbaum, 1997); and Aaron T. Beck, *Prisoners of Hate: The Cognitive Basis of Anger, Hatred, and Violence* (New York: HarperCollins, 1999).

37. For a description of other forms of passive aggression in partner relationships, see John F. Crosby, 1991, p. 162.

38. Richard J. Gelles and Claire Pedrick Cornell, 1990, p. 15. For statistical data on higher rates of violence in the United States compared to other industrial (and nonindustrial) countries, see Ian R. H. Rockett, "Injury and Violence: A Public Health Perspective." *Population Bulletin*, December1998, Vol. 53, No. 4, Table 1, p. 7.

39. On systems theory, see Jason Montgomery and Willard Fewer, *Family Systems and Beyond* (New York: Human Sciences Press, 1988); Kathleen M. Galvin and Bernard J. Brommel, *Family Communication*, 3d ed. (Glenview, IL: Scott, Foresman, 1991); Carlfred B. Broderick, *Understanding Family Process: Basics of Family Systems Theory* (Newbury Park, CA: Sage, 1993; and Chester A. Winton, *Frameworks for Studying Families* (Guilford, CT: Dushkin/McGraw-Hill, 1995), pp. 44–85.

40. On children who are compelled to take over the role of a departed parent, see Nancy D. Chase, ed., *Burdened Children* (Thousand Oaks, CA: Sage, 1999).

41. Murray A. Straus and Richard J. Gelles, *Physical Violence in American Families: Risk Factors and Adaptations to Violence in 8,145 Families* (New Brunswick, NJ: Transaction, 1995).

42. Bureau of Justice Statistics, "Violence by Intimates: Analysis of Data on Crimes by Current or Former Spouses, Boyfriends, and Girlfriends." Washington, DC: U.S. Department of Justice, Office of Justice Programs, NCJ-167237, March 1998.

43. Richard J. Gelles and Claire Pedrick Cornell, 1990, p. 15.

44. For a vivid historical picture of violence against children and the relationship between child abuse and war, see Lloyd de Mause, *The History of Childhood* (New York: Psychohistory Press, 1974).

45. On the incidence and consequences of child abuse and the intergenerational transmission of aggression, see Murray A. Straus, *Beating the Devil Out of Them: Corporal Punishment in American Families* (San Francisco: Jossey-Bass, 1994); Diana Doumas, Galya Margolin, and Richard S. John, "The Intergenerational Transmission of Aggression Across Three Generations." *Journal of Family Violence*, 1994, Vol. 9, pp. 157–175; and Murray A. Straus, David B. Sugarman, and Jean Giles-Sims, "Spanking by Parents and Subsequent Antisocial Behavior of Children." *Archives of Pediatric Adolescent Medicine*, 1997, Vol. 151, pp. 761–767.

46. Murray A. Straus and Julie H. Stewart, "Corporal Punishment by American Parents: National Data on Prevalence, Chronicity, Severity, and Duration, in Relation to Child and Family Characteristics." *Clinical Child and Family Psychology Review*, 1999, Vol. 2, 2, pp. 55–70.

47. On cross-cultural differences in the aggressive emotions of children, see Jo Ann M. Farver, Barbara Welles-Nystrom, Dominick L. Frosch, Supra Wimbarti, and Sigfried Hoppe-Graff, "Toy Stories: Aggression in Children's Narratives in the United States, Sweden, Germany, and Indonesia." *Journal of Cross-Cultural Psychology*, 1997, Vol. 28, pp. 393–420.

48. Michael P. Johnson and Kathleen J. Ferraro, "Research on Domestic Violence in the 1990s: Making Distinctions." *Journal of Marriage and the Family*, 2000, Vol. 62, pp. 948–963.

49. On gender differences in reporting violence, see Jan E. Stets and Murray A. Straus, "Gender Differences in Reporting Marital Violence and Its Medical and Psychological Consequences." Pp. 151–165 in Murray A. Straus and Richard J. Gelles, eds., *Physical Violence in American Families* (Newbury Park, CA: Sage, 1990).

50. The 1998 Bureau of Justice Report, cited in note 42, contains figures on the prevalence and consequences of violence toward women.

51. On black-white differences in domestic violence and killings, see Fox Butterfield, "Study Shows a Racial Divide in Domestic Violence Cases." *New York Times*, May 16, 2000, p. A16.

52. Jan E. Stets and Murray A. Straus, "The Marriage License as a Hitting License." Pp. 227–244 in Murray A. Straus and Richard J. Gelles, 1990.

53. Richard Gelles, "A Life Course Approach to Family Violence." Pp. 225–254 in Sharon J. Price, Patrick C. McKenry, and Megan J. Murphy, eds., *Families Across Time: A Life Course Perspective* (Los Angeles: Roxbury, 2000).

54. James D. Torr and Karin Swisher, *Violence Against Women* (San Diego, CA: Greenhaven Press, 1999).

55. Kathleen J. Ferraro, "Battered Women: Strategies for Survival." Pp. 583–590 in A. Carderelli, ed., *Violence Among Intimate Partners: Patterns, Causes, and Effects* (New York: Macmillan, 1997).

56. Pamela Choice and Leanne K. Lamke, "A Conceptual Approach to Understanding Abused Women's Stay/Leave Decisions." *Journal of Family Issues*, 1997, Vol. 18, pp. 290–314.

Chapter 9 Parents and Children
1. On pressures that are more severe for single parents, see Sara S. McLanahan and Karen Booth, "Mother-Only Families: Problems, Prospects, and Politics." *Journal of Marriage*

and the Family, 1989, Vol. 51, pp. 557–579; also Sarah McLanahan and Gary Sandefur, *Growing Up with a Single Parent: What Helps, What Hurts* (Cambridge, MA: Harvard University Press, 1994).

2. E. Michael Foster, Damon Jones, and Saul D. Hoffman, "The Economic Impact of Nonmarital Childbearing: How Are Older Single Mothers Faring?" *Journal of Marriage and the Family,* 1998, Vol. 60, pp. 163–174; Henry N. Ricciuti, "Single Parenthood and School Readiness in White, Black, and Hispanic 6– and 7–Year Olds." *Journal of Family Psychology,* 1999, Vol. 13, pp. 450–465; Cloe E. Bird, "Gender Differences in the Social and Economic Burdens of Parenting and Psychological Distress." *Journal of Marriage and the Family,* 1997, Vol. 59, pp. 809–823; and Paul R. Amato, "Diversity within Single-Parent Families." Pp. 149–172 in David. H. Demo, Katherine R. Allen, and Mark A. Fine, eds., *Handbook of Family Diversity* (New York: Oxford University Press, 2000).

3. See Kyle Pruett, *Fatherneed* (New York: Free Press, 1999).

4. Larry L. Bumpass and R. Kelly Raley, "Redefining Single-Parent Families: Cohabitation and Changing Family Reality." *Demography,* 1995, Vol. 32, pp. 97–109.

5. For one of the first studies of the negative economic consequences of divorce for women that resulted from changes in divorce laws, especially the addition of "irreconcilable differences" to the list of legal grounds for divorce, see Lenore Weitzman, *The Divorce Revolution* (New York: Free Press, 1985). For more recent longitudinal evidence from the National Survey of Families and Households, see Pamela J. Smock, Wendy D. Manning, and Sanjiv Gupta, "The Effect of Marriage and Divorce on Women's Economic Well Being." *American Sociological Review,* 1999, Vol. 64, pp. 794–812. For cross-cultural evidence on the economic consequences of changes in divorce laws for women, see Mark A. Fine and David R. Fine, "An Examination and Evaluation of Recent Changes in Divorce Laws in Five Western Countries: The Critical Role of Values." *Journal of Marriage and the Family,* 1994, Vol. 56, pp. 249–263.

6. Sarah S. McLanahan and Irwin Garfinkle, "Single Mothers, the Underclass, and Social Policy." *Annals of the American Academy of Political and Social Science,* 1989, Vol. 501, pp. 92–104; also Sarah S. McLahahan and Gary Sandefur, 1994.

7. On the cost of day care for lowest-income women, see "Parents Whose Children Need Day Care Often Face Daily Crisis." *Population Today,* July-August 1998, Vol. 26, No. 7–8, pp. 1–3.

8. On grandmothers and child care, see Ken Bryson and Lynne M. Casper, "Coresident Grandparents and Grandchildren." *Current Population Reports* P23–198, May 1998; Nazli Baydar and Jean Brooks-Gunn, "Profiles of Grandmothers Who Help Care for Their Grandchildren in the United States." *Family Relations,* 1998, Vol. 47, pp. 385–393; and Anne R. Pebley and Laura L. Rudkin, "Grandparents Caring for Grandchildren." *Journal of Family Issues,* 1999, Vol. 20, pp. 218–242.

9. For a good review of studies that relate changing attitudes toward marriage to realistic economic and demographic conditions in the African American subculture, see K. Jill Kiecolt and Mark A. Fossett, "The Effects of Mate Availability on Marriage Among Black Americans: A Contextual Analysis." Pp. 63–78 in Robert Joseph Taylor, James S. Jackson, and Linda M. Chatters, eds., *Family Life in Black America* (Thousand Oaks, CA: Sage, 1997).

10. On high rates of unemployment or underemployment in inner-city black communities despite a booming middle-class economy, see William Julius Wilson, *When Work Disappears: The World of the New Urban Poor* (New York: Alfred A. Knopf, 1997); and, in a more optimistic tone, see his *The Bridge Over the Racial Divide: Rising*

Inequality and Coalition Politics (Berkeley: University of California Press and New York: Russell Sage, 1999).

11. On attitudes toward marriage of older, highly educated, successful black women, see Melinda B. Tucker, Robert J. Taylor, and Claudia Mitchell-Kernan, "Marriage and Romantic Involvement Among Aged African Americans." *Journal of Gerontology: Social Sciences*, 1993, Vol. 48, No. 3, pp. S128–S132.

12. See M. Belinda Tucker and Claudia Mitchell-Kernan, "African American Marital Trends in Context: Toward a Synthesis." Pp. 345–362 in M. Belinda Tucker and Claudia Mitchell-Kernan, eds., *The Decline in Marriage Among African Americans* (New York: Russell Sage, 1995).

13. Jorge Del Pinal and Audry Singer, "Generations of Diversity: Latinos in the United States." *Population Bulletin*, March 1997, Vol. 53, No. 3 (Washington, DC: Population Reference Bureau); also Maxine Baca Zinn, "Diversity within Latino Families." Pp. 252–273 in David H. Demo, Katherine A. Allen, and Mark A. Fine, 2000.

14. See Melba Sanchez-Ayendez, "The Puerto Rican Family." Pp. 199–222 in Charles H. Mindel, Robert W. Habenstein, and Roosevelt Wright, Jr., eds., *Ethnic Families in America* (Upper Saddle River, NJ: Prentice Hall, 1998), pp. 204–205.

15. Sharon M. Lee, "Asian Americans: Diverse and Growing." *Population Bulletin*, June 1998, Vol. 53, No. 2 (Washington, DC: Population Reference Bureau).

16. Two articles that review dozens of studies on this topic conducted during the 1980s and 1990s are Paul R. Amato, Jr., and Bruce Keith, "Consequences of Parental Divorce and Marital Unhappiness for Adult Well-Being." *Social Forces*, 1991, Vol. 69, pp. 895–914; and Paul R. Amato, Jr., and Joan G. Gilbreth, "Nonresident Fathers and Children's Well-Being: A Meta-Analysis." *Journal of Marriage and the Family*, 1999, Vol. 61, pp. 557–573.

17. Daniel Perlman, "Loneliness: A Life-Span Family Perspective." Pp. 190–220 in Robert M. Milardo, ed., *Families and Social Networks* (Newbury Park, CA: Sage, 1988).

18. Daniel Perlman, 1988, p. 218.

19. Nadine F. Marx and James David Lambert, "Marital Status Continuity and Change Among Young and Midlife Adults: Longitudinal Effects on Psychological Well-Being." *Journal of Family Issues*, 1998, Vol. 19, pp. 652–687.

20. For a comprehensive review of these studies, see Sarah S. McLanahan and Gary Sandefur, 1994; also Terry Arendell, "Conceiving and Investigating Motherhood: The Decade's Scholarship." *Journal of Marriage and the Family*, 2000, Vol. 62, pp. 1192–1207.

21. Sarah McLanahan and Karen Booth, 1989, pp. 557–579.

22. On children who manage to thrive even under the worst of circumstances, see Jonathan Kozol's empathic study of black and Latino children in the South Bronx: *Ordinary Resurrections* (New York: Crown, 2000).

23. A classic theoretical paper on this topic is Alice Rossi's "Transition to Parenthood." *Journal of Marriage and the Family*, 1968, Vol. 30, pp. 26–39. See also Pamela M. Wallace and Ian H. Gottlib, "Marital Adjustment During the Transition to Parenthood: Stability and Predictors of Change." *Journal of Marriage and the Family*, 1990, Vol. 52, pp. 21–29; and Jay Belsky and John Kelly, *The Transition to Parenthood: How a First Child Changes a Marriage* (New York: Delacorte Press, 1994).

24. Kathryn McCannell, "Social Networks and the Transition to Motherhood." Pp. 83–106 in Robert M. Milardo, ed., *Families and Social Networks* (Newbury Park, CA: Sage, 1988); Ann Goetting, "Patterns of Support Among In-Laws in the United States." *Journal of Family Issues*, 1990, Vol. 11, pp. 67–90; and Danielle Julien, Elise Chartrand,

and Jean Begin, "Social Networks, Structural Interdependence, and Conjugal Adjustment in Heterosexual, Gay, and Lesbian Couples." *Journal of Marriage and the Family*, 1999, Vol. 61, pp. 516–530.

25. Shelley M. MacDermid, Ted L. Huston, and Susan M. McHale, "Changes in Marriage Associated with the Transition to Parenthood." *Journal of Marriage and the Family*, 1990, Vol. 52, pp. 475–486; also Gayle Kaufman, "Do Gender Role Attitudes Matter?" *Journal of Family Issues*, 2000, Vol. 21, pp. 128–144.

26. Alyson Fearnly Shapiro, John M. Gottman, and Sybil Carrere, "The Baby and the Marriage: Identifying Factors That Buffer Against Decline in Marital Satisfaction After the First Baby Arrives." *Journal of Family Psychology*, 2000, Vol. 14, pp. 59–70.

27. Jack O. Bradt, "Becoming Parents: Families with Young Children." Pp. 235–254 in Betty Carter and Monica McGoldrick, eds., *The Changing Family Life Cycle*, 2d ed. (Needham, MA: Allyn and Bacon, 1989).

28. See Martha R. Burt, *Homeless Programs and the People They Serve: Findings of the National Survey of Homeless Assistance Providers and Clients* (Washington, DC: Urban Institute, 1999); and Children's Defense Fund, *The State of America's Children, Yearbook 2000* (Washington, DC: Children's Defense Fund, 2000), pp. 87–88.

29. For a review of changes in maternity leave and day-care policies in the United States since the end of World War II, see Yvonne Zylan, "Maternalism Redefined." *Gender & Society*, 2000, Vol. 14, pp. 608–629.

30. For research evidence of a similar picture currently among low-income, low-skilled employed mothers in France, Denmark, and other European countries, see Eileen Drew, Ruth Emerek, and Evelyn Mahon, eds., *Women, Work, and the Family in Europe* (London: Routledge, 1998).

31. On the decline in the independence and power of married women who shift to part-time employment after the birth of a child, see Haya Stier and Noa Lewin-Epstein, "Women's Part-Time Employment and Gender Inequality in the Family." *Journal of Family Issues*, 2000, Vol. 21, pp. 390–410.

32. On differences in the psychological stresses experienced by employed mothers and fathers, see Chloe E. Bird, "Gender Differences in the Social and Economic Burdens of Parenting and Psychological Distress." *Journal of Marriage and the Family*, 1997, Vol. 59, pp. 809–823; and Melissa A. Milkie and Pia Peltola, "Playing All the Roles: Gender and the Work-Family Balancing Act." *Journal of Marriage and the Family*, 1999, Vol. 61, pp. 476–490.

33. A classic article on this topic is Hanna Papanek's "Men, Women, and Work: Reflections on the Two-Person Career." Pp. 90–110 in Joan Huber, ed., *Changing Women in a Changing Society* (Chicago: University of Chicago Press, 1973).

34. On differences in marital satisfaction among two-earner parents, see Patricia Voydanoff, "Work and Family: A Review and Expanded Conceptualization." Pp. 1–22 in Elizabeth B. Goldsmith, ed., *Work and Family* (Newbury Park, CA: Sage, 1989).

35. On ethnic subcultural differences in housework by men, see Beth Ann Shelton and Daphne John, "Ethnicity, Race, and Difference: A Comparison of White, Black, and Hispanic Men's Household Labor Time." Pp. 131–150 in Jane C. Hood, ed., *Men, Work, and Family* (Newbury Park, CA: Sage, 1993); and Terri L. Orbuch and Lindsay Custer, "The Social Context of Married Women's Work and Its Impact on Black Husbands and White Husbands." *Journal of Marriage and the Family*, 1995, Vol. 57, pp. 333–345.

36. On differences in the leisure time of mothers and fathers, see Geoffrey Godbey and John Robinson, *Time for Life: The Surprising Ways Americans Use Their Time* (State College, PA: Penn State University Press, 2000).

37. On the effect of a wife's higher income on the willingness of fathers to do housework, see Catherine E. Ross, "The Division of Labor at Home." *Social Forces*, 1987, Vol. 65, pp. 816–833; Arlie Hochschild, *The Second Shift* (New York: Viking, 1989); Julie Brines, "Economic Dependency, Gender, and the Division of Labor at Home." *American Journal of Sociology*, 1994, Vol. 100, pp. 652–658; Barbara A. Arrighi and David J. Maume, Jr., "Workplace Subordination and Men's Avoidance of Housework." *Journal of Family Issues*, 2000, Vol. 21, pp. 464–487; and Theodore N. Greenstein, "Economic Dependence, Gender, and the Division of Labor in the Home: A Replication and Extension." *Journal of Marriage and the Family*, 2000, Vol. 62, pp. 322–335.

38. Pepper Schwartz, *Peer Marriage: How Love Between Equals Really Works* (New York: Free Press, 1994); and Judith S. Wallerstein and Sandra Blakeslee, *The Good Marriage: How and Why Love Lasts* (Boston: Houghton Mifflin, 1995).

39. Glenna Spitze, "Women's Employment and Family Relations: A Review." *Journal of Marriage and the Family*, 1988, Vol. 50, pp. 585–618; also Larry L. Bumpass, Teresa Castro Martin, and James A. Sweet, "The Impact of Family Background and Early Marital Factors on Marital Disruption." *Journal of Family Issues*, 1991, Vol. 12, pp. 22–42.

40. Dana Vannoy-Hiller and William W. Philliber, *Equal Partners: Successful Women in Marriage* (Newbury Park, CA: Sage, 1989), p. 145; also, John M. Gottman, *What Predicts Divorce: The Measures* (Hillsdale, NJ: Erlbaum, 1996).

41. Barbara B. Bunker, Josephine M. Zubeck, Virginia J. Vanderslice, and Robert W. Rice, "Quality of Life in Dual-Career Families: Commuting versus Single-Residence Couples." *Journal of Marriage and the Family*, 1992, Vol. 54, pp. 399–407.

42. On the effects of mothers' employment on child development, see Ellen Galinsky and Judy David, *The Preschool Years* (New York: Viking, 1988); T. Berry Brazelton, *Families: Crisis and Caring* (Reading, MA: Addison-Wesley, 1989); Jay Belsky, "Parental and Nonparental Child Care and Children's Socioemotional Development: A Decade in Review." *Journal of Marriage and the Family*, 1990, Vol. 52, pp. 885–903; Mary Douglas Salter Ainsworth and John Bowlby, "An Ethological Approach to Personality Development." *American Psychologist*, 1991, Vol. 46, pp. 333–341; and Theodore N. Greenstein, "Maternal Employment and Child Behavioral Outcomes." *Journal of Family Issues*, 1993, Vol. 14, pp. 323–351.

43. On time spent with children by working mothers and the academic achievements of children of employed mothers, see also W. Keith Bryant and Cathleen D. Zick, "An Examination of Parent-Child Shared Time." *Journal of Marriage and the Family*, 1996, Vol. 58, pp. 227–237.

44. Chandra Muller, "Maternal Employment, Parent Involvement, and Mathematics Achievement Among Adolescents." *Journal of Marriage and the Family*, 1995, Vol. 57, pp. 85–100.

45. On the stresses created by employers who do not empathize with their employees' responsibilities for their children (especially fathers' need to be with their children), see the case study by Arlie Hochschild, *The Time Bind: When Work Becomes Home and Home Becomes Work* (New York: Holt, 1997); also, Suzanne Braun Levine, *Father Courage: What Happens When Men Put Family First* (New York: Harcourt, 2000).

46. Robert E. Calem, "Tales from the 'Telecommuting' Front. Listen. You Might Be Next." *New York Times*, April 18, 1993, pp. A1, A6; also Phil Patton, "The Virtual Office Becomes Reality." *New York Times*, October 28, 1993, pp. C1, C6.

47. Mellissa Stainback and Katherine M. Donato, "Going to Work but Never Leaving Home." *Population Today*, September 1998, Vol. 26, No. 9, Table 1, p. 3.

48. Kathleen Christensen, *Women and Home-Based Work* (New York: Henry Holt, 1989).

49. Kathleen Christensen, 1989, p. 205.

50. Arne L. Kalleberg and Rachel A. Rosenfeld, "Work in the Family and in the Labor Market: A Cross-National, Reciprocal Analysis." *Journal of Marriage and the Family*, 1993, Vol. 53, pp. 913–925.

51. On sleep deprivation and the desire for more time off by workers in the United States, see the results of a national Harris poll reported by Dylan Loeb McClain, "Forget the Raise, Give Me Some Time Off." *New York Times*, July 12, 2000, p. G1.

52. Harriet B. Presser, "Nonstandard Work Schedules and Marital Instability." *Journal of Marriage and the Family*, 2000, Vol. 62, pp. 93–110.

53. See Harriet B. Presser, "Can We Make Time for Children? The Economy, Work Schedules, and Child Care." *Demography*, 1989, Vol. 26, pp. 523–543.

54. Most of these techniques for reducing work–family role conflict are described in Maureen H. Schnittger and Gloria W. Bird, "Coping Among Dual-Career Men and Women Across the Life Cycle." *Family Relations*, 1990, Vol. 39, pp. 199–205.

55. Anjani Chandra and Elizabeth Hervey Stephen, "Impaired Fecundity in the United States: 1982–1995." *Family Planning Perspectives*, 1998, Vol. 30, No. 1, pp. 35–45.

56. On issues and controversies surrounding the new fertility technologies, see Barbara Katz Rothman, *Recreating Motherhood: Ideology and Technology in a Patriarchal Society* (New York: W. W. Norton, 1989); also Scott B. Rae, *The Ethics of Commercial Motherhood: Brave New Families?* (Westport, CT: Praeger, 1994).

57. Institute for Science, Law, and Technology Working Group, Illinois Institute of Technology, "Art into Science: Regulation of Fertility Techniques." *Science*, July 31, 1998, Vol. 282, pp. 651–652.

58. On biological difficulties in the extension of childbearing to older women, see gynecologist Zev Rosenwaks' "We Still Can't Stop the Biological Clock." *New York Times*, June 24, 2000, p. A15.

59. On the current situation of sperm banks, globally and in the United States, see Jeff Stryker, "Take It to the Bank." *New York Times Magazine*, June 25, 2000, p. 20.

60. An example of this kind of impassioned and often bitter competition was the race to break the genetic code between National Institutes of Health scientists, nonprofit medical research foundations, and Craig Venter, CEO and founder of the privately owned, profit-oriented Celera Genomics Group. See Richard Preston, "The Genome Warrior." *The New Yorker*, June 12, 2000, pp. 66–83.

61. Elizabeth Hervey Stephen, "Assisted Reproductive Technologies: Is the Price Too High?" *Population Today*, May 1999, Vol. 25, No. 5, p. 1, p. 7.

62. Elizabeth Hervey Stephen, 1999, p. 7.

63. Tim B. Heaton, Cardell K. Jacobson, and Kimberlee Holland, "Persistence and Change in Decisions to Remain Childless." *Journal of Marriage and the Family*, 1999, Vol. 61, pp. 531–539.

64. Karen Seccombe, "Assessing the Costs and Benefits of Children: Gender Comparisons Among Child-Free Husbands and Wives." *Journal of Marriage and the Family*, 1991, Vol. 53, pp. 191–202.

65. See Ellen M. Nason and Margaret M. Poloma, *Voluntarily Childless Couples: The Emergence of a Variant Lifestyle* (Newbury Park, CA: Sage, 1976); also Marsha S. Somers, "A Comparison of Voluntarily Child-Free Adults and Parents." *Journal of Marriage and the Family*, 1993, Vol. 55, pp. 643–650.

66. Chris Knoester and Alan Booth, "Barriers to Divorce." *Journal of Family Issues*, 2000, Vol. 21, pp. 78–99. On the topic of less daily stress in homes without children, see Philip A. Fisher, Beverly I. Fagot, and Craig S. Leve, "Assessment of Family Stress Across Low-,

Medium-, and High-Risk Samples Using the Family Events Checklist." *Family Relations*, 1998, Vol. 47, pp. 215–219.

67. These statistics are from a national survey conducted by the Princeton Survey Research Associates and reported in the *New York Times*, November 9, 1999, p. A10.

68. Rosemary J. Avery, *Adoption Policy and Special Needs Children* (Westport, CT: Auborn House, 1997).

69. On the attachment difficulties of older adopted children, see David M. Brodzinsky, Daniel W. Smith, and Anne B. Brodzinsky, *Children's Adjustment to Adoption: Developmental and Clinical Issues* (Thousand Oaks, CA: Sage, 1998).

70. We have no national studies on this topic, but see Karen March, "The Dilemma of Adoption Reunion: Establishing Open Communication Between Adoptees and Their Birth Mothers." *Family Relations*, 1997, Vol. 46, pp. 99–105; and James Gladstone and Anne Westhues, "Adoption Reunions: A New Side to Intergenerational Family Relationships." *Family Relations*, 1998, Vol. 47, pp. 177–184.

71. From a Letter to the Editor, *New York Times*, June 10, 2000, p. A14.

72. The earliest classic sources on child development from the fields of philosophy and sociology focused on the development of a sense of self. See, for example, sociologist Charles Horton Cooley's *Human Nature and the Social Order* (New York: Scribner's, 1964 [1902]) and philosopher George Herbert Mead's *Mind, Self, and Society* (Chicago: University of Chicago Press, 1934), edited by Charles W. Morris. Freudian psychiatrists and psychologists have focused on the emotional development of young children. A major contribution was Erik H. Erikson's *Childhood and Society*, 2d ed. (New York: W. W. Norton, 1964). For a pioneering study of the development of language and reasoning skills by social psychologists, see Jean Piaget, *The Language and Thought of the Child* (New York: Meridian Books, 1926). On the development of morality, see Jean Piaget, *The Moral Judgement of the Child* (Glencoe, IL: Free Press, 1948), and, more recently, Lawrence Kohlberg and Richard Kramer, "Continuities and Discontinuities in Childhood and Adult Moral Development." *Human Development*, 1969, Vol. 12, pp. 93–120.

73. For more recent sources on child development and the interaction between genetics, culture, and childrearing styles, see Jerome Kagan and Howard Moss, *From Birth to Maturity* (New Haven, CT: Yale University Press, 1983); Burton L. White, *The First Three Years of Life*, rev. ed. (Englewood Cliffs, NJ: Prentice Hall, 1985); Benjamin Spock, *Dr. Spock on Parenting* (New York: Simon and Schuster, 1989); and Susanne Denham, *Emotional Development in Young Children* (New York: Guilford Press, 1998).

74. See Arnold H. Buss and Robert Plomin, *A Temperament Theory of Personality Development* (New York: Wiley, 1975), pp. 225–230.

75. Burton L. White, 1985, p. 252.

76. Stanley H. Hall, *Adolescence: Its Psychology and Its Relation to Physiology, Anthropology, Sociology, Sex, Crime, Religion, and Education* (Englewood Cliffs, NJ: Prentice Hall, 1904).

77. For a brief but comprehensive and thorough account of the demographics, values, socialization experiences, theoretical approaches to understanding adolescence, and effects of changes in the economy and government policy on adolescence, see Suzanne K. Steinmetz, "Adolescence in Contemporary Families." Pp. 371–423 in Marvin Sussman, Suzanne K. Steinmetz, and Gary W. Peterson, eds., *Handbook of Marriage and the Family*, 2d ed. (New York: Plenum Press, 1999).

78. Andrew J. Cherlin, Eugenia Scabani, and Giovanna Rossi, "Still in the Nest: Delayed Home Leaving in Europe and the United States." *Journal of Family Issues*, 1997, Vol. 18, pp. 572–575.

79. Stephanie Coontz, *The Way We Never Were: American Families and the Nostalgia Trap* (New York: Basic Books, 1997), p. 131.

80. Frances K. Goldscheider and Calvin Goldscheider, "The Effects of Childhood Family Structure on Leaving and Returning Home." *Journal of Marriage and the Family*, 1998, Vol. 60, pp. 745–756.

81. Nicholas Buck and Jacqueline Scott, "She's Leaving Home: But Why? An Analysis of Young People Leaving the Parental Home." *Journal of Marriage and the Family*, 1993, Vol. 55, pp. 863–874.

82. Lynn K. White and Stacy J. Rogers, "Strong Support But Uneasy Relationships: Coresidence and Adult Children's Relationships with Their Parents." *Journal of Marriage and the Family*, 1997, Vol. 59, pp. 62–76.

83. Rubye W. Beck and Scott H. Beck, "The Incidence of Extended Family Households among Middle-Aged Black and White Women." *Journal of Family Issues*, 1989, Vol. 10, pp. 147–168, p. 147.

84. Jean D. Okimoto, *Boomerang Kids* (New York: Pocket Books, 1989).

85. *Kids Count 2000 Data Book* (Washington, DC: Population Reference Bureau, 2000).

86. David M. Olson, Hamilton I. McCubbin, and Associates, *Families: What Makes Them Work*, 2d ed. (Newbury Park, CA: Sage, 1989), p. 230.

87. Everett Carl Ladd, *The Ladd Report* (New York: Free Press, 2000).

88. See Lynn K. White and Stacy L. Rogers, "Economic Circumstances and Family Outcomes: A Review of the 1990s." *Journal of Marriage and the Family*, 2000, Vol. 62, pp. 1035–1051.

89. The classic research on this topic is T. H. Holmes and R. H. Rahe's, "The Social Readjustment Scale." *Journal of Psychosomatic Research*, 1967, Vol. 11, p. 213.

Chapter 10 Divorce and Remarriage

1. Betty Yorburg, *Families and Societies* (New York: Columbia University Press, 1983), pp. 155–158; Willie Pearson, Jr., and Lewellyn Hendrix, "Divorce and the Status of Women." *Journal of Marriage and the Family*, 1979, Vol. 41, pp. 375–385.

2. William J. Goode, *World Changes in Divorce Patterns* (New Haven, CT: Yale University Press, 1993).

3. Edward L. Kain, *The Myth of Family Decline* (Lexington, MA: Lexington Books, 1990).

4. Reuben Hill, *Families Under Stress* (Westport, CT: Greenwood Press, 1971 [1949]).

5. Theodore N. Greenstein, "Marital Disruption and the Employment of Married Women." *Journal of Marriage and the Family*, 1990, Vol. 52, pp. 657–676.

6. David Lester, "Trends in Divorce and Marriage Around the World." *Journal of Divorce and Remarriage*, 1996, Vol. 25, pp. 169–171.

7. On reasons given for divorce in the 1950s, see William Goode, *After Divorce* (New York: Free Press, 1956). The quote on current reasons for divorce is from Sharon J. Price and Patrick C. McKenry, *Divorce* (Newbury Park, CA: Sage, 1988), p. 34.

8. For a negative view of the changed values and expectations in contemporary marriages, see Norval D. Glenn, "Values, Attitudes, and the State of American Marriage." Pp. 15–33 in David Popenoe, Jean Bethke Elshtain, and David Blankenhorn, eds., *Promises to Keep: The Decline and Renewal of Marriage in America* (Lanham, MD: Rowman and Littlefield, 1996); also David Popenoe, "The Decline of Marriage and Fatherhood." Pp. 312–319 in John J. Macionis and Nijole V. Benokraitis, *Seeing Ourselves: Classic, Contemporary, and Cross-Cultural Readings*, 4th ed. (Upper Saddle River, NJ: Prentice Hall, 1999). For a more positive view, see Stephanie Coontz, *The Way We Really Are: Coming to Terms with America's Changing Families* (New York: Basic Books, 1997), pp. 109–122.

9. Theodore N. Greenstein, 1990, pp. 657–676; and Theodore N. Greenstein, "Gender Ideology, Marital Disruption, and the Employment of Married Women." *Journal of Marriage and the Family*, 1995, Vol. 57, pp. 31–42.

10. Norval D. Glenn, "The Recent Trend in Marital Success in the United States." *Journal of Marriage and the Family*, 1991, Vol. 53, pp. 261–270.

11. Teresa Castro Martin and Larry L. Bumpass, "Recent Trends in Marital Disruption." *Demography*, 1989, Vol. 26, pp. 37–51.

12. Liana C. Sayer and Suzanne M. Bianchi, "Women's Economic Independence and the Probability of Divorce." *Journal of Family Issues*, 2000, Vol. 21, pp. 906–943. For additional evidence on the divorce rate after 25 or more years of marriage (1 percent), see Zheng Wu and Magaret J. Penning, "Marital Instability After Midlife." *Journal of Family Issues*, 1997, Vol. 18, pp. 459–478.

13. Sharon J. Price and Patrick C. McKenry, 1988; Teresa Castro Martin and Larry L. Bumpass, 1989.

14. Teresa M. Cooney and Peter Uhlenberg, "Family Building Patterns of Professional Women: A Comparison of Lawyers, Physicians, and Postsecondary Teachers." *Journal of Marriage and the Family*, 1989, Vol. 51, pp. 749–758.

15. Teresa M. Cooney and Peter Uhlenberg, 1989, p. 747.

16. U.S. Bureau of the Census, *Statistical Abstract of the United States*, No. 162 (Washington, DC: U.S. Government Printing Office, 1999), p. 113.

17. On this topic generally, see D. Alex Heckert, Thomas C. Nowak, and Kay A. Snyder, "The Impact of Husbands' and Wives' Relative Earnings on Marital Disruption." *Journal of Marriage and the Family*, 1998, Vol. 60, pp. 690–703.

18. A. Belinda Tucker and Claudia Mitchell-Kernan, "Trends in African American Family Formation: A Theoretical and Statistical Overview." Pp. 3–26 in M. Belinda Tucker and Claudia Mitchell-Kernan, eds., *The Decline in Marriage Among African Americans* (New York: Russell Sage, 1995); Martin King Whyte, *Dating, Mating, and Marriage* (Hawthorne, NY: Aldine de Gruyter, 1990); and Erma Jean Lawson, *Black Men and Divorce* (Thousand Oaks, CA: Sage, 2000).

19. Deborah Brodie, *Untying the Knot: Ex-Husbands, Ex-Wives and Other Experts on the Passage of Divorce* (New York: St. Martin's Press, 1999).

20. See Frank Furstenberg, Jr., and Andrew Cherlin, *Divided Families: What Happens to Children When Parents Part* (Cambridge, MA: Harvard University Press, 1991); Paul R. Amato and Bruce Keith, "Parental Divorce and the Well-Being of Children: A Meta-Analysis." *Psychological Bulletin*, 1991, Vol. 110, pp. 26–46.

21. Paul R. Amato, "The Consequences of Divorce for Adults and Children." *Journal of Marriage and the Family*, Vol. 62, 2000, pp. 1269–1287.

22. On the great importance of continued emotional support, especially from the father, for the adjustment of children after a divorce, see Judith S. Wallerstein and Sandra Blakeslee, *Second Chances: Men, Women, and Children a Decade After Divorce* (New York: Ticknor and Fields, 1989); Robert E. Emery, *Marriage, Divorce, and Children's Adjustment*, 2d ed. (Thousand Oaks, CA: Sage, 1999); and Kathleen M. Harris, Frank F. Ferstenberg, Jr., and Jeremy K. Marmer, "Paternal Involvement with Adolescents in Intact Families: The Influence of Fathers Over the Life Course." *Demography*, 1998, Vol. 35, pp. 201–216.

23. Robert E. Emery, "Children in the Divorce Process." *Journal of Family Psychology*, 1988, Vol. 2, pp. 141–144.

24. Greer L. Fox and Robert F. Kelly, "Determinants of Child Custody Arrangements at Divorce." *Journal of Marriage and the Family*, 1995, Vol. 57, pp. 693–708.

25. On changes in government policy regarding the kidnapping of children by divorced fathers, see Paula S. Fass, "A Sign of Family Disorder? Changing Representations of Parental Kidnapping." Pp. 144–168 in Mary Ann Mason, Arlene Skolnick, and Stephen D. Sugarman, eds., *All Our Families: New Policies for a New Century* (New York: Oxford University Press, 1998).

26. The Amato and Keith study (1991), cited in note 20, contains a summary of the conclusions of dozens of studies on the consequences of divorce, for girls and boys, of over 80,000 children in the United States. Another excellent source is Mary F. Whiteside and Betsy Jane Becker, "Parental Factors and the Young Child's Postdivorce Adjustment: A Meta-Analysis with Implications for Parenting Arrangements." *Journal of Family Psychology*, 2000, Vol. 14, pp. 5–26.

27. For a rather optimistic review of recent trends in U.S. government family policy, see Karen Bogenschneider, "Has Family Policy Come of Age? A Decade Review of the State of U.S. Family Policy in the 1990s." *Journal of Marriage and the Family*, 2000, Vol. 62, pp. 1136–1159. On the need for change in current government policy to provide more help to children who live with a single, divorced mother, see Judith S. Wallerstein, "Children of Divorce: A Society in Search of Policy." Pp. 66–94 in Mary Ann Mason, Arlene Skolnick, and Stephen D. Sugarman, eds., *All Our Families: New Policies for a New Century* (New York: Oxford University Press, 1998).

28. E. Mavis Hetherington, "Coping with Family Transitions: Winners, Losers, and Survivors." *Child Development*, 1989, Vol. 60, pp. 1–14.

29. Sara S. McLanahan and Gary Sandefur, *Growing Up with a Single Parent* (Cambridge, MA: Harvard University Press, 1994).

30. See Nancy D. Chase, ed., *Burdened Children* (Thousand Oaks, CA: Sage, 1999).

31. On the consequences of divorce, depending on how *old* a child is when parents divorce, see Lianne Woodward, David M. Fergusson, and Jay Belsky, "Timing of Parental Separation and Attachment to Parents in Adolescence: Results of a Prospective Study from Birth to Age 16." *Journal of Marriage and the Family*, 2000, Vol. 62, pp. 162–174.

32. For a major review of survey research on the effects of parental divorce on adult children, see Paul R. Amato and Bruce Keith, " Parental Divorce and Adult Well-Being: A Meta-Analysis." *Journal of Marriage and the Family*, 1991, Vol. 53, pp. 43–58. See also Lynn K. White, "Growing Up with Single Parents and Stepparents: Long-Term Effects on Family Solidarity." *Journal of Marriage and the Family*, 1994, Vol. 56, pp. 935–948; and Du Feng, Roseann Giarruso, Vern L. Bengston, and Nancy Frye, "Intergenerational Transmission of Marital Quality and Marital Instability." *Journal of Marriage and the Family*, 1999, Vol. 61, pp. 451–463. See also the follow-up study by psychologist Judith Wallerstein and her associates 25 years after their initial depth interviews (in the 1970s) with children whose parents had divorced: Judith Wallerstein, Julia Lewis, and Sandra Blakeslee, *The Unexpected Legacy of Divorce* (New York: Hyperion, 2000).

33. Marsha Kline, Janet R. Johnston, and Jeanne M. Tschann, "The Long Shadow of Marital Conflict: A Model of Children's Postdivorce Adjustment." *Journal of Marriage and the Family*, 1991, Vol. 53, pp. 297–309; also Donna Ruane Morrison and Mary Jo Coiro, "Parental Conflict and Marital Disruption: Do Children Benefit When High-Conflict Marriages Are Dissolved?" *Journal of Marriage and the Family*, 1999, Vol. 61, pp. 626–637.

34. On the financial consequences of divorce for women, see Richard R. Peterson, "A Reevaluation of the Economic Consequences of Divorce." *American Sociological Review*, 1996, Vol. 61, pp. 528–536.

35. Tim B. Heaton and Ashley M. Blake, "Gender Differences in Determinants of Marital Disruption." *Journal of Family Issues*, 1999, Vol. 20, pp. 25–45.

36. Lenore J. Weitzman, "The Economic Consequences of Divorce Are Still Unequal: Comment on Peterson." *American Sociological Review*, 1996, Vol. 61, pp. 537–539.

37. Daniel R. Meyer and Judi Bartfield, "Compliance with Child Support Orders in Divorce Cases." *Journal of Marriage and the Family*, 1996, Vol. 58, pp. 201–212.

38. Judith S. Wallerstein and Sandra Blakeslee, 1989, p. 301. On the effects of divorce on older women, see also Namkee G. Choi, "Correlates of the Economic Status of Widowhood and Divorced Elderly Women." *Journal of Family Issues*, 1992, Vol. 13, pp. 38–54.

39. Joseph H. Pleck, "Paternal Involvement: Levels, Sources, and Consequences." Pp. 66–103 in M. E. Lamb, ed., *The Role of the Father in Child Development* (New York: Wiley, 1997); Penny Edgell Becker and Phyllis Moen, "Scaling Back: Dual-Earner Couples' Work-Family Strategies." *Journal of Marriage and the Family*, 1999, Vol. 61, pp. 995–1007.

40. William H. Whyte, Jr., *The Organization Man* (Hawthorne, NY: Simon and Schuster, 1956).

41. See Catherine Kohler Reissman, *Divorce Talk* (New Brunswick, NJ: Rutgers University Press, 1990); and Terry Arrendell, *Fathers and Divorce* (Thousand Oaks, CA: Sage, 1995).

42. Lenore L. Walker, *The Battered Woman* (New York: Harper and Row, 1979); also Catherine Reissman, 1990.

43. Deborah Brodie, 1999.

44. Personal interview.

45. On the role of extramarital affairs in divorces, see Annette Lawson, *Adultery: An Analysis of Love and Betrayal* (New York: Basic Books, 1988); and Emily M. Brown, *Patterns of Infidelity and Their Treatment* (New York: Brunner/Mazel, 1990).

46. On stages in emotional recovery after a divorce, see Diane Vaughan, *Uncoupling: How Relationships Come Apart* (New York: Oxford University Press, 1986).

47. Arne Mastekassa, "Psychological Well-Being and Marital Dissolution." *Journal of Family Issues*, 1994, Vol. 15, pp. 208–228.

48. Arne Mastekassa, "Marital Status, Distress, and Well-Being: An International Comparison." *Journal of Comparative Family Studies*, 1994, Vol. 25, pp. 183–206.

49. Nadine F. Marks and James David Lambert, "Marital Status Continuity and Change Among Young and Midlife Adults: Longitudinal Effects on Psychological Well-Being." *Journal of Family Issues*, 1998, Vol. 19, pp. 652–686.

50. Paul R. Amato, 2000, p. 1282.

51. For some good reviews of research on remarriages and stepfamilies, see Andrew J. Cherlin, *Marriage, Divorce, Remarriage* (Cambridge, MA: Harvard University Press, 1992); Lawrence Ganong and Marilyn Coleman, *New Families, New Responsibilities: Intergenerational Obligations Following Divorce and Remarriage* (Hillsdale, NJ: Erlbaum, 1999); and Marilyn Coleman, Lawrence Ganong, and Mark Fine, "Reinvestigating Remarriage: Another Decade of Progress." *Journal of Marriage and the Family*, 2000, Vol. 62, pp. 1288–1307.

52. Larry L. Bumpass, James A. Sweet, and Andrew Cherlin, "The Role of Cohabitation in Declining Rates of Remarriage." *Journal of Marriage and the Family*, 1991, Vol. 53, pp. 913–927.

53. Larry L. Bumpass, James A. Sweet, and Teresa Castro Martin, "Changing Patterns of Remarriage." *Journal of Marriage and the Family*, 1990, Vol. 52, pp. 747–746.

54. Larry L. Bumpass, James A. Sweet, and Teresa Castro Martin, 1990.

55. Teresa Castro Martin and Larry L. Bumpass, "Recent Trends in Marital Disruption." *Demography*, 1989, Vol. 26, pp. 37–51.

56. Alan Booth and John H. Edwards, "Starting Over: Why Remarriages Are More Unstable." *Journal of Family Issues*, 1992, Vol. 13, pp. 179–194.

57. Lawrence H. Ganong and Marilyn Coleman, *Remarried Family Relationships* (Thousand Oaks, CA: Sage, 1994).

58. Lawrence H. Ganong and Marilyn Coleman, 1994.

59. Lawrence Kurdek and Mark Fine, "Parent and Nonparent Residential Family Members as Providers of Warmth and Supervision to Young Adolescents." *Journal of Family Psychology*, 1993, Vol. 7, 245–249.

60. Lynn K. White and Alan Booth, "The Quality and Stability of Remarriages: The Role of Stepchildren." *American Sociological Review*, 1985, Vol. 50, pp. 689–698. See also Marilyn Ihinger-Tallman and Kay Pasley, "Stepfamilies in 1984 and Today—A Scholarly Perspective." Pp. 19–40 in Irene Levin and Marvin B. Sussman, eds., *Stepfamilies: History, Research, and Theory* (New York: Basic Books, 1997); and Karen Bogenscheider, "Parental Involvement in Adolescent Schooling: A Proximal Process with Transcontextual Validity." *Journal of Marriage and the Family*, 1997, Vol. 59, pp. 718–733.

61. Frances Kobrin Goldscheider and Calvin Goldscheider, "The Effects of Childhood Family Structure on Leaving and Returning Home." *Journal of Marriage and the Family*, 1998, Vol. 60, pp. 745–756.

62. Paul R. Amato, "The Implications of Research Findings on Children in Stepfamilies." Pp. 81–87 in Alan Booth and Judy Dunn, eds., *Stepfamilies: Who Benefits? Who Does Not?* (Hillsdale, NJ: Erlbaum, 1994).

63. Personal interview.

64. For reviews of these differences, see Lawrence H. Ganong and Marilyn Coleman, 1994; and Marilyn Coleman, Lawrence H. Ganong, and Mark Fine, 2000.

65. E. Mavis Hetherington, "An Overview of the Virginia Longitudinal Study of Divorce and Remarriage with a Focus on Early Adolescence." *Journal of Family Psychology*, 1993, Vol. 7, pp. 39–56.

66. See Andrew J. Cherlin, "Remarriage as an Incomplete Institution." *American Journal of Sociology*, 1979, Vol. 84, pp. 634–650.

67. Lawrence Kurdek, "The Nature and Predictors of the Trajectory of Change of Marital Quality of Husbands and Wives Over the First 10 Years of Marriage." *Developmental Psychology*, 1999, Vol. 35, 1283–1296.

68. A popular description of effective techniques for resolving conflicts in remarriages by two psychotherapists who specialize in treating these problems is Emily B. Visher and John S. Visher's *How to Win as a Stepfamily*, 2d ed. (New York: Brunner/Mazel, 1992).

Chapter 11 The Middle and Later Years

1. See Pauline Boss, *Family Stress Management* (Newbury Park, CA: Sage, 1998).

2. On stresses during the transition from adolescence to adulthood, see William S. Aquilino, "From Adolescent to Young Adult: A Prospective Study of Parent-Child Relations During the Transition to Adulthood." *Journal of Marriage and the Family*, 1997, Vol. 59, pp. 670–686.

3. Becca Levy and Ellen Langer, "Aging Free from Stereotypes: Successful Memory in China and Among the American Deaf." *Journal of Personality and Social Psychology*, 1994, Vol. 66, pp. 989–997.

4. For a clearly written, often cited account of the physical aspects of aging by a cell biologist, see Leonard Hayflick, *How and Why We Age* (New York: Ballantine Books, 1994). For more technical accounts of the physiology, psychology, and sociology of aging, see James E. Birren, ed., *Encyclopedia of Gerontology* (New York: Academic Press, 1996); and James A. Birren and K. Warner Schaie, eds., *Handbook of the Psychology of Aging*, 4th ed. (New York: Academic Press, 1996).

5. On myths about aging and loss, see Ski Hunter and Martin Sundel, eds., *Midlife Myths* (Newbury Park, CA: Sage, 1989); and Richard A. Kalish, ed., *Midlife Loss* (Newbury Park, CA: Sage, 1989).

6. Robert C. Atchley, *Continuity and Adaptation in Aging: Creating Positive Experiences* (Baltimore: Johns Hopkins University Press, 1999).

7. Two popular and highly influential sources on the midlife crisis written by research psychologists are George Vaillant, *Adaptation to Life* (Boston: Little, Brown, 1977), and Daniel J. Levinson, *The Seasons of a Man's Life* (New York: Knopf, 1978).

8. See the analysis of life histories of this generation collected by sociologist Glenn H. Elder, Jr., in *Children of the Great Depression* (Chicago: University of Chicago Press, 1974).

9. On the increased job opportunities of older workers in the current job market and myths about their abilities, see psychologist Ken Dychtwald's *Age Power: How the 21st Century Will Be Ruled by the New Old* (New York: Tarcher/Putnam, 1999). See also Geoffrey Brewer, "Out to Pasture, Greener Pasture." *New York Times*, June 21, 2000, pp. C1, C9.

10. For a review of over 150 studies of older workers (in their 50s and beyond), see Mildred Doering, Susan R. Rhodes, and Michael Schuster, *The Aging Worker: Research and Recommendations* (Beverly Hills, CA: Sage, 1983).

11. Elaine M. Brody, *Women in the Middle* (New York: Springer, 1990).

12. Yoshinori Kamo and Min Zhou, "Living Arrangements of Elderly Chinese and Japanese in the United States." *Journal of Marriage and the Family*, 1994, Vol. 56, pp. 544–558.

13. For a case study of men who are caregivers, see Phyllis B. Harris and Joyce Bichler, *Men Giving Care: Reflections of Husbands and Sons* (New York: Garland, 1997).

14. Donald G. Fowles, *A Profile of Older Americans* (Washington, DC: American Association of Retired Persons, 1989). See also Nan E. Johnson and Jacob J. Climo, "Aging and Eldercare in More Developed Countries." *Journal of Family Issues*, 2000, Vol. 21, pp. 531–540; and Kevin Kinsella, "Demographic Dimensions of Global Aging." *Journal of Family Issues*, 2000, Vol. 21, pp. 541–558.

15. For the actual prevalence of women "caught in the middle," see Glenna Spitze and Vern L. Bengtson, "Continuities and Discontinuities in Intergenerational Relationships Over Time." Pp. 246–268 in Vern L. Bengtson, ed. *Adulthood and Aging* (New York: Springer, 1996); and Nazli Baydar and Jeanne Brooks-Gunn, "Profiles of Grandmothers Who Help Care for Their Grandchildren in the United States." *Family Relations*, 1998, Vol. 47, pp. 385–393.

16. Kurt Luescher and Karl Pillemer, "Intergenerational Ambivalence: A New Approach to the Study of Parent-Child Relations in Later Life." *Journal of Marriage and the Family*, 1998, Vol. 60, pp. 413–425.

17. On widespread and continuing feelings of obligation to care for older parents, regardless of past histories and social circumstances, see David Eggebean and Adam Davey, "Do Safety Nets Work? The Role of Anticipated Help in Times of Need." *Journal of Marriage and the Family*, 1998, Vol. 60, pp. 939–950; and Catherine H. Stein, Virginia A. Wemmerus, Marcia Ward, Michelle E. Gaines, Andrew L. Freeberg, and Thomas C. Jewell, " 'Because They're My Parents': An Intergenerational Study of Felt Obligation

and Parental Caregiving." *Journal of Marriage and the Family*, 1998, Vol. 60, pp. 611–622.

18. Donna L. Hoyert and Marsha M. Seltzer, "Factors Related to the Well-Being and Life Activities of Family Caregivers." *Family Relations*, 1992, Vol. 41, pp. 74–81.

19. Alexis J. Walker, Hwa-Yong Shin, and David N. Bird, "Perceptions of Relationship Change and Caregiving Satisfaction." *Family Relations*, 1990, Vol. 39, pp. 147–152.

20. Personal interview.

21. Robert C. Atchley, *Social Forces and Aging*, 9th ed. (Belmont, CA: Wadsworth), p. 348.

22. See Thomas E. Johnson, Gordon J. Lithgow, Shin Murakami, and David R. Shook, "Genetics." Pp. 577–586 in James E. Birren, ed., *Encyclopedia of Gerontology*, Vol. 1 (New York: Academic Press, 1996). See also The Johns Hopkins Medical Letter, "Health After 50." December 1998, pp. 4–6.

23. On the physical health of older people in the future, see the article by physician-gerontologist Robert N. Butler, "Future Trends." Pp. 387–390 in George L. Maddox, ed., *Encyclopedia of Aging*, 2d ed. (New York: Springer, 1995).

24. William S. Aquilino, "The Likelihood of Parent-Adult Child Coresidence: Effect of Family Structure and Parental Characteristics." *Journal of Marriage and the Family*, 1990, Vol. 32, pp. 405–419.

25. Peter L. Uhlenberg and Theresa M. Cooney, "Family Size and Mother-Child Relations in Later Life." *The Gerontologist*, 1990, Vol. 30, pp. 618–625.

26. Beth J. Soldo and Martha S. Hill, "Intergenerational Transfers: Economic, Demographic, and Social Perspectives." Pp. 187–216 in George L. Maddox and M. Powell Lawton, eds., *Annual Review of Gerontology*, Vol. 13 (New York: Springer, 1993).

27. Peter L. Uhlenberg and Theresa M. Cooney, "Divorce for Women After Mid-Life." *Journal of Gerontology*, 1990, Vol. 45, pp. S3–S11.

28. Charlotte Perry, "Extended Family Support Among Older Black Females." Pp. 70–76 in Robert Staples, ed., *The Black Family: Essays and Studies*, 6th ed. (Belmont, CA: Wadsworth, 1999); William H. Meredith and Douglas A. Abbott, "Chinese Families in Later Life." Pp. 213–230 in Bron B. Ingoldsby and Suzanna Smith, eds., *Families in Multicultural Perspective* (New York: Guilford Press, 1995); and Catherine Chilman, "Hispanic Families in the United States: Research Perspectives." Pp. 96–111 in Mark Robert Rank and Edward L. Kain, eds., *Diversity and Change in Families* (Englewood Cliffs, NJ: Prentice Hall, 1995).

29. On conflicts between immigrant parents and their native-born adolescents, see Jeanne M. Tschann, Elena Flores, Lauri A. Pasch, and Barbara Vanoss Marin, "Assessing Interparental Conflict: Reports of Parents and Adolescents in European American and Mexican American Families." *Journal of Marriage and the Family*, 1999, Vol. 61, pp. 269–283.

30. Charlotte Perry, 1999, pp. 70–76.

31. Pyong Gap Min, "The Korean American Family." Pp. 223–253 in Charles H. Mindel, Robert W. Haberstein, and Roosevelt Wright, Jr., eds., *Ethnic Families in America* (Upper Saddle River, NJ: Prentice Hall, 1998).

32. Jean Pearson Scott, "Sibling Interaction in Later Life." Pp. 86–99 in Timothy H. Brubaker, ed. *Family Relationships in Later Life*, 2d ed. (Newbury Park, CA: Sage, 1990).

33. Richard J. Gelles and Claire Pedrick Cornell, *Intimate Violence in Families*, 2d ed. (Newbury Park, CA: Sage, 1990), p. 113.

34. Gerald Handel, "Beyond Sibling Rivalry: An Empirically Grounded Theory of Sibling Relationships." Pp. 105–122 in Patricia A. Adler and Peter Adler, eds., *Sociological Studies of Child Development*, Vol. 1 (Greenwich, CT: JAI Press, 1986).

35. Deborah T. Gold, "Sibling Relationships in Old Age: A Typology." *International Journal of Aging and Human Development*, 1989, Vol. 28, pp. 37–54; Thomas R. Lee, Jay A. Mancini, and Joseph W. Maxwell, "Sibling Relationships in Adulthood: Contact Patterns and Motivations." *Journal of Marriage and the Family*, 1990, Vol. 52, pp. 331–340; and Ingrid Arnet Connidis and Lori D. Campbell, "Closeness, Confiding, and Contact Among Siblings in Middle and Late Adulthood." *Journal of Family Issues*, 1995, Vol. 16, pp. 722–745.

36. Victoria H. Bedford, "Sibling Relationships in Middle and Old Age." Pp. 201–222 in Rosemary Bleiszner and Victoria H. Bedford, eds., *Aging and the Family: Theory and Research* (Westport, CT: Praeger, 1996).

37. Jennie Keith, "Age in Social and Cultural Context: Anthropological Perspectives." Pp. 91–111 in Robert H. Binstock and Linda K. George, eds., *Handbook of Aging and the Social Sciences* (New York: Academic Press, 1990).

38. Leo Simmons, *The Role of the Aged in Primitive Society* (New Haven, CT: Yale University Press, 1945).

39. William H. Meredith and Douglas A. Abbott, "Chinese Families in Later Life". Pp. 213–230 in Bron B. Ingoldsby and Suzanna Smith, eds., *Families in Multicultural Perspective* (New York: Guilford, 1995).

40. Timothy H. Brubaker, "Families in Later Life: A Burgeoning Research Area." *Journal of Marriage and the Family*, 1990, Vol. 52, pp. 959–982; also Katherine R. Allen, Rosemary Blieszner, and Karen A. Roberto, "Families in the Middle and Later Years: A Review and Critique of Research in the 1990s." *Journal of Marriage and the Family*, 2000, Vol. 62, pp. 911–926.

41. For a more technical review of biological changes in old age, the demographic effects of advances in medicine, and the implications of increased longevity for families and societies, see Ian K. Ross, *Aging of Cells, Humans, and Societies* (Boston: W. C. Brown, 1995). On ways to help maintain health and delay the onset of disability, see John W. Rowe and Robert L. Kahn, *Successful Aging* (New York: Pantheon, 1998).

42. On the importance of maintaining contact with grown children, see Lynn K. White and John N. Edwards, "Emptying the Nest and Parental Well-Being: Evidence from National Panel Data." *American Sociological Review*, 1990, Vol. 55, pp. 235–242. For a report on the results of an AARP survey on contact between the two generations, see Tamar Lewin, "Grandparents Play Big Part in Grandchildren's Lives, Survey Finds." *New York Times*, January 6, 2000, p. A16.

43. Andrew J. Cherlin and Frank F. Furstenberg, Jr., *The New American Grandparent* (New York: Basic Books, 1986), pp. 188–193.

44. Margaret Mead, *Blackberry Winter* (New York: Morrow, 1972), p. 72. See also Margaret Platt Jendrik, "Grandparents Who Parent Their Grandchildren: Effects on Lifestyle." *Journal of Marriage and the Family*, 1993, Vol. 55, pp. 609–621.

45. Colleen Leahy Johnson, *Ex Familia* (New Brunswick, NJ: Rutgers University Press, 1988).

46. On the importance of their own grandparents in the relationships of grandparents to grandchildren, see Valerie King and Glen H. Elder, Jr., "The Legacy of Grandparenting: Childhood Experiences with Grandparents and Current Involvement with Grandchildren." *Journal of Marriage and the Family*, 1997, Vol. 59, pp. 848–859.

47. Lillian Troll, "The Contingencies of Grandparenting." Pp. 135–150 in Vern L. Bengtson and Joan F. Robertson, eds., *Grandparenthood* (Newbury Park, CA: Sage, 1985), p. 135.

48. On class and ethnic differences in the grandparent role, see Vern L. Bengtson, "Diversity and Symbolism in Grandparental Roles." Pp. 11–25 in Vern L. Bengtson and Joan F.

Robertson, 1985; also Valerie King and Glenn H. Elder, Jr., "American Children View Their Grandparents: Linked Lives Across Three Rural Generations." *Journal of Marriage and the Family*, 1995, Vol. 57, pp. 165–178.

49. Maximiliane F. Szinovacz, "Grandparents Today: A Demographic Profile." *The Gerontologist*, 1998, Vol. 38, pp. 37–52.

50. Charlotte Perry, "Extended Family Support Among Older Black Females." Pp. 70–76 in Robert Staples, ed., *The Black Family*, 6th ed. (Belmont, CA: Wadsworth, 1999).

51. Kenneth J. Doka and Mary Ellen Mertz, "The Meaning and Significance of Great-Grandparenthood." *The Gerontologist*, 1988, Vol. 28, pp. 192–197.

52. David A. Karp, "The Social Construction of Retirement Among Professionals 50 to 60 Years Old." *The Gerontologist*, 1989, Vol. 29, pp. 750–760, p. 750.

53. Robert C. Atchley, "Retirement." Pp. 437–449 in James E. Birren, ed., *Encyclopedia of Gerontology* (New York: Academic Press, 1996); and Jill Quadagno and Melissa Hardy, "Work and Retirement." Pp. 326–345 in Robert H. Binstock and Linda K. George, eds., *Handbook of Aging and the Social Sciences*, 4th ed. (New York: Academic Press, 1996).

54. On marital satisfaction and conflicts when the wife continues working after the husband retires, see Gary R. Lee, "Marital Satisfaction in Later Life: The Effects of Nonmarital Roles." *Journal of Marriage and the Family*, 1988, Vol. 50, pp. 775–783; Maximiliane E. Szinovacz, "Couple's Employment/Retirement Patterns and Marital Quality." *Research on Aging*, 1996, Vol. 18, pp. 243–268. On less heated arguments among more attached and committed couples, see Maximiliane E. Szinovacz and Anne M. Schaffer, "Effects of Retirement on Marital Conflict Tactics." *Journal of Family Issues*, 2000, Vol. 21, pp. 367–389.

55. Douglas E. Crews, "Cultural Lags in Social Perceptions of the Aged." *Generations*, Spring-Summer 1993, pp. 29–34.

56. The results of the AARP poll were reported in a newspaper article by Douglas Martin, "To Be Old, Gifted and Employed Is No Longer Rare." *New York Times*, January 13, 2001, Section 3, pp. 1, 12.

57. Victor C. Cicerelli, "Family Support in Relation to Health Problems of the Elderly." Pp. 212–228 in Timothy H. Brubaker, ed., *Family Relationships*, 1990, p. 218.

58. David S. DeGarmo and Gay C. Kitson, "Identity Relevance and Disruption as Predictors of Psychological Distress for Widowed and Divorced Women." *Journal of Marriage and the Family*, 1996, Vol. 58, pp. 983–997.

59. Herbert H. Hyman, *Of Time and Widowhood: Nationwide Studies of Enduring Effects* (Durham, NC: Duke University Press, 1968); and Jane K. Burgess, "Widowers." Pp. 150–164 in Catherine S. Chilman, Elam W. Nunnally, and Fred M. Cox, eds., *Variant Family Forms* (Newbury Park, CA: Sage, 1988).

60. On changes in agricultural and industrializing societies, see Helena Z. Lopata, *Widows: The Middle East, Asia, and the Pacific*, Vol. 1 (Durham, NC: Duke University Press, 1988); for changes in advanced industrial societies, see her Vol. 2, *Widows: North America* (Durham, NC: Duke University Press, 1998).

61. On changes in Italy, see Marlise Simons, "Casualties of Change in Italy: Old People Left Behind." *New York Times*, August 26, 1999, p. A1.

62. For recent changes in various immigrant subcultures in the United States, see Ruben G. Rimbaut, "Ties That Bind: Immigration and Immigrant Families in the United States." Pp. 3–46 in Alan Booth, Ann C. Crouter, and Nancy Landale, eds., *Immigration and the Family* (Mahwah, NJ: Erlbaum, 1997).

63. James J. Lynch, *The Broken Heart: Medical Consequences of Loneliness* (New York: Basic Books, 1989).

64. Orjan Hemstrom, "Is Marriage Dissolution Linked to Differences in Mortality Risks for Men and Women?" *Journal of Marriage and the Family*, 1996, Vol. 58, pp. 366–378; and Linda J. Waite and Maggie Gallagher, *The Case for Marriage* (New York: Doubleday, 2000), pp. 47–64.

65. Gloria D. Heinemann and Patricia L. Evans, "Widowhood, Loss, Change, and Adaptation." Pp. 142–168 in Timothy H. Brubaker, ed., *Family Relationships in Later Life* (Newbury Park, CA: Sage, 1990).

Index

"Dowry deaths," 67
Dowry systems, 53
    in India, 66–67

Economic conditions, family violence and, 160
Economics, 11
Education
    effects of, 223–224
    egalitarianism and, 43
    global trends in, 64
    women and, 154
Educational achievement, 197
Egalitarianism
    changes in attitude toward, 43
    defined, 38
    in marriage, 57, 74
Egg donors, 179
Elderly. *See also* Grandparents
    caregivers and, 209–212
    gay and lesbian, 141
    gender differences and, 87
    global trends in, 64
    life stages of, 96
    loneliness of, 168
    longevity, 96–97
    medical technology and, 211–212
    normal biological aging, 215–216
    retirement and, 218–219
    rural communities and, 86–87
    social status of, 214–215
    widows and widowers, 219–222
Elizabeth, Queen of England, 72
Elopements, 146
Empathy, 7
Employed mothers
    divorce and, 193–194
    effects on children, 174–175
    leisure time of, 173
    marital satisfaction of, 173
    media portrayals of, 128
    nonstandard work hours for, 177
    two-career marriages, 173–174
    working at home, 175, 176
Employee dating, 115
Empty nest stage, 15, 96
Engagement announcements/parties, 112
Ethics, 87
    Confucian, 19, 84

Ethnic diversity, 21
Ethnic families
    American concerns with, 78–79
    assimilation and acculturation of, 80–82
    childrearing practices of, 83–84
    contact between generations, 212, 213
    defining ethnic origin and race in, 79–80
    divorce and, 195
    extended family relationships in, 83
    familism, 39, 83
    husband–wife relationships in, 83
    poor, 76
    power, in family relationships and, 156
    single-parent households of, 166–168
    stereotypes and generalizations of, 80
    unmarried young adults in, 83
Ethnic minorities. *See also specific ethnic groups*
    familism, 39, 83
    issues in defining, 79–80
    marriage rates of, 129
    new upper class and, 72–73
    retirement and, 218
Ethnic origins
    defined, 79
    social class and, 84–85
Ethnocentrism
    lower middle class and, 74–75
    upper working class and, 75–76
Europe
    delayed home leaving in, 186
    family forms in agricultural societies, 53
Experiments, 8
Extended families
    agricultural societies and, 29–30, 53
    defined, 29
    horticultural societies and, 53
    households, 31–32
    in the United States, 30–32
    old upper class and, 71–72
Extended family relationships
    differences among ethnic families and, 83
    in middle age, 209–214
Extramarital sex. *See also* Sexual fidelity
    in living-together relationships, 132
    in the United States, 108–109

Failure, self-blame and, 40–41